To My Friend J...

I hope y...
better than I w...

Gay "Doc" Lewis
~2011~

NOTHIN' BUT A THING

G.L. "Doc" LEWIS

Published in the United States of America.

ISBN-10: 1463649002

ISBN-13: 978-1463649005

Non-fiction

This book is dedicated to all the gallant Marines and Navy Corpsmen of the 1st Force Reconnaissance Company, 1st Marine Division (REINF) Republic of South Vietnam, many of whom are portrayed in this work. Semper Fi.

ABOUT THE COVER

These are the men of 1st. Force Recon team "Countersign" as they prepare to be extracted from a weeklong radio relay mission at a once beautiful, French resort high atop BaNa Mountain in August of 1967.

Kneeling left to right:

PFC George Johnson   Corporal Jerry Maynard

Standing left to right:

PFC Dave Arthurs, Lance Corporal Ed "Pee Wee" Palmer, Lance Corporal Ed Unkle, Navy Corpsman Gary "Doc" Lewis and Lance Corporal "Billy" Gilmore (killed in action September 1967)

PREFACE

It's safe to assume that anyone who has endured battle has a story…this is mine; as I saw it from the perspective of a nineteen-year-old boy.

This work is a personal narrative of my time in Vietnam. It is not a 'blood-n-guts' story. Rather, it's all about the true to life, every day wartime experience that I encountered as a Navy corpsman serving with the Fleet Marine Force.

The characters and events are real. Some names have been changed simply because much time has passed and age erodes some memory or that identifying them would serve no useful purpose. However, actual names of most of those I served with in 1st Force Recon platoons have been used to recognize their service and honor them as friends and comrades-in-arms.

Obviously, literary license has been taken in dialog content between characters in order to maintain the spirit of each scenario from my point-of-view. While some interpretational discrepancies' may have occurred, the narrative content is true to reality and spirit.

I apologize to anyone who feels neglected or slighted by the contents of this work.

Molly,

The memory of your dad inspired me to write this.

May he eternally rest in peace.

IN COUNTRY

It was mid-June, 1967. As the tail ramp of the glistening, C-130 Hercules was being lowered a slight, smooth-faced, young man barely past puberty joined the ranks of thousands of other young men entering the unfamiliar world of *what am I doin' here*? A brilliant, white light penetrated the darkened cargo bay temporarily blinding him and all the other troops onboard the aircraft. With the light came a sudden, over-powering belch of hot air mixed with diesel fumes that viciously forced its way into his lungs, literally taking his breath away. The interior of the airplane instantly transformed into one, gigantic, sauna-like oven. Overwhelming heat and humidity shocked every pore in his body to ooze a warm flood of prickly sweat. Through painful, squinting eyes he managed to see the loadmaster standing tall in the center of the ramp, extending his arms with thumbs pointing upward, signaling all those onboard to get up and get off *his* airplane. "Anything you FNG's leave behind belongs to me, except your trash. Deep-six that shit in the trash bags or take it with you," he bellowed.

One wide-eyed Marine private quizzically blurted out, "Hey sergeant. What's FNG?"

The seasoned Marine airman gloated, knowing full well someone would be gullible enough to ask. "Fuckin' New Guy, you dipshit, now get off my fuckin' airplane."

Grabbing their gear, the troops scurried out of the plane's belly only to be confronted with even more intense heat when they stepped off unto concrete tarmac. A blistering 140 degree plus temperature penetrated through thick-soled, leather, combat boots; sautéing feet as if they were standing on a huge, concrete griddle. Most of them never experienced being cooked in such a fashion. Freshly starched, olive-drab utility uniforms, recently laundered at

Camp Butler in Okinawa, became drenched and sticky with perspiration. Boots that were painstakingly spit-shined to a mirror-like finish went drab from the rays of the scorching sun. All the effort the young Marines made to look squared-away vanished within minutes after touching down in the hellish heat of Da Nang airbase.

The smooth-faced, youngster involuntarily doubled over while gasping shallow breaths as he stepped off the cargo ramp. "You OK Doc?" a fellow troop asked putting his hand on the young man's shoulder.

"Yeah man, I'm okay," he struggled for air. "Just wasn't ready for this kinda heat."

Doc is the generic nickname given to Navy corpsmen. It becomes an honored nickname when Marines refer to him as "my Doc" or "our Doc." In the Corps, or as some prefer to call it "the crotch," there's a distinction between corpsmen who serve in hospitals, dispensaries or ships and those who serve with Marine field units. There's a finer distinction between those who serve in aid stations or field hospitals and those who serve alongside the Marines on the battlefield. For those corpsmen, "Doc" has a different ring to it. For now, Gary Lewis is just Doc Lewis. His official rate of Hosptialman is the equivalent to Lance Corporal in the Corps, a low-echelon enlisted troop. Hailing from the coal fields of western Pennsylvania, Lewis was just three weeks out of Field Medical Training School at the Camp Pendleton Marine Corps base just outside Oceanside, California. That's where he became indoctrinated to the Fleet Marine Force, or FMF. It was a six week training course packed into three intense weeks. It's where he was instructed in Marine Corps protocol, tradition and history. According to the Geneva Convention corpsmen are non-combatants but, he learned to "protect the patients" by using weapons like the M-14 rifle and .45 caliber pistol as well as becoming familiar with hand grenades and Claymore mines. He also learned to disembark from transport ships down cargo nets into pitching and heaving landing craft and to erect heavy canvas General Purpose tents just in case someone needed a field-expedient aid station. He was introduced to digging individual fox-holes into rock-hard, parched California earth using a slightly larger than a tablespoon *entrenching tool*. Twenty-mile forced marches and nighttime land navigation using a map and compass only served to reaffirm being lost. Essentially, except for the physical conditioning and mental harassment Marine recruits go through in boot camp, Navy corpsmen receive a respectfully scaled-down version of infantry training. More importantly, it's where he received his most critical instruction- that of saving the lives of wounded Marines. That would be his job. He didn't realize it then but, from the moment he stepped from the plane onto the hot tarmac, he would undergo a thirteen month metamorphosis from a Beatles lovin', 19-year-old boy into a 20-year-old combat tested veteran.

As the group milled around near the tail of the aircraft, a sudden thunderous roar reverberated through the air around them. A pair of Marine F-4 Phantom fighter jets blasted past them overhead on their way to a mission somewhere...maybe over North Vietnam? As if choreographed, the group shielded their eyes in unison as they followed the jets cutting through the heavy air, climbing and disappearing into the blinding sun. The noise of afterburners faded away while only a trace of engine exhaust marked their trail against the bright sky.

While their attention was diverted by the fighters, a Marine corporal garbed in faded, green jungle utilities and scuffed up, canvas-sided, jungle boots rode up on a bicycle, stopping in front of them.

"OK, you men listen up," he commanded their attention. "Get your gear and muster over there where it says "Transient Area." He pointed to a wooden, open air structure next to the airfield about a hundred yards from where they were standing. It was barely visible through a shimmering, reflecting mirage between them and the building.

"Get in the line that begins with the first letter of your last name. Do you understand?"

"Yes, Corporal," someone replied in typical gung-ho fashion.

"OK, then. It's going to take a while to process all of you, so have your orders ready when you get in line... Understand?" No response came but, the corporal continued on anyway. "You can leave your gear in the processing area but, make no mistake, we have thieves in Vietnam so, I would suggest not to leave your shit unguarded. You figure out how to do it. Any questions? No. OK, move out." The corporal turned and peddled back across the tarmac toward the staging area as the group followed behind like

ducklings trailing their mother. Another pair of Phantoms took off and again the group watched them climb.
"Nice an' quiet 'round here ain't it," PFC Nobody commented to no one.

Once inside the open-air facility the replacements did as they were instructed. Handing over in their orders they congregated outside until their names were called for assignment to their new units. The corporal spoke the truth. It was taking a while but, one by one, young Marines were assigned units.
"SYMANSKI, DAVID D., MEADER, ROBERT J., WILSON, MARK G." a squeaky-voiced, Lance Corporal Evans rapidly spouted off, "You guys are going to One-One. Saddle-up. Your transportation is waiting for you out front."
"Hey, I know somebody in One-One!" Private Symanski excitedly blurted out as he gathered up his gear.
"Don't get too excited," Evans responded as he handed Symanski back his orders. "They got in some deep shit yesterday in a 'ville' about a click south of here. You just might be replacing who you know."
The Lance Corporal's remark jolted Symanski. He tossed a half-smoked cigarette on the deck, stepped on it and joined the other two walking away.
The other men either cat-napped or passed the time in conversation. Some of them recollected basic training and AIT. They spoke of Jacksonville and San Diego. Some proudly showed pictures of girlfriends or hot cars. Every so often Lance Corporal Evans returned to call out more names. Sometimes he announced a single name; sometimes he announced a few together. Two Marines, who joined the Corps together, went to basic and AIT together, suddenly found them separated, each wishing the other well and making good-intentioned but, most likely false promises to stay in touch.

The afternoon passed agonizingly slow for those still waiting. Even though the Marines were shaded by a corrugated, metal roof, there was no escaping the relentless heat nor, was there respite from the stench of jet fuel and diesel fumes that mixed with strong, foul and unrecognizable odors. The activity on the airfield was also non-stop. Aircraft of all types and from all branches of the military continuously took off or landed. Even a few commercial airliners shared the runway. They seemed particularly out of place taxiing between the array of military aircraft. Occasionally, faint reports of distant artillery could be heard through the immediate concoction of noises. In the midst of all the activity, the replacements were becoming bored and tired of the hurry-up-and wait routine. They were all eager to get to their units and see some action. Hours passed since they landed and only about half of the troops got assigned units.

More time passed when a Marine Gunnery Sergeant came out of a room behind the counter and approached the troops. He was wearing a clean set of pressed jungle utilities with rolled-up sleeves that fit snuggly around well-formed, tanned biceps. Lewis noticed a faded tattoo of the Marine Corps eagle, globe and anchor insignia etched on the sergeant's right forearm. *'Lifer',* he thought. A crisp, starched and blocked cover accentuated the typical high-n-tight haircut. The troops started to get to their feet.

"As you were," the sergeant insisted, loosely extending a hand, halting them. "How you men doin'", he asked.

"Good Gunny," someone lied for all.

The sergeant forced a smile. "How'd I know you'd say that?" He paused momentarily before continuing. "I know it's hot and miserable for ya'll right now but trust me when I tell ya, you'll get used to it pretty damn quick. Ya'll been sittin' here a while, probably longer than ya should. Well, we can't help that. We're gonna git ya assigned just as fast as we kin, so bear with us for a little bit longer. We're tryin' to git ya'll outta here by ta-night. "IF….I repeat IF, we can't, we'll git ya a place to rack out and git ya outta here first thing to-ma-ra," he stated firmly. Scanning the young faces he spotted Lewis. "Doc," he mused. "Looks like you could use a Doc yourself. Somethin' a matter lad?"

"No Gunny, it's just the heat. That, and... Well, I think we're all pretty hungry"

The sergeant wrinkled his brow and bellowed "You mean you men ain't et yet?"

Their silence indicated to the sergeant that no one had eaten.

"Somma-na-fuckin-bitch," He turned an evil-eye toward Evans behind the counter. "Somebody's gonna git a bodacious ass chewin'," he growled.

At that moment a large, black Marine toting an M-14 rifle came into view from behind the slatted, wooden fence. The shirtless brute was wearing a filthy, frayed flak-jacket over a massive but

somewhat flabby, sweat-soaked, torso. His trousers were torn and dust-covered, while his boots had all the black leather scrapped away. The camouflaged helmet cover was faded and personalized with graffiti. A crinkled pack of Cools was tucked snuggly in the cover band. He was definitely not the poster-board version of a Marine the young troops have come to mentally recognize. The big man spotted the sergeant, which immediately prompted him to do an abrupt about face and quickly duck out of sight.
Fortunately for the Marine, the Gunny didn't notice him enter or leave.
"OK," Gunny continued, "Chow don't go down for a couple more hours yet so, there's a box full of them there leftover C-rats behind the counter. You men go help yourself to whatever ya think ya kin stomach." With that offer, Gunny made his way back behind the counter, saying something indiscernible to the Lance Corporal as he passed then, disappeared through a passageway in back of the building.

After rummaging through the pile of cans everyone found something to snack on. Each man retrieved the ubiquitous P-38 can opener that was tethered to dog-tag chain around his neck and began opening their selected fare in an impromptu race to see who could open their's fastest.
When the black Maine reappeared group watched him with bewildered curiosity as they casually consumed the meager rations.
The big man scoped the area for any sign of Gunny. Satisfied the coast was clear; he strolled across the deck to a nearby *water buffalo*, removed a canteen from the web-belt, placed it under a spigot and filled it with the warm, heavily chlorinated water. As he replaced the cap and returned the canteen back into its cover, he looked around at the fresh, clean faces. "Anybody here from Cleveland?" he asked, displaying a large, toothy, grin.
No one answered. "How about A-lanta?" he queried again.
"I'm from Macon," a light-skinned *brothe*r eagerly replied.
"Macon! Did you hear what I said? I said A'lanta....b'sides, ain't nothin' in Macon worth talkin' about anyhow."
The young troop chose to ignore the comment and continued spooning processed cheese on a tasteless, cardboard cracker.
"Who you with?" one new guy asked the Marine.

"I'm with India 1/5…here to pick up one of you sorry ass FNG's."
"Yeah. Who?"
"Man…I just do the hauling. I don't know who…don't care who. I just drive," he responded uncaringly, while making his way to the counter.
Soon he and Evans returned to the group. "GOR-KO-CHE"….."GOR-KU-COW", the Lance Corporal struggled with the name.
"Gorocowski," a voice corrected the pronunciation.
"BENJAMIN J.?" Evans asked.
"Yeah, that's me."
"India Company, one-five" the Lance Corporal said, handing over a packet of orders. The black Marine stepped forward. "I'll get your bag. You must be really tired from all your hard sittin' around on your squeaky-clean ass all day."
"I'll get my own gear," Gorkocowski retorted. "I gotta use the head first."
"No time for that now. Gotta di-di. If we ain't back by curfew we'll be in a boo-koo deep shit."
"Curfew," Evans remarked. "That's not 'til nineteen-hundred!"
"I plan on makin' a little stop in Dogpatch first, if ya know what I'm saying?" the Marine confided to Evans in a sly, muffled voice, gently elbowing him in the ribs.
"Come on," he instructed the replacement with a nod of the head. "You got any MPC or greenbacks?" he whispered as they departed.

More time passed without anyone being called. It was getting late in the afternoon and the entire remaining group used the time to grab some sleep simply out of boredom. There was a noticeable lull in activity around the airfield. Aircraft returning from their missions occasionally broke the abnormal silence. Lance Corporal Evans came out from behind the counter. "Aw-right, listen up," he squealed. "I got one more assignment. Where's LEWIS, GARY L?" No one responded. He called out again, "LEWIS, GARY L." No response came. Attempting to assert more authority than he actually had, he barked an ominous warning "LEWIS, if you ain't here, you're AWOL."
One of the young Marines pointed to a figure lying in a corner, sound asleep. "I think that's him."

Evans walked over to the reclining body and kicked at the boots. "Hey. Wake up."
The corpsman twisted slightly then bolted upright, shaking and clearing his head. Evans repeated himself, "Are you Lewis?"
"Yeah."
"Gary L?"
"Yeah."
"I got your orders here, Doc."
Sheepishly, Lewis got to his feet.
"You're going to the First Medical Battalion. It's just up the road by 327."
"327. What's that?" the doc questioned.
"Hill 327. It's where the PX and *Slop-chute* is. A very popular hang-out." Evans answered handing over the sealed, brown envelope. He continued, "They said they're going to send someone to come get you…probably should be here in about ten…maybe fifteen minutes."
"What time is it now?" Lewis asked Evans without thinking to look at his own watch.
Evans raised his wrist. "Sixteen forty-two. Why?"
"Cause I'm hungry. I don't want to miss chow."
"You won't. They got chow all the time up there," Evans assured. Evans then announced that whoever didn't have their name called was going to have to remain overnight in the transient barracks.

When the green, cracker-box, type ambulance with a large red cross painted on its side pulled up next to the transient facility, Doc Lewis was already waiting outside. The driver yelled out the opened passenger side window. "You the one going to First Med?" Lewis nodded.
"Stow your gear in the back," the driver instructed. "Then climb aboard up here."
The young driver pulled his M-14 closer to his side making room for Lewis to climb aboard the dust-laden cab. Once his passenger got situated, the driver put the vehicle in gear and pulled away. It wasn't long before the driver managed to gear the vehicle up to a much too dangerous speed. The road was congested with pedestrians, bicycles, motor scooters, mini-cabs, military vehicles, a few Honda cars and VW Beetles. Lewis even noticed a conspicuous pink and white, American-made, 1955 DeSoto parked at a dilapidated Esso Station. Behind the wheel was a

middle-aged, blond female. The sight was totally unexpected and out of place prompting Lewis to wonder who she was and what on earth was she doing there. Most of the Vietnamese wore cone-shaped, straw hats on their heads, a utilitarian design a thousand years old and dressed in both silky black pajama-looking clothing as well as western and European-style wear. Market vendors openly displayed products that were either pirated or black-marketed. Not displayed was under-the-counter contraband. Whisky, pornography, even handguns could easily be obtained if one wanted.

The ambulance driver seemed unconcerned that recklessly weaving in and out of traffic produced a few close calls. Clamping both hands on the oversized steering wheel the private controlled the vehicle's mass as it bumped and bounced over the potholes.

"Where you from Doc?" the driver inquired, briefly taking his eyes off the road.

"Pennsylvania," Lewis answered quickly, hoping the private would pay attention to his driving.

"NO SHIT, so am I," the PFC exclaimed. "Where in P.A.?"

"Pittsburgh." Lewis came back quickly again.

"HEY, I'm from Uniontown. Know where that is?"

"Yeah, I've been there a couple times, for track meets back in hi…HEY, LOOK OUT!"

The young driver quickly maneuvered the vehicle to the left then back to the right, narrowly missing an old man squatting down close to the road. The near-miss didn't seem to faze the driver. Bewildered, Lewis just stared across at the driver, who didn't bother to slow down at all. A moment later, a young woman on a bicycle, wearing a white sarong, jumped off the bike, managing to avoid a collision with the ambulance as it rounded the corner approaching the notorious section of Da Nang called Dogpatch. Doc saw her in the side mirror, shaking her fist and screaming what sounded like Vietnamese profanity. Everywhere, dozens of smiling children raised their little index fingers high in the air, calling out "GI number One-VC number Ten" as the vehicle sped past them. The erratic driving concerned Lewis to the point he had to say something.

"Hey man slow down a little. Give these people an even chance," he urged.

"Bullshit Doc. I slow down and one of these cute little V.C. might be inclined to toss a grenade in. No way, not me," the driver insisted as he laid on the horn.
"This here stretch is Dogpatch Doc," The private informed his passenger. "The whole place is off-limits to G.I.'s."
"Why?" the doc asked.
"I don't know for sure but, I heard that the ladies will cut your throat while you're doin' it. What makes it worse is that they'll do it on the upstroke!" he laughed at his own macabre humor.
Doc looked around at both sides of the road as they drove through, noticing that most of the buildings appeared to be nothing more than shanties. They seemed to be constructed from anything available, plywood, cardboard, corrugated metal. Some of them were sided with hundreds of flattened-out, tin cans; product labels still visible. A few had signs written in Vietnamese. It was difficult to distinguish whether the signs were there for advertisement or an integral part of the structures. He also noticed that there weren't very many military-aged, males around. Just as the vehicle was about to leave the Dogpatch area, Doc Lewis caught a glimpse of a familiar figure sneaking out from a side door of one of the shacks. It was the black Marine who was at the airfield earlier, with Private Gorokowski trailing close behind. They disappeared from view when the vehicle finally slowed down as it approached a sandbagged checkpoint, manned by a solitary Marine armed with an M-14, who casually waved them on.

The driver gave Lewis a narrated tour. "Over here on the left is the Sea-Bee compound; down that road on the right is the 3rd MP's." He retrieved a Marlboro from a plastic container and lit it with a Zippo "Up here on the left is the PX," he advised in a puff of smoke. "There's the beer-garden there. You can buy two cans of whatever beer they have at the time. Once in a while it's even cold." He took another drag and continued, "There's a library and bowling alley, too."
Doc leaned forward, barely being able to see through the cloud of dust. He saw what he guessed to be about thirty or forty, ragged looking Marines in flak-jackets and helmets, sitting in the dirt, resting their backs against the shady side of a large, metal building, their rifles locked and loaded, close at hand. They appeared to be savoring every ounce of their ration of beer. A

thought ran through Doc's mind that the beer was their reward for surviving something.... maybe something frightening and un-survivable. His thought was interrupted as the ambulance slowed to a stop. Up in front of them a 2-1/2 ton *'deuce-and a half'* stopped in the road to give a group of fellow Marines a lift. They helped each other climb up into the open bed and get situated among others already onboard. Jerking forward, the truck belched a cloud of diesel exhaust from its stack, kicking up a cloud dust as it moved. This accommodation occurred twice more before the driver pointed out the 1st Medical Battalion compound on the right. "There's your new home Doc."
Lewis looked out the window downward toward a congestion of metal roofed, wooden buildings of assorted sizes clustered among stands of banana trees. The entire area was situated below the main road on a sloping hillside. It wasn't how he imagined it. He envisioned uniform rows of large, general purpose tents with red crosses painted on them. It didn't appear that much thought was given to the layout of the compound. Lewis surmised the two largest buildings were constructed first and all the others grew outwardly from them in all directions. Most of the buildings were built on piers above ground. The Sea-Bees built those from stud framing with plywood half-walls around the sides. Screening material was attached to the upper half of the sidewalls to keep the insects out but still permit much needed ventilation to pass through. These *'hootches'* are where the troops live. The two larger structures were the obvious medical facilities. All the buildings had corrugated metal roofing. The western side of the compound abutted a high-traffic, dirt road that eventually intersected with Highway One several miles to the north. The east side opened to an expanse of rice paddies between the compound and the city of DaNang. The perimeter was surrounded by a mix of barbed-wire and concertina type razor-wire. Outside the perimeter in nearby paddies, Vietnamese, rice farmers labored knee-deep in muddy, bacteria infested water, accompanied by children riding on the backs of large water-buffalo. A Marine sentry was posted at the entrance to the property next to large, red sign with yellow lettering read 1st MED BN. 1st MAR Div (REIN) RVN."
The entrance road, like all the other dirt roads in the area, was liberally saturated with diesel fuel in an attempt to keep down the dust. After the guard waved them through, the driver proceeded

down the grade toward a parking area just in front of a screened-in hut. Bringing the vehicle to a stop he announced, "Here we are Doc."

Lewis climbed out and took a look around, absorbing everything. It all looked so unreal. The driver retrieved his weapon as he got out of the vehicle, walked to the rear, opened the back door and pulled out the passenger's sea-bag. "Don't forget your shit."

Turning to face the driver Lewis asked "Where do I go now?"

"Right here, Doc," the private replied, motioning toward the hut with a head gesture.

"OK," the corpsman acknowledged. "Thanks for the lift."

"Anytime Doc, anytime," he responded, walking away in the opposite direction.

Inside, Lewis saw two other corpsmen about his own age tending to paperwork. One seemed to be struggling with a Remington typewriter, the other was leafing through a folder. Both were wearing plain, white, tee shirts tucked in cotton fatigue trousers. Two, large, free-standing, electric fans provided circulation, and strains of Johnny Cash's *'Ring Of Fire'* was coming from a reel-to-reel tape recorder perched on top of one metal file cabinet. One man stopped typing when he glanced up to notice Lewis standing there.

"You need something," he asked.

"I'm reporting in" Lewis answered.

Reluctantly, the young man got up and made his way to the counter with an out-stretched hand. "Let me see your orders."

Lewis handed them over. The clerk opened the manila envelope, pulled out the papers and quickly looked at the first page. "Stand by," he instructed, taking the entire package into a room at the rear of the building. A minute later he returned with an older man, carrying a coffee cup and dressed in the same informal attire. "Lewis" the man questioned.

"Yes, sir," Doc affirmed.

"Welcome aboard Lewis. I'm Chief McKinney," he introduced himself as the senior NCO in charge of the corpsman in the outfit—the *head honcho* then, reached out to shake Lewis's hand. Following that order of business the Chief said that he would have more time to go over things in more detail tomorrow and that the priority now was to get the new corpsman billeted.

"Rappaport," the Chief called out to one of the ad hoc yeomen.

"Yes Chief," Rappaport responded.
"Take Lewis here; get him a rack up with the Ward gang. See that he gets squared away," the Chief ordered politely.
"Aye, Aye, Chief," he replied obediently in traditional naval jargon.
The Chief once again addressed Lewis. "Come back here tomorrow morning sometime after chow. We'll get you processed in then."
Lewis nodded, confirming that he understood.

Outside, he heaved the sea-bag, balancing it over his shoulder as Rappaport lead the way along pathways worn in the dirt between the rows of hootches. As the pair climbed the gentle slope toward their destination, Rappaport pointed out the triage area, the operating rooms, two wards and x-ray room. When they stepped on a straight section of corrugated, steel covered boardwalk, Lewis caught the welcomed scent of food. Rappaport explained that the building up a short flight of steps to his right was the galley and the screened-in structure on his left was the mess deck. To Lewis' disappointment, Rappaport also advised that they stopped serving about fifteen minutes earlier. "Damn," Lewis cursed. Picking up on new medic's apparent frustration Rappaport spoke up. "They serve sandwiches for midnight chow if you want. That's at twenty-three thirty," then added, "Breakfast starts at oh-six hundred."
Stepping off the boardwalk back onto the dirt path they continued up past three more hootches. "Here's the head," Rappaport said as he pointed to an unimpressive plywood, four-hole outhouse. "Up there behind it are the showers. You have to get there first thing if you want warm water." Maneuvering around to the back of the last building in the row, he highlighted that the small plywood building about thirty feet away was their enlisted club. "You can get beer, soda and some *Ge-dunk* there. They got a pool table and a T.V." He then opened the screened door at the back of the hootch and directed the new corpsman inside. "Here's your digs my friend," saying as he held the door open until they passed through then let it slam shut behind him.
Lewis looked around. His immediate attention was drawn to three canvas cots with mosquito netting framed over them in a tent-like fashion. Near each cot was a green, wooden, foot locker. Dusty blankets and pillows strewn over the cots and several articles of

military and civilian clothing along with various colored bath towels were draped over a make-shift clothesline strung along the wall. The deck looked as if it hadn't been swept down for weeks. Clumps of dried mud and small piles of dust collected in the corners. Candy wrappers, flattened-out cigarette butts and empty soda cans were scattered on the deck near each cot. A conspicuous Miss April centerfold was tacked to the wall beside one corner cot. Overhead, four, bare, light bulbs hung from pull-chain fixtures were crudely attached to the ends of electrical wire with friction tape. It appeared by toiletries set on shelves above each cot that three other people were billeted there. Lewis was stunned that he was supposed to live there. He gave a bewildered look to Rappaport who responded, "Don't worry. This is just the temporary hootch. Once you get assigned a watch they'll move you someplace permanent."

Unconvinced, Lewis dropped the sea-bag then took a few steps toward a single, folded cot lying in the dust. Picking it up he undid the straps, unfolded it and began setting it up. He found that one of the end pieces that stretched the canvas taut was missing but, it simply didn't matter right now if his rack sagged a little. He was tired and hungry and for now just wanted to get himself somewhat situated. Selecting an unoccupied corner he pushed the cot along the deck with his foot until he got it into position.

Rappaport assisted by lifting the sea-bag and placing next to the cot before making an offer. "I'll see if I can scrounge you up a blanket and pillow from the Surge. Ward." Before leaving he added, "You can take your shirt off if you want. The work uniform is tee shirts unless you leave the compound, then you have to be in the full uniform of the day but, you have to wear a cover all the time outdoors. I'll be back in a few minutes," he said as he exited.

"OK man. Thanks, I appreciate it." Lewis sat down on the edge of the cot. Removing his cover and shirt he sat quietly for a few seconds before reaching into his pocket for a smoke. He drew the first puff deeply into his lungs, holding momentarily before exhaling. Flicking ashes on the deck between drags he peered out through the screen. It was still hot even though the sun was casting long, day ending shadows. He observed a couple of men in flip-flop shower shoes walking up toward the shower. Another man in a towel was leaning over one of the spigots at the water buffalo, brushing his teeth, rinsing and spitting waste on the ground near his feet. He watched as another corpsman carrying a copy of the Stars and Stripes hurried to the four-hole'r. Turning to look out the opposite side of the building he spotted tiny, specks in the distance… helicopters descending near the place he would later know as Marble Mountain. A convoy of six-by's rumbled past on the road above.

He tossed the cigarette on the deck, snuffing it out with the bottom of his boot then laid back on the cot. He never heard Rappaport returning with the blanket and pillow.

The screen door slammed. Lewis shifted his body in the sagging cot before opening his eyes wide enough to catch a blurry figure moving past his cot, shower shoes flopping as he walked. It took moment for him to realize where he was and sensing by the brightness that he slept longer than he should have. It was mid-morning and the metal-clad roof was heating the hootch to near cooking temperature. He felt dampness under his chin, around his eyes and armpits. The sweat made him feel uncomfortably warm and sticky. Propping himself with his elbows he watched the person who has just passed. A tall, thin young man stood as the far end of the hootch. He dropped the towel from around his waist and replaced it with a pair of white, boxer-style, 'skivvy' shorts. Lewis reckoned that he had just come from the shower. The young man turned around. "Sorry man. I didn't mean to wake you," he apologized to Lewis.

"No problem," Lewis uttered in wake-up stupor.

The man continued to speak as he pulled up a pair of utility trousers. "Get in yesterday?" he asked.

"Yeah. Last night." Lewis answered looking at his watch. "Shit, nine-forty-five. I missed chow again," he groaned.

"Yeah. Sure did," the man confirmed. "But you didn't miss much," he tagged.

The comment didn't ease Lewis's hunger pangs.

Lewis forced a move to sit up on the edge of the cot. He realized that except for his utility shirt he had fallen asleep fully clothed. He spotted a blanket and pillow that he apparently had kicked onto the dusty floor.

Pulling a white tee shirt over his head the man walked toward Lewis, shower shoes flip-flopping with each step. "I'm Jason Bennett… and you are…?"

"Lewis. Gary Lewis," accepting Bennett's handshake.
Using his tee-shirt as a towel Lewis wiped the sweat from his face and brow then reached to retrieve a Viceroy. He lit it and took a puff.
"Those things will kill you," Bennett warned politely.
"I'll take my chances," Lewis rebutted equally polite.
"Where you from?" Bennett inquired.
"Pennsylvania, you?"
"California. Oceanside actually. I'm a brat. My dad's a retired gunnery sergeant. Man, was he disappointed when I joined the Navy instead of the Marines. He mellowed out some when I became a corpsman. Now look where I am… Semper fi, semper fi."
Bennett returned to his cot. *Flip-flop, flip-flop, flip-flop*. He sat down, powdered Desenex between his toes, reached into the foot locker, pulled out a pair of brown socks and slipped them over his feet. Then he put on a pair of used jungle boots, carefully lacing them through each eyelet, following up by stretching a blousing rubber around each boot and tucking the bottom of his trousers securely under and around each boot. It appeared to Lewis that he process was ritualistic even though he knew it was typical military routine. Bennett turned. "Hey man, I'll show you around later if you want."
"I dunno. I gotta go see the chief this morning to finish up reporting in," Lewis said exhaling smoke and flicking ashes on the floor.
"Well, I guess you gotta do what you gotta do," Bennett paused while slipping a tan colored web belt through his trouser loops. "Listen, I'm going to the PX to try and get a fan. You want anything?"
"No. I don't think so. Thanks anyway."
"It's OK." the man said as he buttoned his shirt and put on a cover. "I'll talk to you later." SLAM.
Lewis stomped out the cigarette and prepared to take a much needed shower.

The cold water felt good on his body as it trickled out of the shower head. He recalled what Rappaport had told him about the hot water situation but, it didn't matter. He just enjoyed the refreshing cold water. After a few minutes under the stream however, he actually began to get chilled and started to shiver. A

paradox ran through his mind '*How can it be hot and cold at the same time?"*
Upon approaching the hootch, he saw Rappaport waiting for him thought he screen.
'*Shit, I must be in trouble with the chief,*' he thought since it was so late and the chief told him to be at the office after breakfast.
"What's up?" Lewis asked as he entered anticipating a hostile reply.
"Nothing bu-cu," Rappaport calmly answered. "I'm just going to show you where you're going to be assigned and get you familiar with the place. That's all."
Lewis hesitated before questioning, "What about the chief? I was supposed to see him this morning."
"Don't worry about him…he's busy…had to go to the Navy Hospital in DaNang to pick up some meds." Rappaport leaned toward Lewis and continued in a half-whisper. "He's got the hots for a nurse lieutenant there…thinks he has a chance of getting some ass."
Upon hearing that Lewis let out a sign of relief. "Whew. Man I thought I was going to get chewed out big time!"
"Nah, he's not that hard-nosed. Actually, he's kind of laid-back. You just do your job and keep out of trouble and he won't bother you…it's that simple." As Rappaport spoke, Lewis couldn't help notice a peculiarity in his mannerism…he kept his eyes shut when he talked. "Besides," Rappaport continued, "He's a real pussy-hound. All he talks about is pussy, pussy, and pussy. It's a good thing we have plenty of penicillin! He leaves the compound a lot on *military business*." Both men snickered.
Lewis removed the padlock from his sea bag and pulled out a clean uniform. Rappaport advised him that he might want to wash all his uniforms to get the starch out before wearing them; that starch and perspiration is not a good combination is this climate because the combination irritates the skin, causing unbearable itchy rashes. Lewis acknowledged the advice and continued dressing.
The two took the same path taken the day before. Lewis caught the smell of food being prepared for lunch as they passed the mess deck. It teased him. He was determined not to miss lunch today. Rappaport showed him the mail room where he could pick up and send mail, explaining it was open every day. They took the path to the bottom of the hill where a helicopter landing pad was

located. This is where they bring in the casualties. It was about 75 feet away from "receiving," the triage bay where the wounded were carried in and treated according to the seriousness of their wounds. Rappaport gave him his assignment. "This is where you're assigned. You'll be working mid-watch from twenty-two hundred until oh-six-hundred. There will be a Doc on duty with you," he said referring to a physician and not a corpsman. Lewis was aware of the distinction. When a corpsman refers to a Doc he means a doctor, not another corpsman. Lewis continued to check the place out. It was nothing more than a large wooden-floored, platform covered with the ever present metal roof. It was open on two ends, one from the helo pad, the other lead to the operating room, x-ray and the wards. Overhead a dozen or so incandescent light bulbs hung down from electrical cords. There were at least ten canvas litters, each resting on a set of metal horses evenly spaced along the half-walls, five on each side. Next to each litter were an IV stand and a gooseneck light. Behind the litters was a continuous shelf stocked with various supplies; Syringes, bandages, splints, cravats, instruments, IV solutions, surgical gloves, face masks, and an array of other medical necessities. There were water-filled buckets and mops located nearby along with a water hose, used to wash the blood off the deck. Out of sight next to triage was the morgue holding area, where bodies were placed before being picked-up by the graves registration unit. Lewis began to feel a little apprehensive about his first assignment. Maybe it was too much responsibility for him. Maybe he'll screw up and let someone die. '*God, don't let me screw up!*' he thought silently. Not wanting to let Rappaport sense his feelings he asked, "Hey man, I forgot to ask your first name. You already know mine."

"Well, it's Mel, actually it's Melvin," he reluctantly confessed, "but everyone around here calls me 'Heeb', you know, short for Hebrew, since I'm Jewish and all."

Lewis acknowledged with a quick nod.

"What do you prefer?" Lewis asked sincerely.

"I kinda like Heeb…now that I'm used to it," he answered, smiling in appreciation that the new guy even bothered to ask.

"What shall I call you by?" Heeb returned politely.

"Lew works for me."

As they continued the tour they passed by the wards that were constructed in the same manner as the hootches. Lewis could see inside through the screening. From what he could tell there were about twelve beds packed in close quarters, most of which were occupied. Two, oscillating, electric fans purred in a futile attempt to provide some comfort from the heat. Heeb explained that some of the wounded would recover from less serious wounds and be sent back to their units. Others, with more critical injuries, were here just long enough to stabilize for transport to the Naval Hospital in DaNang, or to hospital ships USS Repose or Sanctuary. The ships were positioned off the coast of Vietnam in the South China Sea in an area called Yankee Station. Some of the wounded would be sent to the Naval Hospital in Yokosuka Japan, Subic Bay or even back to the states.

At least two corpsmen were on duty at each ward. They were kept busy changing dressings, passing out medications, changing IV's, taking vital signs, charting records, assisting with patient hygiene, emptying bedpans and numerous other tasks, all for the well-being of the patients. It was common for ambulatory patients to assist the corpsmen in accomplishing other menial but, time-consuming tasks, such as bringing in meals from the mess hall for the bedridden or collecting linen and towels for laundering. They were eager to help the corpsmen as well as their bothers-in-arms.

Lewis spotted a Marine major, accompanied by his First Sergeant, unceremoniously pinning a Purple Heart medal on the pillow of one unconscious Marine. It was a small token of appreciation for spilling blood for his country in combat. Someone took a photograph of the modest event.

Heeb pointed out a passageway where several troops were congregated. "Down there to the right is Sick Call. If you're sick you'll need to go there and see the Doc first thing in the morning. You'll see more corpsmen thee than *jarheads*." Again Lewis acknowledged with a quick nod. After a while they covered most of the compound. Rappaport located the Dental ward, the Chaplain's office and chapel, the motor pool, supply and hootches where the small contingent of Marines lived. It wasn't long before Heeb suggested chow. It was exactly what Lew was waiting to hear.

When the pair got in the chow line about twenty others were in front of them. They picked up the ubiquitous, stainless-steel, compartmented food tray and eating utensils and waited for the serving line to open. Most everyone was chatting and joking around, making sarcastic wisecracks about the food. The comments didn't bother Lewis. He was hungry and didn't care what was being served.

After finally stuffing his belly with the ever-present military fare of 'something-over-rice,' bread and butter, a solid fudge brownie and gulping down three glasses of a watered-down, orange-flavored liquid resembling Kool-Aid, Lewis picked up an apple and stuffed it in his trouser pocket to eat later on. The two men lifted the trays and made their way back up behind the mess where they found five, large, galvanized steel garbage cans. The first container was for scraps that fell from the tray when it was slapped against the inside of the can, forcing food to be released. The next three cans were equipped with kerosene emersion heaters to heat the wash water. The last can was filled with cold rinse water. The procedure after scrapping was to dip the tray into the first hot, soapy water can and scrub it down with a hard-bristled brush, then dip again in the second hot water can, followed by a dip in hot rinse water and finally the last dip in cold water rinse. At the end of the line there was an old, weathered, Vietnamese man, dressed in rags, collecting the trays and stacking them for re-use. He humbly bowed to each man who handed him a clean tray, smiling broadly, exposing a toothless mouth. His wage was the privilege to root around the leftover garbage for scraps of food. The sight tore at Lewis's heart but the only thing he could do was accept it for what it was. As he handed over the tray a UH-34 Sikorsky helicopter passed closely overhead. Everyone turned to look skyward. It was landing at the helo pad.

"They're bringing in casualties." Heeb advised his new friend. "The shit must have hit the fan somewhere," he added.

The information didn't require a response.

"OK, now you have to go to the mailroom and fill out an address card," Heeb told Lewis.

"Do you remember where it is?"

"Yeah, I think I can find it."

"OK. I gotta get back to the quarterdeck now. Remember, report for duty at twenty-two hundred. It would be better if you got there early to relive whoever is on duty. Oh yeah, I almost forgot, be sure to stop off at the chow hall before you go to get your midnight meal. It'll be a couple of sandwiches and a piece of fruit or something. OK, any questions?"

"No, I don't think so…wait a minute," he quickly added. "Where can I get a pair of those jungle boots? These things are killing me."

"Sorry man," Heeb shrugged his shoulders, "We don't issue them here. The best way is to go to graves registration and see if they have any your size that won't be needed any more. That's the way everyone else gets them."

Absorbing Heeb's recommendation, the thought didn't appeal to the young corpsman.

"Thanks a lot Heeb. I'll see you around," Lewis promised.

The helicopter roared as it lifted from the helo pad and headed across the open rice paddies toward DaNang.

Heeb hollered back. "Try to get some sleep. You'll need it."

Lew went to the mail room and filled the address card as requested then made his way back to the hootch. One step inside he saw Bennett sprawled out on his cot in his skivvies. He also spotted a brand new fan tied securely to the rafter above him, blowing a steady stream of air directly down on the reclining body. Lewis was careful not to let the door slam. He didn't know if Bennett was sleeping and didn't want to wake him if he was. He also noticed that the other two cots across from Bennett's were still vacant. Sitting down on the edge he lit up a smoke, letting it dangle from his lips. He sat there silently a few minutes pondering his austere surroundings, wondering if he'll be assigned a different hootch anytime soon. He couldn't unpack his sea bag without having the means to stow his clothing. Constantly digging into it is a pain. He definitely needed a foot locker or something. Snuffing out the cigarette he laid back resting his head on the newly acquired pillow. It was uncomfortably hot again, the sweat still seeping from his pores. *'I'm going to have to get myself one of those fans too,'* he thought. Lying there he struggled to fall asleep but couldn't. A combination of heat, constant rumbling of truck traffic on the nearby road, anxiety of his new assignment, lack of creature comforts, uncertainty of what lies ahead, all gelled together in his active mine, preventing him to relax enough to catch some zee's. Discouraged, he rose from the cot, grabbed his cover and quietly exited the hootch.

At the water buffalo he placed his head under the spigot and deluged it in water. It felt good but was only a temporary relief

from the heat. Not knowing what else to do to occupy his time, he walked to the 'club' to check it out. The hillside location forced him to climb a few steps to enter. Inside he saw a few handmade, cocktail tables and chairs scattered around a single large room, a pool table that has seen better days and a small, elevated bar with a few barstools against the back wall. A flickering, black and white television set was precariously situated on top of a makeshift bookcase, showing an episode of *Car 54 Where Are You*, the volume turned down. The bookcase housed a variety of paperback books with a hand printed piece of paper taped to the front which
Read "Take One-Give One." Nancy Sinatra's song "*These Boots*" was coming over the Armed Forces Radio Network from a radio resting on the bar. Also on the bar were a half a dozen, empty tin cans, painted red with the text "BUTTS" stenciled on the side. The walls were bare except for several Playboy center-folds and photograph of Ho Chi Minh's head centered in the cross-hairs of a rifle scope. For sale on a counter behind the bar was an assortment of small bags of potato chips, pretzels and corn-curls. A canister of Slim-Jims sat next to the chips. A small chalkboard above the counter read "*Olympia & Blatz*" indicating the current beer selection. Underneath that text was scribbled "*2 cans per man.*" One a small shelf was a checker set, a Monopoly game and a few decks of playing cards. Lewis surmised that as humble as it was, it was still better than some folks had. A red-headed young man came from a room behind the bar lugging in a case of Blatz.
"Sorry man, we don't open 'til six-teen hundred," he informed Lewis.
"That's OK. I just wanted to take a look around," Lew said. "Hey, is it alright if I take one of these books?" he asked pointing to the bookcase.
"Sure. Go ahead."
Thanking the man, Lewis searched for a title. After about a minute of fumbling through the assortment he chose a coverless copy of "*To Hell and Back*" by World War Two hero Audie Murphy. "Thanks again," he said leaving the building. The man acknowledge with weak, half-assed salute.
Walking down the grade back toward his hootch, Lewis noticed another helo approaching the compound across the rice paddies from the south east. There was no doubt it carried more casualties. He was tempted to go to receiving and observe what

was going on but finally decided against it, figuring he'll get his share of action in time.

Passing in close proximity to the four-hole'r Lewis's nostrils absorbed the strong, unpleasant odor of human excrement mixed with diesel fuel permeating the heated afternoon air. These outhouses were made from plywood. Four, open holes were cut into a bench-like seat without any provision for privacy. Tucked away underneath each hole was half of a 55 gallon drum, partially filled with diesel fuel. Every so often someone, usually as a form of summary punishment, would be tasked with removing the containers and burning off the contents. This disagreeable job was called *"burning the shitters."* He was wondering to himself if he would be able to use the facility without puking when the time came. He knows that eventually he would have to vacate his bowels so; he developed a plan in his mind to go in the middle of the night when no one else was around. That way, he reasoned, no one could see him vomit or hold his nose while doing his business, thus avoiding the possibility of unwanted embarrassment.

Back in the hootch, Bennett was sleeping but there was still no sign of the other two, whoever they are.

The remainder of the day dragged by. Lewis read a couple of chapters in the paperback, took a couple cat-naps, went to evening chow, took another shower and go ready for his first duty assignment. Bennett was also preparing to go to work. Lewis found they both worked the same mid-watch, but Bennett worked on the ortho war

"Well, how'd your day to Gary?" Bennett asked as he cut the strings holding the fan to the rafter.

"Pretty damned slow," Lewis replied. "What are you doing?" he inquired in the same breath.

"Man, I'm taking this to work with me. We got thieves around here. There's nothing more inviting for somebody to steal than an unsecured fan," Bennett answered in a matter-of-fact tone. Lewis accepted the logic.

Curious about the two empty cots Lewis decided that now would be a good time to inquire. "Hey Jason, what's going on with those two?" he asked lighting up a smoke while pointing to the cots.

"Well," Bennett struggled to find an answer. "Let me put it to you this way. They diddy-bopped in here a couple of weeks ago. I don't think anyone knows they're here. After the first three days without getting a duty assignment they disappeared...been gone ever since."

Lewis responded. "You mean they've been gone for ten days and no one even knows…or cares." Lewis added in disbelief.

"Hey man, it's not that no one cares…it's that no one knows they're gone in the first place. Don't give me that shit about not caring. Who knows! They might be Air America people, undercover spies gone out on a mission."

Lewis heard of Air America. He knew it was a bogus cover for the C.I.A. but he didn't think anyone at a medical facility could be involved with the kind of operations the C.I.A. conducts.

"YOU KNOW!" Lewis asserted, "Why didn't you report they were gone? They could be captured or dead somewhere!"

"They could be, but it's not my job to babysit them. Hell, I don't even know them other than their names. Jarvis and Jones, that's their names. The J-J twins. Besides, who the hell are you to reprimand me…Hospitalman." Bennett snapped, inferring that he out ranked the young sailor.

Lewis didn't like Bennett's attitude. He shook his head and decided it was better just to drop the subject, for now.

The two grabbed their covers and went to the chow hall for their brown-bag meal. Once there, they separated. "See ya later man," Bennett bid.

"OK," Lewis replied half-heartedly.

As the young man entered the triage bay he noticed a few corpsmen just sitting around smoking and talking. Everything seemed to be quiet. There were no patients on litters and the area appeared to be in order. He walked toward the group. One of the men came over to him, "You my relief?" he questioned the new man.

"Well, I was told to report here for the mid-watch tonight."

"Great, you're early." He said without bothering with an introduction "Here's the deal. Everything is cleaned and stocked, except for the Dextrose. It's in the boxes around the corner, it needs to be shelved. Doc Van Hussen is the duty medical officer tonight. He's already in the M.O.'s office catching some zee's. S-2 is reporting a possible rocket attack on DaNang tonight so don't be surprised if you get some work."

Lewis acknowledged every comment with an uneasy nod. He could feel the anxiety twisting his gut. Nervously he asked, "Is anyone else on duty with me?"

“Nope. You’re it.” Seeing Lewis’s apprehension he added. “If something big goes down, you’ll have a lot of help most ricky-ticky. Don’t worry.”
The other two came over checking out his new leather boots and starched, cotton utility trousers.
“FNG, Woooooo,” one mocked as all of them left the area together, leaving Lewis alone. He had never felt any more alone than now. He couldn’t help but feel like an abandoned child. *‘Christ, why couldn’t they let me work with somebody until I get up to speed,’* he thought. *‘They got no right to just put me here by myself.’*
He took a second look around hoping someone else was thee. No one was.

Lighting up a Viceroy he casually walked to the edge of the platform floor where it dropped one step to the ground and looked out over the rice paddies toward the city. Far off in the distance, beyond DaNang, he could see about a half dozen, flickering, illumination flares slowly etching a smoky, snake-like path against the dark, moonless sky. Lights from the city glowed faintly near the horizon. It was quiet-almost too quiet for a country immersed in war. He wondered how long the stillness would last before casualties would arrive. In his solitude, he recalled the short tour of duty he had in the E.R. at the Naval Hospital in Jacksonville, Florida, where he performed training, prior to Camp Pendleton. He supposed this would be similar, except for the cleanliness and the presence of female nurses. In particular, he remembered one night when a teenaged, dependent’s daughter was brought in semi-conscious after a car accident. She was wearing only a red, flowered bikini. The impact of the crash forced the evacuation of her bowel in the bikini. The doctor ordered him to clean her. He didn’t want to. He reasoned that because she was a female, a *Corps-wave* should be tasked to do the job. He mentioned it to the doctor, who didn’t buy it. It was a very unpleasant experience.
He flicked a half-smoked cigarette out onto the ground without putting it out. Time drifted by slowly because of inactivity and the absence of anyone to talk to. He wished he brought the paperback with him. Restless, he picked up the brown-bag meal and sat down crossed-legged on the floor. It was a few minutes after mid-night and he was ready for a sandwich. Opening it he

found two, cold Span sandwiches with a slice of American cheese on white bread, and orange and a half-pint, carton of *Reamers Blend.* He ate everything including the juicy orange. He spent the next couple of hours smoking cigarettes, just waiting for something to happen, secretly hoping nothing would. According to his wristwatch, it was 17 minutes past 2 A.M. and everything was still quiet. He was beginning to get sleepy. As if a switch was turned on, he suddenly remembered what the other corpsman said about the Dextrose needing to be placed on shelves. It was a simple enough task and would occupy some of his time. He opened the carton containing 12 glass bottles of 5% Dextrose I.V. solution. Removing two bottles at a time he carefully placed one on the shelf behind each litter. He didn't know what to do with the empty carton so he just left it where he found it. Another hour passed and three more cigarettes spent. He kept glancing at his watch. The hands didn't appear to move although the second hand indicated it was running. By this time the night air was getting cooler. Every once in a while he felt a mild chill on his thin, bare arms. '*Tomorrow I'll bring a shirt and a book,*' he reminded himself.

He watched as the distant flares continued to drop throughout the night and wondered what was happening out there. It brought back memories of his first year of sea duty aboard the destroyer Leonard F. Mason. He spent time as a corpsman 'striker' trainee aboard her before going to Hospital Corps School in San Diego. The ship provided naval gunfire support operations along the coast of Vietnam. It was almost *de ja vu* as he recalled standing on deck at night and watching flares floating down toward the earth far inland. From his perspective then, being that far out at sea, it was a distant war, except when the ship had firing missions. The whole ship shuttered as salvos from her 5 inch guns sent rounds screaming to targets far away. He recollected thinking about how much better he had it than those fighting on shore. He never knew that the Marines didn't have their own medics like the Army and that it was Navy corpsmen who got assigned to Marine Corps units. It was a shock when he learned that fact in Corps School. Worse yet was trying to explain to his mother how he all of a sudden was in the Marines. It seemed so long ago yet, less than 18 months passed since then. '*Now look at me!"* a thought interrupted his reminiscence.

Lewis was struggling to stay awake. It was 4:14 A.M. when out of nowhere the urge to use the *'four-holer'* sneaked up on him. Sharp contractions in his bowel reinforced the urgency. Even though there wasn't anything going on, he was reluctant to leave triage unattended. After a few seconds elapsed he logically reasoned that the general order of not leaving your post until properly relieved didn't pertain now, since a doctor was supposedly on duty although, he hadn't actually seen him. He stepped off the platform and made his way toward the outhouse. Upon approaching it in the darkness he heard moaning sounds coming from within. He paused, cocked his head and listened closely. He recognized the slapping sounds. "*Holy-shit, some son-of-a-bitch is jerking off!*" Not wanting to barge in on whoever it was inside, he quietly backed down the path, thinking he should approach again making some noise to alert the person first. On second thought, maybe he should just wait until the guy was finished, after all, it shouldn't take too long. He decided on the latter and returned to triage. After several minutes of increasing discomfort he again made his way to the outhouse. It was vacant when he got there. Surprisingly, the odor was tolerable. Diesel fumes covered most of the fecal stench. It was totally dark inside. Not wanting to feel around he brought out his *Zippo*, giving him just enough light to find the holes and toilet paper and complete his business. Finally relieved of two days of backfill he returned to the triage bay where he immediately grabbed a bottle of Isopropyl alcohol and washed his hands.

5:05 A.M. brought the airfield in Da Nang to life. Phantoms taking off with fully thrusting afterburners engaged, created thunderous roars even from the distance. Sunrise was just beginning to break the darkness of the tropical sky. Lewis spotted at least four pair of brightly burning engine exhaust trails cutting through the pre-dawn pink and purple backdrop.

Lewis was thankful nothing happened to embarrass him during his first duty day in Vietnam. He could barely wait for his relief to show up. It was a long and boring night and all he needed to do now was wait it out for another 45 minutes. He figured two more cigarettes would sustain him until then, lighting up one he continued to scan the expanse of rice paddies to the east. For a few moments it was a peaceful setting with the sun coming up, highlighting scattered wisps of fog clinging low on the paddies. Then, out of nowhere, he heard the distinct sound of helicopter rotors *'popping'* and was shocked to see two CH-46 Sea Knights skirting the compound three hundred years away, about 100 feet from the deck and descending. *Butterflies* filled Lewis's stomach as he thought they might be bringing in wounded troops. He could feel himself trembling with reluctant anticipation while questioning his next move. *'What should I do now? Should I get Doc? Should I call out for help? Who should I call? I don't know! I don't know what to do!"* Eyes wide open, he focused on them intensely for what seemed to be hours but, breathed a sigh of relief as they passed by and continued northward, disappearing behind an outcropping of banana trees. Never having been exposed to that kind of stress before, he vowed to get the answers to his questions before his next watch.

Although he already served a little more than two years in the Navy, he always had someone else directing him and never had to made decisions on his own. He didn't like how it made him feel. '*Damn it,*' he cursed in anger under his breath, '*this kind of shit pisses me off. Someone should explain to me what I'm supposed to do.*' He didn't hear the person approaching next to him. "Nice quiet night huh?"

The unexpected voice startled him enough to give a quick jerk.

"Sorry, I didn't mean to sneak up on you," a fully uniformed man apologized quickly.

Lewis turned, spotting officer's bars and medical corps insignia on the man's jungle shirt. He correctly surmised the man was Doctor Van Hussen then responded more or less respectfully.

"Sir, you nearly scared the crap out of me!"

"I'll be more careful next time," the doc promised with a pleasant smile. The physician's demeanor eased Lewis's tension.

"Yes sir, nice quiet night," he answered the doc's first question.

"Yeah, we don't get many quiet ones around here. Did you manage to get any sleep?"

"Sleep sir? On duty?"

The medical officer explained. "I don't mind if anyone catches some sack time when nothing's going on. As a matter-of-fact, you should get as much rest and nourishment as you can. There's no telling when you might have to work sixteen or twenty hours straight. We don't want anyone to keel over from sleep deprivation or make needless mistakes when it can be avoided." The words sounded more like a demand than advice.

"What about the choppers coming in?" Lewis asked reflecting inexperience. The doc picked up on Lewis's youthful, naïve personality and inexperience despite the attempt to conceal it.
"The pilots always radio ahead…someone will get the word to us and give us time to get ready."
Lewis nodded that he understood and was about to ask another question when the doc interrupted him before he could utter a word.
"Well then, I guess I'll see you again tomorrow night, right?" Van Hussen predicted.
"Sure thing, Sir. See you tomorrow night."
The doctor turned and disappeared into the planked corridor toward the M.O.'s office.
Lewis sensed satisfaction after initially speaking with Doctor Van Hussen. He liked the man and hoped they could work together as a team.

It was twelve minutes past six when Lewis' relief appeared carrying a canteen cup full of coffee. It was the red-haired corpsman he met at the club the day before.
"Sorry I'm late man, the chow line just wasn't fuckin' movin'. Got anything to report?"
Lewis stared hard into the man's bloodshot eyes, trying to convey his disapproval for him being late. "No. It was quiet all night," he snipped.
"OK partner, you're officially relieved."

Tired and not very hungry Lewis passed by the chow hall. Back at the hootch he noticed the J-J twins still didn't show up. Bennett wasn't back from his watch either '*He's probably at chow'* Lewis reasoned. He sat down on the edge of the cot and removed the heavy boots from his aching feet. Reaching for a cigarette he found only one left in the
Pack. '*God, I can't believe I went through a full pack*!" Not bothering to light it he fell
back against the pillow. At ease with himself for making it through his first day he drifted off to sleep. The last thing he remembered hearing was the familiar flip-flop of shower shoes of people walking to the shower.
His slumber lasted less than three hours. SLAM, the door jolted him awake.

"Lew, wake up," Heeb instructed in a hurried voice. "The chief wants to see you *most sko-shee*."
Shaking out the cob-webs Lew inquired. "Why?"
"He thinks you screwed up bu-cu last night!"
"How?"
"Don't know. He sent me go get you. Better hurry."
Already in uniform, all he needed to do was put on his boots. The pair hurried toward the CP. Chief McKinny was waiting for him. Without as much as a salutation the chief began his interrogation.
"What the hell did you do with the carton of Dextrose solution last night?" he inquired outright.
Lewis swallowed. "I put them on the shelves like I was told to."
"Well, who the hell told you to do that?"
"I don't know his name, just the guy I relieved."
"Those bottles were there to be sent to one-one's aid station this morning, did you know that?"
"No sir, I didn't. No one told me that!"
Sensing Lewis was telling him the truth the chief looked him in the eye. In a near whisper he declared, "Well, I'll find out who told you to do that and I have *his* nuts in the ringer. In the meantime…you go back…get all those bottles and bring them back here. Make it so…NOW."
"Aye, aye Chief," Lewis quickly responded to the order without hesitation.
As he hurried to triage he searched his memory for the last time he was chewed out as an individual but nothing registered.
In the triage Lewis saw the duty corpsman attending a grimy, young semi-conscience Marine lying naked on the first litter, sweating and shaking uncontrollably. His uniform and boots were piled up on the floor under the litter. Lewis didn't remember hearing a chopper land. Two I.V.'s were running, one in each arm. Wet towels were placed across the patient's forehead, under the back of his neck, in his armpits and in the crotch area.
He didn't detect any blood or wounds. The corpsman removed a thermometer from the troop's rectum and announced the reading to the M.O. standing behind him. "One-oh-five-point two…up point two from last."
The doctor calmly responded to the reading with a diagnosis followed by instructions, "Possible malaria, get him in the tub STAT and prepare for transport to hospital." He jotted something

on a chart before changing his order. "Belay my last…make it transport to Repose."
"Repose, Aye sir," the duty corpsman repeated to confirm his understanding.
The M.O. turned his attention to Lewis. "Can I help you?" the doctor questioned in a sort of snobbish way.
"Yeah," Lewis answered but wished he hadn't.
"Excuse me," the physician retorted.
"I mean, Yes Sir."
"That's better. Now what can I do for you young man?"
During his brief time in the service Lewis had come across a few officers-of-the-lines who were this arrogant but not one medical officer. This doctor seemed to be strictly career Navy and he reasoned that by the way the duty corpsman responded in the traditional nautical language, this person might be difficult to deal with.
"Sir, I mistakenly put the Dextrose on the shelves during my watch last night. Chief McKinny ordered me to come down here and bring them back. He said they were
needed at an aid station this morning, "Lewis explained as best he could.
"Well, you can't have them. We also need it here. You go back and inform your Chief McKinny if he has a problem with that to come see Lieutenant Commander Ebersen-Witmore."
"But sir…" Lewis started to plead before being interrupted.
"What is your name and what do you do?" the Commander asked abruptly.
"Lewis, sir. Hospitalman Gary Lewis."
"Hospitalman? May I inform you that you might not see Petty Officer unless you learn to do as you're instructed."
Lewis was dumbstruck by that remark. 'Ass-hole' he thought resisting the temptation to take a swing at the belligerent son-of-a-bitch. It took all the false respect he could muster to dismiss himself from the situation. "Sir, I'll relay the information to the chief. May I go, sir?"
"You may," the arrogant bastard smugly permitted.
Instead of just turning around and walking away, Lewis brought himself to attention followed by a nicely executed about face before smartly stepping out. On his way back to the CP he could feel his anger over that confrontation increasing with each step.

He laid odds in his mind that someday, somebody with less self-control than he will do that man well-deserved harm.

Heeb hollered back to the chief when Lewis entered the orderly room. "Chief, Lewis is here…" then leaned close to Lewis and continued in a song-like whisper…"and he's empty-handed."
The first thing McKinny noticed was that Lewis wasn't holding the Dextrose. "What's going on Lewis?" the Chief demanded.
Lew glanced at Heeb then back to the Chief. He managed to compose himself before explaining to the Chief what transpired in triage. McKinney accepted the explanation with some reservation and dismissed the young corpsman. "That's very interesting Lewis. It sounds like a bunch of crap but, hell I believe you. I'm going to get to the bottom of this thing before the day's over. Carry on."
Without hesitation. Lewis departed the orderly room. "Aye, aye Chief."

On the way back to the hootch he took time to eat lunch. Sitting by himself in the chow hall he pondered the morning's events. He couldn't believe he got chewed out twice in one day. "I don't like it here already' he told himself. Looking around at other people he noticed that there seemed to be cliques. It was a social moray that he never felt party to. He preferred to be selective when choosing friends and seldom gave in to peer pressure.
Finishing lunch he cleaned the try, remembering to offer a friendly smile and modest bow to the old Vietnamese man. It made him feel good.
By the time he got back to the hootch, Bennett was again sprawled out under his fan, sound asleep and snoring loudly. The two other cots were still empty.
Reaching into his sea bag he pulled out a tablet and pen. It was a good time to write home.

Hi Mom,
Well, I made it here safe and sound. Thought I'd take a few minutes to jot you a note. You know I'm not much for letter writing but I suspect you're anxious to hear from me. It's really hot here, probably around 100. I sweat all the time.
I'm assigned to the medical battalion in Da Nang. It's safe here and I get a lot of good food, so you don't have to worry about me.

I can tell you I'm not thrilled about being here; I would rather be back on ship seeing the world, ha ha. Hope you're feeling well. That's about all for now. I'll write again soon. Take care and tell George I said Hi. God Bless.

Love,
Gary

With a sense of accomplishment Lewis put the letter in an envelope, addressed it and placed a stamp in the corner. He immediately took it to the mail room where the clerk told him he didn't need a stamp. "Just write "FREE" where the stamp should be." He was instructed.

He deemed himself stupid because he already knew outgoing mail was free. He just wasn't thinking.

The remainder of the afternoon was spent reading the paperback and napping. Every so often he fanned himself with the book, glancing enviously at Bennett's fan. 'I *gotta get one of those'* he reminded himself before his eyelids closed.

"Hey Gary…Gary."

Hearing someone beckon he woke from a sound sleep.

"Yeah …yeah…what?" Lewis answered without opening his eyes, still wanting more sleep.

"Hey man, it's chow time. You going?"

Frustrated, he opened his eyes. It was Bennett. He pondered the question then replied.

"Nah, I want to get more zee's," he said rolling over on his side.

It was after nine-thirty that evening. Lewis slept through chow and then some but managed to wake in time to shower and dress before heading out for his watch in triage. He remembered to bring the paperback utility shirt and fresh pack of *Viceroys*. He presumed that Bennett had already left for work. Casually, he walked along the path alone. The evening air was a little cooler than the night before and the night sky was dark but clear and sprinkled with a billion twinkling stars. Half way to the chow hall he heard a series faint '*womps'* coming from the direction of DaNang. He didn't recognize the sound. Slowing his pace he turned to look back toward the city. From the high vantage point he could make out the entire area surrounding the city, about three miles away as the crow flies. Far away sirens began to scream from many directions. Suddenly, a huge, yellow-white fireball lit up the entire area. The sight was hypnotic, gluing Lewis's eyes

on the giant flash. A few seconds into the trance an increasing rumbling sound followed by a tremendous shock-wave hit with enough force to violently rattle all the building in the compound and buckle his legs. It was the loudest blast he had ever heard. The first thing that entered Lewis's mind was the enemy had the atomic bomb. Remembering grade school drills he ducked for cover in a nearby ditch. Fearing another, closer blast he remained there trembling, his heart racing. He had never experienced such a massive release of adrenalin. *'This is the real shit*! A few more seconds passed when he heard footsteps running by and voices shouting "incoming." Raising his head above the crest of the culvert he saw subdued silhouettes of people rushing toward the *'receiving'* area. He didn't think that anyone had spotted him hunkering down; he was glad of that. From all the activity he knew that something big was happening and that he should get to his station as quickly as possible. Jumping to his feet he darted along with the others. As he ran a weird thought entered his confused, adolescent mind. He wondered if he should stop and pick up his brown-bag lunch first. He wisely chose not to.
When Lewis arrived at 'Receiving' he saw about twenty other corpsman, Marines and doctors already there, including Doc VanHussen and the corpsman he relieved the night before. The one who told him to shelve the Dextrose. Not knowing exactly what to do he approached the corpsman. He wanted to question him about the Dextrose but determined it wouldn't be the appropriate time.
"Hey, am I supposed to relieve you now?" Lewis asked trying to catch his breath.
"Yeah, you're supposed to but, I'm not leaving just yet. We'll be getting a lot of casualties tonight…they'll probably be coming in all night long."
Uncertainty prompted Lewis to ask concurrent questions. "So, what's going on now? What should I do?"
"There's nothing we can do but wait for the helos…they should be getting here pretty soon."
The man really didn't answer the questions but, Lewis figured he'd find out what he should do when the time came. He decided to learn who the corpsman is instead "By the way, what's your name?"
"Sam," he answered simply.
"OK, Sam, I'm Lew."

“Lew,” he repeated, acknowledging that he heard it. “Just stand by,” then excused himself to be with the other corpsmen standing near the edge of the platform.

For a few long minutes Lewis just nervously stood thee attempting to figure out exactly what was about to take place. He observed the other corpsmen and Docs milling about in groups. They appeared to be too calm for the situation yet, somehow, Lewis sensed they were all uneasy.

“FIVE OUT” someone yelled. Everyone on the platform began disbursing in different directions. It seemed that they all had been through this before and that everyone except him knew their duties.

The familiar sound of rotor blades popping indicated the first chopper was inbound.

In less than a minute the CH-46 touched down on the helo pad, rear ramp already extended. After the chopper landed someone in triage turned on floodlights to illuminate the area. A half dozen Marine litter bearers crouching in the rotor-wash rushed to the rear ramp, entering two at a time. The first pair inside exited carrying the first bloody casualty into triage, followed by another and then another. The sequence was repeated until seven casualties were brought in. The chopper lifted off the pad immediately, making room for the next one. In triage Doc VanHussen and another doctor who Lewis hadn’t met yet were busy assessing the injuries. Four corpsmen hurried to cut away uniforms to expose wounds.

Sam positioned himself between two litters attempting to cover two men at a time. Lewis just stood there helplessly not knowing what he should do. Sam looked up, spotting him and barked “YOU, Lew, get your ass over here NOW!”

Lewis rushed over, scared but eager to help somehow.

“Take this man’s vitals,” he ordered.

Van Hussen stepped in and addressed the man. “Where do you hurt Marine?” he asked while quickly scanning the body.

“All over Doc, it hurts bad, it’s burning me all over,” the young Marine muttered.

The Doc determined that while the body had been peppered with shrapnel, no damage was done to the vital organs, never-the-less he ordered x-rays.

“You’ll be OK, just hang in there, we’ll have you fixed up in no time,” the Doc reassured before moving to the next litter.

"Goddammit, write down his vitals," Sam barked at the new corpsman.

Low did as he was instructed then took it upon himself to move to the next litter to do it again. He was shaking so badly that he could hardly attach the blood pressure cuff to the man's bloody arm. Looking at the young, unconscious, Marine's dirty, pale face he could tell that he wasn't in very good shape. "What's his BP?" Sam demanded as he cut through the uniform. Lewis couldn't hear diastolic through the stethoscope because of all the external noise. The second attempt was more successful. "Eighty-four over Fifty-eight," he reported. Sam noticed the Marine's extended belly hollering out, "Doc, I think we got an internal bleeder here."

The other physician moved in quickly, forcing Lewis out of his way. He felt the hard, distended stomach then, pinching a fingernail he asked, "What's this man's B.P.?"

Lewis repeated it. The Doc ordered to someone within ear-shot, "Get his man to O/R. STAT." Two corpsmen rushed over with a gurney, transferred the body, and then wheeled it quickly toward the operating room.

Lewis moved to another litter and repeated taking vital signs and jotting them on a form someone else had already begun to fill out and stopped when he saw all the vitals were already noted. Sam was working on a patient in the middle litter pushing an I/V. Lewis noticed a large battle dressing saturated with blood secured around the man's abdomen. Sam instructed the rookie to take a bottle of saline from the shelf and pour it slowly over the dressing. Lewis knew from training not to place a dry dressing over exposed internal organs as someone had done to this man, guessing that whoever tried to help him wasn't a corpsman or medic. Lewis complied with the order. The bloodstained excess poured off the canvas and onto the floor. Sam called out "We need a Doc here!" Van Hussen weaved his way through the rush. Bending over the body he closely examined the wound very carefully and gently tugged and probed at the dressing. Sam began a quick, cursory brief. "Also looks like a couple broken legs; left arm fracture; multiple shrapnel wounds

Below the trunk, including the genitals; minor burns all over; slow pupil response and…."

"And," the doctor interjected, "a broken pelvis. We'll need pictures…X-ray then O/R."

Van Hussen leaned in closer to the barely conscious man's ear. "Listen Marine, you're hurt pretty bad but, we'll get you fixed up. You need to hang in there."
The Marine struggled with a barely audible grunt, indicating that he heard what the Doc said.
The Doc's and corpsmen busily continued attending the other casualties. "ANOTHER BIRD INCOMING,' someone alerted the staff. About the same time a deuce-and-a-half pulled up close to the platform between triage and the helo pad. The driver shouted out,
"WE GOT WOUNDED HERE!"
Someone shouted back "OK, BUT YOU GOT TO MOVE THE TRUCK. WE GOT CHOPPERS COMING IN!" Litter bearers followed the vehicle as it moved away. The driver parked it, jumped out and helped lower the heavy, tail gate. Three walking wounded slowly climbed down off the truck bed assisted by the litter team. One body remained motionless on the bed floor. A corpsman climbed up on the bed while the litter team raised an open litter to him. Lewis watched the corpsman as he knelt down, disappearing behind the truck's side rails. A moment later he stood up and called out, "I need a Doc to pronounce." Hearing that, Lewis knew someone's mother would never see her son alive again. The thought cut deeply. The other doctor climbed up and a few seconds later climbed back down. Litter bearers carried the body over to the graves registration holding area, hidden out of sight behind a plywood wall.
Someone turned off the floodlights when the second helicopter descended. As it came into view, Lewis didn't recognize it as any kind of aircraft he had seen before. It was small, shiny aluminum fuselage, partly painted white, with large, dark lettering spelling out U.S. AIR FORCE along the side. It had two rotors side-by-side instead of in-line and twin, boom-like tails. He thought it was a strange looking. Two teams of litter bearers started approaching the rear of the aircraft when one of them tripped and fell in the darkness. Lewis dispatched himself to assist the injured man who advised Lewis that he would be OK and for him to go help the litter team. Another Marine jumped in saying "That's OK, I got it."
The helo's kept arriving with wounded troops most of the night. Doctors, corpsmen and litter bearers continued to work feverishly until near dawn when there was a lull in the activity. It was after

7 A.M. when Lewis was finishing up with cleansing and debriding a relatively minor laceration injury. More than two hours passed since the last chopper arrived with two injured and one dead. The morning watch was tasked with the clean-up. The platform was slippery with blood and cluttered with remnants of dressing wrappers and shredded uniforms. A young physician and the red-headed corpsman from the relieving watch came over to the litter where Lewis was. The Doc examined Lewis's work before announcing "Good job. We'll finish with the sutures. You can go now."

Lewis backed away meekly replying, "Yes sir," then turned to the wounded Marine.

"Good luck, take care of yourself."

"Thanks doc," the man replied, "you too."

Lewis looked around the triage, disbelieving what had taken place thee. He saw Doc VanHussen having a discussion with that bastard Ebersen-Witmore. He overheard what he thought was the evenings casualty count …"thirty-seven, three D.O.A." The numbers were far less than what it seemed.

It suddenly dawned on him that he hadn't eaten, smoked a cigarette or relieved himself all night. It was far different from the previous night. He was ready for a smoke but couldn't remember where he put the shirt and book. Thinking back he didn't recall bringing them with him. A light bulb went off…he must have left them in the ditch.

During the trek back to the hootch the events of the night ran through his head. Being the new kid on the block he thought he had performed well despite of all his inexperience and insecurities. He didn't screw up, that was the most important thing. He felt both relief and satisfaction. When he got to the ditch his shirt wasn't there, neither was the paperback. "Shit," he uttered aloud. He wondered who would take them but, it really didn't matter since he figured he wouldn't get them back anyway. Inside the hootch he saw Bennett standing there naked on one leg trying to put on a pair of skivvies. He just came from the shower. Lewis spotted his shirt and book lying on the cot. "I found your stuff on the ground, you must have dropped them when the bu-cu shit happened," Bennett confessed.

"Hey, thanks, I guess I did. Yeah, that was something huh?" he expounded while searching a pocket for the cigarettes.

"Sure was! I got eight patients on my ward…don't know how many the others got."
"I heard somebody way we got 37 wounded and 3 K.I.A.'s" Lewis sadly submitted.
"Does that count the ones who didn't' make it through surgery?" Bennett seriously asked.
The thought hadn't occurred to Lewis. "Hell, I don't know?" he answered painfully.
Sitting down on the cot he pulled a cigarette from the pack and lit up.
Observing the rookie's pain Bennett tried to ease his remorse.
"Man, you really need to get out of those clothes and get cleaned up."
Looking down at the sweat-soaked, bloodied tee-shirt and trousers he agreed. "Yeah…I guess I'd better," he said exhaling a lengthy trail of smoke.
The cold shower felt good on Lewis's body but it didn't detract from the night's emotional experience. All he could think about was the number of casualties and how they came in one after another and how he wished he possessed the skills and demeanor that Sam displayed. He scrubbed hard trying to remove the dried blood from his face and arms and under his fingernails. He wished he could wash the vivid images from his mind too but knew he never could. That night would become a haunting, life-long memory. He stopped scrubbing when he heard another chopper arriving. 'I don't know if I can take 13 months of this.'
Clean, but not refreshed, he returned to the hootch. Bennett was already snoring, the fan purring away. The other two cots were still empty. Lewis laid down in his skivvies, his body fighting with his mind to find sleep. It took about twenty minutes when his body finally won.

It was after 3 in the afternoon when Lewis woke up, uncomfortably immersed in his own perspiration. A '*piss hard-on'* was emerging from the front of his shorts, signaling him it was time to urinate. Before heeding nature's call, he lit a cigarette, then donned his trousers and shower shoes and made his way to the 'piss tube' buried deep in the ground near the outhouse. Still groggy, he stood there relieving himself with his eyes shut, the cigarette dangling from his lips, and the sweltering afternoon sun blanching the back of his neck. After shaking off the last drop, he took a few steps to the nearby water buffalo where he wished his hands and splashed water on his face, then opened his mouth under the spigot, gulping down several mouthfuls of the tepid, nasty tasting liquid. Thirst satisfied, he returned to the hootch.

Bennett was awake, still in his skivvies, sitting back under the fan's breeze in a folding, lawn chair that he procured earlier in the day from somewhere. He was leafing through a copy of the Star & Stripes while listening to '*Help Me Rhonda*' coming from a transistor radio owned by one of the missing guys. He appeared to be totally relaxed and unconcerned of anything going on outside the hootch. Upon seeing Lewis he lowered the paper,

"Hey man, you doing OK now?"

"Yeah, I guess so."

"How bout a cold Coke?" he offered retrieving a bottle from a small ice chest on the floor beside the chair.

"Sure," Lewis happily accepted. "That sounds great."

Bennett opened the bottle and handed it to the rookie. Lewis took a swig, letting the cold, bursting bubbles tickle his mouth.

"Ummm, that's good. Thanks" he said relishing the familiar taste.

"You're quite welcome, that'll be a buck."

"Huh?"

"Just kidding."

Lewis sat down on the edge of Bennett's cot asking, "So, how long have you been at First Med.?"

"About a month. Got here, let's see…four more days and it'll be a month exactly. Hell, I'm new here myself, so-to-speak…but I'm not an F.N.G. like you."

Lewis didn't like that title but thought it better not to let it show that it bothered him.

"You been in this hootch all that time?"

"Yep."

"That's funny, Rappaport told me that this is a temporary billet," Lewis insisted.

"Yeah, he told me that too…what can I say," replied shrugging his shoulders.

They both took another swallow of Coke simultaneously. Just then Heeb entered. SLAM.

"Speak of the fukin Devil," Bennett proclaimed. "We were just talking about you."

"Oh yeah," Heeb answered back shutting his eyes. "Well, I don't fuck and I'm not the devil so, what exactly were you guys saying about me?" Bennett and Lewis both chuckled at Heeb's mannerism.
"We were just discussing how you told us both that this is just a temporary hootch."
"Holy Moses, that's what I came to talk to you about. You guys must be psychic or something." The two got another chuckle.
"So, what's going on now?" Bennett queried.
"First, these two guys," Heeb paused and pointed to the empty cots. "They're outta here. It seems that they," Heeb paused again to make quotation marks in the air with his fingers, "borrowed" a mighty-mite a few days ago…ran it off the deep water pier after a few drinks and whatever with the ladies in Dogpatch. Right now both of them are at the Navy Hospital…hurt pretty bad. The JAG's going to send somebody later to help recover their belongings so don't touch anything, OK?"
Unfazed by the news Bennett remarked "Sounds like Leavenworth to me."
"That's not all," Heeb continued. "The Chief is going to move some people around. You'll be getting some new *hootch-mates* sometime in the next day or two."
"Shit," Bennett cursed, disappointed by the news. "Looks like we'll have to field day this place."
"Well, it needs it, don't you think?" Lewis responded.
"I suppose it does but remember, you're the E-3 new guy here," Bennett came back.
Lewis nodded acknowledging that he was the low man on the totem pole.
Sticking up for his new friend Heeb addressed Bennett. "It's a team effort. Everybody has to do their share…just like all the other hootches."
Lewis and Bennett looked at each other. "OK," Bennett reluctantly agreed. "Here's to the team," he added, raising the nearly empty bottle, gesturing an impromptu toast before gulping down the last swallow.
"One more thing," Heeb looked directly at Lewis. "That thing with the Dextrose. It's all squared-away so, don't worry about it."
Surprised, Lewis asked "How?"
"It's a long story; just don't worry about it, OK?" Heeb answered back.

"OK."
"Alright then, I gotta get back…catch you later." SLAM
Immediately after Heeb was out of ear-shot Bennett began to dictate the 'rules' to Lewis.
"Now that the Jew-boy is gone and nothing will get back to the Chief, let's get something straight right now. E-3's and below will do the field-day'n in this hootch. E-4's and above will supervise. This is still the military, got it E-3?"
Jarred by Bennett's remark and attitude Lewis's gut feeling was to lay into him with a right cross but realizing that a physical assault on an NCO would only get him into serious trouble and since Bennett outsized him by about 40 pounds, he'd probably get his ass kicked, he had no choice but take it. "That's the Navy way…Petty Officer," Lewis came back facetiously, handing Bennett the empty Coke bottle then walked back to his cot fuming inside. Lewis understood the lowest ranking men got the menial, dirty jobs but he couldn't understand Bennett's bigoted remark. It disgusted him. He made up his mind then and there to avoid Bennett as much as possible. He got in uniform and went to chow.
Seeing Sam in front of the cow line Lewis remembered Heeb saying the Dextrose incident had been squared-away. Curious as to how, he decided to ask Sam about it before chow was over. Carrying the try filled with some sort of meat loaf and runny mashed potatoes Lewis approached the table to sit down in an empty seat across from Sam and his buddies.
"Hey guys," Lewis opened with an unobtrusive salutation.
"Hey rookie," one of them responded. It was the one who called him an FNG two days earlier on his first watch in triage.
"Lew," Sam acknowledged and bestowed an invitation, "have a seat." Lewis complied.
Noticing everyone at the table was gulping down their meal so quickly, Lewis assumed that they were still on watch and were there only for the short period of time it took to eat and get back to relieve someone else for chow. Lewis figured it wouldn't hurt to ask about the Dextrose now. Facing Sam he started off somewhat meekly and apologetic.
"I was told not worry about the Dextrose thing. I hope I didn't get you in any trouble."
"Everything's copasetic," Sam calmly replied, then followed up by explaining that there were two boxes of Dextrose solution

there that evening. One was meant for triage the other for the aid station. Someone from the 1/1's aid station must have come in and discretely picked up their box without telling anyone. Searching his short-term memory a few seconds Lewis happily responded, "Yeah, now I remember. You said '*boxes*' not '*box*'! That means I didn't screw up after all!"

"That's what it means. You did what you were told to do," Sam enlightened him. What Sam didn't divulge was the fact that the corpsman sitting next to him was on duty with

him that night and knew that the troop from 1/1 picked up the Dextrose but, he forgot to tell Sam.

"By the way," Sam added, "thanks for your help last night. You catch on quick."

"Thanks," Lewis smiled.

With that over with Sam and the other two corpsmen got up to go back to their watch.

"See you later," Sam predicted.

"Later, aye," Lewis beamed.

Pleasantly relieved by Sam's story, Lewis casually consumed the stuff on his tray without regard to the taste or texture. Pondering what Sam revealed, but totally unaware of the real facts, he laid blame on the guy from the aid station for his run-in with Ebersen-Witmore. Thinking he still didn't like that name, he decided to give the ass-hole a new name, something more befitting his character. '*Let's see..how..about Ebersen-Witless..no..Witless-Witmore..that has a ring to it..no, just a simple Witless should do.'* Satisfied with the new, secret pet name he finished his meal. After remembering to smile and bow at the old man in the scullery he nonchalantly made his way back to the hootch. When he got there he saw a jeep parked beside it. "*Must be the JAG,"* he assumed. Once inside his assumption proved to be correct. A Marine Second Lieutenant, an MP Corporal and Chief McKinney were there taking inventory of the two men's personal belongings. They all looked over at him when he let the door slam. Bennett was there also, kneeling on the floor, packing items away in the foot lockers and sea bags as the officer identified them to the MP, who was making notations on a clipboard. Not knowing what else to do Lewis offered up, "Can I be of help?"

"McKinney come toward him and in his normal mild-mannered voice asked, "What's your name again?"

"Lewis, Chief."

"That's right…Lewis. You just got here didn't you Lewis?"
"Yes Chief, three days ago."
"Uh-huh," pointing down at the cot he continued, "What's this?"
Lewis looked to where the Chief was pointing. Slightly befuddled he answered, "That's my rack Chief."
"Your rack...you sleep on this do you?"
"Yes Chief."
"Not very comfortable is it?"
"Not really Chief."
"Where's the cross piece?"
"I don't know Chief. It wasn't there when I got it." Lew explained.
"I'll buy that. I see the canvas is beginning to rip too. Well, here's what I recommend you do. Either shit a cross piece or, when they're finished up over there," the Chief turned his head in the direction of the others," you take one of them racks there and deep-six this one. Is that clear?"
"Yes Chief. It's clear."
"Good." The Chief gave him a half smile before continuing.
"Then, you and Bennett over there, give this deck a good sweep-down, swab-down, fore and aft. It's a pig-sty in here."
"Yes Chief, I'll make it is so," Lewis answered, resolved since he's the lower rank he'd do the work.
"No," the Chief corrected "you ***both*** will make it so."
Overhearing the Chief's orders Bennett got to his feet. "Chief, I'm a Petty Officer Third," he stressed; hoping that bit of information would exempt him from the detail.
McKinney knew what Bennett was up to but he didn't let it change his orders. "Yes, I know you're a Petty Officer, Bennett. And having had attained such a high, salty, rank in my Navy, you surely must have gained a great deal or expertise along the lines of field-day. Therefore, I expect YOU to give Hospitalman Lewis here instruction ***by example*** on the proper techniques of conducting a field-day part. Is that clear?"
Frustrated by the defeat, Bennett huffed, "Yes Chief, it's perfectly clear."
"Good, I'm glad we came to this understanding. I want to see this shit-hole be spic-n-span by noon tomorrow."
The unexpected dressing down the Chief gave Bennett delighted Lewis. It was obvious that the Chief didn't particularly care for him either.

"I think we're finished here Chief," the lieutenant announced in typical second lieutenant military bearing. "I think we got all the personal gear. Everything else is issue, it belongs to you."
"Yes sir, is there anything else we can help you with sir?"
"You can get this stuff loaded in the back of the jeep," the officer replied.
Instinctively, Lewis and Bennett both acted on the request without being ordered to. Lewis spotted the transistor radio on Bennett's shelf. Deliberately wanting to rile Bennett he spoke up, "I think that radio there belongs to one of these guys Chief."
The Chief first looked at the radio then at Bennett.
"Oh, yeah, I must have forgotten. They said I could borrow it, sorry." Bennett lied; everyone knew it. He handed it over to the corporal.
As the jeep drove off, Chief McKinney reminded both Lewis and Bennett before departing, "Tomorrow, noon, I'll be back to inspect. Carry on."
Bennett couldn't wait until the Chief was gone before tearing into Lewis. "You idiot! Why'd you have to mention the radio? Jones did say I could borrow it. Now, because you have to be so stupid, we don't have nothing to listen the groovy sounds with."
Pleased with himself for being honest Lewis didn't allow Bennett's ear-beating bother him. He smiled at Bennett saying "I'm not a thief," then simply walked away.
With a little more than an hour left before he had to go on watch Lewis didn't want to return to the hootch just yet. He thought a moment before he decided to go up to the club for a soda. There were about fifteen people there smoking and joking, he didn't recognize anyone. He was hoping Heeb would be there but wasn't. Finding a space to stand at the bar he ordered a Coke from the same red-head he had not yet met. He observed the beer selection was whittled down to just Blatz. The red-haired corpsman place a bottle of Royal Crown in front of him. "I'm sorry, I asked for Coke," Lewis apologized nicely.
"I'm sorry too, we don't have Coke. We have RC, that's all. That'll be twenty-five cents"
Lewis accepted the drink and handed over a quarter. A *Bonanza* rerun was being aired on the TV while overtones of *"I Wanna Hold Your Hand'* was barely audible from the radio. A group of four was playing partners at the pool table, each taking turns using

the only cue stick they had between swigs of Blatz. The smoke irritated Lewis's eyes.

It was difficult for him to comprehend how these medical people could seem so unaffected by the nature of their jobs. All the sick, injured, maimed and dead these guys have to deal with on a daily basis must have really calloused them all, he thought. It was getting too smoky. Lewis walked outside to finish his soda. Sitting on the club steps he tried to prepare himself for the watch tonight. Physically, he felt good—emotionally he wasn't sure. He prayed it wouldn't be a repeat of the previous night. His thoughts were broken by a sudden blitz of mosquitoes targeting him everywhere, even though his heavy cotton trousers. Abruptly, he stood up swatting at the buzzing vermin. He realized that he was sitting under the lights, attracting all the insects in Vietnam, including the blood-thirsty, malaria carrying kind. He retreated back inside angry with himself for being so stupid. Forty minutes of continuous itching passed before he left the smoky haven to go to work. He stopped by the hootch to retrieve his book and another pack of Viceroys. Bennett wasn't there.

When Lewis arrived at 'receiving' he saw Sam there directing two grimy *'grunt'* Marines in helmets and flak-jackets with M-14's slung on their shoulders assisting a third marine hobbling on one leg. "Put him on that litter," Sam calmly directed, pointing to an empty station.

"He got shot in the foot Doc," one reported as the pair lifted the wounded man up onto the litter.

"With what?" Sam asked.

"AK," said the other.

"Ouch," Sam remarked semi-seriously, judging from the experience that the injury wasn't life-threatening. Making a quick decision he looked at the rookie "Corpsman Lewis here will take care of you," then turned to the wounded man. "Just lay back and get as comfortable as you can, I'll let the Doc know he was a paying customer."

Pulling Lewis aside he gave his report before being relieved from watch. "Everything is stocked and in order. There's one KIA in 'graves holding'. They should be here anytime to pick up the body. Robertson is the Duty Doc and…as always ...S-2 says DaNang might get hit again tonight."

The last comment penetrated Lewis's gut but he hid it from Sam. "Got it," he said, understanding the report. "You're relieved." He took one step toward the litter then turned. "Hey Sam."

"Something else?" Sam questioned.

"Yeah. Who's the KIA?"

Without any indication of sensitivity Sam replied, "I don't know, some poor bastard from 1/5. The '*skinny's*' on the tag. Anything else?"

"No, nothing else"

Lew stashed the brown bag meal and paperback in a nearby cubby hole before turning his attention to the young '*grunt*'. The muddy, canvas-sided, jungle-boot was soaked with blood.

"Before we take off the boot I need to take your blood pressure and pulse. Its stuff the Docs need to know." Lewis informed.

"You gotta do what you gotta do Doc."

After making a note of the readings Lewis pulled the goose-neck lamp close to the litter and retrieved a pair of scissors. "I'm going to cut the laces and take off your boot. It's going to hurt a little," he warned in advance.

"It's OK Doc, pain builds character."

The young man's profound remark caused Lewis to pause for a second to absorb the meaning. He couldn't help but wonder if the young troop meant what he just said or simply wanted to impress his buddies with 'gung ho' manliness. Actually, it really didn't matter, he like the phrase and framed it in his mind, thinking that he may use it someday.

After the laces were severed, Lewis began as gently as possible to pull the tug at the boot. Enduring the pain the Marine tightly gripped the sides of the litter while clinching his teeth, determined not to cry out. Lewis tossed the boot on the floor then proceeded to cut away the drenched sock, tossing it on the floor also. The two grunts stepped forward to get a closer look.

"Shee-it, you mean we 'humped' your ass all the way here for THAT?" one blurted out.

Everybody let out a small laugh.

Lewis examined the wound. The bullet passed through between the ankle and Achilles tendon. Grabbing a gauze pad he dabbed at the blood still oozing from the holes when Doc Robertson appeared. Lewis recognized him as the Doc with Van Hussen from the night before, The 'grunts' stepped back while Lewis moved aside for the Doc.

“Well, what do we have here?” Robertson asked.

Trying to appear as professional as possible Lewis rattled off, “G-S-W, T-N-T left foot, 110 over 68, 94.”

“Uh-huh,” the physician acknowledged as he leaned over, pulling the lamp in closer.

Stymied, one of the ‘grunts’ whispered to Lewis “What did you just say?”

Lewis explained, “Gun-Shot-Wound, going completely through the left foot, his blood pressure is 110 over 68 and pulse is 94 beats a minute.”

“Oh.”

While carefully scrutinizing the wound, Doc Robertson, in his easy-going manner, began asking unimportant questions to the young casualty.

“Where you from Marine?”

“A little town called Eureka Springs, Arkansas sir.”

“Arkansas, huh?” Never been there. I hear it’s pretty country though.”

“Yes sir, it is…AHHH,” the youth cried out from pain when the Doc touched his ankle.

“Sorry,” the Doc apologized as he stood up. “Here’s what’s going on. I don’t think you have any damage to your bones, but we’re going to get some X-rays to make sure. I’ll have orthopedics check it out tomorrow. They might want to ship you out to the Repose.”

Concerned, the Marine asked, “When can I get back to my unit Doc?”

“I can’t say for sure. It all depends on the full extent of your injury and how long it takes to heal. Besides, you might not want to go back after seeing all those pretty, big-tit, nurses on the Repose!” The young man strained a smile that ricocheted onto everyone else’s face.

Writing notes on the patient’s chart Doc Robertson addressed Lewis. “Clean and dress the wound, give him Demerol, 50 milligrams, IM. I’ll send in someone from X-ray, they’ll take him to the ortho ward from there.”

“Yes sir,” Lewis replied as the Doc handed him the chart.

“Take care of yourself Marine,” the Doc said departing the triage.

The two ‘grunts’ kidded their comrade as they watched Lewis administer the Demerol and dress the wound. “You maggot son-of-a-bitch, we know you let the ‘gook’s shoot you on purpose just

so you can see some boo-koo tit. Maybe next time we get in a fire-fight, I'll throw my foot out to get shot at too!"
"Bullshit, I saw both you bastards not getting off one round. I'll bet neither of you even has to clean your pieces."
"You know what sweetie, talk like that hurts our feelings."
By the barrage of playful jabs, Lewis gathered that these guys cared about each other; that a close camaraderie existed in their unit that he didn't see in the medical battalion. He imagined that most combat units shared the closeness.
"OK, all finished," Lewis announced just as the corpsman from X-ray walked in pushing an empty wheel-char. Both Marines helped their friend off the litter into the chair and
bid him farewell as he was wheeled away. "See ya later man, don't knock-up any of those nurses." "Or squids," the other laughed referring to the sailors.
After their buddy disappeared from sight one of the Marines asked Lewis if there was anywhere they could get some food and place to sleep for the night, explaining that it was too dangerous to drive back to their unit in the dark. The request put Lewis on the spot. Looking at his watch he told them the chow hall was closed but then remembered he had a brown bag meal and offered it to them. "About the best I can do for you guys is a couple of sandwiches."
Realizing the corpsman was offering them his meal the men refused. "Nah Doc, we can't take your lunch."
"No, it's OK. I want you to have it. I had a big dinner earlier. Besides, I only eat it to kill time anyway."
They gave in to Lewis's insistence as he handed over the bag. Lewis smoked a cigarette watching them devour the SPAM and cheese sandwiches and share the Blend. They even shared a hard-boiled egg slicing it in two using a well utilized K-BAR knife. One of them let out aloud belch just before lighting up a Marlboro. Not knowing whether or not he would get into any trouble, Lewis took it upon himself to offer them empty litters to sleep on for the night. He qualified the offer by telling them that if casualties start coming in they would have to give them up and get out of the area. They agreed. Within a few minutes they were snoring, rifles by their side. Lewis turned off the bank of lights above the litters. Shortly thereafter the 'graves registration' showed up. It was difficult to see a body bag being treated like a sack of flour but the reality is that it doesn't hurt the d

The watch was passing as slowly as his first night on duty. Alone, Lewis sat of the edge of the platform smoking and watching the flares drifting downward. Occasional dim 'pops' from small arms fire, too far away to be of concern, broke the relative silence. Lewis leaned forward, folding his arms onto his lap and lowered his head.

Something startled him awake. He looked around before getting to his feet. It was still dark, the grunts were still sleeping soundly; no one else was around and he didn't hear any choppers. His mind was playing tricks on him he reasoned. He took a reading from his watch; it was nearly 4:30 in the morning. He figured he had slept almost three hours in the same position, accounting for the stiffness in his neck and back. Putting both hands behind his neck he massaged it while rotating his head in small circles. He heard something and stopped the motion to listen closer. He heard it again but couldn't make it out, then once again. The noise seemed to be coming somewhere up behind the chow hall then, it dawned on him. It was the cooks getting prepared for breakfast. The handling of pots and kettles echoed to the nearby buildings. Satisfied that he learned the origin of the noise and the cause of his sudden wake up, he lit a smoke and waited for his watch to come to an end. A half-hour had passed before the jet noise from the airfield woke one of the grunts who abruptly sat up. Getting his bearings, he woke his buddy. "Hey shit-maggot, time to di-di."

Both of them crawled off the litters, clutching the M-14's and walked over to Lewis. "Hey Doc, we gotta get goin', they'll be wonderin' where we are. Thanks for everything man, we really appreciate it."

"No problem guys. If you're over back this way look me up, OK?"

"Don't take this the wrong way Doc but, I hope we never see you again, if ya know what I'm sayin'"

They climbed into the jeep and drove off. '*Yeah, I know what you're sayin'* Lewis thought as they disappeared around the corner.

While walking back to the hootch after having a fairly decent breakfast, Lewis thought about the detail ahead. Despite grabbing a couple hours sleep he was tired and really didn't feel up to anything laborious but, he know that Chief McKinney will have a conniption if the hut isn't squared away by noon. He doubted that

Bennett would comply with the Chief's directive, preferring to let him do all the work. When he entered the quarters he was surprised to see that Bennett had already started the field day. Clouds of dust kicked up as the Petty Officer furiously swept little piles of dirt into the center of the floor. He eyed Lewis but didn't say anything and just kept sweeping. Lewis was tempted to follow the Chief's orders explicitly and let Bennett show by example but, reasoned that doing so would just create more animosity between them. That wouldn't serve any purpose. The task should be a team effort. Tossing the paperback on the cot he began picking up the larger articles of trash and placing it an empty cardboard box. After depositing the trash in a dumpster he returned to the hootch with a swab and bucket of water. By that time Bennett had finished with the sweep down so Lewis began swabbing down the deck just like he had done so many times aboard ship. Neither man spoke to one another. The heat had dried the deck almost as fast as Lewis could swab it. Before long the entire structure was as clean as it could possibly get. The men lined up cots evenly spaced along the deck, each choosing a side, leaving a clear pathway down the center. They neatly folding the blankets and ponchos on their own cots and stowed away any loose article in sight. Lewis placed his sea bag under the new cot that he picked up earlier so it wouldn't give a cluttered appearance. They had finished just before lunch and was expecting Chief McKinney to appear at any time. Both men received a certain sense of satisfaction from their labor. The hootch at least appeared to be ship-shape.

McKinney arrived as he said he would. Without bothering to enter he stuck his head in the door just before noon, giving a quick scan before proclaiming "Looks good. Now keep it this way." Then he scurried away as if he had something important to do.
Bennett had no problem expressing himself. "That bastard!"
Lewis couldn't help but think that Bennett was looking for some recognition and praise for the work and gathered that he would take all the credit if given the opportunity to do so. Tired from lack of sleep and working feverishly in the heat, Lewis decided to finally sack out. Stripping to his skivvies he watched Bennett muttering and throwing a hissy-fit as he left for chow. *"Good! Maybe now I can get some shut-eye,"* Lewis whispered under his breath.

A week had passed since the two had field-day'd the hootch. During that time three more corpsmen had been assigned to live there. Hospital Corpsman 3rd Class Angel Rodriguez, Hospitalmen Johnnie Sherman and Francis A. Wilfong. Petty Officer Rodriguez had been at 1st Med. nearly seven months, making him senior over Bennett and in-charge of the hootch. From the day he moved in he immediately showed a dislike for Bennett, as did the other two. Rodriguez was a likable Hispanic from Los Angeles. It was rare to see him without a pleasant smile on his face. He had been in the Navy more than three years and had his eyes set on being a career man, a "lifer" in military lingo. Both Sherman and Wilfong hailed from Ohio. Sherman called Youngstown, Ohio his home while Wilfong came from the small town of Zanesville.

The two were a study in contrasts. At six feet-three inches tall and about 230 pounds, Sherman was a hulk of a young man. In high school sports was his forte', especially football. His athletic ability had won him scholarships at several small colleges. Unfortunately, his academic mind didn't respond well to study. Rather than being drafted into the Army, he chose to enlist in the Navy. Wilfong, on-the-other-hand was a pale, skinny, blonde-haired young man who displayed distinct feministic mannerisms although, he didn't impress the others as being a queer. He was extremely soft-spoken and introverted. Nevertheless, his presence in the hootch did indeed provoke an uneasy atmosphere. Everyone except Bennett accepted Wilfong's mannerisms for what they were—just mannerism's.

"That little faggot better never come near me," Bennett proclaimed to the men in the hootch when Wilfong wasn't there. "If he does I'll cut his tiny nuts off." He threatened.

Rodriguez jokingly responded, "Hey man, how you know his nuts is tiny?"

Flustered, Bennett came back, "'Cause all fags got tiny nuts. That's what makes 'em fags. Everybody knows that."

"You a wrong hombre' man. You'd be better off just to keep your mouth shut. You hear me?"

"You don't go telling me what to do," Bennett snapped. "Just 'cause you're senior to me don't give you the right to dictate to me. I got freedom of speech 'ya know."

"Not in my Navy you don't."

Lewis and Sherman stood out of the way, watching the two as tension built up.
"Your Navy! exclaimed Bennett. "Your Navy! Since when do wetbacks have a navy?
The smile left Rodriguez's face. He coolly crossed the floor toward his newly acquired adversary. Angel got nose to nose with Bennett, jabbing a strong, stiff finger in his chest, pushing him backwards.
"For your information man, I was born in L.A. I didn't swim no river man. If I ever hear you call me or any of my brothers a wetback again, we'll see who cuts whose nuts off. Comprende?"
Bennett retorted, "Hey man, you just assaulted an NCO. I got witnesses." He said looking toward Lewis and Sherman.
Angel turned his head looking at the two subordinates.
"I didn't see anything," Lewis reported smoothly.
"Me neither," Sherman agreed.
Bennett, sensing defeat, backed off. "Hey man, I'm sorry. I didn't mean to.................."
"No man," Angel interrupted, pointing a finger in Bennett's face. "You did mean to. If you did'n meant to you wouldn't have said it."
The confrontation ended when Angel wisely turned his back and walked away.
Doc Lewis was disappointed that Angel didn't tear into Bennett with his fists, after all, he did deserve a good ass-whoopin'.

Lewis had been at 1st Med. for almost a month before he got his first letter from home. Every day he stopped by the mail room to check if he had gotten any mail. Every day he was disappointed. But, not that day. It was from his mother and postmarked a week and a half earlier. He didn't waste any time opening it. Sitting down under the shade of a banana tree he glued his eyes on every word.

Dear Son,
I received your letter this morning. I was so excited and happy to get it I cried. It's comforting to learn that you're not involved in any combat and are eating well.
If you only knew how I worry about you. My heart aches when I see the news on TV and hear about all those boys dying for this useless war. Oh how I pray for your safe return home. Now I

know how grandma felt when Uncle Frank and Uncle John were in the war. A mother always worries about her children, no matter how old they get.

I have some other news for you that you probably didn't expect. George and I got married last Saturday. I know this might be a bit of a shock to you but your old enough to know that mother needs someone to take care of her.
Please try to understand that he will never take the place of Daddy, no one can but he is kind and treats me well.

We'll be moving up to an apartment on Benton St. next month. This place is too big for just the two of us.

I'm sorry I have to make this short. I have to get ready for work. I'm doing waitress work at the Greek's on Main St. They'll fire me even if I'm one minute late.
Remember, I love you Gary. God be with you. *Mother*

As welcome as the letter was, he wasn't prepared for the marriage part. He had met George while on leave three months earlier and didn't like him. Since his real father died of cancer at age 47 back in '59, his mother remarried to an over-the-road truck driver in '62 and divorced a year later. Now she remarried again. He understood that his mother was only 52 years old and relatively still attractive and needed companionship but this jerk left a lot to be desired.
He could picture them in his mind going out to the Lithuanian Club on Saturday nights, drinking beer and dancing then sleeping it off all day on Sunday. He didn't like his vision. His dad and her never behaved that way when he was alive. He just couldn't comprehend how his mother took the slide downhill. His thought was cut short when he heard someone addressing him.
"Hey Lew, finally get some mail?"
Looking up, Doc Lewis saw a silhouette backlit from the sun brightly glaring behind the figure. He didn't have to see the face since he recognized the voice as he friend Heeb.
Squinting he answered. "Yeah, finally." He got to his feet, folded the letter and placed back into the envelope. "What's up?
"Not much," Heeb replied. "Just lookin for Bennett. Have you seen him?"

“No. Not today. Of course, I’m not actually looking for him either.”
“Well, I gotta find him. The Red Cross confirmed that his dad passed away yesterday. The Chaplin is waiting for him at the orderly room now. We’re cutting orders for emergency leave for him. I gotta go. If ‘ya see him send over but, don’t tell him why. OK?”
“OK. If I see him.” Lewis promised.
Luck had it that Lewis ran into Bennett a short time later, before Heeb did. He was returning from the PX at Hill 327
“Hey Bennett, Heeb’s been looking for you,” Lewis kept his promise.
“Oh yeah, what’s that Jew-boy want now?” he responded with his typical demeanor.
Biting his tongue while attempting to maintain his composure, Lewis just calmly answered back. “I think it’s pretty important. You’d better go to the orderly room on-the-double.”
Bennett made the detour rather than going back to the hootch.

The night was cool, dark and rainy when Lewis reported for duty at the triage. Except for the rain pelting hard against the tin roof, it was unusually quiet. All the litters were empty. He received the customary report from Sam as he relieved the watch.
“We received 17 casualties. Four we’re K.I.A.s . Graves already picked them up. The others are either admitted or transported elsewhere. We got one Viet Cong P.O.W. with a concussion. After we patched him up the M.P.’s took the fucker away. Everything here is cleaned up and stocked. Oh yeah, your buddy Ebersen-Witmore is the duty M.O.”
“Great,” Lewis responded sarcastically.
“Yeah. Other than that, there’s nothing more to report,” Sam finished.
“I guess you’re relieved then” Lew came back.

The watch passed slowly. Lewis figured that the weather kept the V.C. from conducting their attacks and reasoned that there would not be too many, if any, incoming casualties that night. The lack of patients didn’t bother him at all. Over the past month he felt that he had seen his share wounded young men, not to mention the scores of bodies that were killed-in-action. The images of the K.I.A’s were especially difficult to get out of his mind. So many of their faces looked uncommonly familiar. He couldn't help but search his memory, wondering where he met them yet; he knew that he had never seen any of them before. Even the wounded haunted him. Over the short period of time he had been in Nam, they seemed to appear in wholesale numbers. Every type of wound imaginable passed through the triage at some point over the past month. Bullet penetrations and shrapnel in every part of the body was common place. Burns, concussions, fractures, malaria and a myriad of other injuries and illnesses filled the triage nearly every day. Even the smallest of lacerations needed to be treated against infection in the tropical climate. He was amazed at the skill demonstrated by the dedicated Docs who miraculously pieced shattered bodies back together to the point of being transportable back in the states. He even had to admit that Witless-Witmore saved men from nearly impossible odds of survival. There had been times when buckets of water had to be thrown across the floor to wash off large pools of slippery blood. He recalled one badly wounded Marine arriving with cardboard from a C-ration box serving as a battle dressing placed over a stomach wound and secured in place with thin-gauge communication wire. He couldn't imagine the corpsmen in combat having to resort to such crude, lifesaving methods.

The first rule is to stop the bleeding by using anything that's available. Fight the infection later.

Lew's thoughts were suddenly interrupted by a nearby roll of thunder. A constant curtain of water fell from the edge of the tin roof into deepening puddles at the edge of the triage deck. He lit a cigarette and stared out into the wet darkness, welcoming the coolness of the wind and rain. Out of the darkness he saw a poncho-clad figure sloshing through the flood coming toward him. As the figure got closer he recognized it as his friend Heeb.

"As you were," Heeb blurted out as a joke as he stepped up unto the triage deck.

"What are you doing out in this weather? You think you're some kind of duck?" Lew mused.

"Nah, even ducks wouldn't be out in this," he answered. "I just finished up some paper work and was heading over for midnight chow. I thought I'd drop by and tell you the latest skinny."

"Oh yeah, what skinny?"

"Well, your buddy Bennett left this afternoon. It looks like he won't be coming back. I guess he's looking at a hardship

discharge when he gets back to the world. He said he's the only one left to support his mother now that his father died."
"Hey, I'm sorry to hear about his dad but, I can't say that anyone here will be disappointed about that asshole not coming back."
"You're right on target there my friend. Chief even made everyone drop what they were doing just to expedite Bennett's orders. Chief, himself called around just to find the first available flight outta here. He found an Air Force C-141 heading back to Hickam earlier and had Corporal Marks drive Bennett over. I guess he's somewhere over the Pacific by now."
A selfish thought popped into Lew's head. *'I wonder if he left his electric fan behind?'*
Another roll of thunder shook the air.
"OK man, I'm hattin' out to chow now. You want me to bring you back some coffee or somethin'?" Heeb thoughtfully asked.
"No thanks man. I'll talk to you tomorrow. See ya."

Alone once again, Lewis' ever busy mind continued processing random thoughts and ideas. He dwelled mostly on questioning his worthiness as a corpsman. He admitted to himself that he gained a lot of experience in the triage but, somehow it just wasn't satisfying enough for him. He wondered if he could be more useful out in the field with a combat unit. He didn't place much value on his work at 1st Med. Most of his time seemed to be spent prepping the wounded for the Docs. Stripping off clothing, taking vital signs, cleansing wounds, starting IV's, giving injections, applying dressings, stocking supplies and filling out paperwork just wasn't his bag. Even though he knew his work was important in the overall scheme of things, it just wasn't fulfilling enough for him. The nights when the triage was heavy with casualties and his adrenalin pumped at a hundred miles an hour in all the confusion and rushing around trying to help save lives is what he liked the most. He felt that it was when he was at his best. It was when he had the most confidence in himself. He thrived on the action. Some nights were like that but, most of the time they weren't. Most nights he just sat around reading a paperback, smoking cigarettes and waiting. He wondered how his friend and fellow corpsman, Jack Johnson was doing at 1/1. He and Jack had become friends during their clinical training at the Naval Hospital in Jacksonville, Florida. They were ordered to Camp Pendleton together, as well as to the transient facility in Okinawa.

That's where they became separated. He had heard that Jack got assigned to the infantry unit about a week before he himself came in country. During his time at 1st Med. he had seen several wounded Marines from 1/1 pass through triage and wondered if Jack was the corpsman who treated them in the field. The notion entered his head that if Jack ever got hit, he might be the triage corpsman on duty who would have to attend to him. It was a notion that he forced aside because he didn't want anything to happen to Jack and he didn't want to think about it.
'Maybe I should transfer to a combat unit.' He thought. The idea somehow appealed to him. The only problem he had was trying to decide which unit to ask for a transfer to. The 'grunts' always seem to get into the shit and the odds of getting killed were pretty high. The artillery might be a possibility. 'Arty' fire bases are usually far back from the action but, they're normally isolated and come under attack frequently because of their support value. He recollected that back at Camp Pendleton, the two drill sergeants were always going at each other about which units were better. One D.I. advocated for the grunts. Strength in numbers was his logic. The other D.I. insisted that Recon was the way to go. Six-man teams 'snoopin'-n'-poopin', undetected through the jungle was far safer. Lewis reasoned that both type units had their advantages as well as disadvantages. However, being young and unfamiliar with the Corps and direct combat, he wasn't sure of what to do. The one thing he was sure of was that more grunts came in wound than did Recon Marines. He did recall a Corporal Allen from 1st Recon had died sometime in July but, he didn't know the circumstances. He reasoned that one dead from Recon as opposed to maybe forty or fifty K.I.A.'s from grunt outfits during the month he been there, the chances of surviving his tour of duty were better with Recon. He also thought of the Civil Action Program, where small groups of corpsmen and Marines actually live with the Vietnamese in their villages. The CAP is meant to help win over the hearts and minds of the indigenous people through providing security and medical care. He saw the problem with that is too many of the people were also the VC at night. He heard stories of entire CAP teams being slaughtered by the very people they came to help. To his way of thinking it was too dangerous. Besides, he didn't particularity like the Vietnamese anyway. He 'deep-sixed' that idea.

Lew mauled over the idea of transferring throughout his watch. The rain had subsided and the clouds began to disperse nearer to daybreak. He imagined that the heat and humidity would be stifling as the day progressed. He knew it would be difficult to sleep in those conditions. Two things didn't occur during this watch that he was grateful for. The first being no casualties came in and the second was that Everson-Witmore didn't show his face anytime during the night.

Another cigarette found its way to his lips as the sun came up over the top of the hills behind the compound. He watched wisps of steam develop over the low-lying valley when the sun's heat found the leftover puddles and the broad leaves of nearby banana trees. As welcome as the end of watch was, it was still only the beginning of another routine day at 1st Med. The oncoming watch relieved on time.

Tired from the all-night watch, Lew abstained from eating breakfast and continued his way back to the hootch.

"GOOOOOOOD MORNING VIETNAM," blasted from the radio at the chow hall as Lew walked past. The daily salutation was followed by a sarcastic remark about an Army attack on a Viet Cong controlled village or *'ville'* near Saigon. That preceded an equally, eye-opening, drum-rolling, blast of *"Wipe Out"* that gradually faded as he walked away.

The hootch was empty when he arrived. There was no sign of the Bennett's fan.

"Damn," he muttered as the door slammed shut behind him. He spotted a handwritten note on Bennett's empty cot.

I'm not coming back. You guys can have whatever I left behind.
Good Luck and stay safe, Jason.

Wanting to take advantage of the situation Lew closely examined the vacated space. The only item that would be worth having was the fan and it was obviously not there. Disappointed, he stripped to his skivvy shorts and laid down on the dusty, canvas cot. Physically tired but not sleepy he tossed restlessly. He could hear the ever present rumbling of six-by's rolling along Highway1 behind his hootch but, by now he had become accustom to their noise and dust. Once again his mind generated thoughts about requesting a transfer to a combat outfit. As his mind worked the pros and cons, sleep crept up upon him unexpectedly. Before long he was out to the world.

It was mid-afternoon when woke up in the usual, heat induced, body dampness. Sluggishly propping himself up on his elbows hew saw Angel sitting on his cot under a stream of air blowing from the fan that Bennett had left behind. It disturbed him that Angel laid claim to the fan.
"Dammit man, I wanted that fan," Lew stated with obvious disappointment.
"Hey guy, I was here first. You snooze-you lose. That's the way it is man. You know that." Angel commented. "It ain't my fault he didn't give it to you."
Lew reluctantly accepted the fact. "Yeah, I know…but I really wanted to have it anyway. Can I buy it from you?" he offered.
"No man. You ain't got enough dinero," Angel half-laughed.
Lew lit up a smoke while maneuvering into a sitting position.
"Tell you what man," Angel grinned. "I'll let you have it if you blow me"
Lew knew Angel well enough to realize that he was just kidding. Pretending to give the proposition some thought, Lew played a countering bluff. "OK," he answered Rodriguez's smile disappeared, "You go to hell man."
Lew burst out in laughter knowing his bluff worked.
Angel caught on to the joke and laughed along with Lew. "You a bastard man."
The jovial carryings-on between them broke any tension over the matter of the fan.
"Tell you what", Angel began. "I think me an' you can share the fan. You can move your rack next to mine an' we set it to move back and forth so both of us can get the air."
Pleased with that idea Lew responded "Yeah. I think that'll work!"
It only took Lew a few minutes to rearrange the cot and move his gear next to Angel.
"Look here man," Angel started while adjusting the oscillator switch. "When I'm not here you can get all the air." He flipped the switch again. "When you ain't here, I get the air. When both of us are here we switch it so it moves back and forth like this. We both get the air."

Lew happily agreed with the arrangement but asked, "What if neither one of us is here?"

"Hey man, you gotta know that I'm going to chain it to the rafter with a padlock. I don't thin that anyone is going to take but, you never know," Angel beamed with satisfaction.

"Chain, aye," Lew agreed in support of the idea.

Angel then locked the fan to blow air in Lew's direction. "OK man, it's all yours now. I gotta get to my watch" He secured his footlocker, donned his cover and left the hootch.

Lew sat in the comfort of the breeze, savoring what little coolness it offered.

For the next half hour he sat there listening to helicopters coming in with wounded while he relaxed, smoked cigarettes and gave more thought to transferring out of 1st Med.

The screened door opened. "Hey sailor, don't you got the life of Riley," Heeb quipped seeing Lew all mellowed out.

"Hey Heeb," Lew greeted him pleasantly. "You skatin' again? How'd you get away from Chief?"

"Easy. He's in Da Nang again."

"Seems like he spends more time there than he does here," Lew responded.

"Seems like it," Heeb agreed.

Heeb sat down on Angel's cot. "Want a Coke?" Lew offered sensing that Heeb was going to stay a while.

"Nah, I just wanted to see if you wanted to go to China Beach tomorrow. Maybe do some swimmin', drink some beers and check out some *round-eye* girls."

"I don't know." Lew hesitated briefly. "I was thinking about doin' something else."

"Oh yeah, like what?"

Before answering Heeb's question Lew sat on the edge of the cot directly in front of him and looked him squarely in the eyes.

"Heeb," he started, "I was thinking about asking for a transfer to a field unit tomorrow."

Rappaport's jaw dropped in disbelief. "What? Are you out of your gentile mind?"

"Not really."

"Yes you are. Man, don't you know when you got it made? You got hot food and showers here and we're pretty safe. You got a good chance of being killed out in the field or even worse. You can get all shot up and be a vegetable for the rest of your life." Heeb attempted fear as reasoning.

"Yeah, I'm aware of all that but............"

"But what?" Heeb interrupted. "You see the grunts who don't get to shower for a month or more. All those guys eat is cold, C-rats all the time. Man, they don't even sleep in cots or have shelter most of the time. Wait 'til the monsoon season. That rain we got last night is nothing." He pointed to the fan. "They don't have fans either." Heeb paused momentarily. "You see all the wounded *Jarheads* our own age comin' in all shot up. You see the body bags being carted away. You go to the field and you could be one of them. You want that thought for a whole year?"

Lew took a deep breath before answering. "Of course I know all that. I think I can deal with all the shitty stuff. Listen. I'm not satisfied with my job here. I think I can handle the field for a year. I need to be where I can do some good."

"What do you think you're doing here? Don't you consider this 'doin' good?"

"Yes, but not enough. I feel like I'm just an orderly, not a real corpsman."

Heeb jumped to his feet. "What are you sayin'? Everybody here aren't," he fingered quotation marks in the air, "real corpsmen?"

Exasperated, Lew looked up his friend. "No. I didn't say that. I just think that I can do more good in the field than I can here. It's a personal thing."

Heeb threw his arms up in the air in defeat. "OK. It's your life but, I think you're an idiot. I think you're making a big mistake."

"Thanks for your support," Lew remarked facetiously.

Heeb attempted another argument against his friends transfer. "I can't support you for wanting to kill yourself. Don't you realize that when the shit hits the fan and somebody calls 'corpsman up' you'd be the one who has to get his ass up and go through the bullets when everyone else is duckin' for cover?"

"Yeah, it's a scary thought but, the way I see it is when somebody does call for a corpsman that's when I'll be needed the most. Maybe I can actually save a life instead of taking a ....a rectal temperature."

"You know what," Heeb instilled a counter-thought. "The Chief might not even let you have a transfer. I didn't want to tell you this but, the Chief has plans for you."

"Yeah, what plans?"

Heeb sat down, looked Lew straight in the eye, lowered his voice so he wouldn't be overheard by anyone outside the hootch and began, "You gotta promise you won't repeat this."
Lew nodded his promise.
"Chief is going to promote you and let you take over for Sam when he rotates back to the *world* next month."
Surprised, Lew spouted out, "Me! Why me?"
"Shhhh. He thinks you got enough experience and that you're ready for promotion."
Lew lowered his head for a few seconds, quietly absorbing Heeb's words before he came back. "No," he said firmly. "I want to go to the field. As a matter-of-fact, I'm going over right now and put in for a transfer."
"Did you forget, the Chief is in Da Nang," Heeb reminded.
"Yeah damn it, I forgot"
After a couple of seconds of awkward silence Heeb finally gave in to his friend's conviction.
"OK, I give up trying to convince you that you're making a mistake. You're right. It is your life."
Glad that the debate had ended, Lew let go a deep, relaxed breath then, with all sincerity he could muster added, "Ya know, I'm kinda glad you tried to talk me out of it. You're a good friend."
Heeb silently replied with a slight, appreciative, smile. "So, where you gonna transfer to?"
"I haven't made up my mind yet. I keep thinking about Recon."
"RECON! You're outta you fuckin' mind!" Heeb blurted out in disbelief. "Do you know what those psychos do?"
"Actually, no."
"Well, I do. They sneak around the jungle for weeks at a time trying to find '*Charlie*'. They patrol right in the V.C.'s backyard and if the V.C. finds them first, it's all over. I heard of entire patrols being wiped out. I heard that one patrol was sent into North Vietnam and never was heard from again. Man, they kill monkeys and snakes for food, and eat them raw. They get blockage 'cause they're not allowed to shit because it stinks and the smell gives their position away..........."
"Whoa," Lew stopped his friend before he delivered any more absurdities.
"What! Don't you believe me?" Heeb responded.
"No. I think that's all bullshit."

"Bullshit, huh? I'll tell what's bullshit. Its bullshit when a friend of mine goes off his rocker and jumps into something he doesn't know anything about. That's bullshit."
"Hey man, relax. Just take it easy. I said I was thinking about Recon. Maybe they don't even need corpsmen. Maybe I'll go to the grunts instead." Lew guessed.
"The grunts. That's just about as bad." Heeb spouted off before gaining a little composure. "Listen. I'm being square with you. The truth is that I just don't want to see you go. The fact is that you're the only friend I got here," he said meekly.
"I appreciate you friendship Heeb. But, I have to do what's right for me. I think the field is right for me."
Rappaport absorbed Lew's words. Disappointment showed in his face. "You're right. You need do what's right for you," he conceded once again, barely finishing his sentence as Wilfong entered the hootch. Lew welcomed the disruption. The conversation with Heeb had been played out long enough and he saw no need to extend it any further.
"Gentlemen," Wilfong greeted them politely as he passed by without noticing that Lew had relocated next to Angel. Neither Lew nor Heeb responded to the new guy's salutation. They weren't being deliberately ignorant, for the moment they just were involved with other thoughts.
"So," Heeb broke the silence. "Do you want to go tomorrow or not?"
"Huh?" Lew forgot about the earlier invitation.
"China Beach, remember?"
"Ah….no. I have other things planned. But thanks anyway."
Heeb rose from Angel's cot. "OK, but you're going to be sorry when you miss out on all the nice, round-eye chicks flaunting their tits and asses all over the beach."
"Hey man, the last thing I need is getting all horned up with twelve more months to go on my tour," Lew humorously advised.
"OK, see ya later man. See ya later too Fonggy," he added, unwittingly nicknaming the new guy as he left.
Lew looked over his shoulder at Wilfong standing there dumbstruck with a hand raised in a farewell gesture
"Fonggy?" Lew inquired.
Without having a response, Wilfong just shrugged his shoulders.

When Lew arrived at triage for his watch that night he found it busier than usual. He counted seven casualties on the litters being attended to by Sam and couple of other corpsmen as well as Doc Van Hussen. Even though the staff was busy, the urgency wasn't present. It was obvious that none of the men were injured badly enough to warrant the Doc to concentrate on any one man for more than a few minutes. Lew stashed his lunch in the normal cubby-hole before approaching Sam for report. Walking past one of the litters he gave the patient a double-take. He barely recognized the face of the young private who had waited with him at the transient facility on the first day in country. He was the one who was lured into Dogpatch by the black Marine who picked him up. Lew couldn't remember the man's name, but he positively remembered the face. He paused in front of the litter a moment. It was clear that the young, now Lance Corporal, didn't recognize him as the corpsman who shared the six-hour, C-130 plane ride from Okinawa.

Lew tried not to stare but couldn't help himself. Even though the face was dirty and unshaven, it somehow looked older than the 19 years recorded on the paperwork. Sam came over to where Lewis was standing. "Ready for report?" Lew nodded and the two moved to a corner of the triage. Sam began. "These guys came in earlier this afternoon. They're all peppered with shot from a Claymore mine that was accidentally triggered when some asshole sat down on that thing-a-ma-jig that sets it off."

"No shit," Lew commented.

"No shit. These guys were lucky that they were too far away to get the full impact. Most of the BB's barely penetrated the skin. We debrided anything that needed it, cleansed and dressed the wounds. They all could have probably been treated at the company aid station instead of being sent here but, we got 'em anyhow"

"So, why are they still here?"

"Doc said he wanted to keep them overnight. He ordered a temp ward be set up in that empty hootch down the hill, so they can all be together. He said if no signs of infection are present, he'll release them back to their unit tomorrow. Right now a couple guys are setting up the cots. It should be ready any time now. That's about it. Oh yeah, wait a minute. They're all ambulatory."

"OK, I understand they're all ambulatory. You're officially relieved sir, Lew answered in an upbeat vain.

“Relieved, aye. Good luck,” Sam offered as he tilted his head in the direction of Van Hussen giving Ebersen-Witmore his report.
“Oh hell,” Lew muttered when he turned to see Witless coming on as the duty Doc. He watched carefully as Van Hussen and Ebersen-Witmore seemed to be having a disagreement. After a minute of heated whispering between the two, Lewis sensed that Van Hussen got the better of Witless, who snorted out some kind of probably meaningless remark toward Van Hussen as he surrendered the watch. One of the Marines
got Lew’s attention. “Hey Doc, Can I grab a smoke?”
“Did the Doc say you couldn’t?”
“No.”
“Well then, smoke ‘em if you got ‘em. Just go over there off the platform,” Lew pointed out the location.
Taking advantage of the permission all seven ‘grunts’ got up from the litters and advanced toward the edge of the platform.
“Oh hell,” Lew commented “I think I’ll join ya.”
Before Lew could light up, Ebersen-Witmore called out to him.
“Lewis. You can socialize on your own time. Right now you need to prepare your stations in case we get a mass casualty call.”
“Yes Sir,” Lew reluctantly obliged, while wishing he could just deck Witmore one time without being court-martialed.
Lew began tidying up the stations and surveying for replenishment of supplies when Ebersen-Witmore came over to him. “You realize of course that you should have asked my permission for these men to smoke,” he uttered. “After all, I am in charge here.”
Miffed, Lew restrained his reply. “Sir, these men are ambulatory with superficial wounds. There’s no reason not to let them grab a smoke, is there?”
“Actually Lewis, there’s no reason for these men to be here at all. We shouldn’t be expending our time and resources when their own company aid station could have dealt with such minor injuries,” Witmore smugly remarked.
Lew felt the blood boiling in his veins. His face flushed red with anger and wanted so badly just to choke the life out of Witmore when one of the Marines cried out, “DOC, DOC…..something’s wrong with Mad-dog!”
The Doc and corpsman ran over to where the men were standing around their buddy laying on the ground, twitching and crying out that his stomach hurts badly.

"Quick, you men get him back on his litter," Witmore commanded without so much as to make a preliminary assessment of the man's sudden complaint.

Lew grabbed the stethoscope and cuff for a blood pressure check and compared it against the one taken earlier. He informed Witmore of a drop from the baseline reading.

"What's going on with you young man?" Witmore asked the Marine.

"I dunno Doc. I just felt a sharp pain in my belly then got dizzy and dropped. It hurts fuckin' bad Doc."

"Uh huh," Witmore responded while unbuckling the man's belt and pulling his trousers down to mid-thigh. The exposed flesh revealed a small, blood spotted, puncture in the lower abdomen region. Witmore looked up over his glasses at Lewis. "Get this man's x-ray," he directed.

"Sir, none of us got x-rays," one of the 'grunts' informed the M.O..

"You didn't have x-rays taken?" the physician repeated then added in a huff, "Why do I have such an incompetent staff."

He again looked up at his corpsman. "Well, what are you waiting for? Go alert the techs that I'll be needing pictures STAT, "he snapped at Lewis.

Lew ran to the x-ray room and brought back two technicians pushing a gurney. Witmore was jotting down notes on the man's chart. Without bothering to look up he coldly ordered Lewis to "Push a Ringers before they take him away." Lew didn't have any difficulty in finding a good vein to start the IV. Within a minute the man was hurried to x-ray.

"What do you think Doc?" Lew somberly inquired of Witmore who was walking toward the O.R.

The M.O. turned to his corpsman. "I think someone had a lapse of professional medical procedure Lewis. I think this young man may have a perforated colon that should have been diagnosed hours ago. I think he'll survive. I think I'm going to review a certain person's medical competency." Witmore turned away, and then turned again. "Oh yes," he added. "And I think you need to learn to keep uninvited bystanders away from the triage when a doctor is with a patient."

Even though the last comment infuriated him, Lew held back his urge to follow up with a targeted obscenity. He took a deep breath

to afford him time to calm down. The remaining Marines gathered around the corpsman. "Hey Doc, what's his problem?"
one asked.
"That's just the way that asshole is," Lew replied, not knowing any other appropriate answer to the question.
An hour passed when another corpsman entered the triage. Lew recognized the man but didn't know his name. "The temp ward is ready for them now," he informed Lewis.
"Great. Maybe they can get some rest," Lew remarked. "OK, Marines" he got their attention. "The Doc here will take you to your quarters. Get your gear and follow him."
"What about Mad-dog?" one asked.
"All I can say right now is that if his injury is what the Doctor suspects, he won't be going back with you tomorrow."
The 'grunts' grabbed their gear and departed the triage. A few of them thanked Lew as they meandered behind the other corpsman. Doc Lewis watched them, as they filed out, keeping an eye on the Lance Corporal who didn't recognize him.
The remaining hours of his watch proved uneventful. The clam afforded him time to further think about transferring. He battled with the pros and cons but, by the end of the watch he had made up his mind, finally deciding that he would request a transfer to Recon.

The following afternoon Lewis went the orderly room. Upon entering he was surprised to see Heeb there. "What are you doing here? I thought you were going to the beach today."
"I had paperwork to do. Some idiot wants to transfer outta here," Heeb replied as he handed his friend a request for transfer document. "Just sign where the X is," he instructed. "We'll take care of the rest."
Lew examined the form letter for a moment. It specified the gaining unit was the 1st Reconnaissance Battalion, 1st Mar Div (Reinf) RVN.
"Once you sign it, there's no changing your mind," Heeb cautioned.
Lew hesitated a few seconds, as if he had second thoughts.
"Gimme a pen," he finally resolved. He scribbled his signature then handed the paper back to Heeb. Dismayed the clerk placed the completed form in the Chief's 'IN' basket. "There, it'll be processed through the normal channels."

“Got any idea how long it’ll take?” Lew inquired.
“A few days … maybe a week.”
Satisfied that he had done the right thing, Lew thanked his friend as he turned to depart.
Disappointment reflected in Heeb’s voice. “Anytime, my friend.”

On the way back to his hootch, Lew stopped by the mail room. Two others were in line in front of him. One got a couple of letters while the other received a shoe-box sized package. Lew moved up in front of the opened, half-door. “Got anything for Lewis?”
“I don’t think so Doc but, I’ll check.” The mail clerk sifted through a stack of letters. “Nope, nothing here for Lewis. Sorry.”
He wasn’t actually expecting any mail so, not getting any wasn’t a big disappointment.
“OK, thanks.”

Angel and Sherman were involved in a game of cards when Lew entered the hootch.
Both were stripped to their skivvies, sitting under breeze of the fan humming overhead and listening to the popular, female, disc jockey, Chris Noel broadcasting over Armed Forces Radio. Angel was clinching a smoldering cigar between his teeth, concentrating on the hand he was holding. Sherman was sitting on the edge of Lew’s cot. Angel’s foot locker served as a card table, positioned between the cots. Sweat dampness appeared from the pores under Sherman’s eyes when he looked up to see who came in. An exchange of greetings wasn’t necessary. Lew sat on the unoccupied potion of his own cot, eagerly anticipating removal of his hot, leather boots.
“You mind if I sit here?” Sherman thoughtfully asked.
“Nah.” Lew answered as he pulled one boot off.
“Sheeee-it hombre,” Angel delighted. “A pair of deuces. I win again. Ah Ha!” He collected the five, individually wrapped Slim-Jims in the pot before declaring, “That’s all for me man. I know when to quit when I’m a face.”
There was sudden pause followed by laughter.
“Ahead,” Sherman was quick to correct him. “You mean ‘to quit when you’re ahead.”

Lew forced back a laugh, knowing that Angel was more proficient in speaking English than he pretended and that he was just jagging the new man.

"Ah ha, gottcha man. You oughta give me another Slim-Jim just for being a dumb-assed, new guy," Angel quipped.

Aware he had been taken in by Angel's, good-natured prank, Sherman tossed him another Slim-Jim. "There, I hope you choke on it," he laughed as he returned to his own cot.

With both boots removed, Lew stretched out on the cot and let the breeze hit him. Angel pushed the foot locker back out of the way. Except for the *whirr* of the fan and the music from the radio, the hootch went quiet until Wilfong returned from taking a shower.

SLAM!

His slender, white frame was draped only in a towel. Standing next to his own cot he dropped the towel to get dressed.

"Holy Mother of Mary!" Angel exclaimed. "Look at that monster!"

Sherman and Lewis turned to look. It was obvious that Angel's surprise came when he saw the size of Wilfong's endowed manhood.

"Holy cow!" Sherman added in disbelief.

Embarrassed by the attention, Wilfong quickly grabbed the towel and covered his pubic area. "Haven't you ever seen a man's penis before?" he retorted

"I ain't never seen nothin' like that, except maybe on a donkey," Angel blurted out.

"Me 'neither," added Sherman. "Man, that's some sausage."

Lew was as surprised at the size of Wilfong's penis as were the others but, chose not to remark about it, preferring to let them do any teasing.

"Man, I hope you never get married," Angel began again. "You'll kill your woman with that dong."

"Hey," Sherman followed up. "Now we can call him 'Big-Dong Wilfong."

"Yeah," Rodriguez mused. "Maybe we can ship him out to 'Dong Ha,"

Sherman took another jab, "You better be careful around him. If you get him mad he might desert and join the Viet Dong!" The two men broke up with self-induced laughter, obviously enjoying their own brand of torment. Even Lew cracked a smile at the humor. The laughter became so intense that tears began to roll down Sherman's face and forced snot to drip from his nose. He fell to the floor and doubled over from laughing so hard. The display of comical antics eventually caught up with Lew and developed into an involuntary barrage of uncontrollable laughter from the trio. Wilfong wasn't amused. He quickly slipped into his trousers, then folding his arms sat on the edge of his cot while his tender, youthful face produced the sternest looking scowl he could muster. The 'mean' look was ineffective and only served to incite even more laughter from the three.

Disgusted by his *hootch-mates'* behavior, Wilfong got up and announced, "I don't have to take your crude insults," then stormed out. SLAM.

The laughing soon waned after the victim disappeared. Within a few minutes, the laughs became snickers; composure settled in and humor transformed into more serious conversation.

"Ju know," Angel began, "I'm glad I don't got what he got."

"Me too," Sherman agreed.

"Anybody with something like that is sure to have problems with it later in life," Lew predicted.

"No doubt,' Sherman acknowledged.

"Don't they got operations that can fix that?" Angel inquired seriously.

That particular question once again triggered Sherman's off-beat humor. "Sure. It's called a 'pecker-ectomy'. The quick-witted remark produced smiles from Lewis and Rodriguez but, not belly laughs Sherman hoped for.

The subject was dropped and everything went back to normal, routine, monotony.

Wilfong returned after Rodriguez had left for his watch on the surgical ward and Sherman reported to the chow hall for two weeks of mess duty. With only the two of them in the hootch, Doc Lewis picked up on the deliberate manner that Wilfong chose to ignore him. He watched as the young man sat down on the edge of his cot with his back toward him. Lew didn't have any desire for them to become enemies and couldn't understand why Wilfong would find the teasing so terribly offensive. After all, a lot of men would like to be that endowed, he reasoned. Lighting a cigarette, he got up and walked over to Wilfong. Attempting to make amends for the earlier behavior Lew spoke first. "I think you should lighten up a little bit. No one meant to offend you."

"Well, it sure seemed like it," Wilfong snapped back.
"True skinny, we didn't." Lew sincerely offered.
"You could have fooled me," Wilfong snipped again.
Lew guided his words, trying not to come across as being condescending. "Listen, you've been in the Navy long enough to know how people joke around and kid each other. Think about it," he followed up. "If they didn't like you, they wouldn't be so up front……they'd talk behind your back."
"I'm sorry but, I don't accept that. I know what people say about me. Do you know what it's like for everybody to stare at your thing all the time? I've been dealing with it since junior high. I can't even shower unless no one else is there. I'm tired of it." Wilfong spilled out.
Lew took a moment, searching for a good response. "You know, I just don't understand why you would be so sensitive about your…ah….dick. Most men would brag about it if they had it."
"Not if they went through what I go through," he began to shed some light on the discussion. "I certainly realize I'm not the most manly type guy. Well, here it is. I've been propositioned so many times by other men I'm afraid to show myself anymore." He confided. Lew was jolted by the sudden outpouring of candor. The revelation thrust him in an awkward situation, having never discussed such a matter before he didn't know how to handle it. *"Why is he telling me this stuff?"* he thought, wishing it was someone else who was dealing with it. Desperately wanting to conjure up the right words, Lew took a deep breath to buy time. "Hey man, you just have to ignore what people say. This is the military. If someone approaches you, report them," Lew attempted a diplomatic response.
"I did that once at Great Lakes but, it only got worse. I got a blanket party in return." Wilfong recalled, almost coming to tears remembering that he was pretty badly beaten up. It was at that instant that Lew realized Wilfong just might be a little light on his toes. Wanting to clarify things Lew drafted the courage to come to the point. "Are you ……I mean…ah…do you like girls?"
A strange look came to Wilfong's face. "If you're asking if I'm queer, let me say this…..I'm as queer as you are."
Not being a homosexual, Lew accepted the answer at face value nevertheless; he wasn't completely comfortable with it. Hiding his uncertainty he responded with a simple "OK" and let it go at that. The dialog between them came to an abrupt but welcomed

end when the door opened and Chief McKinny stomped in with a piece of paper in his hand. “LEWIS,” he barked. “What the hell’s this crap about a transfer?”

The Chief’s unexpected intrusion intimidated Lewis to the point of temporary speechlessness. “Well,” the Chief demanded, “I’m waiting.”

Lew forced a coating of slava down his throat. “Ah, yes Chief” he proceeded “I put in the request this afternoon.”

“I know that Lewis. What I want to know is why?”

“I just think I can be of better service out in the field Chief.”

“Oh you do, do you?” McKinney made the statement a question.

“Yes, I do Chief.” Lew confirmed. “I want to be there when it counts; when a corpsman is needed the most,” he insisted, adding “I want to put my field training to positive use. Maybe I can do something that will give a Marine a chance to make it home alive.”

The Chief gave his subordinate a penetrating look as he raised the signed paperwork “ I have half a notion to recommend denying this here transfer,” he huffed.” I don’t think you have enough experience for the field.”

Lew knew better. He guessed that the Chief was just trying to encourage him to change his mind. Thanks to Heeb, he also knew what the Chief had intended for him after Sam rotated back. The Chief wouldn’t have made that plan if he didn’t think he had the experience.

“I’m sorry Chief, I really want to transfer to a combat unit.”

Sensing Lewis’ determination the chief made another half-hearted attempt to sway him.

“Listen lad,” he started out unusually soft-spoken “You’re doin’ a real good job here…..you have friends here. Hell, we’re a family here. Are you sure that this is what you want to do?”

“I’m sure, Chief.”

A reluctant, but friendly smile came to the Chief’s face. “You know Lewis, I don’t want to do it but, I’m going to recommend your transfer to the old man anyhow.”

“Thanks Chief.”

“Yeah,” McKinney unwillingly replied. “You’d better start packing your gear. This ain’t going to take long.” He pursed his lips, finalizing their conversation, then turned and left the hootch.

“Transfer?” Wilfong’s meek voice asked.

“Yeah. You better keep your mouth shut about it too.” Lew warned.

Rappaport caught up with Lewis at the Club later that night. Lew was sipping on a Royal Crown cola and watching an episode of “Combat” on Armed Forces Television; killing time before his watch at triage.
“Hey Lew,” Heeb called out.
“Hey man, what’s going on?”
“I’m glad I found you. Chief said for me to track down your ass down and let you know you don’t have to pull your duty tonight.”
Lew was stymied. “Why not?”
“Because my friend, you’re outta here tomorrow morning. The Chief walked your transfer through and called Recon for a report date. You’re supposed to report there tomorrow.”
“TOMORROW!” Lew exclaimed. “I don’t understand. Why so soon?”
“Beats the shit out of me. I guess there’s a high turn-over rate for corpsmen there.”
The news created a massive churning of ‘butterflies’ in Lew’s gut. Nervously, he lit up a cigarette and wondered what he got himself into.
“You need to get your shit together and report to the orderly room at 0800 hrs. We’re cutting your orders now.”
Stunned, all Lew could say was “Oh shit.”

The following morning before breakfast Lew assembled the belongings that he gathered up and stowed away the night before. Since he didn’t accumulate anything more than when he arrived there, it was an easy task. One sea-bag full of cotton utility uniforms, toiletries and a few small personnel items was his complete inventory.
Before he left the hootch for the last time he took a look around. Angel was snoring away soundly under the fan. Lew adjusted the switch to keep it the air blowing directly on Angel. Wilfong was fast asleep also. He didn’t want to wake them and felt guilty for not doing so to say farewell but, reasoned that they probably wouldn’t care anyway. He spent a minute reminiscing about the past five weeks. He never did get to meet those two missing guys. The thought of Bennett angered him. He wondered how Bennett would have dealt with Wilfong’s feministic mannerisms.

Shouldering his sea-bag he exited the hootch, carefully holding the door so it wouldn't slam behind him.

Heeb greeted him when he entered the orderly room. "Oh-eight-hundred, right on time."
Lew scanned the room. "Where's Chief?"
"Beats me," Heeb answered. "He don't have to be here you know."
"Yeah, I know."
"Besides," Heeb added. "You aren't exactly on his top ten list."
Lew shrugged.
"OK, here's your orders and medical records," Heeb handed him a sealed envelope. "The only thing you have to do now is stop by the mail room and fill out a change of address card."
"That's it," Lew questioned.
"Yeah, that's all." Heeb forced a disappointed smile. "Oh yeah. I got a driver to take you down to Recon. That's him over there," Heeb said pointing through the screen at a Marine Lance Corporal standing next to a mighty-mite.
"Great. Thanks man." was all Lew could say.
Heeb stepped from behind the counter and offer Lew his hand. "I'm sorry you made this decision and I'm really sad to see you go."
"Hey man, don't go soft on me. Look," Lewis pointed out to his friend, "I'm only a couple miles from here. I'll get back to visit you from time to time. We can got to 327 and have some beers together. Hell, you can even come over sometime."
"Yeah man, I guess we can do that," Heeb acknowledged.
"Sure we can," Lew tacitly promised. The two shook hands to solidify their friendship.
"You don't know it but you're the only friend I ever had." Rappaport whispered to himself as he watched Lew get into the vehicle and ride away.

SWIFT, SILENT, DEADLY

First Reconnaissance Battalion was only about a "click" northwest of 1st. Med. along a diesel-sprayed, gravel, road called Highway 542. The kidney jarring trip from place to place under the scorching, mid-morning sun lasted an excruciating 10 minutes. Pulling into the compound the Jeep passed under large red and yellow portal that read "CAMP REASONER" and another smaller sign underneath read "1st Reconnaissance Battalion, 1st Mar Div (REIN). The place looked similar to 1st Med. although, it was absent of larger structures. The same type hootches were scattered about in a seemingly hap-hazard manner taking advantage of every available piece of hillside real estate. One could imagine that from the air it would resemble a semi-circle shape with a large open dirt area in the center, probably used as some sort of parade ground or '*grinder*'. The driver stopped in front of a small wooden building that wasn't typical. It had full-height walls with a small red cross painted above the door.

"I guess this is where you need to go Doc," the driver spoke louder than necessary. "It's the battalion aid station."

"OK, thanks man."

Lewis got out, pulling his sea bag awkwardly from the back of the jeep. As the driver backed away Lewis dropped the sea bag at the foot of the steps leading up into the building. Inside a lone corpsman was sitting in a lawn chair, reading a paperback under

the ubiquitous electric fan. Lowering the book he gave new man the once over. "Let me guess, you're the new corpsman."
"Yeah, you guessed right," Lewis smiled.
Putting aside the book the man got up, offered his hand and identified himself.
"Bob Stottlemeyer, HM3."
They shook hands. "Gary Lewis."
"Glad to have ya aboard Lewis…but, we didn't expect you here so soon."
"Me either," Lewis responded and handed over the orders.
"I only need your medical jacket," Stottlemeyer said as he opened the package to retrieve it. "The rest of the stuff goes over to the Company office." He returned the envelope.
"Come over from First Med did ya?"
"Yeah."
"Wassa matter, too quiet for ya over there?" Stottlemeyer asked tongue in cheek.
"No, just too clinical for me," Lew replied not wanting to let on that he just didn't care for the place or most of the people. "I think I'm more of a field type person."
"Field huh? Well, if it's the field you want, you came to the right place brother."
Stottlemeyer then took the time to inform Lew that the aid station was more of a records keeping station, than a treatment facility. Except for minor injuries anyone needing medical attention would be sent to sick call at First Med. He explained that all the platoon corpsmen need to spend time in the aid station when not on patrol and keep tab of their men's immunizations and to administer the shots for those who need them. He was further instructed on the filing system and was told that if a Marine in his platoon needed to report to sick call, his corpsman would be the person to pull the record. Essentially, each corpsman was responsible for all the medical needs of the troops in his platoon. He stressed that the corpsmen have to make sure the men took their weekly dose of *Chloroquine Premiquiin* anti-malaria tablets, as well as keeping a stockpile of salt tablets. After the briefing and tour of the aid station Stottlemeyer got down to the assignment part.
"They need a corpsman in Force Company. Your boss is HM2 LaPorte. He's the senior NCO in Force but he's out in the bush now but", he added "when they get back I'll let him know you're here so he can assign you where he wants. In the meantime, I'm

going to put you with the fifth platoon for a few days. Their Doc is Paul Roshong but, he's on R and R so they don't have a corpsman right now. He should be back sometime this week."
Everything was new and confusing. "What's Force Company?" Lewis asked, having never heard of it before.
"Basically, it's that same as the other companies but, in Force you parachute and scuba dive and go to special Recon schools. They're supposed to be a cut above the other companies. Kinda like Marine Corps *Green Berets."*
"Sounds bitchin'," Lew responded enthusiastically.
"Yeah, it's a good outfit." Stottlemeyer reinforced Lewis's perception. "Hey listen, I can't leave the Aid Station but if you go over there," he pointed out the direction, "cross a little foot bridge, the first hootch past the *shitter* is fifth platoon. You can find a rack there, then just stand by until I get someone to relieve me then I'll show you around a little later."
"Alright, sounds good."
"OK but, before you do that, run your packet over to the office," the Petty Officer said opening the door and pointing to its location.
"OK, will do."

Once again Lewis heaved the sea bag on his shoulder and set out toward the Company Office. Along the way he passed a small, open-air kiosk. Inside was a small Vietnamese man posing as a barber giving a high and tight haircut to one Marine while another waited his turn. Hanging from the wall was a display of trinkets and plaques that were for sale.

Inside the office the he handed over the packet to the clerk on duty behind the counter. Finding everything in order the clerk nonchalantly welcomed Lewis to the unit then released him to go about his business. Walking across the dirt open area, he spotted the chow hall on the hill to his left. Nearing the outhouse he saw another Vietnamese man dressed in rags, wearing the traditional cone hat and stirring a flaming mixture of diesel fuel and human excrement with a long wooden pole. Dark smoked bellowed skyward. The man paused to offer up a series of modest bows as Lewis strolled by. He was reminded of the indigent *tray coolie* back at First Med and politely acknowledged the man with a smile.

Arriving at the first hootch he opened the screen door and stepped inside.
It appeared to be the near twin as the one back at the medical battalion except this one had a more orderly appearance. One shirtless Marine was inside sitting on the edge of his cot engrossed in a letter. Interrupted from his reading, he looked toward me. "Can I do something for you?" he asked abruptly.
"Maybe. They sent me here. Is this the Fifth Platoon hootch?
"Uh huh. Who sent you here?
"The corpsman at the aid station. He said I was assigned to the Fifth platoon for a few days."
"OK…ah….just…ah…help yourself to an empty rack and make yourself at home." The Marine proposed.
Two cots without blankets, in the center of the row appeared empty. Lewis tossed the sea bag down claiming one. The Marine went back to reading.
"Where is everyone?" the Doc inquired.
"Out in the bush," the Marine snipped, annoyed by the interruption.
It was apparent that man didn't want to be bothered with questions at the moment. Eyeing a butt can on the floor next to the rack; Lew retrieved a cigarette, lit up and waited for the Marine to finish reading his letter. He read it once then once again before folding it and placing it under his pillow.
"First letter I got in two weeks," the man remarked.
Lew couldn't help but notice a dressing on the man's shoulder.
"What's the bandage for?"
"Got shot. It's nothing really, just a graze but, it was enough to keep me outta the bush for a little while. I need to get it looked at tomorrow. That reminds me …I need to change the bandage."
"Here, let me do it," Lew offered his expertise. "Where the stuff?"
The Marine supplied the corpsman with a bag of dressing material and ointment. "You got a name?" Doc asked.
"Shiftbauer, but they call me 'Shifty"
"Shifty Shiftbauer, sounds like a race car driver's name. Where you from Shifty?"
"A little town south of Pittsburgh Pennsylvania called Uniontown."
"Uniontown! You're the second person I've met from Uniontown in a month." recalling the other was the Marine who drove him from the air field to 1st Med. on the first day in country.

"I'm from Pittsburgh myself," Lew stated then changed the subject. "This wound looks like its healing real good."
"Ya know, I've never been to Pittsburgh." Shifty admitted.
Lew's curiosity got the best of him. "How'd you get shot?"
"The *gooks* found us and opened up. I got down prone, laid down some fire when an AK round grazed me but felt like it blew my shoulder away. We broke contact and Doc patched me on the run to the LZ where we got extracted. That's about all there is to it," Shifty downplayed the scenario.
"There, that'll do it," he said smoothing out the last piece of adhesive tape.
"OK, thanks Doc," Shifty said.
After the wound was dressed Lewis and Shifty conversed about the outfit for nearly an hour. He told Lewis about how the platoons were divided into teams; discussed aspects of different type of missions; went over the command structure, chow times and a myriad of other things that Lewis couldn't either remember or fathom. Getting the feeling that Lewis's mind was saturated with too much information, Shifty mentioned it was time for chow. He grabbed a steel food tray, a canteen cup and utensils from beside his cot then moved to Roshong's cot and gathered *his* utensils *for* the new corpsman to use and mentioned that he would have to get some of his own before Roshong returned. He also stopped Lewis from leaving the hootch without a shirt. Unlike the medical battalion, around here you didn't leave the hootch without being in full uniform.

On their way to chow Shifty pointed out the location of the shower. Passing by the '*shitter'* the Vietnamese man was still tending to his task. "That's Ho Chi," Shifty informed the new Doc. "At least that's what everybody calls him."
"We've met," Lew said.
"Yeah, well listen to this." Shifty asked the man "What's new Ho Chi?"
The old man came to attention, raised his hand in salute and replied "Gunny Sucks"
The pair laughed. "I think that's all the English he knows…and I taught him," Shifty grinned proudly.
The closer the two got to the chow hall the louder the sound of metal cups clanking against metal trays became. Lew noticed that some of the Marines in the line were sporting fresh camouflage

face paint. It appeared that on some faces a great deal of care was taken to detail the green, black and brown patterns.
"Those guys are going out on patrol in a little while. They supposed to go to the head of the line," Shifty informed.
After finishing a hefty portion of stew over rice the two took their trays to the same type of trash can scullery as at First Med except here there was no Vietnamese *'tray coolie'* . Everyone had to clean their own mess gear.
Walking back to the hootch two UH-34 helicopters banked sharply and descended behind a row of hootches to a landing pad at the bottom of the hill just beyond. The noise ended when the pilots shut down the engines. Shifty explained that a team was *'hatting out'* and sometimes the *chopper drivers* need to get briefed on the mission, further explaining that sometimes they don't need a briefing and just lift off when the troops are on board.

Inside the hootch Lew removed the thick cotton shirt and heavy leather boots. Even though by now he had become acclimated to the tropical conditions he still relished removing those articles, especially the boots. Shifty kicked back on his cot for a little afternoon nap. Contented, Lewis did likewise.

Their lazy afternoon nap was suddenly shattered by loud shouting. "GET UP, GET UP! Jolted by the beckoning both men sprung up in their cots. Shifty spoke excitedly "What the hell's going on?"
Out of breath, the messenger broke the reply between gasps of air, "Killer Kane..... is in some shit.......... Dixon wants ....every swingin' dick to muster ......for a reactionary force...... get your 782 shit together......... and muster at the chopper pad.... ASAP," then took off to relay the message elsewhere in the compound.
Panicky, Lewis asked Shifty a string of questions, "What's this all about?" What am I supposed to do?" What's a Killer Kane?"
Shifty hurriedly tried to explain it all to the new corpsman while he gathered his gear and rifle. "Killer Kane is one of our teams, they got themselves in some shit and the Old Man wants us to go help 'em. You gotta go too. Take Doc's gear there," he pointed to it hanging from a nail.

Lew rushed to grab the web gear and the medical kit. The belt and suspenders were too large and need adjusted but he couldn't bother doing it now. Nervously fumbling with the laces it seemed to take forever for him to secure his boots when it dawned on him, "Hey, I don't have a gun!"
The Marine forgave him calling it a gun, "Don't worry 'bout it. If the shit's that bad you'll be too busy to use it anyway."
"You're right," Lewis came back. Just as he stood up another issue entered his mind.
"Wait a minute," he told Shifty "You can't go. You're under doctor's orders not to go to the field."
"Bullshit," the Marine barked back.
"Bullshit my ass. If you go, you'll be disobeying a direct order. Hell, you can get court marshaled for that!" Continuing to argue his point "I'm a corpsman. I have an obligation to report you if you go, and I WILL, Lew insisted. "You can't go until a doctor says you can go!"
"But Doc," Shifty began to plead.
"Don't 'but Doc' me. Think about it. If I let you go, ***I*** can be court marshaled. You're already under prevailing orders. You can't get in trouble following those orders."
"It's not about the orders."
"I know it's not, believe me but, you HAVE to obey the orders." Lewis played a trump card. "What would you do if Doc Roshong told you not to go?"
The last comment quieted Shifty.
"Now, how do I get to the chopper pad?"
Shifty reluctantly gave in. Laying the M-14 on the cot and removing the web gear he despairingly said "Just follow those guys."
Lew looked through the screen and saw scattering of young men hustling across the grinder, weapons-in-hand, toward the landing pad. He bolted out trying to catch up.

All eyes turned to Lewis as he approached the gathering point in his cotton stateside utilities and leather boots, borrowed 782 gear and to top it off, without a weapon. Upon seeing the disarrayed youth the sergeant in charge stopped barking out orders and called him over to where he was standing. "Who the hell are you," he demanded "and what the fuck are you doing here?"

Shaken, Lewis's voiced cracked in response "I, I'm a new corpsman, I just reported here this morning." The sergeant understood the new Doc's situation but, didn't want an inexperienced corpsman on this particular mission, especially one without a weapon but, since the CO said to muster every available man, he no choice but to comply. The sergeant gave a quick look around before selecting one individual to help the rookie corpsman get with the program. Spitting out a plug of tobacco he volunteered someone. "Owens, take care of the Doc… looks like he could use some help."
"Right Sarge," the young veteran obeyed, signaling Lewis to come to him.
The sergeant continued his instructions loud enough for all to hear. "The birds are on the way. Everybody grab two bandoliers of 762 and two frags each. Ski and Fish get the claymores, Hambone, you got the 79 rounds. EVERYBODY, make sure you fill your canteens and do it quick. You can '*camy up*' in the chopper."
Lewis felt as out of place as he looked. "Doc," Owens said, "first thing, take off that damned white tee-shirt and lose the collar brass," referring to the black metal rank and caduceus emblems pinned to Doc's shirt collar. Fumbling with the buttons Lew hurriedly got out of the green cotton utility shirt and pulled the tee-shirt over his head, tossed it to the ground, removed the insignias then put the utility shirt back on. Owens helped the corpsman adjust the borrowed 782 gear. "Here," he handed Lewis two fragmentation grenades, "put these on like this," he said showing Lewis how to snap the *'frags'* on the canvas belt between the ammunition pouches. He then cris-crossed two bandoliers of 7.62 ammunition over Lewis's head... "Since you don't got a weapon you can *'hump'* some 60 rounds too!" Nervously, Lewis nodded agreement as Owens added the extra belt of 7.62 rounds to the burden. Lewis immediately felt the weight of the ammo biting into his sweaty neck.
"Go fill you canteens," Owens instructed. Lewis rushed to the water buffalo, topped off the two canteens, and rushed back to Owens as two CH-46 helicopters were making their approach... Lewis could feel his heart pulsating rapidly as the choppers got closer. The sergeant was on the PRC 25 radio, communicating with the pilots.

He gave the handset back to the radioman standing next to him and began shouting out commands over the rotor noise. "WE'RE TAKING TWO BIRDS. SKI, YOU GET HALF THE MEN ON THE SECOND BIRD, I'LL TAKE HALF WITH ME" He gave a quick look "OWENS, YOU AND THE DOC GET ON THE FIRST BIRD WITH ME." Owens gave the sergeant a 'thumbs up' sign. Crouching low, holding onto their *bush hats*, the two teams entered the choppers from the tail ramp. Lewis followed Owens closely. Nervous excitement raced through his body as this was the first time he had been in a helicopter. As soon as the men sat down on the webbed, troop seats the pilot throttled the engines to maximum torque, forcing the bird to shutter and shake as it broke free of its own weight. It was an awesome experience for the rookie corpsman to feel the surge of power as the chopper climbed higher. He wished he could look out the window to watch the ground fall away below but, knew better than to try. The temporary coldness at the high altitude was a welcome relief for all onboard. Once airborne, Owens pulled out a small plastic bottle of insect repellant and squeezed some of the liquid into his hand then, rubbed a stick of green and loam colored camouflage paint into the liquid, creating a paste like mixture that served a two-fold purpose of keeping insects away and disguising facial features. He handed a small stainless-steel mirror to Lewis to hold up while he applied the paint to his own face in order to show Lewis what to do before handing it off to him to do likewise. He applied the paint to his face and behind his ears as well as his exposed arms and fingers. Lewis awkwardly did the same as the pilot constantly recovered the helicopter from sudden bursts of atmospheric winds. Owens gave Lewis a 'thumbs up' indicating the *camy job* was good enough.
Lewis sat there, self-conscience of his fear, hoping it wasn't noticeable. He watched the faces of the others. From what he could gather, everyone was cognizant of their own fears also. They were in the air about 20 minutes when ear drums popped and the temperature inside the chopper began warming up as it descended. Even though there was no need to, the crew chief pointed downward to let all on board know the chopper was approaching the LZ. Without instruction, each man pulled out a full magazine and locked and loaded their rifles. The door gunner yanked back the bolt of the 50 caliber machine gun mounted in an open-air window and positioned himself to let loose a barrage of

deadly fire if necessary. Lewis could feel his insides twitching. The tension combined with heat and humidity made him nauseated. *Oh God, don't let me puke now.* The last couple hundred feet of the approach felt as if the chopper was falling from the sky. There was a distinct change in engine noise as it neared the ground. When the ramp was lowered he could see debris flying all around and tall strands of 'elephant grass' was being blown flat from the rotor wash. "GO,GO,GO" the crew chief shouted out. The men ran off the chopper as quickly as possible, each side branching off to form a semi-circle perimeter just beyond the sweep of the rotor blades. Lewis followed his mentor as closely as possible but, as luck would have he tripped over something, falling to his knees, landing on a cactus plant. The needles penetrating deep into his right knee forced him to grimace but he wouldn't let out a cry of pain. The helicopter lifted off hurling more debris toward him. Hiding his face from the projectiles he lost sight of Owens who was crouching down in the grass just ahead of him. '*Oh God, where's Owens?*' Just then he caught a glimpse of someone partially concealed signaling him. It was Owens. He crawled over getting as close as possible to him without actually making physical contact. The second helicopter set down discharging the troops in the same manner then lifted off without incident. The two groups formed up into one full circle defensive perimeter. Everyone remained silent and motionless, listening closely for any indication of the presence of *'Charlie',* waiting for the enemy to open up on them with everything they had. Lewis's heart was pounding so hard he knew it sounded like a bass drum to the Viet Cong. What made matters worse was the heat, humidity and throbbing pain in his knee. Perspiration dripped from everyone's face, washing away the '*camy*' paint and saturating uniforms to the point of near immobility. Nearly five full minutes went by without anyone making a motion or sound. Reasoning that if the VC were going to attack they would have done it by now, the sergeant attempted radio contact with *Killer Kane.* The troops relaxed slightly but didn't let down their guard. Lewis began to pull the needles from his knee. Slowly, one by one, he pulled them out using his fingers. It hurt but it wasn't unbearable pain. He remembered what one Marine told him back at First Med, *"Pain builds character."* Owens watched the new corpsman refrain from wincing. After Lewis removed the last prong, seven individual blood stains merged into one, covering the knee cap through the heavy trousers. He sat there another minute holding his hand tightly over the knee.

Word passed back to them in whispers *"Killer Kane, two-five meters...move out ...pass it on"*

Owens relayed the message. The troops rose to their feet and moved as quietly as possible through the razor sharp grass that easily cut their exposed skin. As they moved Lewis wondered what he got himself into. Here it is, a hundred degrees, a hundred percent humidity, his knee throbbing in pain, heavy bandoliers cutting into his neck, grass lacerating his flesh, sweat pouring into his eyes, Asians wanting to kill him, with a group of people who don't know or trust him, he feels like puking and a headache coming on to boot. '*What the hell am I doing here?'*

Within a few minutes the reaction team hooked up with Killer Kane down in a grass covered depression. They were so close to the LZ the choppers nearly landed on top of their position. The sergeant made his way to Killer Kane's patrol leader while the rest of the team reinforced Kane's perimeter. Owens and Lewis hunkered down near the center of the perimeter. They sat there quietly for several minutes. Hearing shuffling in the nearby grass Lewis turned to see what it was. A camouflaged figure approached them crawling on his knees. The man whispered "You the corpsman?" Lewis nodded. "I'm Doc Conners. I saw your Unit One and figured you're the Doc."

"I'm Lewis, just got here today."

"I figured that."

"You need some help? Got anybody hurt?" Lewis asked as if he should.

"Nah, nobody hurt, except you," Conners whispered back, noticing Lewis's blooded trousers.

"It's nothing." Lewis assured.

Conners could see that Lewis was showing signs of dehydration. He dug into his shirt pocket and pulled out a small plastic bag. Taking out two salt tablets he handed them to Lewis. "Here, take these and drink some water. You're sweating too much. I better get back. See ya later."

Lewis carefully and quietly pulled the canteen from its pouch, put the salt tablets in his mouth and took several swallows of the warm water. He sat there quietly, nervously watching Owens for tell-tale signs of what he should do next.

KRACK KRACK KRACK somebody opened fire. There was no return fire. Lewis's head nearly exploded at the unbelievably loud report of rifle fire. Owens raised his weapon preparing to let go some rounds.

"WHAT'S GOING ON? WHO THE HELL FIRED?" an authoritive voice hollered out from a concealed position.

"I DID SIR…I THOUGHT I HEARD SOMETHING," another hidden voice shouted.

"WHERE?"

"UP IN THE TREE LINE, JUST IN FRONT ABOUT TWELVE O'CLOCK."

Suddenly there was an eerie silence, everyone's weapon trained on that location while all ears strained to catch what the rifleman claimed to have heard.

A good five minutes passed without anyone making a move or sound. Lewis never witnessed such self-discipline. It seemed like an hour to Lewis as the scorching sun chose only him to torture, draining the moisture from his body. Sweat was pouring from his brow into his eyes but he was afraid to move to wipe it away. On top of everything else he could feel his leg beginning to cramp up. He desperately wanted to shift his weight but feared the movement would somehow compromise all of them. He endured the agony as long as he could. Just as he was about take the chance of adjusting his position word came down that they were to move out.

The word spread that Killer Kane's platoon leader, Lieutenant Finlayson, was satisfied that the enemy had withdrawn. The reactionary team was ordered to return to the LZ for an *'extraction'*, team Killer Kane would follow shortly afterward. Lewis picked up some grumbling from the troops who were uneasy about using the same LZ that they came in on, fearing that the VC could have set up an ambush there. Never-the-less, they moved out, back-tracking along the path they created through the elephant grass. The team fanned out around the LZ. Soon two CH-46's appeared overhead. The radioman maintained communications with the pilots as the sergeant tossed a yellow colored smoke grenade. From the radioman's communication Lewis gathered that some kind identification process was going on for the pilots to know who tossed the smoke.

The bird set down with the ramp already lowered, rotor wash blasting clear anything loose. The team scurried inside one by one leaving the last man, lugging the M-60 machine gun, to cover them before he entered. Anyone who could, positioned their M-14's out of the open starboard side windows and began peppering the jungle opposite of Killer Kane's location with bursts of automatic fire. The 50 caliber gunner got in the act, shredding apart small trees and most likely killing anyone unlucky enough to be hiding behind or near them. The entire cargo bay filled with smoke and acrid smell of ignited gunpowder that eventually dissipated as the chopper ascended. A full measure of relief came when the chopper attained altitude and smiles began to appear on the men's sweat stained faces. The cold air gave credence that they were out of danger. Those who smoked pulled out cigarettes from plastic, protective containers and lit up. Lewis reached into his shirt pocket only to find a mangled, sopping wet, useless pack of Viceroys. Seeing the doc's predicament Owens offered up one of his Marlboros. Lewis smiled, gratefully accepted it and deeply inhaled the comforting smoke.

Back at Camp Reasoner, the battalion commander, LtCol Stinemetz, Force Company CO, Captain Dixon and Force Company First Sergeant was there to meet them as they disembarked from the choppers. Even though no one said it, they all knew that the committee was actually there for Killer Kane's return and not the reactionary team. The 1st Sergeant handed each man a cold *Budweiser* as they walked off the steel grated landing pad. Lewis really didn't want a beer but, he didn't want to call any more attention to himself by not taking one either, so he obliged. He followed Owens to the 'weapons point' where everybody cleared their weapons and turned back in unused ammunition, grenades and claymores. Owens turned to Lewis, "We're all done here Doc, nice meetin' ya. Go take care of your knee."
Lewis thought there should be more to it than just departing and going their separate ways but, in point of fact, there wasn't. "OK, see you around Owens. Thanks"

Shifty was waiting back at the hootch when Lewis hobbled in. He noticed the bloody knee. "You get *dinged* Doc?"
"No, I fell on some cactus needles," Lewis admitted, limping to his cot.
"Hell of a first day, ain't it?"

"Yeah. One hell of a first day." Lewis answered while seeing two more helicopters approach the pad. *'That must be Killer Kane finally coming back,'* he thought.
"Listen, why don't you get yourself squared away, take a shower and I'll buy you a beer later." Shifty suggested.
Lewis couldn't wait to shower and tend his injury. "Sure, Why not." he replied.

The sun was almost set when they passed by the Company Office. Fresh from their patrol, the Killer Kane team was assembled out in front for a group photograph that included a display of assorted weapons and a large Viet Cong flag they captured that day. Lewis recognized Doc Conners sitting in the middle with a broad, country boy, looking grin across his dirty face. Others were smiling also, and some looked very serious. Lewis couldn't determine if the team was exhibiting a sense of pride for capturing the weapons or that they survived combat without having anyone shot or killed. He concluded that it was probably a little of both.

Team "Killer Kane"

The 'club' was nothing more than an open air pavilion situated on the top of the highest point in the compound. It overlooked the same broad expanse of rice paddies that could be seen from 1st Med. From this vantage point one could see the highway snaking around the base of the mountains rising upward behind them. Far off in the distance the city of Da Nang was barely visible and Marble Mountain appeared to be a mere mole hill. The helicopter pad was mostly perceptible below, allowing anyone at the club to watch the teams come and go. About half way up the rise on the left, between the club and helo pad, was a modest hillside amphitheater where movies were occasionally shown against an egg white, painted plywood screen and rare USO shows were performed on an equally modest plywood stage.

The mood at the club was as sociable as Marines get. Country western music emanated from the reel-to-reel tape player. Everyone seemed to be enjoying their allotment of cold beer and conversation. Discussions ranged from weaponry to questioning individual ancestry. Lewis gathered that only a group of the *tightest-knit* people could get away some of the remarks being made without blows being exchanged. He liked the camaraderie. Shifty pointed out that the few men wearing gold 'jump wings' on their shirts were members of Force Company…his unit.

It was dark when the pair finished more than their ration and returned to the hootch.

Lewis laid back in the cot. He placed his hands behind his head, stared aimlessly at the metal roof and tried to filter through all the events of the day. Shifty turned out the lights.

It was after nine in the morning when Lewis woke up to the sound of choppers landing. He rose to look around. Shifty wasn't there which meant he probably went to 1st Med to have the doctor assess his wound. Lighting up a cigarette he sat on the edge of the cot thinking about what he was supposed to do that day. The five beers he consumed the previous evening didn't help in the thought process. He took a couple more hits from the cigarette before Stottlemeyer came in. "Hey man, you gonna sleep all day or what?" he joked.

"No." he responded sluggishly. "Just taking my time letting my brain catch up with my head."

"Oh yeah, I know how that feels," he said speaking from experience. "I heard you went out with the reactionary team yesterday."

"Yeah, watta shocker that was."

"Ya know, I don't ever remember anyone going out on their first day."
"I guess I set a precedent huh?"
"Probably." He paused for a rebuttal but none came. "Anyway," he continued, "LaPorte's team just came back. He'll probably want to meet you sometime today so be available. Don't di-di anywhere, OK?"
Lewis tried unsuccessfully to blow a smoke ring, "Sure."
The screened door open. Doc Conners stuck in his head. "Hey, what's this, a corpsmen's convention?"
"Come on in turd breath." Stottlemeyer invited with obvious familiarity
Conners entered,"Just wanted see how the knee is doing."
"Knee?" Stottlemeyer puzzled.
Lewis 'fessed up' "Yeah, I fell on a cactus yesterday." He raised the trouser leg to show them. It looked inflamed but not swollen. Seven small, dark dots marked where the needles entered.
"Sheee-it. Does it hurt?" Stottlemeyer asked.
"Nah" Lewis lied.
Conners injected some humor "Maybe you'll get a Purple Heart for that."
Stottlemeyer came back quickly "He would if he was in the Army." The three laughed.
"Well, I gotta di-di. We're going to the PX, anybody need anything?" Conners asked. Stottlemeyer declined but Lewis asked for cigarettes.
"Viceroys, two cartons. Got it. Pay me when I get back." Conners said as he started to leave.
"Hey." Lewis stopped him. "And one of those plastic cigarette boxes."
"Right, a plastic box."
"OK, enough already with the bullshit." Stottlemeyer said to Lewis. "Get ready, I'll be back in ten minutes to take you to meet LaPorte."
"Ten minutes, aye," Lewis mumbled.

Stottlemeyer knocked on the screened door of the E-6' s hootch. It was a courtesy to the senior NCO's to knock before entering.
"Enter," a voiced directed from inside.
The men entered and made their way past small, tidy cubicles of semi-private living space that senior enlisted enjoyed. LaPorte's

space at the far end of the hootch was more open than the others. He was sitting in a lawn chair with nothing more than a towel wrapped around his waist, doing something with the gear he used on patrol. It was obvious that he was preparing to shower. "Mike, here's our new corpsman Gary Lewis," Stottlemeyer introduced him. Laporte simply said "Hi" as he extended his hand.
Lewis took the healthy looking, medium built man to be maybe 165 pounds, in his mid-twenties. His blonde hair was close cropped and despite the camouflage, Lewis could make out rose colored cheeks behind the washed out face paint.
"Lewis just got in yesterday and was lucky enough to *hat out* with the reactionary team just a few hours after he reported in," Stottlemeyer thought LaPorte should know.
"Trial by fire, eh" LaPorte asked stiffly.
The new corpsman didn't know how to address LaPorte. Calling him Mike was too familiar; Petty Officer was too formal, LaPorte was not appropriate, he chose nothing.
"Yeah, I guess," Lewis answered modestly without an address.
The senior asked Stottlemeyer, "Where'd you put him?"
"Fifth platoon until Roshong gets back."
"OK but, when Roshong returns, have him," pointing to Lewis, 'take over the 6th platoon."
LaPorte turned to Lewis offering up some information. "Our situation here is that we have six platoons and only five corpsman. You might be in for a lot of work. As it stands now, you might find yourself running back-to-back patrols." Lewis nodded but didn't fully understand. LaPorte once again turned to Stottlemeyer. "Who's all in the compound?"
"Ah, let's see…Mickelson and Conners are here...yourself…. Roshong should be back from R & R tomorrow."

"Have Conners help him get squared away with gear and draw a weapon," LaPorte instructed. "Yeah, get him some *jungle Ute's* and boots too. He can't be expected to go in the bush wearing that shit." He added.
"Conners went to the PX with his team this morning." Stottlemeyer reported.
"Well then, have Mickelson take care of it," LaPorte answered back tersely. "Tell him that when he gets this man squared away to come back here. I'll take him up to meet the 'Old Man later"
"OK."

LaPorte then addressed Lewis. "Welcome aboard Gary. We expect a lot from you and if you have any problems, come see me."
"I'll sure do that," Lewis pledged.
During an uneasy moment it appeared that LaPorte wanted the conversation over with so he could get back to getting himself squared away. Saying nothing more the two retreated.

"We'll *hat out* to the second platoon to see if we find Doc Mickelson," Stottlemeyer said. "That's the 6th platoon's hootch there," he indicated to Lewis pointing to a solitary building situated down in a small ravine. "That's where you'll go when Roshong gets back."
"Awright," Lewis acknowledged as they took the short stroll to the second platoon hootch. The pair entered. "Doc around?" Stottlemeyer asked one of three men who were sitting around cleaning their rifles.
"He be up at the aid station Doc," one answered.
"Thanks."

Mickleson was inside the aid station trying to wash out a foreign particle from one of his men's eye. Stottlemeyer introduced him to the new corpsman and informed him of what LaPorte had directed. Mickleson apologized and stressed that he was unable to comply with the senior NCO's order because he was going to escort the man to 1st Med. for a doctor to look at his eye. Everyone understood the priority. Stottlemeyer decided that *he* would accept the responsibility of taking the new man around, figuring it wouldn't matter just as long as Lewis got the equipment he needed. Both of them walked to the large, metal supply building.
"Corporal Van, how are you this fine day?" Stottlemeyer greeted the supply clerk.
"Just fuckin' duckie Doc. What can I do ya for?"
"This is Lewis. He's our new corpsman. He needs some gear, jungle Utes and boots."
"7-8-2 we gots. Boot's n Utes we ain't gots. How about some K-Bars? We gots plenty of K-Bars."
"No utilities?" Stottlemeyer asked in disbelief.
"Nope. We should be getting some in next week. We might have some boots. What size you wear?" he asked Lewis.

"Eight," Lewis answered hopefully.
"Uh huh, eight, let me see," He looked over the few pairs he had on the shelf and rummaged through a cardboard box on the floor. "Nope, can't help you there either. Maybe next week."

The news disappointed Lewis. He was in country more than a month and was still wearing the heavy stateside utilities and leather boots.
"Oh well, he still needs all the other shit." Stottlemeyer said equally disappointed.
The corporal handed Lewis a clipboard and instructed him to initial beside each item that was issued. One by one every piece of equipment was accounted for and checked; belt, suspenders, ammo pouches, canteen, canteen cup, canteen cover, ruck sack, ruck frame, helmet, helmet liner, helmet chin strap, helmet head band, helmet cover, flak jacket, food tray and utensils The list went on until everything necessary was issued except for uniforms and boots. Lewis was loaded down with everything to carry back to his hootch. Stottlemeyer helped carry part of the burden. They dumped all the equipment on Lewis's cot. Shifty had returned from 1st Med. and was gathering his tray for chow.
"Hey, Shifty, how'd it go? What did the Doc say?" Lewis inquired immediately.
"He said I can go to the bush. I just have to keep it clean and dry." Shifty answered happily.
"Good," the new corpsman came back.
Stottlemeyer advised Lewis that they would have to go to the armory to draw a weapon after lunch. Shifty volunteered to take him instead, claiming he didn't have anything else to do. "Great," Stottlemeyer replied. "Then, when you're finished with that, you can stop by the aid station and pick up your Unit One. After that you should be all set."
"Yeah, except for uniforms."

After lunch Shifty escorted the new corpsman to the armory.
"Here you go Doc. A brand new, used M-14 one-each, sling, bayonet, scabbard, gas mask, waterproof bag, gas mask carrier, filters and ten magazines. Just sign here," the armorer said, showing him where to sign the hand *receipt* for the weaponry.
"I thought corpsmen were supposed to get 45's?" Lewis quizzed.

“Not in this movie Doc. You’re a rifleman first, then a Doc. Besides, the last thing you want in a firefight is a forty-five. Trust me.” Lewis took the man at his word and signed the receipt.
The armorer stressed, “Memorize the serial number Doc. That’s real important.” He handed over a canvas pouch of gun cleaning gear. “Here, you don’t have to sign for the cleaning shit,” he added
Shifty bumped in the conversation asking the armorer “Did you get any *skinny* about us getting the new M-16’s yet?”
“Ya know, you’re about the millionth prick that asked me that today. The only thing I know is that supposedly, we’re going to get them within the next week or two. I did hear that there’s no cleaning shit for them though. And another thing,” he emphasized “They’re reconditioned, not new! LBJ probably spent too much on his barbeques for us to get new stuff instead of Army hand-me-downs.”
Lewis thought he’d add his two cents worth. “You think that’s bad, the Navy’s still using M-1’s”
“That don’t matter,” the armorer replied sarcastically. “Squids don’t shoot at anything anyhow.”
Lewis didn’t like the term *squids* but chose not to rebut.
“Anything else I can do for you guys?” the armorer asked.
“No. I guess we got it all,” Shifty answered. “See ya later Guns.”
“Thanks,” Lewis followed up.

The next couple of hours was spent in the hootch trying to assemble all the gear he was issued. Shifty helped him fit and organize the ruck-sack and web gear.
“Doc, it’s real important to keep this gas mask dry. You need to seal it up real good in the waterproof bag and stow it where you can get to it quick. Once the filters get wet you’re in deep *kimchee* and might as well throw it away ‘cause it’s useless.”
He showed how to apply green duct tape to the snaps and anything else that would get caught in the *‘wait-a-minute vines’*, explaining that when you get snagged you inevitably say ‘wait a minute’. He instructed Lewis to put duct tape tabs on the bottom of the ammo magazines that would make it easier to pull them out from the ammo pouches, and to roll the rubberized poncho tightly for more storage inside the ruck. He explained to load the ruck with the heavier articles near to top for better balance and less strain on the lower back and items requiring less frequent access

near the bottom. He advised that in time, Lewis would figure out what was best for him; that he would have to adjust for each patrol. He clarified that every patrol served a different purpose and could range from one day to two weeks duration; that some patrols required carrying more ammunition while others required more food and water. He stressed that whatever he chose to take he would have to hump. Longer patrols meant more food and water and 'C' ration cans were heavy. He advised the new doc to allow for one, full meal a day and eat candy bars and cheese or peanut butter with Cracker's at other times. Shifty went on to explain that the pack gets lighter as the patrol gets longer because the food and water is consumed.

"Everybody humps an extra belt of M-60 machine gun rounds, including you Doc."

Lewis was astonished by the cumulative weight. "Just how much does all this shit weigh?"

"Anywhere from 80 to 100 pounds, sometimes more," Shifty replied. "Sometimes you can't get up on your feet. You have to put the ruck on the ground, slip your arms in the straps and roll on your stomach, prop yourself up on your knees then get to your feet."

"Damn. You could really get hurt if you fell the wrong way." Lewis pointed out.

"Yep, but you'll get used to it after a while," Shifty said as he got up to fetch a can of ammunition "Here's some ammo. We might as well load up those magazines too."

As the men sat there inserting one round at a time into the magazines Doc Conners came in with Lewis's cigarettes. "Here you go buddy, that'll be four and a half bucks. Two dollars a carton and twenty-five cents each for the two plastic cigarette cases. I figured you might want two."

"Hey thanks a lot man, I really appreciate it." Lewis reached into his wallet and pulled out his last five dollar bill. Embarrassment flushed across the new doc's face. "Damn, I'm broke," he whimpered.

"Let's see, what's today?" Conners thought out loud.

"Thursday." Shifty answered quickly.

"OK…so…..the eagle shits next Tuesday, the first of the month." Conners whipped. "Tell you what," he said to the new doc. "You keep the fin and pay me Tuesday, OK?"

"You sure?" Lewis said in an apologetic voice.

"No problem. I got plenty." the veteran Doc smiled. "Oh, by the way." he added "I saw Stottlemeyer on the way here. He said to remind you that you'd better get your ass up there and pick up your Unit One."
"Holy crap!" Lewis exclaimed like a child who forgot his homework. "I forgot all about that!" He dropped everything, grabbed his utility shirt and cover and darted toward the door.
"Hey, come see me in my hootch when you're done there. I might have something else for you."
"OK. I'll be there in a little while," Lewis answered back.
"FNG," Shifty laughed good naturedly.
"Fuckin'-A," Conners concurred nodding his head.

LaPorte was at the aid station talking with Stottlemeyer when Lewis entered.
"Good, you're here. I was just about to send someone to get you," LaPorte began.
"I came to get my Unit One," the new doc informed the Petty Officers.
"I have it all ready for you, everything should be there. You might want to customize it yourself when you get a chance. Whatever you do, keep track of the Morphine. You'll have to account for every dose you use or don't have. I'm dead serious." Stottlemeyer insisted. "Also," he added handing him a small tube. "Here's an Atropine injection. Keep it in your gas mask."
Lewis accepted the items, nodding that he understood the instructions.
"If you gentlemen are finished," LaPorte broke in, directing his speech to Lewis "I'll take you over to meet the C.O. now."
"Sure," Lewis simply replied.

When they entered the Company Headquarters, the same clerk that Lewis turned in his orders to asked their business. "Captain, Doc LaPorte's here to see you," he announced.
To Lewis's surprise the commander came out of his back room office to greet them, rather than having them go in. The First Sergeant accompanied him. Lewis suddenly recollected them both from when they came to the medical battalion after one of their men was wounded. La Porte began. "Sir, this is our new corpsman, Hospitalman Gary Lewis. He came over to us from

First Med." The commander smiled and extended a hand to Lewis, formally identifying himself "Captain Dixon." Lewis's hand felt demure clasped in the commander's strong, firm grip. "It's good to meet your sir," the young medic responded, thinking that he bared an uncanny resemblance to actor Aldo Ray, with his bull neck and raspy voice.

The commander continued, "This is my '*Top*', Master Gunnery Sergeant Henderson.

The sergeant refrained from a handshake, "Lewis, welcome aboard."

"Top." Lewis matched the sergeant's acknowledgement.

The clerk handed the C.O. Lewis's personnel jacket. The Captain opened it up and scanned a couple of pages. LaPorte added to the mix. "Gary spent time aboard ship off the coast a couple years ago Sir." That information made it obvious to Lewis that the senior corpsman had already looked into his personnel file.

"So, Doc, what made you volunteer for Recon?" Dixon asked while he continued to review the folder.

Caught off guard by the question, Lewis hesitated before answering; attempting to conjure up an answer he thought the Captain would want to hear.

"Sir, I just wanted to be part of an outstanding unit."

"I'll buy that," Dixon replied although, Lewis sensed that he didn't. "I see you got an Article 15 for dereliction of duty. Want to tell me about that?"

"Well, sir," Lewis swallowed. "Aboard ship, we had a muster for inspection and my shoe polish dulled from standing so long in the sun. The Chief Boatswains Mate wrote me up for not properly preparing for an inspection."

"Uh huh. Sounds like something a Boatswains Mate would do. Well, I think if you don't have at least one Article 15 in your career, you're doing something wrong," he smiled. "Just as long as it's only one."

"Yes Sir," Lewis agreed, relieved by the commander's tolerant attitude.

"Well Doc, we certainly need our corpsmen. Without you guys a lot of my men wouldn't be around. I mean that sincerely. You take care of my men while you're here…they'll take care of you and so will I."

"Yes Sir I will."

The skipper extended his hand once again as a signal to terminate the talk. “Glad to have you with us Lewis.”
The new corpsman realized the meeting was over. “Aye Aye Sir.”
“LaPorte, stand by,” the captain ordered.
Since the meeting was so informal, Lewis was uncertain if he should just casually leave or come to attention and about face. He snapped to attention then casually walked out. The meeting with Captain Dixon made Lewis feel good. He gathered that the man could be trusted and would truly look out for the men under his command.

Lewis heard loud country and western music and laughter coming from Doc Conner’s hootch as he approached it. Through the screen he saw several troops whooping it up. Once inside he noticed that several men were taking turns drinking from a fifth of Jack Daniels while almost tripping over an empty Wild Turkey bottle on the deck. One young Marine was sprawled out unconscious on a corner cot.
“Lewis, come on in,” Doc Conners beckoned. “Hey everybody, this is Doc Lewis.”
A series of Hi’s and hello’s came from everywhere.
“Haaayyy Doc, you ole *‘pecker checker’* you,” an inebriated individual spouted out.
“You come to see ah,…….ah….ole what his name off?”
Lewis recognized Owens, his mentor from the day before then answered, “Yeah, sure, old what his name.”
Conners came over to where Lewis was standing to enlighten him.
“We’re celebrating Corporal Anderson di-di-ing back to the *World* tomorrow.”
Not knowing Anderson, the only thing Lewis could come up with was “Groovy.”
“Yeah, this time next week he’ll be a PFC.”
“Huh?” Lewis didn’t understand what Conner’s meant.
“Private Fuckin’ Civilian.”
“OK, I get it.”
Conners went on. “Since you and him are about the same size I thought you might want his jungle Utes. He won’t need them anymore. He said you could have a couple sets and a pair of boots too.”

Surprised by the offer, Lewis thought he'd better take advantage of it. "Sure, if they fit."
"They will," Conners assured. "He's over here, come with me." Conners introduced Lewis to Anderson. "Hey Doc, have a schnort," the happy corporal offered Lewis the half empty whiskey bottle. Reluctantly, Lewis took a swig. It burned his throat and made his eyes water. "Whew, that's some heavy duty shit," he gasped.
"Go'head, have another," the corporal offered.
"No thanks. I don't think I can handle much of that."
"OK, shoot yourshelf," Anderson slurred.
Both docs found humor at Anderson's state. "I think you have some utilities for the doc," Conners reminded him.
"You're right, I…. al……almosht forgot." the corporal recalled while swaying slightly. "Comin ze here." He slapped his hand against a wooden foot-locker. "Here ya go Doc, Ah take it all. You kin take thish locker too." Anderson insisted.
Lewis thought it was his lucky day. "The locker too! Are you sure?"
"Yep, I…(hiccup)....I'm shure."
Lewis saw two sets of clean but well used used, jungle utilities folded neatly in the locker and a pair of slightly used jungle boots. The leather was hardly scuffed and the canvas was still green. He looked at the size. *'Eight, perfect'*. He felt like a kid at Christmas. "Hey man, I really appreciate this, thanks a lot!"
"No prob-lem-oh…(hiccup)...oh..oh. I think I better sit down, ha..ha." he fell straight down, his butt hitting hard against the floor, still gripping the neck of the bottle. A second later his head dropped. He was out of it. The Docs laughed and shook their heads. Conners turned to Lewis. "Better get out of here while you have a chance," he suggested.
"Yeah, I think so. Hey man thanks for setting this up for me."
"You heard him, 'No prob-lem-o'."

Lewis struggled carrying the bulky locker back to his hootch in the heat but, somehow managed to get within fifty feet when Shifty came out to lend a hand.
"Hell Doc, you shoudda came and got me."
Breathing heavily and salty sweat dripping from his heat-flushed face he answered back, "I didn't think it would be this hard to carry." He took a deep breath. "Anyway, I made it this far."

Inside the hootch the first thing Lewis did was try on the newly acquired jungle uniforms. They fit him well. So did the boots. He couldn't believe his luck. "Looks like I'm pretty well set," he beamed, satisfied his month-long search had ended.
The Marine sat down on his cot and grinned, "Sure looks like it Doc."
"I wonder what I should with these things?" Lewis asked, referring to the cotton utilities.
"Save 'em to exchange for new jungles when they come in."
"Yeah. I probably should do that, thanks," he said tossing them in the foot locker.

Lewis spent the time up until evening chow getting even more squared away; folding clothing and arranging it neatly in the foot locker, finishing loading ammo into the magazines, buffing the new, used boots and organizing his Unit-One. He was thrilled that he could stop living out of a duffle bag. Meanwhile, Shifty had his nose stuck in a Louis L'Amore paperback, only occasionally looking up to check on Doc Lewis' progress.

After the pair returned from chow they casually lounged around the hootch, playing blackjack for toothpick stakes and having idle conversation until they became bored.

At the end of this busy day Lewis laid in his cot reflecting about everything that occurred over the past couple of days. Intermittently his thoughts were interrupted by Shifty's loud snoring but, it didn't prevent him from drifting off to sleep.

"HONEY, I'M HOME," someone shouted in song as the door slammed.
"What the.........," Shify began to curse at the intruder before he recognized Doc Roshong through blurry, morning eyes.
Lewis raised his head off the pillow to get a look at who woke them so early. He saw a slender, long-faced, young man dressed in badly wrinkled, short-sleeved, kakis at the door. The young man's facial features reminded Lewis of Stan Laurel of the Laurel and Hardy comic team.
"Haaaaay Doc," Shifty spoke out, "Welcome back."
"I can't say it's good to be back to this shit hole but, it's good to see your ugly face."

Roshong spotted Lewis. "Who's your new bitch?" he jested. "The minute my back is turned you find someone else."
Doc Lewis was dumbstruck by the remark but, gathering from what he had heard about Roshong's comical antics he surmised the comment wasn't meant as demeaning.
Before Lewis had a chance to respond Shifty blurted out, "That's Doc Lewis….your replacement."
Roshong's face suddenly looked puzzled and perplexed, knowing he still had four months to go before the end of his tour.
"Replacement?"
"We got word that you came down with terminal V.D. on R and R so, LaPorte expedited a replacement." Shifty said with a serious face.
"Bullshit," Roshong challenged.
"Me no bullshit you G.I.- you my numba-one turd. You boo-koo dinky-dow. You go home now." Shifty came back mocking Vietnamese whore-talk.
Roshong realized that Shifty was pulling his leg. "You asshole," he laughed before extending a hand to the new Doc. "So Lewis, welcome aboard."
"Thanks," Lewis muttered sheepishly as he received the handshake.
Roshong dropped his travel bag on his cot and looked around, checking out the area to see if it was as he left it. "I see nothing's changed around here."
"Nope," Shifty confirmed. "Everything is still the same."
"The team in the bush?" Roshing came back to Shifty with a question answer.
"Yeah. They hatted-out four days ago. So, how was R and R?"
"Great! Man, you should see the beautiful round-eyes in bikinis. Thousands of 'em. Everywhere….just like picking apples from a tree."
"I know you Doc. With your devious mind, you only picked the bad apples."
"Maybe. Maybe not." Roshong remarked ambiguously.
Doc Lewis sat up in his cot. Convinced he wasn't going to get back to sleep he pulled out a smoke and took a deep drag.
Roshong glanced at Lewis as if he didn't approve of smoking but, didn't say anything. Shifty got up from his cot and left the hootch to relieve himself before heading to the showers.

While Roshong unpacked his bag the two Docs engaged in the typical, new guy, question and answer routine. "Where you from? Where'd you go to boot camp and Corps School? Where'd you do clinical training?"
Judging from their conversation Lewis began to understand why Paul Roshong was highly regarded by the Marines in his platoon. He possessed a pleasant mix of humor and seriousness and knew when to apply each trait. It seemed obvious that he would rather be with Recon than elsewhere. Preparing to shower, Roshong stripped down to his skivvies. Doc Lewis got up from the cot, grabbed his own "douche kit" and towel and accompanied Roshong to the showers. Along the way Lewis explained LaPorte's plan. Paul offered to show him where the 6th platoon hootch was and help him with the move after breakfast.

Both Roshong and Shifty helped the new Doc make the move to the 6th platoon hootch. Lew managed to carry his sea bag, rifle and 782 gear while Roshong and Shifty carried the foot locker down to the isolated hootch surrounded on three sides by banana trees.
A group of Marines were sitting in a semi-circle in front of the hootch, cleaning their weapons after returning from a patrol the previous evening.
Roshong took the initiative. "Hey you jarheads," he sung out using the Vietnamese word for nurse. "Here's your new bok-*chi.*"
Lew suddenly became flushed as the men scrutinized him.
"Ah right," one man exclaimed. "We finally got our own Doc."
"Hi guys," Lew greeted his new platoon.
"Be gentle with him," Roshong pleaded in jest. "Don't throw him away after you take turns with him like you did with your last corpsman."
"Darn," another Marine played along, drawing scattered laughs.
The ranking corporal in the group stood up and opened the door for them. "Just find an empty rack Doc and make yourself at home," he suggested with a smile.
"OK, thanks," Lewis replied.
"There's an empty cot in the middle," Shifty pointed out. "How 'bout there Doc?"

"It's OK with me." Lew answered, tossing his sea bag on the empty cot while his helpers edged the foot locker against the wall between that and an adjacent cot.
"Whew!" Roshong gasped, "What ya got in there Lewis, bricks?" The question didn't require an answer.
"Hey, thanks guys. I really appreciate your help," Lewis sincerely commented.
"Don't mention it." Roshong applied his humor. "I wanted to get your ass out anyway. We can't have two corpsmen in the same hootch.. People will talk you know." The comment drew its intended smiles.
Shifty then reminded Doc Roshong that they needed to go up to aid station.
"Yeah, I forgot," Roshong acknowledged. "We gotta di-di mao."
"See you later Doc," Shifty bid Lewis as the pair made their way out the door.
"OK, see you guys later, and thanks again."

Lew turned his attention to getting settled in and squared-away. He noticed that this hootch collected more dust than the others he had been in. He guessed that because of its close proximity to the helicopter landing pad it simply got the brunt of the dust and debris
the rotor wash kicked up. There was an abundance of Playmate of the Month centerfolds fixed to the roof, probably as an incentive to stay alive. Ruck sacks and web-gear were scattered about and half-filled boxes of left-over or unwanted C rations were tucked away under all of the cots. A cache of sodas and a small refrigerator occupied an unclaimed corner space. He noticed the conspicuous absence of electric fans. A few of the personal shelf spaces above the cots displayed cherished photographs of wives and girlfriends back in the states. One Polaroid photo was of a 'cherry' '57 Chevy Bel-Aire coupe with a beautiful, blonde girl standing beside it wearing only a pink, cowboy hat. Lew wondered which one the guy would prefer if he had to make a choice.
It didn't take long to get situated in his new surroundings. Thinking that he was half-assed, squared-away, Lew went outside to get acquainted with the men of his platoon.

Sitting on the front step he watched and listened to the men as they continued cleaning their M-14's and made idle conversation. The mid-morning sun beat down on them but, it didn't bother them or their new corpsman. After more than a month in-county, he became acclimated to the unpleasant heat and humidity. Lew was cut short of lighting a cigarette when one red-haired, freckle-faced man thought to start an introduction process. "Hey Doc, what's your first name?"
"Gary."
"I'm Dobson," he began. "That's O'Neil, Baker, **Sergeant** Collins, he just got his **buck sergeant** warrant," Dobson emphasized the rank then continued with the introductions in the order the men were sitting. "There's Simmons, McAllister, Hoffman and last but not least," he added fanfare, "soon to be Mister Civilian himself, Rodney Keenan."
Lewis recognized the new sergeant as the corporal who opened the door. Overwhelmed by the onslaught of new faces he fashioned a semi-apology "I hope you don't expect me to remember all your names real soon."
"Nah Doc, you'll just be quizzed this afternoon," the new buck joked.
"Wait a minute," Dobson broke in. "This is only Team 'Bumble Bee'. The other half of the platoon, Team 'Quaker Oats' is still in the bush."
"Well, all I can say is that I will eventually place a name with a face but, not by this afternoon," the Doc assured the group as he got around to lighting up the cigarette.
After the introductions he continued to carefully watch the men clean and examine their weapons, noting that they removed the .762 rounds from the magazines and wiped the ammo clean also. He never realized that so much attention was given to cleaning both weapons and ammunition. It was clear that the Marines staked each other's lives on the care and maintenance of their individual weapons. Simmons, the tall, thin, dark black Marine was going over the M-60 machine gun with particular care. Dobson finished with the rifle and began working on the stubby, M-79 grenade launcher. It dawned on the corpsman that he should probably offer to help. No sooner than he asked, he was put to work loading up the magazines with the clean ammo. It was close to lunch time when the group finished and policed-up the area in front of the hootch.

“You going to chow Doc?” Dobson asked. The corpsman nodded in reply.
“Why don’t you come with us to the PX instead?” the red-head invited. “We got the whole afternoon off.”
Lew didn’t have to even think about it. “Ok, I’ve been wanting to go there for a month.”
The Doc quickly donned his shirt and cover and ran out to where Dobson, O’Neal and Barker were waiting.
“Doc, Doc, Doc,” Dobson shook his head in disbelief. “You have to take your rifle with you anytime you leave the compound. Didn’t anybody tell you that?”
“No.”
“Well, go get it, we’ll wait for you, and don’t forget to lock and load a full magazine.”
When Lewis returned with his M-14 the four of them made their way across the grinder and up the hill to the main gate. It didn’t take long for them to get a ride in the back of a six-by. As the truck passed 1st Med. a chopper was landing. Lew looked down on the compound trying to catch a glimpse of anyone he knew. He didn’t recognize anyone. The truck made four more stops to pick up riders before it got to Hill 327. Lewis barely remembered passing here on his first day in-country, it seemed so long ago and a lot has happened since then. Everyone got out and made their way to the metal PX building, initially ignoring the beer garden around the corner. Inside the shelves were stocked with necessities as well as a modest variety of luxury items. Lewis was looking for an electric fan but none were available. It didn’t really matter because he forgot that he only had a five-dollar MPC in his wallet. He was happy just to browse around see what the place offered. All the hard-to-get luxury items have been sold; fans, refrigerators, folding lawn chairs, foot lockers, transistor radios, tape players, television sets and what astounded him the most….Honda motorbikes. Many of the administrative ‘pouges’ based around Da Nang actually buy either Hondas or Vespa motor scooters for personal transportation. It was a common sight to see a serviceman in uniform riding down the road on a motor bike wearing a flak-jacket, helmet and having a rifle slung across his back or a .45 strapped to his leg.
With so many Marines in the place Lewis got separated from the others. After conducting a cursory search without spotting anyone he came with he decided to go outside and search. Instinct

directed him to the beer garden where he found Dobson and O'Neal.
"Have you guys seen Baker?" Lew asked.
"Yep". Dobson replied. With a can of cold Coors in his hand he pointed to where a hoard of Vietnamese boys were in the business of shining the boots of G.I.'s for as much money as they could get.
"He's over there."
Lew's eyes found Baker in the throng of Marines and Sea Bees. He was having his boots buffed by a little boy who had a big smile on his face. The kid was stretching a piece of cloth over the toe of Baker's boot and slap-buffing a hundred miles an hour, finishing up with a "One dolla G.I."
"One dollar!" exclaimed Baker, just teasing the boy, having every intention of giving him the buck. "That's robbery. What are you gonna do with a dollar?
"I give to fa-da"
"Yeah, I'll bet your father's name is Ho Chi, huh?"
"NOOO. No Ho Chi. Ho Chi numba ten…you numba one, No Ho Chi. I no V.C.
V.C numba ten. You dinky-dao"
Baker laughed and handed the boy a greenback instead of MPC. The boy took the money and hurried away in search of another customer.
"I didn't think we're allowed to have greenbacks." Lew stated.
"We're not supposed to but everybody has some," Dobson went on to explain. "Sometimes you just can't buy what you want with MPC or "P's so, you keep a few dollars American on hand. Just don't worry about it." Lewis accepted the logic.
After the four of them consumed their two-can, ration of cold beer and 'smoked-'n-joked' for another hour or so, they hitched a ride back to Camp Reasoner. Lewis enjoyed the spending the afternoon getting acquainted with his new team members.
The remainder of the day and evening was spent on leisurely conversation with others in the team who didn't go with them to the PX. A few of the men went to the Recon Club for a few more beers before settling in for the night. Doc Lewis wasn't among them. He preferred to just stay in the hootch and get as much sleep as possible.

Three days of typical 'down-time' between patrols had passed for Team Bumble Bee without much going on. It was a routine of reading paperbacks, playing cards, going to the PX, writing letters, playing handball or volleyball and just shooting the breeze. The men got the word to get ready for another patrol on the fourth day after Lew joined the team. It was Sergeant Collins's first assignment as patrol leader as well as Doc Lewis' first patrol ever. The sergeant made the announcement just before noon chow that day. "Listen up. We're 'hattin'-out' tomorrow at thirteen-hundred. There's going to be a team briefing this afternoon at fifteen-hundred at the company briefing room. Be there." Collins paused momentarily. "Before you ask, I don't know where we going or how long we'll be out. Make sure you tell anyone who isn't here. Got it?" No response indicated that everyone understood. Lew wanted to ask a thousand questions but chose not to. He was suddenly apprehensive about going on his first recon mission but, didn't want it so show. Sergeant Collins left the hootch without having to say anything more. Everyone heard and fully understood their new sergeant's order thereby, negating any need for questions.

Doc Lewis accompanied O'neil for chow. On their way back two 'husses', CH-34 helicopters descended for a landing, kicking up dust that blew back toward their hootch.

Lewis wondered if they were going to take the 'husses' when the team left for patrol. To his thinking they were ancient aircraft leftover from the Korean War. Back in the hootch some of the men were already busy preparing for the next day's patrol. Lew noticed that each man had a unique way to get ready. One man sharpen his K-Bar knife while another would adjust web gear and still another would empty everything inside the ruck sack and place the contents on his cot to inventory. Baker used brown duct tape to cover the flash suppressor of the rifle and secure the sling holders in place. Closer examination revealed that no one had slings attached to their rifles. Lewis promptly removed the sling from his own rifle and borrowed the tape to duplicate whatever Baker and the others did. It was an impromptu monkey-see, monkey-do learning process; gathering in whatever he could from the more seasoned Marines. It wasn't long before they could prepare no further, having to wait and hear the details of their mission.

The team was seated in the briefing room at 1500 sharp. Captain Dixon informally began by introducing a young, clean-cut First Lieutenant from S-2 to commence the briefing.
"Gentlemen. We went over the intel you brought back from your last patrol in Happy Valley. Your debrief indicated that you guys heard a lot of wood chopping at night, throughout the night, nearly every night you spent in the bush in this area," he pointed out the area on a map hanging from the wall. "This activity is not consistent with your everyday, indigenous wood choppers, firstly because, civilians don't labor in the jungle at night and secondly because there's no access roads that we know of in that particular area that will support transportation of that much timber. We can only conclude that something else is taking place in the area. Whatever is going on there we want to know about it. We believe the V.C. or possibly the NVA is constructing something on a fairly large scale. It may be a rocket launch site or an encampment or bridge. Obviously, we need to know ASAP. We don't want another rocket attack like the last one." That comment triggered a vivid, momentary flashback in Lewis' mind of that night at 1st Med. The lieutenant finished up "If this area is important to the VC or NVA, you can expect it to be heavily protected, booby-trapped or possibly even mined"
Captain Dixon took over. "Your insertion LZ is here." he pointed to the spot on the topo map. "It may be 'hot'," he cautioned, indicating the possibility of receiving enemy ground-fire upon landing. "You'll follow the ridgeline northward at your discretion. You already know that the terrain is steep and mostly under a double-canopy of trees. Since the activity is occurring at night you'll need to listen and try to pinpoint the exact location and learn what is going on there. Plan on five days in the bush. Your extraction LZ will be your call but it looks as if there's a suitable clearing about two clicks on the eastern side of the ridge in this area. As always, an enemy prisoner takes priority, then your extraction will be immediate after capture. Any questions?"
"Sir, what's the skinny on friendlies?" Collins asked.
Dixon looked at the lieutenant for help with the question. "We have no confirmation on friendly troops being anywhere in your AO."
Dixon added, "And remember, this area is a "Free Fire Zone. Anything or anybody in the area is a bona-fide target. 'Arty' and

air support is available but, you'll be out of range for any naval gunfire. Any questions?"
"What's the weather lookin' like Sir?" Hoffman spoke up.
"Mild and pleasant, high in the mid-sixties," the lieutenant remarked, drawing wishful chuckles from everyone, and then added, "Actually men, it's going to be pretty much the same, hot and humid."
"Any other questions? Dixon asked. No responses came. "OK. Team leaders and RTO's stand by. Everyone else, you're dismissed. Good luck."

Doc Lewis strolled back to the hootch along with the other men. He observed that they didn't seem to be as apprehensive about the patrol as he was. Private McAllister even displayed 'gung-ho' bravado. "Wouldn't it be bitchin' if we could capture a 'dink' prisoner?" he commented with youthful, male enthusiasm. "I heard that the whole team gets three days R & R at China Beach if they bring a P.O.W."
"Is that dead or alive?" O'Neil asked.
"Live stupid. What good's a dead prisoner?"

As the men waited for Sergeant Collins to return, several of them took the time to write letters home. Lew heard about a traditional 'last letter' that was never mailed unless someone didn't make it back and wondered if these guys were writing that letter. Thinking that it was a good idea, he also took the time to do just that….just in case.

Dobson and Lance Corporal Hoffman returned with one case of C-Rations for each man
on the back of a Mighty-Mite. Each man grabbed a cases and began to sort out what meals they cared to take. Right off the bat the men began to barter for the meals they liked the most. "I'll trade Ham-an-Muhta-fuckas' for anything else," Simmons made the first offer.
Doc Lewis, not knowing the menu fare asked Simmons what he was referring to.
"That's what we call Ham and Lima Beans Doc. Nobody likes 'em."
"I'll give 'em a try. What do want to trade for?" the corpsman obliged.

"Well. Nobody likes peaches and pound cake either. If you have 'em I'll take 'em off your hands," Simmons answered not letting on that the combination was a favorite among most troops.
Doc Lewis searched through the rations looking for the commodities. "No, I don't have them, sorry."
"What do 'ya have that you want to get rid of?" Simmons queried.
"I don't know. I haven't had much of this stuff to know what I like and what I don't like. Why don't you just pick out something?" Lew suggested.
"I'll take those meatballs and beans if 'ya don't mind."
"Don't let him fool you Doc," Hoffman interfered with the transaction. "Those are pretty good."
Simmons confessed, tossing the ham-and-limas aside. "Yeah Doc, I'm bein' straight with 'ya, they're pretty good. You go ahead and keep 'em."
"OK."
The team spent about an hour packing and repacking their rucks. Doc Lewis learned a little from each man as he stuffed and jammed the backpack. Satisfied that he could fit nothing more in, he struggled to strap the bag closed.
"Hey Doc," Dobson stopped him. "How about your medical kit? You need to put it inside your pack. Our last Doc put his right on top, where he could get to it fast."
Lewis thought a moment before answering. "I thought I'd carry it separate."
"NOoooo Doc. You don't want the '*gooks'* to see it. Man, that tells 'em you're the 'bok-chee' and they'll take you out first.." Dobson warned him.
A dumbfounded look emerged on the corpsman's face.
"Yeah Doc," O'Neil added. "Don't you know there's a bounty on your head?"
Corporal Keenan broke in. "It's a fact Doc. They got rewards for killing an officer, a radioman and …a corpsman. They figure if they can ding a corpsman first, he won't be able help anyone else when they get shot. Killing one corpsman is like killing five regular Marines. This ain't no John Wayne movie Doc. Corpsmen don't wear red crosses either."
"Damn!" Lew murmured in disbelief, and then started out repacking to make room for his Unit-One.
"A couple other things you should know Doc," Keenan advised "We don't wear rank in the bush and we don't salute officers."

"If you don't like some asshole like Simmons, just salute him in the bush. It don't need to be an officer," Dobson joked.
"Kiss my beautiful black ass," Simmons came back good-naturedly.
"Better make more room Doc," Keenan said as he placed a block of C-4 plastic explosive and a bandolier of M-60 rounds on the corpsman's cot. "You'll have to 'hump' this stuff too."
"Holy shit! How am I supposed to carry all this stuff?"
A few chuckles arose from the Doc's exasperation.
"You're not done packing yet Doc." Keenan once again advised. "You still have to fill your canteens and get issued grenades tomorrow."
The corpsman couldn't say anything. He just shook his head in disbelief.
Dobson offered additional encouragement. "Doc, just remember this. The longer we're in the *'boonies'* the lighter the pack gets. We gotta eat the C's and drink the water."
Doc Lewis drew a deep breath then let out a surrendering moan as he continued to rearrange the overstuffed backpack.

Everyone finished with their packing and were preparing to go to evening chow when Sergeant Collins came in. "OK guys, stand-fast a couple minutes. Just to let you know nothing's changed. They only gave me three maps," he said as he handed one to the assistant patrol leader, Corporal Keenan, one to the radioman, Lance Corporal Hoffman and kept one for himself. Pointing to Keenan and Hoffman he instructed, "You two get together with me after chow." Both men nodded their understanding. "As always, no beer for you guys tonight but, they're going to show a movie called Casino Royale at twenty-hundred. You might want to see it. I hear it's pretty funny. That's all I got, anybody have anything else?" No one answered. "All right then, carry on."

As the men were returning from chow, a voice called out over the clanking noise of the metal food trays. "LEWIS" The corpsman turned to see LaPorte calling him. Lew broke away from the group and made his way over to where LaPorte was standing. He wasn't sure why the senior corpsman called him over but sensed it wasn't a good sign. The little tension he felt was broken when he spotted a slight smile on LaPorte's normally somber face.

"I understand you're going out on your first patrol tomorrow," LaPorte began.

Lew nodded confirmation.

"Your men helping you? Anybody giving you a hard time about anything?" he probed.

"No, everybody's real helpful," Lew answered then asked, "Why"

"Just wanted to know that's all. I try to keep informed about my corpsmen," he replied. "I don't get to learn much when my corpsmen don't tell me things." He paused to let his words sink in. "You should stop by the aid station more often and look into your men's medical records. You'll probably find most of them need immunizations." LaPorte's words began to sound more like a scolding than an inquiry. "Did you pick up salt tablets and malaria pills for your men yet?"

"No, I wasn't aware that I was supposed to," came Lewis' excuse.

"Bullshit Lewis." LaPorte began to cite barrage of corpsmen's responsibilities. "You need to understand that your job is not just patching people up. You have to keep the men healthy too! You got to make sure they get their shots. You got to make sure they take their malaria pills every week. You got to make sure they drink enough water and take salt tablets. You got to make sure they keep their feet dry. Hell Lewis, I want you to take better care of them than their mother's did." Lew absorbed the message as LaPorte's way of helping him rather than chewing him out.

"Yes Sir, I understand." Lew calmly responded. "I'll make sure they get taken care of in the future," he assured his boss.

LaPorte nodded. "OK, I'll take your word right now but, just make sure you do. After all, these men depend on you. They're not as dumb as you might think. If they sense that you're not looking out for them, you'll get no respect from them. By the way, don't 'Sir' me anymore, I work for a living." Lew heard that particular statement at least a hundred times before. "Call me Mike," LaPorte gave informal permission.

"OK, Mike."

"One other thing," Mike said with deep seriousness. "I know you've been told this before but, I'll say it again. For your own well-being, don't get too close to any of them."

"I understand. Thanks for the advice," Lewis tried to end the conversation.

The senior corpsman also wanted to get back to doing whatever he was doing earlier. "Ok Lewis, good luck on your patrol. See you when you get back."
"OK. Thanks again Mike."
Before heading back to his hootch, Lew walked up to the aid station where he picked up some Cloriquine-Premiquine and salt tablets.

Later that evening some of the men went to see the movie while others stayed in the hootch and relaxed. Doc Lewis was among those who stayed behind. He found it difficult to relax with the uncertainty of his first patrol looming in his mind. It was after 2200hrs when Dobson turned out the lights. Doc Lewis just laid in his cot staring at the darkness, letting the time idle by. He eventually got a few hours' sleep.

After morning chow everyone in the team assembled at the hootch. Lewis noticed that he was the only one who wasn't dressing out in 'Tiger-Stripes', the popular green and black camouflaged uniforms. He also noticed that everyone else was wearing 'bush-hats'. He didn't have one. Since no one mentioned it, he never thought to obtain one. He thought that everybody wore helmets and flak jackets, just like all the grunts he'd seen. It was so obvious that Recon wore soft covers yet, it didn't occur to him that he didn't have one. Every time he went left the hootch he wore the traditional Marine Corps soft cover. His stupidity humiliated him however; it didn't go un-noticed that he didn't have a bush-hat.
"O'Neil," Sergeant Collins called out. "Take Doc up to Ho-Chi's and get him a cover and make it quick"
Lewis found out that the trinket shop/barber shop in the compound was called Ho-Chi's.
When they returned the Doc was sporting a brand-new, green and brown camouflaged bush hat that cost him his last five dollars. It suddenly occurred to him that today was the first of the month, meaning it was payday, and he still owed Doc Conners money. He mentioned it to O'Neil, who said that they will have to wait until after they return from patrol to get paid. He told the Lewis that they would get together as a group and go over to the Division Disbursing Office to get paid. He further advised the Doc to take out the amount of money that he needed for the month

and suggested to leave most of his pay on the books and let it accumulate. Satisfied with that bit of information, Lew thanked O'Neil.

Everyone was busy getting the last minute stuff taken care of. Things like wrapping toilet paper, cigarettes and matches in plastic bags, filling canteens with water and locking personal items away consumed the few remaining hours before mustering at the helo pad. Each man took time to meticulously 'camo-up' their faces and any exposed skin.

Doc Lewis handed out the malaria pills and ordered every man to take one. He also distributed a handful of salt tablets in plastic bags that he prepared the previous evening to each man with the instructions to take one tablet with water every couple of hours. Sergeant Collins swallowed the malaria pill and instructed everyone to do the same.

"OK men, do what Doc says." After ensuring each man complied he barked out the order. "Now let's 'hat' out."

Doc Lewis nervously followed the lead of the others, first strapping on the gas mask around his waist and left leg, then slinging the suspenders of web gear over his shoulders, and finally slipping his arms through the shoulder straps of the overburdened ruck sack. The added weight of eight, canteens filled with water pulled him backwards, nearly forcing him to fall on his back. Dobson quickly reached out to stabilize him. The corpsman could hardly keep his balance under the weight of the 80 pound pack but managed to find that slouching over helped steady the cumbersome weight.

The team made their way to the munitions point near the helo pad where they each received three fragmentation grenades, a few colored smoke grenades, CS tear gas grenades and a few claymore mines. After the men secured the additional munitions Collins called the men together.

"Listen up. Here's the order of march. Simmons, you take point with the M-60. Dobson you back up Simmons. I'll follow Dobson, Hoffman will be behind me with the radio. Doc, you follow behind Hoffman. O'Neil behind Doc with the extra Prick 25. Then Baker and McAllister, and Keenan, you're rear guard. Is everybody clear on that?"

All confirmed their understanding before the sergeant brought out the map that he folded flat inside a plastic bag. A grease pencil

marked the patrol route. He showed it to every one before explaining, "We're going to be inserted here. It's the same LZ that was identified at the briefing. We're going to 'hump' northward along the ridge line about half-way up the side of the hill. We're not going to follow any trail we find but, we will mark its location and note its direction and how much use it gets. Hoffman, 'sit-reps' will be given every hour. It's the same as before. A girls name used in a sentence means 'all secure'. Keying the handset twice means 'affirmative, we're all secure'. Everybody got that?" The sergeant saw a puzzled look in the corpsman's face. "Doc, you got it?"
Lewis nodded timidly "I think so," he replied but was still unsure. Sergeant Collins continued. "No talking, use hand signals." Remembering that this was the corpsman's first patrol Collins inserted an extra tasking "Somebody go over the signals with Doc while we're waiting for the choppers. The pilots have been briefed so we're going to jump on just as soon as they touch down." The sergeant assigned Dobson to take the second 'bird' along with McAllister, Keenan, O'Neil and Doc Lewis.
The team didn't have to wait too long. Two CH-34, Husses appeared coming from the direction of Da Nang. Doc Lewis saw Hoffman lift the handset to his ear and began to communicate with the choppers. When they landed the crew chiefs gave the 'thumbs-up' signal for the team to climb aboard. Rotor wash blasted dust and twigs the men's faces as they approached in single file, fighting against the blinding whirlwind under the burden of their packs. The choppers lifted off as soon as the last man struggled inside. Doc Lewis surprised himself with the burst of physical energy he mustered up to climb aboard, even though the crew chief assisted him slightly. The open-sided choppers gave an excellent aerial view of the Recon compound below, confirming it was the crescent shape that Lewis imagined. The choppers ascended northward for several minutes before turning west, climbing over the range of steep hills that separated the Da Nang valley from the rest of the country. Even though this was the doc's first patrol, he wasn't as apprehensive as he was when he went out with the reactionary force a couple of weeks earlier. He was more concerned with the chopper falling out of the sky than anything else and hoped his freshly camouflaged face concealed his fear. It seemed as if they had only been in the air a few minutes when the change of pitch in the chopper's engine

indicated that they were descending. Dobson pulled a magazine of ammunition from its pouch and locked-and-loaded his rifle. The others followed suit. As Lewis loaded his own M-14, he finally began to feel the same nervous anticipation that he felt once before. He could see the first chopper approach the LZ. It wasn't landing, it was hovering about fifteen off the ground and the men were jumping out into a field of tall, sharp elephant grass. As the first chopper pulled away the second chopper moved into the same hovering position. The men had to jump to the ground. From such height Lew was sure that someone would get hurt, especially with all the weight in the packs forcing the body to twist awkwardly before impact with the ground. His turn to jump came before he had a chance to position himself for a least likely injury. The crew chief hurriedly pushed him off the aircraft.

He somehow managed to land on his feet although the weight of the pack twisted him into a roll that absorbed the brunt of the impact. Within seconds the chopper lifted off,

leaving the team isolated on the ground. Forming a perimeter and concealing themselves in the tall grass, the sergeant 'lipped' if anyone was hurt. Surprisingly, no one was injured. They waited quietly for any sign of the enemy before moving out. Satisfied that they hadn't been observed, Collins checked the compass reading against the map, pointed out the direction of travel then signaled for the team to move. Each man fell in to his assigned position as Simmons lead the way through the grass toward the steep, heavily vegetated, ridge in front of them. The patrol cleared the elephant grass only to be caught up in a thicket of vines and bramble. Assuming the thicket was impassable Collins redirected Simmons to go around it. More than an hour had passed as the team agonized in the afternoon heat and humidity before they cleared the thicket. Auerbach mimed breaking an invisible stick that signaled the team to take a welcome break. Every man quietly lowered his body to the ground, half-reclining against the pack while retrieving a canteen, carefully taking only one, full mouthful and washing it around in the mouth before swallowing it. The rest gave Doc Lewis time to reflect on what he observed on this first leg of the mission. He noticed that every man traveled 'turtle slow' and deliberately avoiding making any noise; painstakingly pushing aside branches and vines while watching foot placement , avoiding stepping on twigs that could snap. He also found that every man maintained an interval of about 15 feet from the man in front. When moving he noticed that every man pointed his weapon in the opposite direction from the man in front. Once more Sergeant Auerback checked the map. He snapped his finger to get Simmon's attention then pointed out the direction of travel once again. Collins pumped a clinched fist twice as the signal to move out again. Once out of the thicket the team filed up the steep, tree covered hillside. It was dark under the double-canopy of trees as very little sunlight penetrated the thick, green foliage.

Everything looked prehistoric. Heavy vines, lush ferns and small bushes all combined to surround the tightly packed trees. The stink of rot and decay permeated the air. Lew wondered if this musty smell was the 'jungle rot' his uncle, who served in the 'Big War', told him about when he was a small boy. The men moved as quietly as possible, enforcing 'noise discipline' that impressed Lewis. He scrutinized the men's faces, attempting to pick out what they all were scanning for. It was obvious that were looking for signs of the enemy but, Lew sensed that they were also looking for other things beyond human form. They scanned overhead, on the ground and to the left and right as they moved. Suddenly a raised, clinched first stopped the patrol in its tracks. Hoffman turned around to silently relay communication to Doc. First he pointed to his eyes then, pointed to something tied to a nearby tree. At first Doc didn't understand what was going on but, quickly caught on when he barely made out a concealed, tree branch with long, pointed, bamboo spikes attached to it tied back against its trunk. He realized that this was a V.C. booby-trap that, if tripped, would spring forward and impale anyone unlucky enough to be caught within its arc. Lewis nodded to Hoffman the he got the message then turned around and relayed the warning to O'Neil who, in-turn passed it down the line until everyone was aware of the object. The team moved out once more, each man looking for a tripping mechanism as they passed by. Logic told the Doc that this trap seemed out of place yet, he reasoned if there's one, there's probably more. As if hit by a brick, he suddenly realized that this was indeed a deadly dangerous place. Cautiously, the team climbed the hillside until they reach a small, semi-flat surface about half-way from the crest that was surrounded by heavy brush and large ferns but, also permitted an unobstructed view of the adjacent hillside. Sergeant Collins determined that they would use this area as their 'harbor site' for the night.

The men sat down forming a tight, defensive perimeter. After a few minutes of silence, they all quietly removed their packs and settled in, getting as comfortable as the hard, damp ground would permit. Doc Lewis welcomed slipping out of the binding, shoulder-straps and relieving the burden from his aching back. Darkness was coming upon the jungle quickly because of the heavy cover. Lew sat quietly as he watched the others for direction. He could hear whispers coming from Collins and Hoffman as he watched the sergeant run his finger over the map, then whispered instructions to Hoffman, who then whispered into the radio handset. Within a few seconds Hoffman lipped the message to Collins then repeated it down the line "On the way". The Doc didn't understand the message until a screeching, high-pitched, whistling sound pierced his ears from overhead, followed by a loud KA-RAK-BOOM that shook the valley and echoed through the jungle. Through an opening in the foliage a plume of white smoke rose up against the dark green background on the next hill over. Lew then understood that the sergeant called an artillery round. It scared him to think the round traveled overhead, barely clearing the top of the hill above them. He had heard stories about 'short-rounds' failing to reach their targets and falling on friendly troops but, this put his nerves in full tension.

"Relax Doc," O'Neil whispered. "The Sarge located that round on the map relative to our position. If we have to call in 'arty' the 'guns' will already have that round as a control point. Then we can direct their fire from it." He explained. Even though the corpsman learned the reason, it didn't quench his fear of artillery shells flying above his head. He wondered if the others had the same reservations.

Satisfied that he had established a control point Collins put the map away and then mimed spooning food into his mouth, silently signaling the men that it was OK to chow down. Everyone reached into their packs and pulled out a tin of C rations. Doc Lewis selected a can of boned turkey. Using the ingenious P38 can opener he punctured the tin and slowly eased it around the lip of the can. He remembered that Shifty had once instructed him to hold his hand tightly around the can to muffle any noise. O'Neil pulled out a bottle of Louisiana Hot Sauce and offered it to the corpsman to 'doctor-up' the bland fare. Lew found the cold meat with sauce added to be tolerable. When both men finished O'Neil instructed Lew to cut out the bottom of the can and fold the tin flat. He then dug a small hole in the ground to bury and hide all their waste. The rule was to not leave any signs of their being there. It was totally dark when all had finished eating. It was time to catch some sleep. The men would each take one hour watch, keeping the radio handset to their ear, beginning with Simmons and continuing through in the order of march. Lew calculated that he would get about four hours sleep before it was his watch. If everything remained uneventful, he reasoned, the first man and last man would be fortunate enough to get a full night of uninterrupted sleep. He lowered his aching body into a fetal position, resting his head on his curled up arm and closed his eyes. The stench of the ground entered his nostrils while incessant buzzing of mosquitoes around his head interfered with his comfort. The noise of chirping crickets, 'whopping' birds and howls of exotic unknown creatures, combined to keep him uneasy in the dark, spooky jungle. Although he was extremely tired he could only find sleep in short increments.

"Doc.....Doc, it's your watch" Hoffman whispered while nudging the corpsman with the handset. "They'll ask for a sit-rep on the hour. When they do, don't say anything, just click the handset twice and pass it over to the next man."

Doc Lewis took the handset from Hoffman and sat upright, resting against the backpack with the handset receiver pressed against one ear. Cautiously, he shielded the luminous dial on his wristwatch to check the time. It was 5 minutes after one in the morning. He had another 55 minutes before his watch was over.

The jungle was completely dark and eerie. He couldn't tell if the moon was out or not because of the thick canopy overhead. Except for bits of dim phosphorus light emitted from decaying vegetation on the ground, he couldn't even see his hand in front of his face, rendering his vision useless. He had to rely on his sense of hearing for any indication of danger. He heard tales that the V.C. where such masters of quietly sneaking up on unwary troops that they would cut the throat of one man and leave the others alone just to play physiological games with their minds. The thought prompted Lew to be intensely cognizant of the jungle noises. He strained to hear even the slightest unusual sound, fearful that if he failed to recognize someone sneaking up on them they all could die.

He couldn't believe how active the jungle was at night. They were surrounded by creatures, birds and insects making intuitive calls and chirps that echoed throughout the forest. Occasionally, distinctive rustling of small animals racing across the ground near them sent hasty surges of adrenalin through his startled body, temporarily raising his pulse and paralyzing his breathing. As the minutes passed, his imagination began to take hold of his senses, leaving him to question every sound he heard. *'What was that? Where's that coming from?'* he kept asking himself. At one time during his watch everyone in the patrol was awakened abruptly by a falling tree branch that crashed to the ground only a few feet from their 'harbor'. It was an anxious moment as they all instinctively reached for their weapons. After the men collected their composure and returned to their slumber Lew once again looked at his wristwatch. Fifteen minutes remained until his turn was over. As he sat motionless he began to get drowsy and welcomed the thought of sleep. Even though it didn't do any good he constantly scanned the darkness in effort to keep awake. A few minutes before the end of his watch he heard an unusual noise. Holding his breath he cocked his ear in the direction of the sound.

He made it out to be some type of movement but couldn't tell who or what was moving. It sounded fairly close and that there was more than one source. He remained perfectly still, determined to identify the noise before awakening anyone prematurely. As the sounds got closer he raised his M-14, posturing for a fire-fight. He shook near uncontrollable with fear as he slipped his finger through the trigger guard. He was only seconds away from opening up when he realized that the sounds where coming from high in the trees. Suddenly, he realized that a group of nocturnal monkeys, swinging from limb to limb were the culprits that triggered his fright---not the enemy. Relieved, he lowered the rifle, grateful that he held off firing. He was so caught up in event that he almost failed to hear someone faintly calling on the radio. "Bumble Bee..Bumble Bee….If you're in the backseat with Sally, key your handset twice." Lew hurriedly grabbed the handset and keyed it two times, then listened for a response. "Roger Bumble Bee, I copy. Break-Break - Jelly Bean…Jelly Bean…..If you're in the haystack with Helen key your handset twice." Lew heard the two 'clicks' obviously coming from another patrol somewhere. "Roger Jelly Bean, I copy." Then there was silence over the net. Lew turned to his relief "O'Neil….it's your watch," he whispered as quietly as he could while guiding O'Neil's hand to the radio. At last, he could finally close his eyes.

Lew felt someone gently shaking his shoulder. "Doc, wake up. Doc." It was Hoffman rousing him awake. Forcing his eyes open he could tell that it was daylight. He slept soundly despite being uncomfortable. He didn't know if his body was aching from 'humping' the hills the previous day or from sleeping on the hard ground. Looking around he saw most of the men eating but Keenan was smoking a cigarette. Lew wanted a smoke more than food so he pulled one out of the plastic box and struck a match that emitted a loud 'snap' as it swiped across the strike-strip. All heads turned to look at him. By the look in their faces it was obvious that he did something wrong. O'Neil leaned toward him and issued a stern reprimand. "Doc, don't strike the matches so hard. Use a lighter if you gotta smoke." Embarrassed by his obvious mistake the corpsman acknowledged with a nod. After a few quick inhales he butted out the cigarette and 'field-stripped' it, burying the remnants deeply into the ground. Afterwards he opened a can of Ham and Eggs and finding it to his liking, ate it hardily. After the team finished with their morning meal Sergeant Collins signaled to move out.

Hours passed as the team made their way along the difficult course of travel, ever aware that the enemy could find them out if they made the slightest mistake. Collins called for several breaks during their day-long march that ended uneventfully just before dusk. The harbor-site for the night was located between large boulders that protruded out from the extremely steep terrain. Once again an 'arty' shell screamed overhead and impacted where Collins could see the smoke. The night was spent the same as the night before except that the order of watch moved up by one man. There were no sounds of wood chopping that night or the previous night. If anyone was chopping wood it would have echoed for miles. The only sounds coming from the jungle were from the creatures who inhabited the jungle.

The third day was a carbon copy of the previous days with the exception of being more physically demanding. Collins decided to change direction from northward to eastward. This meant that the bearing was toward the extraction LZ but, the terrain was much steeper than shown on the map. The new route took them to the fringes of impassable thorny, overgrowth near the crest of a hill that wasn't located on the map. They could have cut their way through using machetes but the noise would give them away. Instead, Sergeant Collins directed the patrol to set up a defensive perimeter while Dobson and Simmons scouted ahead to look for a way around the obstacle in order to get to the top of the ridge before nightfall. The pair returned within a half an hour and informed the sergeant that they found a suitable route. Collins let the two men rest a few minutes before continuing on with the patrol. The way to the top of the ridge was arduous, forcing the men to grab unto vines and saplings in order to make the climb up the nearly vertical hillside, taking one step at a time, searching for footholds that would bare their individual weight. The men struggled their way to within a few meters from the top. When they stopped they could see a small clearing just in front of them at the very crest. Sergeant Collins held their position in the tree line to give them concealment. The clearing looked as if it had been intentionally blown out as an LZ by a previous recon patrol some time back. The fallen trees were decayed and their bases were splinted like an explosive toppled them, rather than being cut down. It was a sure sign that it was used as an extraction LZ. All the vegetation within in the clearing was in the process of regeneration as indicated by high grasses, young sapling trees and a scattering of flowering bushes. Collins halted the team while he and Simmons carefully skirted around the tree line to the opposite side of the clearing, avoiding being exposed in the open. Simmons returned within a few minutes informing Corporal Dobson to move the patrol around the clearing to where Collins was waiting. Word passed that this is where the team will harbor for the night. Thinking that the VC was smart enough to figure out the expedient LZ might be used again by the Americans, Collins wisely assumed that it might be booby-trapped. As the men settled in, Collins carefully belly crawled through the grass, probing a path, up to where a large bush provided concealment in the center of the clearing.

Doc Lewis and the others watched him from the tree line as he cautiously raised his head slightly above the grass to get a view of the surrounding hills and valleys. After making observations he raised a clinched hand to his ear, signaling Hoffman to bring up the radio. The radioman followed Collin's exact path until he rendezvoused with the sergeant. Within a few minutes an artillery round exploded in the valley below, leaving its unmistakable plume of 'willy-peter' smoke rising in the air. The two, once again, snaked their way back to the harbor site. Unlike the previous harbors, Collins directed Dobson, McAllister and Baker to set up the Claymores on the slope below their position and instructed Simmons to position the machine gun to cover the clearing. It was a precaution that reinforced the Doc's thinking of the danger.

After finishing off a can of cold beans-and-wieners and a tin of fruit cocktail, Doc Lewis got to his feet and quietly moved several feet away from the rest of the men to relieve himself. He learned earlier in the patrol that the standard practice was to kneel as close to a tree as possible and control the flow so it wouldn't make the splashing sound that might give them away. He also learned to dig a 'cat-hole' for solid waste and to leave no trace of it behind.

As darkness fell, the clearing beyond the tree line afforded an unobstructed view of the night sky. Brightness of a full moon cast shadows and gave clear detail to the bushes, trees and grass in the clearing. A billion stars dotted the dark heavens beyond a few strands of wispy, translucent clouds, while an occasional shooting star dissolved in its own path. Even with all the sounds of the jungle, everything seemed peaceful although, everyone knew that could change in a heartbeat.

For the new corpsman, the watch was even longer than the night before. The moonlight reflecting off shiny leaves in the clearing tended to play tricks with his vision. At times he thought he spotted something moving and strained his eyes to determine what it was, only to realize that the source was simply his imagination. The longer he sat motionless the more drowsy he became. He was constantly forcing himself to keep his eyelids open. At one point he caught himself falling asleep when his head abruptly dropped and jerked him awake. More than anything else, he wanted to

sleep….just five minutes. He was about to check the time when he faintly heard something coming over the radio. Thinking it was time for a 'sit-rep' and the welcomed end of his watch he positioned the receiver to his ear, poised to key the handset twice. To his amazement, the transmission was in scratchy Vietnamese. The surprise jolted his sleepiness into being fully awake. He was hearing it but didn't know what to do. Thinking he should let somebody know, he decided to wake up Hoffman who was sleeping next to him. "Hey Hoffman, wake up. Listen to this."
The Marine stirred then took the handset from Lewis and listened to the chatter for a few moments before handing it back to the corpsman. "It's OK Doc, they're either probing the net or using the same freq. I don't know what they're sayin' but by the way it's broken up my guess is that they're not too close. Keep listening. If it starts to get louder and clearer, let me know."
"OK," Lew whispered back.
Hoffman rolled over and went back to sleep. Not being familiar with the 'prick-25' radio, Lew didn't know the range it had. For all he knew the V.C. chatter could be originating from as far as twenty miles or as close as one mile. One thing was for sure…the enemy was in the area…somewhere. The uncertainty prompted the corpsman to be even more alert and wiped away all inclination of dosing off. Keeping the handset pressed against his ear he listened intently at the babble, trying to figure out if it was getting any clearer. That would be a sure sign of the enemy getting closer to the patrol's position. Just as suddenly as it started, the chatter stopped. Doc preferred that it continued. At least then he could tell if it was getting closer. Now there was uneasy doubt embedded in his mind but, he remained vigilant for the rest of his watch.
It seemed to take hours before another transmission came over the net. This time it was the one he wanted to hear. "Jelly Bean, Jelly Bean..If you're pumpin' Peggy let me know" He heard the obligatory keying of a handset followed by another transmission. "Roger Jelly Bean, I copy…break…break…Bumble Bee, Bumble Bee…if you're kissin' Kathy…let me know." Lew keyed the handset twice and listened for conformation. "Roger Bumble Bee, I copy….." He was about to pass it over to O'Neil when he detected that it wasn't the end of the transmission. "Break, Break…Porky Pig, Porky Pig….If you're banging Bertha let me know." Two subsequent keying told Lew that yet another recon

team was in the bush somewhere. "Roger Porky Pig…good copy. Over and out"
Satisfied that the 'sit-rep' was accomplished Lew nudged O'Neil. "O'Neil, it's time for your watch."
The groggy Marine pushed himself into a sitting position and took the radio from Doc who advised him of the V.C. communication and another recon team on patrol.
"Keep your ear to the radio. I heard 'gooks' talking earlier. Hoffman said to let him know if it sounded any louder but they quit talking before I could tell. I think there's another recon team called Porky Pig out there too."
O'Neil didn't seem to be fazed by the report. "OK Doc" he returned the whisper.
Lew tried to find some comfort on the hard ground but couldn't get settled in. His mind wandered with nervous apprehension about the chatter he heard and the mosquitoes buzzing around his ear annoyed him to the point where he just gave up trying to repel them. After a few minutes of restless movement O'Neil tersely whispered, "Doc, You need to settle down. Quit moving around so much."
Lew didn't appreciate the scolding but, he understood what the Marine meant. Determined not to compel O'Neil to admonish him again, Lew forced himself to refrain from any movement regardless how uncomfortable he became. He attempted to control his breathing and let his tired body find its own rest. Feelings of lightheadedness and numbness engaged his senses, allowing exhaustion to capture a few hours of much needed sleep.

The Sun was shining brightly when Hoffman woke him. "Hey Doc. I need the radio battery."
Awaking in a mild stupor, Lew seemed to be surprise that it was morning and everyone
was still alive. Clearing his head of cobwebs he opened his backpack, pulled out the battery and handed it to the RTO. He gave himself another minute to waken fully before opening a can of spaghetti and meat balls for breakfast. Curious, he spoke quietly to O'Neil. "Did you hear the 'gooks' at all on your watch?"
"No Doc. Nothin'."
Lew thought deeply, questioning his own memory. He wondered if he just accidentally fell asleep and dreamed he heard the VC

chatter. After all, when people are extremely tried, they can hallucinate. He turned to Hoffman. "Hey, did you hear the VC chatter last night?"

"Yeah Doc, I told you to keep an ear on it."

"I did, but they quit talking."

Apparently unconcerned, Hoffman just shrugged his shoulders and went back to eating breakfast.

The Doc assumed that he probably shouldn't worry about it either, reasoning that these men were a lot more experienced than he.

After the men finished burying trash, landscaping and recovering the Claymores, Collins signaled for them to move out. They slowly moved eastward down the side of the heavily forested hill until they came upon a rippling, mountain stream at the bottom. They crossed the cold, thigh-deep, water one man at a time, carefully balancing themselves as they traversed along the slippery bottom. After the team successfully forded the stream and the last man cleared, the patrol leader called for a halt when the 'squishing' of wet feet inside boots became too noisy, directing everyone to rest and put on dry socks.

It was nearly noon when the team reached to crest of the hill, once again pausing to rest and eat. Doc Lewis relished every minute that he wasn't hiking in the heat. Even a few minutes reprieve from the physical strain of near vertical climbing gave him the chance to catch his breath and regain some strength. Even though he wasn't in the same physical condition as the others he still prided himself in keeping up with them under the same rigors confronting them all. After finishing up some ham slices he and Keenan lit up a smoke and leaned back against the truck of a large diameter tree. He was enjoying the break so much that he hardly noticed an uncomfortable, dull pinching sensation on his inner thigh. Pushing his hand down inside his trousers to scratch he touched a slimy object and withdrew the hand quickly. Looking at it he noticed it was covered in blood.

Rising to his feet he dropped his trousers only to see a large, black, blood-swollen leech fastened to the skin of his inner thigh and another one a few inches below it. The sight of them gorging themselves so close to his penis with blood trickling down his leg shocked him. He knew enough not to try to pull them off but, couldn't recall how he was instructed to remove them when O'Neil intervened. He removed the cap from the bottle of insect repellent and squirted a few shots of the liquid on each ugly parasite. Almost immediately they squirmed and dropped off the Doc's blood-smeared leg. Lew was so relieved that he ignored the slight, residual stinging of the repellent in the wounds. O'Neil whispered, "It's easier that way Doc."

"Thanks."

Sergeant Collins gave the men time to check each other out for more leeches before continuing with the patrol. Both Hoffman and the sergeant had the blood-thirsty parasites attached to their legs and having been accustom to such attacks, removed the vermin themselves.

Collins made his way back to inform each man what his plan was. "We're going to hump toward the extraction LZ. We'll harbor about a hundred meters away from the LZ and call in for extraction tomorrow morning. Keep as quiet as you can. No smoking from here on out. Got it?"

Each individual confirmed understanding.

It was dusk when the team reached their harbor site. Collins selected a very well concealed knoll that overlooked their LZ. It was an isolated, football field, sized patch of elephant grass surrounded by an expanse of tree covered hills and mountains. The team settled in for the long night of watch standing. Collins chose not to call in an 'arty' position that evening but, he did have the Claymores set out again.

As the corpsman assumed his watch he could barely keep his eyes open. He was tired and the only thing on his mind was getting the patrol over with and getting back to Camp Reasoner, taking a shower and sleeping on a comfortable cot. On several occasions he closed his eyes followed by a quick jarring of his head that snapped him awake again.

As the watch progressed he continually found himself forcing his eyes open. It wasn't until he heard the start of the 'sit-rep' that he realized that he had fallen asleep for a few minutes. Thinking that he might have been the cause of the entire team's death because he fell asleep on his watch, created an emotion of extreme self-guilt. "Repeat, Bumble Bee, Bumble Bee, I say again, Bumble Bee, Bumble Bee…if you're happy with Harriet, let me know." He clicked the handset twice and passed it over to O'Neil without saying a word.

Morning came quickly. Sergeant Collins was already on the radio calling for a rendezvous with the choppers at the prearranged LZ. Lew was guilt-ridden about his dozing off during his watch and sensed that the men were aware of it but, it didn't show in their faces. He thought that if they really knew, someone would have already mentioned it to him. Maybe he only dozed off for a minute or two? Maybe he only imagined that he fell asleep? His thinking was broken by the men donning their packs; getting ready to move out. When everyone was ready the sergeant held the compass in his hand and pointed out the direction of travel to Simmons who began to forge their path through the heavy concentration of vines and brush toward the LZ. The patrol had to crawl on their hands and knees most of the way as they were forced to weave, snake-like through the 'wait-a-minute' vines and thick undergrowth, finally reaching their destination nearly an hour later. Doc never realized that such a short distance could take so long to travel but, then again, he never had to crawl through a Southeast Asian jungle before either.

Collins ordered the men to spread out and conceal themselves along the fringe of the elephant grass and the tree line while they anxiously waited for the choppers. Another hour passed before word came down that the 'birds' will be delayed until sometime in the afternoon. The news disappointed the team but everyone except Doc had been through it before and it came as no great surprise to them. Most of the men took advantage of the delay by taking cat-naps. McAllister brought out a paperback. Hoffman kept his ear to the radio. Doc Lewis just sat there impatiently, wishing the choppers would come soon. Even in the shade the sweltering heat and humidity caused sweat to soak through everyone's jungle uniforms, giving the effect of damp, heated suits. The buzzing of exotic insects, especially the large, shiny, green, flies sporadically broke the near unbelievable silence. Doc observed that it was almost too quiet. The normally conspicuous sound of birds and monkeys calling out wasn't there. McAllister, noting the eerie silence, pulled his attention away from the book. Hoffman also lowered the handset away from his ear. The unusual quiet prompted Collins to bring a finger to his lips as a signal for all to keep quiet. He followed up by pointing to his eye then cuffing his ear and pointed toward the depth of the jungle. The gesture was repeated down the line. Each man froze with his weapon held in the ready while they scanned and listened for any

sign of movement. Doc Lewis could feel his heart pumping, anticipating danger. The flies and sweat didn't seem to matter now. *"Oh God, they found us. They know we're here."* The thought raced through his brain. The well-disciplined Marines held steady, taking care not to move or make a sound. They remained in that position for several long minutes when a muted squelch caught the radioman's ear. The chopper pilot was trying to make communication with the team.
Collins took the handset from Hoffman and in a quick voice whispered, "Roger A-Train, this is bravo-bravo six. We're at the playground. I.D. smoke, over."

"Good copy Bravo-Bravo Six. We'll I.D. smoke in four mike, over," the pilot advise that he was about four minutes away from the pre-arranged LZ.
The team heard the familiar sound of rotors popping in the distance. Collins keyed the handset, "A-Train, this is Bravo-Bravo Six, I have a visual. Be advised this may get hot. I repeat this may get hot, do you copy? Over"
"Roger, Bravo-Bravo Six, I copy. It may get hot, over"
As the two CH-46's made their approach Collins ordered Dobson to throw a yellow, smoke grenade in a bare spot in the grass, hoping the grenade would not ignite the grass into an inferno that would prevent the choppers from landing. When the bright yellow cloud bellowed upward the pilot radioed back, "Bravo-Bravo Six, I identify yellow smoke."
"Roger, A-Train, good I.D., over"
"We're comin' in," the pilot announced as the first chopper seemed to just drop from the sky while the second helicopter continued overhead in straight flight. The ramp was already lowered when the chopper's wheels touched down. Without having the need for silence any longer Collins shouted for everybody to get in the chopper. "Hurry up, get your asses movin'." The men scurried quickly through the rotor blast, reaching the ramp and once inside took positions at the open windows, aiming their rifles though the portals at the tree-line. As the chopper lifted off the gunner let go a sustained burst from the .50 caliber 'Ma Deuce' into the trees below. The Marines onboard followed suit, peppering the jungle with all the fire power at their convenience. It was the same tactic used with the reaction team on Lewis' first experience a few weeks earlier. The cabin was

engulfed in thick gun-smoke as empty casings flew everywhere. Since they had not taken fire from the enemy, Doc assumed that the fire power was a precautionary measure and got into the fray, emptying his M-14 at no particular target on the ground. The chopper barely cleared the trees at the top of the ridge as it ascended to altitude. Everyone breathed easy knowing that they may have eluded enemy contact, even though they didn't know for sure that the enemy actually was encroaching on them. The cool air comforted the men. Doc Lewis relaxed and took the opportunity to light up a much desired cigarette, satisfied that he had completed his first combat patrol in Vietnam. He scrutinized the men's dirty, paint smeared faces. There were a few smiles and some conversation but, for the most part, the mood was somber. The corpsman surmised that for the team, it was just another patrol under their belt.....debiting time against their thirteen month tour of duty.

After the helicopters touched down at Camp Reasoner the team disembarked and made their way over to the ammo point to clear their weapons and turn in the hand grenades and Claymores. First Sergeant Henderson was waiting there, issuing each man a can of cold Falstaff and to inform them that the C.O. wanted to debrief immediately after the men dropped off their 782 gear.

Captain Dixon was waiting at the debriefing room with the lieutenant from S-2. The men, filthy and reeking from the nearly week-long accumulation of body stench, took their seats as the captain began.

"Men, it's good to see that you all made it back safely," he gave pause. "Corporal Keenan, I understand that this is your last patrol."

'Yes Sir, it is," Keenan smiled broadly. "Five days and a wakeup."

"I'm glad you made it through your tour. Wanna extend?" he added semi-seriously.

"Negative Sir, I want to go home to my wife and finally see my little baby girl."

"Well, I truly understand that. Good luck to you and your family."

"Thank you Sir."

"Now," Dixon continued, "Let's move on. Sergeant Collins, you can get it rollin'."
"Yes Sir. We followed the patrol route that was mapped out pretty closely. Unfortunately, we didn't hear any wood chopping or see any activity in the area. We did come across an old booby-trap that looked to be rotting away but, it must have been years old."
The lieutenant interrupted. "What kind of trap was it sergeant?"
"Sir, it was a horizontal, whip type with long, bamboo spikes attached to the tip. We looked for a tripping device but couldn't find one. It probably was permanently formed in a bent back position"
"Uh huh. Was it on or near a trail?"
"No Sir, we didn't get near any trails. It was just out in the middle of nowhere"
The lieutenant thought a moment before speaking. "I'm only speculating but, I think it may have been a training aid to teach rookie V.C how to make hasty traps during the early days when they controlled the valley. Go on."
"There was enemy chatter coming over the net from time to time but, the transmission was weak and garbled. We picked it up two nights ago in this area," Collins pointed out their harbor site location on the map. "Actually, it was Doc who heard it first and Hoffman made confirmation."
Dixon remarked, "Damn, sounds as if they were within a few miles from you."
The comment bothered Doc who had no previous knowledge of the radio's operational range.
Again, the lieutenant asked a question, "It's probably too much to ask but, do you have any idea what they were saying?"
No one responded.
"OK, continue."
"We also came upon an expedient LZ on top of this ridge," Collins once more pointed to the map. "We figured it might be booby-trapped or mined so we skirted around it. It might be possible to use it later on. The only other thing I can add is that I think the gooks knew we were in the area and they were following us. I think we avoided contact by a matter of minutes just before our extraction. That's about all I have sir."
"Thanks Collins. Anybody else have anything?" Dixon asked looking around the room.

Hoffman raised his hand. "Sir, the Vietnamese chatter we heard could have been coming from a lot further away than just a few miles. If the gooks were usin' a more powerful transmitter we could have been pickin' up their shit from ....who knows where...maybe China. There's a lot of variables involved..............." Dixon stopped the radioman in mid-sentence. "I get the message Hoffman, thanks for your input. Anybody else?"
"Yes Sir, I got somethin'." Simmons spoke up.
"Go ahead Simmons."
"Sirs, I been point a lot. This is some of the baddest terrain I ever saw. Its steeper than it shows on the map and it's real hard to 'hump'. It's nothin' but covered with vines, thorns and bushes. You know what I'm sayin' sir?"
"We'll keep that information in mind for future patrols, thanks Simmons. Now, anybody else?" When no one answered Captain Dixon released the team. "Ok then men, good job. You're dismissed."

Within an hour everyone had showered and shaved. It was especially refreshing to Doc Lewis who had never been so grubby before. The first order of business after cleaning up their bodies was cleaning their weapons and web gear. They had about an hour to accomplish the task before evening chow. The team sat in front of their hootch sharing the cleaning gear, just as they did when Doc first met them, only this time he was one of them. The conversation and joking around made the job seem easier and quicker. The 'short-timer', Keenan broke out in a cadence song. *"Four more days and I'll be home..hon-neeee,...hon-neeee. Four more days and I'll be home ..ba-aabe...ba-aabe, Four more days and I'll be home...I can't wait to get you alone....honey, oh ba-aabe be mine."*
McAllister jokingly responded to the entertainment. "No you won't man. Who you tryin' to shit. We all know you love it here so much you're gonna extend for six more months."
"Bullshit! Private Asshole" was the best come-back Keenan could think of.
Simmons butted in. "Is that it? Is that all you gots? Man that's the weakest come-back I heard in all my days."
The laughter and joking continued as The Dave Clark Five's song of '*Catch Us If You Can*' was barely audible in the background.

Doc Lewis took his eyes of what he was doing and seriously asked Keenan. “Hey Keenan, what’s your little girl’s name?”
“Audrey. Audrey Jane. She’s eight months old now. Man, I can’t wait to see her. All I got is a picture when she was six months old. Want to see it?”
Doc really didn’t want to but, feeling obligated, he agreed. “Sure.”
Keenan pulled the snapshot from his wallet and handed it over to the corpsman. “She sure is a doll,” Doc offered kindly.
“I think so too Doc,” Keenan proudly responded. “I can’t wait to hold her.”

After chow the men agreed to go to the ‘club’ and have a couple of beers. It was there that Doc Lewis was approached by LaPorte.
“Lewis, I wanted to get with you after you got in from the bush. How was your first patrol?”
“I don’t know. I really don’t have anything else to compare it with except that it was pretty physical.”
“Yeah, most of them are but, at least you didn’t get in any bad shit.”
“No, you’re right but, I think we were close though.” Lew advised as he brought the beer to his lips.
“Well, that’s not what I want to talk to you about right now”, LaPorte set the stage before informing Lew of another move.
“They need a corpsman with the First platoon. I’m assigning you there tomorrow.” He took a sip from his beer. “It’ll be your permanent billet.”
The unexpected news didn’t sit well with Lewis initially. He was tired of being moved around like a foster child but, since LaPorte was in charge, he had no choice but to accept the order.
“First platoon, huh?” Lew tried to hide his disappointment.
“That’s affirmative. Get with Sergeant Sitas in the morning. He’ll be expecting you.”
Remembering that he owed people money and hadn’t seen a pay in more than a month, Lew squeezed in a request. “Before I make the move, would be OK if I went with the guys from the third platoon to the Disbursing Office in the morning to get paid?”
“I don’t have a problem with that. Just make sure you move tomorrow.”
“Will do.”

The men returned from Disbursing just before lunch. Doc Lewis figured that he didn't need much spending money so, he only withdrew $50 from his entitlement. He also signed up for an allotment to send $100 to his mother every month and left the balance on the books. Finally being able to repay Doc Conners gave him a satisfying sense of relief.

THE MIDNIGHT SKULKERS

Carrying his rucksack, 782 gear and rifle, Doc Lewis stuck his head inside the door at the First Platoon hootch and questioned a scruffy looking Marine Lance Corporal at the far end. "First Platoon?"

"Yeah."

"I'm looking for Sergeant Sitas, is he here."

"Nah. He's in the hootch up there." The Marine pointed to the hootch on higher ground next door.

"OK, thanks man," the Doc acknowledged as he turned toward the next hootch. He stepped inside the building.

"Sergeant Sitas?" he asked a beefy, blonde-haired, farm boy looking type Marine seated in a lawn chair, reading a copy of the Star and Stripes.

"I'm Sitas, you Doc Lewis?" he answered and asked in one continuous sentence.

"That's me, Sarge."

The Marine put the paper down. "Come on in," he summoned. "I was expecting you this morning."

"LaPorte said I could go and get paid this morning before I reported here."

"Doesn't matter," the sergeant extended a hand. "I'm just glad to get a corpsman in the platoon. Have a seat."

As Lew sat on the cot, Sitas began questioning him further. "So, I guess you pretty new to Recon."
"Yeah, I'm the FNG," Lew grinned. "Been here a little more than two weeks but," he wanted to stress he wasn't altogether new in country, "I was at 1st Med for a month before that."
"First Med huh? That's good. At least you have some medical experience. Most of the Docs come straight from Pendleton."
The sergeant went on to explain that the platoon was broken down into two teams. One team was called "Countersign" the other was "Dogma". He advised Lew that he would be assigned to team Countersign's hootch below but, would run patrols with both teams.

"This is Dogma's hootch…they're out in the bush for a couple more days, when they get back I'll introduce you to them. I'm Countersign's team leader, Sergeant Johnson is Dogma's team leader. As it stands right now we don't have a platoon leader. As a matter-of-fact, we're kinda lean on troop strength over-all. Countersign has five men, including myself……six now that you're here. We're supposed to get a couple more FNG's sometime soon so, we'll be revamping the team almost from the ground up."
Lew appreciated the sergeant's candor.
"OK Doc, that's all I got, You got anything?"
"No. Not right now."
"OK, you might as well get squared away down below," he told Lew adding "somebody should be there, if not, just grab an empty rack."
Lewis shook the sergeant's hand and departed.

The Lance Corporal was still there when Lew re-entered. "You the new Doc?" he gruffly asked.
"That's right," Lew answered in a kinder manner.
"Well Doc, just find yourself a place to live. There's lots of empty racks," the Marine pointed out.
Before scouting out an available space, Lew walked over to the man and introduced himself. "I'm Lewis," he offered his hand.
The Marine returned the courtesy. "Unkle, Lance Corporal Ed Unkle."
The two shook hands "Good to meet you, Unkle."
"Yeah, me too."

Lew determined that this Marine doesn't mince words. He presumed that the man would undoubtedly speak his mind. After looking around Lew spotted an empty cot in the corner next to the door. "What about here?" he asked Unkle.
"Sure, it's all yours."
Lew dropped the web gear, ruck and rifle on the deflated, rubber air mattress and laid claim to the area. His other belongings were still at the 3rd platoon hootch but, he needed help to carry the stuff. Reluctantly, he asked Unkle for help. "Hey Unkle, could you help me carry my other shit over here?"
"I can't right now Doc, I gotta go to the armory. Sorry 'bout that. Why don't get one of them guys in the 3rd platoon to help you?"
"Yeah, I guess I'll have to."

Dobson was good enough to lend the corpsman a hand carrying the footlocker over to the 1st Platoon hootch. Lewis wanted to get settled into the new digs before chow, saving the most difficult task of blowing up the rubber air mattress until last. After nearly twenty minutes of strenuous huffing and puffing that left him light-headed, the mattress was finally inflated to the firmness he desired. Two Marines entered the hootch as Doc was spreading a sleeping bag over the mattress. One of them was a small-framed, young, man that didn't bare any resemblance to the poster image of what a Marine should look like.
He spoke out first "Hey, we got ourselves a Doc!" he said excitedly. "Welcome aboard Doc." He placed his rifle and a bag of goods he purchased at the PX on the cot directly across from Lew's, following up by offering his hand and introducing himself. "I'm Palmer.....around here I'm 'Pee-Wee', he grinned. "That's Maynard, our distinguished Corporal," he continued. Doc acknowledged the introduction by shaking both men's hands and telling them who he was.
"Where are you from back in the world Doc?" Pee-Wee asked in an upbeat voice.
"Pittsburgh P.A."
"Holy shit. I'm from Sharon. That's about 50 miles north."
"Yeah, I heard of it," the Doc submitted. "But I've never been there."
"I've been to Pittsburgh a few times to watch the Pirates play, but that's about it."

Corporal Maynard got into the mix. "What the hell's a Pirate? They some kinda Navy puke?"
Pee-Wee jokingly barked back "Eat shit maggot. Just 'cause you're short don't mean you can belittle our Navy brothers, especially when Docs around."
"I can take it," Lew smiled.
At that moment Unkle came back into the hootch with news. "Hey, guess what? I just got the *'skinny'*; we're getting the M-16's any day now!"

"That's just 'scuttle-butt'. They been sayin' that for weeks," Maynard doubted.
"No," Unkle stressed. "This is the real 'poop'. I was just at the armory and the 'pieces' are already there…in crates….just waitin' to be unpacked and inventoried."
"Holy shit," Pee Wee blurted out. "That'll probably mean we all have to get qualified on them. I almost didn't qualify on the fourteen."
"I held one of them," Unkle spouted out. "They feel like toys. Give me my Fourteen any day."
"You ever see a Sixteen, Doc?" Pee Wee asked.
"Only with the Army troops."
"I hear they're havin' problems with them jammin' up," Unkle smirked. "I guess people are gettin' killed because of it too!"
Maynard added "I understand they fixed that problem by chrome-plating the chamber."
"Even if they did fix it, you can't beat the stopping power of a Fourteen. Them Sixteens are nothing more than glorified twenty-two's," Unkle affirmed. "Give me a Fourteen any day."
Doc Lewis sat there listening to the men exchanging views about the weapons for nearly twenty minutes before Pee Wee finally brought the arguments to an end. "Hey, it's chow time. Anybody going? Hey Doc, you going to chow?"
"Yeah, I'm starvin'."
The four grabbed their trays and made their way to the chow hall together.

After returning from chow Lew couldn't help but notice a drawing of a helmet hanging over Maynard's cot. It was laid out in numbered grids from 1 to 99. Most of the grids were filled in with a green crayon. Only numbers 1 through 17 were left uncolored. What appeared to be boot toes protruded from under the helmet and the word 'SHORT' was printed below.

Always inquisitive, Lew asked Maynard, "What's that for?"

"That's a 'Short timer's calendar Doc." he answered and further explained that when a person has less than 100 days left on his tour he's considered a 'short timer'. "Every day beginning with 99 you're supposed to color in a block in descending order until none are left blank. That's when your tour is over and you go back to the world."

"Don't worry Doc, you won't need one of those for a while," Pee Wee laughed.

Lew took the comment good naturedly. "I don't suppose I will." Then he spotted another drawing hanging over the doorway. "Now, what's that?" he inquired as his eyes strained to make out the silhouette of a small, dwarf-like figure with a long nose and big, white eyes, running at full throttle; a long, neck-scarf trailing behind in the wind.

Pee Wee spouted out, "That's the 'Midnight Skulker' Doc. That's what we are….

Gremlins who skulk through the jungle at night…unseen…unheard…destroying everything out to stop us."

Doc studied the artwork momentarily then, with a big grin on his face proclaimed, "I like it."

It was then that the door opened and a tall, thin, gaunt-looking, young Marine wearing the ugly, G.I. issue black-framed glasses and sporting a shaved head walked in.

Pee Wee welcomed him, "Hey Weasel, how'd it go?"

"I don't know. I think it went pretty well. They said for me to come back in a couple weeks for another audition. I don't how those people think?" the Marine responded seemingly dejected. He sat on the cot next to Lew and looked at him blankly. "Hello," he uttered nonchalantly. "Hi…ah….Weasel, is it?" Doc replied.

"You the medicine man?" the Marine asked.

Before Lew could reply Pee Wee answered for him. "That's Doc Lewis. He just got here today."

Weasel extended his hand toward the corpsman. "I'm Russ, Russ Whelchel. They call me Weasel. They got a nickname for just about everybody."

"Good to meet you…….ah," Lew paused not know how to address the man.

"Weasel. Just call me Weasel like everybody else."

Lew accepted the Marine's permission to call him by the nickname but, got the feeling the man really didn't care for it. "OK, Weasel." He also couldn't help but notice the Marine had locked up the pair of drum sticks that he carried in with him.

It was almost dark when Unkle suggested a card game. "Anybody want to play some poker? Doc, you play poker?"
"No thanks. Never learned."
"What! A 'squid' who don't play poker!"
"Sorry," Doc apologized.
"OK, suit yourself."
Unkle and Pee Wee moved over to Maynard's cot where the three of them started the first of several hands.
Weasel got up from the cot and unscrewed the light bulb above him as well as the next one in the middle of the hootch. The only light shining was over the men playing cards.
Both Doc and Weasel turned in for the night. The joking and cigar smoke coming from the far end of the hootch didn't bother them enough to keep them awake.

It was after eight in the morning when Doc woke to the sound of clanking food trays. Unkle and Weasel were still sleeping soundly but Pee Wee and Corporal Maynard were nowhere in sight. Lighting up his first cigarette of the day Doc pondered what he should do to with the free time. He wanted to purchase a set of 'Tiger Stripe" utilities sometime and today would be a good day to do just that he reasoned. Grabbing a towel and 'douche kit' he made his way to the shower, finishing the cigarette along the way.
After showering and approaching the hootch he heard a tapping rhythm coming from inside. He saw Weasel was sitting on the edge of his cot in his skivvy shorts, beating the drumsticks on a towel-covered, hard-back book. Doc could tell that the young man was intent on pounding out an imperfection by the manner that he kept starting the beat over and over.
"Shit man, can't you do that when nobody's trying to sleep?" Unkle barked out while propping himself up in his rack.
Weasel stopped in mid-beat and put away the sticks without saying anything, letting Unkle get back to sleep.
Doc sat on the side of his cot that faced Weasel. "Hey Weasel, what's with the drumming anyway?" he inquired.

"I'm trying to get into the Division Band at headquarters. That's where I was yesterday…auditioning. They said I was good enough. I'll probably get in when someone rotates out," he answered the corpsman's question proudly.
"Were you in the high school band?" Doc inquired further
"Yep, four years. I signed up thinking I'd be in the Marine Band but that never happened."
As the two of them continued the conversation, Doc got the impression that the only thing Whelchel wanted to do in life was to be a member of the prestigious Marine Corps Band. He was confident that he would get his chance.
After a while Lew became bored with all the band talk, "Where you from back home?" he shifted the topic.
"Liberal, Kansas," Weasel replied simply then returned the question. "What about you?"
"Pennsylvania. Pittsburgh actually."
"I think Pee Wee's from Pennsylvania," Weasel expounded.
"Yeah. We already talked about that." Doc said as he stood up and put on his shirt and cover. "Well, I want to go buy some Tiger Stripes. Catch you later."
"Later."

Lew bought his Tiger Stripes from Ho Chi's little trinket and barber shop along with a small, yellow, South Vietnamese flag that had three red stripes centered horizontally along its length. He intended to make a stencil of the "Midnight Skulker' and paint the icon on the flag, marking each patrol he made.

Two new men were in the hootch when he returned. Pee Wee and Unkle were giving the FNG's the skinny about the outfit. Pee Wee broke off their impromptu indoctrination to introduce them to the corpsman. "This is the Navy's contribution to the team, Doc Lewis. Doc, this is PFC George Johnson and PFC Dave Arthurs. They're our newbies."
Lew shook both men's hands, "Glad to meet you guys," Lew tried to sound sincere.
Authors was a muscular, freckle-faced, red head and Johnson was a brown-skinned Negro with a few freckles on his nose. During the course of the day Lew found out that Arthurs was actually a Scotsman who enjoyed boxing and who had left his homeland in Scotland to enlist in the Marines for the excitement. Johnson was

a friendly man who hailed from Baltimore. As the new men settled in Doc busied himself by cutting out the stencil and using a permanent marker painted on one 'skulker' indicating his first patrol. He hung the flag next to his cot and wondered how many more patrols were in his future.

That evening Corporal Maynard came in with two pieces of information. First, the men would exchange their M-14's for M-16's the following morning. The second bit of info was that the team was to go to a place called BaNa to set up a radio relay outpost in two days.

"Sergeant Sitas will brief us on the mission tomorrow after the weapons exchange," was his initial comment. "I'm told this BaNa place is an old French resort up on a mountain top overlooking Happy Valley."

"How the hell can we set a relay when we don't have a radioman?" Unkle questioned.

"Beats the shit outta me," Maynard answered.

"What's a radio relay?" the corpsman inquired.

Maynard explained to Doc. "That's where they set up a big antenna and radio to contact teams on deep patrols to relay the messages that are out of range of the 'pricks' Doc," referring to the standard, short ranged PRC 25 radios.

Lew nodded that he understood.

The remainder of the evening was spent once again cleaning the M-14's and removing the ammo from magazines. Johnson and Arthurs were the only two in the platoon who had trained and qualified on the new weapons and spoke highly of them.

The next morning the men turned in their rifles for the new M-16's. Most of the men remarked how light weight and toy-like the rifles were. Johnson and Arthurs gave the men instruction on how to tear down, clean and operate the new weapons. The 'Old Salts', Pee Wee, Unkle and Maynard immediately removed the slings and began taping up the buckles and the openings in the hand grips. Johnson, Arthurs and Doc did likewise. Sitas walked in as the men were loading the magazines with 5.56 ammunition.

"Make sure you men only load 18 rounds in the magazine…not twenty," he instructed adding "They'll jam with twenty rounds." Rather than stopping their progress for a pre-mission briefing he stood in the center of the hootch and gave them the mission information. "Corporal Maynard may have already told you that

we're going out to set up a radio relay tomorrow morning at 0900hrs. We'll be out for about a week so, plan accordingly. This place is some kind of old resort called Ba Na. I don't know anything more except that we have to take along a two-niner-two antenna and boo-koo batteries. There's going to be a radioman from the air wing coming with us. He'll be here sometime today so, expect him. Everybody got that?" No one responded. "There's no need to 'camy-up' or take helmets or flak jackets." He further advised. "Get yourselves squared-away and be ready in the morning, OK?" Sitas gave a glance toward Doc and the other two new guys. "You men all squared away and ready?" Johnson and Arthurs nodded. Since Lew didn't bother to answer the sergeant spoke to him directly. "Doc, you ready?"
"Yeah, I'm ready but, I want to remind all you guys to take your malaria pills, OK?"
"That's right," the sergeant agreed. "Take those horse pills like the Doc says. Anything else?..... No? OK, I'll see you in the morning."

Everyone in the hootch spent the rest of the day getting ready for their morning mission. For the corpsman the most time-consuming task was loading the magazines one round at a time. Private Johnson came to his rescue by showing him how to put the rounds into clips then, insert the clip into the magazine while forcing the rounds down into the magazines. In return for the tip Doc Lewis showed Johnson the way to put tabs of duct tape on the bottom of the magazines in order to pull them out of the ammo pouch more easily and faster.

Doc took his new Tiger-Stripes down to the shower to wash them out so he could wear them on the mission. He was hanging the uniform over a make-shift clothesline tied between two hootches for the hot sun and constant breeze to dry them quickly when a voice shouted out "Hey Doc." Lew turned in the direction of the voice to see Unkle, Johnson and Arthurs carrying five gallon 'jerry cans' down to the water buffalo. "Since you ain't doing nothin' why don't you give us a *huss*?" Unkle spouted out.
Lew guessed that the word 'huss' meant something akin to help or favor. "Sure. What are we doing?"

"We have to fill these with water to take with us. I'll fill 'em, you guys can carry 'em down to the helo pad, then all we got to do is load 'em on the choppers tomorrow."
Doc thought a moment before replying. "I have a better idea. Why don't we just carry them down to the pad now and fill them from the water buffalo that's down there, that way we don't have to lug them so far?"
"Oh shit, Doc. I forgot there's a buffalo down there," Unkle remembered. "Yeah, that's what we'll do."
While the men were carrying out the task two CH-46's approached the pad and descended for a landing. A Recon team filed out of the rear of the aircraft, ducking the rotor blast and made their way over to the munitions point. "That's Countersign, our other team returning," Unkle informed the others. "The big black guy is Sergeant Johnson, the team leader," he pointed out, as if the men should be told. "Looks like they all got back OK."
After the choppers lifted off, the men lined up the 'jerry cans' next to the metal grating of the pad and returned to the hootch.

Sergeant Sitas was inside with the temporarily assigned radioman when the men returned.
He had already been introduced to Maynard, Weasel, and Pee Wee. Sitas spoke out "You guys take care of the water?"
"Yeah, we got it," Unkle answered.
"Good. This is our radioman for this mission, Lance Corporal Gilmore. You guys can introduce yourselves later. He came over T.A.D from the air wing in Da Nang and will be with us for a few days. Corporal Maynard, get him squared away."
Maynard nodded as a means of acknowledgement.
Sitas issued a final directive before leaving. "Make sure you all got your shit together tonight because they moved up the takeoff time on us to oh-eight-hundred. And make sure everybody gives Gilmore the *huss* he needs. Clear?"
"Got it Sarge," Maynard confirmed.
After the team leader left Corporal Maynard assigned Gilmore a cot next to Weasel's before issuing logistical orders. "Pee Wee, you and ah….." he selected one of the newbies,…"Arthurs go up and draw twelve cases of 'C's' and have them delivered at the pad first thing in the morning." Another order followed. "Unkle, you and Johnson take a frag order for two cases of frags, one case of CS, six each of red, yellow and green smokes, six Claymores and

three bandoliers of 79 rounds. Oh yeah," he added. "Draw a case of C-4 too."
Unkle seemed irritated. "You want anything else? Maybe a fuckin' mortar?"
"Just do it," Maynard came back sharply. "Weasel, you and Gilmore go get the batteries he needs." He then addressed Lewis. "Doc, you just do whatever Doc's do."
"I'll go with them. Maybe they'll need help carrying the batteries," Doc offered.
"OK"
As the three of them made their way across the grinder Weasel struck up conversation with the radioman. "Hey Gilmore, where's home?"
"Alexandria, Louisiana," he admitted proudly.
"Uh huh. I'm from Kansas and the Doc's from Pennsylvania. What's your given name?
"It's William but I like Bill. Bill sounds more Marine-like," Gilmore grinned.
"Hey Weasel," the corpsman spoke. "What's Pee Wee's real name? I know yours is Russell but, I haven't heard him called anything else but Pee Wee."
"Ed. I guess that's short for Edward or Eddie."
"It is," the Doc confirmed before asking, "Isn't that Unkle's name too?"
"Yep. Sure is"
Weasel and Gilmore exchanged more of their Marine Corps background as they walked, leaving the corpsman out of the conversation although, Doc didn't mind since he couldn't relate to anything except a few weeks at Camp Pendleton. Eventually Weasel got around to talking about his desire to be a musician. Lew watched for Gilmore's reaction.
"Good," Gilmore spoke with sincerity, looking Weasel straight in the eye. "You should do what you want to do in life otherwise; you might as well be a shoebox."
Doc immediately knew that he liked the radioman.

Everyone completed their details before chow ended, affording them time get their fill of rolled pork slices and runny, mashed potatoes.

During the course of the evening everyone made final preparations for the mission the following day. PFC Johnson gave Doc Lewis more instruction on disassembling and cleaning the M-16. Ruck sacks were packed with more personal items since all the 'C's' and water would be carried separately. The Dave Clark Five's song of '*Catch Us If You Can"* once again came over the Armed Forces radio. Pee Wee belted out, "HEY, that's us. That's OUR team song OK?"
No one disagreed as Pee Wee turned up the volume and began doing a jig while attempting to sing along with the music. His clumsiness made the antics hysterical. The light-hearted time ended with the song and everyone got back to doing what they were doing before the entertainment. The lights went out early that night.

Unkle took it upon himself to wake everyone in the morning. "Reveille, reveille, reveille. Drop your cocks 'n grab your socks…all hands on deck".
Corporal Maynard got into the act. "OK, everybody up! Get dressed and go to the head of the line at chow" he barked out for the benefit of the new people. It was standard practice for teams 'hatting out' to the bush to go to the front of the line.
Doc didn't have a problem getting out of bed as he usually did. As he donned his new Tiger Stripes he saw that everyone except Johnson and Arthurs also were wearing them, including the radioman, Gilmore. For the first time since he had been in Vietnam, he felt as if he actually belonged to a team. He couldn't explain it but, somehow he was eager to get on with this morning's mission.

Most of the team consumed a hearty breakfast before mustering at the helo pad. The entire team seemed to be in good spirits as they chatted with each other while waiting for the choppers to arrive. Doc lit up a cigarette and looked around at the men with idle curiosity. Pee Wee and Unkle dueled with each other with a barrage of quick witted, but good-natured jabs. Weasel had his nose in a paperback. Maynard stood next to Sergeant Sitas and Gilmore, who was monitoring the radio. Johnson and Arthurs sat on the ground next to each other, quietly observing everything that was happening. Gilmore turned and said something to Sitas who then belted out. "OK, five minutes. When the birds land I

want everybody to grab a case of 'C's' and the rest of the gear and put it where the crew chief tells you to. Don't forget anything."
Two CH46's approached low across the rice paddies from Da Nang and touched down fifteen minutes early. The team scrambled to load all their gear before taking seats. Doc Lewis had only been on choppers twice before; the excitement of the lifting off thrilled him each time. He hoped he would never get used to it. The engines roared loudly as the aircraft ascended upward, over the hill that bordered the camp. Doc shifted in the troop seat to get a better view of the ground dropping away. They passed over a long convoy of six-bys and jeeps traveling northward on the highway. He wondered if it was a grunt company going out on an operation. As the chopper cleared the hillside and headed west, all that was below them was full, thick jungle with a few dirt roads cut by combat engineers or Sea Bees. Doc got the attention of the crew chief and made a gesture of puffing on a cigarette. The crew chief gave him the 'thumbs up'. He was able to smoke most of it before the chopper started its descent. The pilots maneuvered the bird into a bank and began to sweep downward in a large circle pattern. The men looked out the portholes to see a complex of white-washed buildings perched atop a mountain peak, brilliantly standing out against the lush green jungle foliage. From the air they saw one, large building and some outbuildings scattered about. Doc imagined that in the old French Colonial days of Indo-China, this must have been a top resort for the rich plantation owners. They were about 500 feet from the ground when the aircraft suddenly shifted erratically. The crew chief frantically shouted out, "WE'RE TAKING FIRE...WE'RE TAKING FIRE". Maynard shouted out, "THEY'RE SHOOTING AT US FROM THAT LITTLE BUILDING TOO!" Doc's eyes opened wide as he spotted some small arms muzzle flashes coming from the outbuilding. The aircraft gunner opened up with the .50 caliber as the pilot throttled to bring the aircraft about in order to distance the aircraft from the ground fire. It suddenly occurred to Doc that the boxes of explosives were sitting on the deck; realizing that if an enemy round penetrated the hull they could all be blown up in an instant. The mental image of that happening sent an overpowering rush of adrenalin through his body. He didn't want to die like that. Unkle let out a burst from his new M-16 when Sergeant Sitas ordered the men not to return fire since they were almost out of range. Word

came down that the mission had been aborted and the choppers were to return to Camp Reasoner.

Captain Dixon met the team when the choppers landed. The pilots shut down the engines and walked over to Dixon and Sitas for some consultation. After a few minutes Sergeant Sitas informed the team to leave all the gear on the aircraft and to just stand-by for further orders then accompanied Dixon and the pilots to Company HQ. The team removed their backpacks and 782 gear and sat down and waited in the heat next to the landing pad. The talk revolved around the aborted mission. Unkle started, "Them fuckin' gooks could have gotten us if they waited a little longer."
"Yeah" Maynard agreed. "You might be right but, from what I saw there was only a few scattered flashes. We're lucky they didn't fire RPG's at us. I don't think there were too many of them either."
"Bullshit," Pee Wee disagreed. "I saw boo-koo flashes comin' from just about everywhere. Man, I don't know where you were lookin'."
Billy Gilmore injected what he heard over the radio. "The pilot reported back that he estimated a company sized unit was down there."
"Then he saw something I didn't ," Unkle retorted. "You guys see anything?" he asked the new men. Only Johnson said he saw flashes.
"What about you Doc?" Pee Wee inquired.
"Oh yeah, I saw some flashes coming from that same building Unkle did," Doc answered exhaling a puff of cigarette smoke, turning his attention to the helicopter crewmembers examining their aircraft for bullet holes. "I wonder if we took any hits?" he asked no one in particular.
"I didn't hear anything hitting us," Maynard responded first.
"Me neither," Pee Wee added.
Unkle strolled over to where the crew chiefs were standing then returned shaking his head, indicating no hits. "Nah, nothin'."

Sergeant Sitas returned a short time later he informed the team that the mission was being scrapped. "We got a reprieve for a while. Headquarters is going to send the grunts up there to annihilate the bastards. We'll be going back when the place is

secured so, for now, let's get all our shit off the birds and turn in the munitions."
That bit of news didn't upset anyone.

During the next couple of days Doc Lewis spent time getting to know the men of the 1st Platoon a little better. Taking the time to talk to each man individually he quickly learned that there was no one that he really had a dislike for. Even though each man had their own idiosyncrasies he felt that he could trust every one of them with his life. He hoped that the men would get to know him well enough to feel the same about him. It was an entirely different atmosphere than he had experienced back at 1st Med. There was a distinct sense of camaraderie here. Since both teams were in the compound and intermingled, Doc had the opportunity to meet and socialize with all the platoon members. Knowing that he would have to run patrols with both teams he set out to introduce himself to the *Dogma* team beforehand. When he went up to Dogma's hootch only a few men were inside. He met the team leader, Sergeant "Findley" Johnson, along with Corporals Pistorino from New York City and 'Bo' Bolinski from Florida as well as Lance Corporals 'Rocky' Schmidt from Minnesota and Rick Rabinold, who everyone called *Rabbi.* The other team members were out and about that day so, Doc would have to meet them some other time. As Lew was leaving, Sergeant Sitas entered.
"Hey Doc, where you going?"
"Ahh, just back to my hootch."
"Good. Pass the word, we're going back to Ba Na again tomorrow and to get ready. If you can, find Maynard and let him know first. I'll be down a little bit later with more poop. Will you do that?"
Lew liked the way Sitas made it more of a request than an order. "Sure thing."

The Doc found the new men, Johnson and Arthurs to be the only ones left in the hootch when he got there.
"You guys know where Maynard is?" he asked.
Arthurs spoke up. "He went to the PX with Pee Wee and that radioman, Gilbert."
"Shit," Doc cursed. "By the way, his name is Gilmore not Gilbert."

"Gilmore, Gilbert, what's the difference. He's only T.A.D. here anyway."
Doc didn't feel he needed to respond to the new man's comment.
"Why? ...What's up Doc?" Arthurs questioned then chuckled at his own remark when he recalled the Bugs Bunny gag line.
Lew let the quip pass. "Sitas just told me that we're going back on that Ba Na mission tomorrow and he wanted me to find Maynard."
"I guess you'll have to wait 'til they get back. If they ain't here, they ain't here."
"Well then, do you know where Johnson and Weasel are?"
Arthurs seemed irritated. "Doc, I don't know where anybody is. It's not my job to babysit people." He paused briefly before adding, "Hey, I think Weasel was going up to Division Headquarters for something."
"I guess I'll just have to let Sitas know that I tried. At least we can get ready, huh?"
"Hey Doc, I've been ready."

Sergeant Sitas appeared to be miffed at Weasel who had just returned from headquarters and had stopped in to speak with him. Doc overheard part of their conversation as he entered the Dogma hootch where Sitas berthed.
"If that's what the Old Man said, it's OK by me," the sergeant scowled. "Doc, you want something?" he questioned in the same tone when he saw the corpsman enter.
"Ah ....I can come back later," Doc replied sensing that this wasn't a good time to break bad news.
"No, it's OK...We're done here," the sergeant half-whispered, staring daggers at Whelchel.
Doc began after Weasel left the hootch. "There's nobody around Sarge. They're all out somewhere....the PX I think."
"That's just fuckin' great," Sitas profaned before calming down slightly. "They'll be back. When Maynard shows up send him to see me, OK?"
"Sure."
"And let the others know whenever they get back too."
"Aye aye, Sarge," Doc obediently answered, avoiding any of Sitas' wrath as he quickly made his escape.

Doc was eager to learn what the tiff between Weasel and Sitas was all about. "Hey Weez, what did you say to piss-off the Sarge?"
Removing his utility shirt, Weasel glanced at the Doc and quietly replied, "I got another audition with the Division band tomorrow. Captain Dixon knows about it. I didn't know about the mission then. That's what he got mad at." Weasel flung his shirt on the cot. "Hell, if I don't go I'll be letting the team down but, if I don't audition I probably won't get another chance."
Doc saw the dilemma Weasel was battling with. "I thought I heard Sitas say it was OK."
"Yeah but he didn't act like it was OK."
"You know what I'd do? I'd go to the audition."
Weasel absorbed the corpsman's words. "Ya know, I think I will go for the audition. They'll be other missions. I just can't let this opportunity slide by….Right?"
"Right."

When Corporal Maynard and the others returned Doc informed them of the rescheduled mission. Except for the frag order, the men got squared away while Maynard and Sitas went over the operation plan.

The following morning the choppers descended on the LZ at Ba Na. From the air everyone could see that the place was no longer as picturesque as what they had seen on their first attempt, the operation by the grunts to take the compound left it a mass of rubble. The company of infantry who took the place left a platoon in place to provide security. As the team disembarked and made their way to the remnants of the main building they passed by the 80 mm mortar crew. Unkle blurted out something to them but Doc couldn't hear if it was a greeting or a playful insult. Sergeant Sitas cautiously lead the team through the clutter of debris of the main hotel up a partially demolished rear staircase that came out onto a second floor hallway which, in turn lead to an open air balcony at the far end of the building.
"This looks like the best place to set up. What do you think Gilmore?"
The radioman looked out over the expanse of jungle down below. "This is good Sarge," he confirmed. "From up here we'll get good reception."

"Good, see to it then. Right now I'm going to go find the grunt leader and check this place out."

When the sergeant left everyone set about with helping Gilmore erect the two-niner-two antenna and had the radio operational within an hour after arriving there. Almost immediately after setting up, radio traffic began. Gilmore started relaying messages just as soon as they came through the station. Everyone except Doc left to take a look around and talk with their grunt brothers. From the high vantage point Doc could see the crew of a 106mm recoilless rifle on the far side of the LZ. Just below them and about twenty yards away was a 60mm mortar crew lounging around inside hand-dug pit surrounded by several layers of sandbags. Riflemen were scattered about in fighting-holes or built-up firing positions, essentially taking it easy; waiting to repel any attack by the VC. All of the grunts were naked from the waist up, not even wearing flak jackets or helmets. One of them had a transistor radio tuned into the popular Cris Noel Show. Doc noticed how seemingly relaxed the grunts were but, also wondered if any of their buddies was killed taking this piece of real estate from the gooks. He imagined that the grunts see action so frequently that they become hardened from their losses. He and Gilmore chatted between messages, talking about fishing, high school sports, hot cars and girls. The longer they talked the more Doc enjoyed Gilmore's company and easy-going manner.

By mid-afternoon the recon men had returned to the perch on the balcony. Sergeant Sitas informed them that they would have to perform perimeter guard at night and assigned two men for each fox-hole on the west and south side of the hotel while the grunts would take the north and east sides. Even though darkness was several hours away the men received their assignments beforehand. Sitas assigned each new man to pair up with a more experienced Marine. Doc and Pee Wee were teamed up together at the first hole on the southwest corner. Unkle and Arthurs paired up as did Maynard and Johnson.

Sergeant Sitas and Gilmore took turns manning the radio. After the men received their assignments Sitas took them around to show them where their positions were located as well as where the Claymores and trip-flares were set up around the perimeter.

Behind them and to the left of the fox-hole that Pee Wee and Doc shared was a foot path cut into an overgrown grass clearing that provided a good thirty-yard, field-of-fire into the tree line beyond. Both men were advised that trip-flares were set up across the pathway and that two Claymores could be detonated from their fighting hole should the V.C. attempt to breach the perimeter from that direction.

Pee Wee asked, “Where’s the path lead?”

Sitas accommodated him. “It goes down past some destroyed buildings, down the hill ‘til it hits the old main entrance road…about a hundred meters”

Pee Wee casually walked over to the fighting hole that was dug into the hill side about 10 meters from the hotel rubble and was concealed within the slope by dozens of trees laid flat from the bombardment. It was large enough to afford protection for both of them but the bottom was a quagmire of thick, wet mud. “Maybe we should build a floor for this thing?” Doc suggested to Pee Wee.

“Yeah Doc, I think we should.”

Sitas spoke up as he led the other men away to their assignments. “Ok, you guys. We still got a few hours before dark. Maybe you should catch some ‘zee’s before setting up house.”

“Yeah Sarge, we’ll do that in a little bit,” Pee Wee agreed as he climbed down into the hole. “Doc, go get some of that rubble. Maybe we can build a floor with it.”

“Ok,” Doc eagerly obliged.

After a few minutes the corpsman returned with a small, wooden pallet instead of rubble rocks.

“Hey Pee Wee, think this will work?” he grinned, proud of his find.

“Yeah Doc, that’ll be great. Where’d you get it?”

“I sweet-talked the mortar crew out of it. They were going to use it for fire wood. I told them we have a better use for it than just burning it.”

“Good job, Doc.”

The Marine and corpsman struggled to make the pallet fit into the hole. Pee Wee excavated a couple of steps into the dirt with his K-Bar that held the platform in place an inch or so above the mud. “There, at least we’ll have dry feet tonight, huh Doc?” Pee Wee happily remarked.

The sun was beginning to set when most of the men woke from taking naps inside the hotel carcass. Doc lit up a smoke as he

traversed the debris piled up in the hallway that led to the balcony. Gilmore was still there tending to a small open fire while minding the radio when Doc spoke to him. "Hey man, don't you get to take a break? You've been doin' that all day."
Gilmore looked up the corpsman as he continued poking at the ashes. "Break where Doc? I'm tired from sitting here but, what else is there to do? After all, this is what I'm here for."
Lew accepted the man's logic but, still felt that he deserved some rest. "Maybe I can talk to the Sarge and see if.........." Gilmore stopped him.
"Doc, I'm a Marine. I'll stick it out here 'til I drop if I have to."
"Yeah, I know you will but, you still need rest. Man, it's not good to exhaust yourself like that."
"Sergeant Sitas is supposed to relieve me in a little while, I'll sleep then, OK Doc?"
"Sure...but let me tell you now, I will talk to the Sarge if you ever want me to."
"I appreciate the offer Doc, thanks."
No sooner than Gilmore said that than Pee Wee and Maynard appeared.
"You about ready Doc?" Pee Wee questioned.
"Ah huh....sure...I'm ready. I just have to get my gear on our way down."
"You'd better take your poncho Doc," Maynard advised. "It'll be gettin' cold up here tonight."

Palmer and Doc hunkered down behind the sandbags used to build up the hole. The setting sun behind the distant mountain range to the west coast long shadows in the valley below, darkening a heavy blanket of fog that was slowly beginning to creep up the hill toward them. All around them jungle creatures called out to one another as wild animals do at night.
"You want first watch Doc?" Pee Wee asked.
"It doesn't matter to me. However you want to work it is fine with me."
"Why don't we just bullshit a little while, unless you're sleepy now."
"No, I'm not sleepy at all. We can shoot the breeze I guess."
During the next couple of hours the men talked about anything that came into their mind...cars, girls, the Navy and Marine Corps, high school antics and more but, eventually ran out of

conversation. The night air became cooler as the time passed, compelling the pair to break out their ponchos for added warmth.
"Why don't you catch some zee's Doc?" Pee Wee suggested. "I'll wake you in a couple hours."
The corpsman didn't argue since he was getting sleepy. "OK," he responded, trying to position himself where he could find any degree of comfort within the tight confines of the hole.

It seemed that he just closed his eyes when Pee Wee woke him. "Doc, it's time for your watch. Doc….Doc."
"Huh…..oh…OK," the corpsman uttered as the men exchanged positions.
After Pee Wee got settled in Lew ducked down to conceal himself lighting a cigarette, being careful not to expose the flame. He repeated the process each time he took a drag, remembering stories of snipers zeroing in on glowing cigarette ambers. Even though the fog was so thick, visibility was only about 25 feet, he didn't want to take a chance of being targeted or give their position away.

During the course of his vigil he became acutely aware that peering out into the fog was useless; he had to rely on his sense of hearing to detect any encroachment by the enemy. Uneasiness crept in as he detected a sudden silence surrounding him. It was as if all the jungle wildlife conspired to play a mean trick on his emotions by simultaneously stopping their chatter. The quiet was nerve-racking. Imaginary sounds penetrated his brain, rendering vivid images in his minds-eye of the Viet Cong stealthily snaking their way up the hillside for the sole purpose of cutting his throat, or worse yet, capturing him and Pee Wee. The thought sent quivers through his body. Clutching the rifle more tightly he poised himself ready to defend the sleeping Marine and irreverently pleaded under his breath '*Oh God, please make this damned fog go away,*' despite knowing full well that miracles just don't happen in real life as they do in the movies. The agony of imagination ended when a real noise came from the trees below. Holding his breath he pointed the rifle in the direction of the noise and cocked his ear to one side, angering himself as his poncho rustled when he moved. *'That's not my imagination'* he established, then held motionless, waiting for the sound to continue. When it did it sounded as if someone was crawling through the fallen trees. *'Shit, it's them!'* He excitedly said to himself pulling on the trigger. Nothing happened. He realized that in the excitement he forgot to release the safety on the selector switch. He frantically engaged the switch to fully automatic and let go a sustained burst. Pee Wee jumped to his feet, aiming his rifle, "What's happening Doc?" he shouted out.

"There…down there…I heard somebody crawling through the trees!" Doc quickly answered. Just then a voice coming from the next Marine position over shouted "GRENADE" that was followed by an immediate loud explosion, which provoked an additional burst of fire from that position.

Even though there was no return fire, the men stood ready for an engagement. Thinking ahead, Doc Lewis fixed a bayonet to the rifle. Pee Wee followed suit. Sergeant Sitas hustled down to them. "What the hell's goin' on here," he demanded.

Doc answered excitedly, "I heard somebody coming up toward us Sarge. I heard it again and opened up on 'em. They tossed a grenade back."

Doc's account angered the sergeant. "Listen to me, Unkle threw that grenade when he heard your fire. It wasn't Charlie." He let the news sink in a moment "All I got to say is that in the morning there better be dead bodies down there. I ain't talkin' monkeys either. You understand Doc?"

"Hey Sarge, I DID," he emphasized," hear somebody."

"Doc, from now on, you don't fire until after we do. Is that clear?" Sitas commanded.

The corpsman felt like a school boy. "Yeah Sarge."

Pee Wee waited until after the sergeant left before commenting to the corpsman. "Hey Doc, don't worry about it man. You did the right thing but, next time wake me up first, OK?"

Lew was miffed. "Hey, I did hear somebody down there. I even waited to make sure before I fired," he insisted.

"I believe ya Doc. I'd a probably done the same thing," Pee Wee tried to reassure the corpsman. "Why don't you try to get some shut-eye now? I don't think I can get back to sleep anyhow."

"Are you sure?"

"Tell you what. I take the guard until I get tired, then I'll wake you. How's that?"

"That's not fair. What if you don't get tired?"

"Then you get more sleep. Now catch some zee's."

"OK. If you insist but, be sure to wake me when you're tired."

"I will Doc, trust me."
Lew thought it would be difficult to sleep. There was too much activity going on in his mind but, he eventually drifted off. He was out for several hours when he felt a tapping at his boot. "Doc, wake up man. You gotta stop snorin'."
"Huh, what's goin' on?" Doc quickly rose half-startled.
"You're snorin' Doc," Pee Wee cited him.
"Oh shit man, I'm sorry," Lew apologized. "What time is it?" he added.
"A little after four. Why? You got a bus to catch?"
"I don't know, I just wanted to know the time." He lit a smoke. "I'll relieve you now OK?"
"Nah, I'm OK. Want some hot coffee?"
"Hot coffee? Here?"
"Sure. Put some water in you canteen cup and give it to me."
The corpsman complied as he watched Pee Wee pull off some puddy-like substance from a rectangular shaped object and place it inside an empty C-ration can on the pallet. The wad ignited when Pee Wee put a match to it. He then put the canteen cup on the rim of the stove can and waited for the water to boil. Doc was impressed. "What the hell is that stuff?" he questioned.
"C-4 Doc."
"The explosive!"
"Yeah, the same stuff. You didn't know you can burn it?
"No, I didn't. I always thought that it would explode."
Pee Wee gave him a lesson while emptying two, instant coffee, bags into the hot water.
"This shit won't explode until you detonate it. I even heard that you eat it if you had to."
"No kidding."
The men doctored up the brew with cream and sugar and shared the guard until sun up.

All the men assembled at the hotel after guard duty ended. Unkle was the first to bring up the question. "What the hell was all that commotion last night?"
"I heard something and opened up, that's all," the Doc answered half-embarrassed.
"So, you're the trigger-happy culprit. Man, when I heard you firing the first thing I did was toss a frag. If somebody was down there, he can kiss is ass goodbye now."

Sergeant Sitas interrupted. "Well, that's what we're going to do before you men sack out.
We going down there and take a look-see. If we find a body we'll give Doc a medal. If not…we'll ride his ass every chance we get."
"OOOOOhh," the men razed playfully.
Lew didn't care for the ribbing he was getting. He felt that he did the right thing but wished he had held off firing his weapon a little longer.
Sitas lead the men down the side of the hill to where Doc thought he heard something. "Pair up and spread out…be careful…if you find anything give a holler. Doc, you and Pee Wee come with me."
The trio examined the area closely, finding nothing of significance. The sergeant commented, "I don't see no body or blood down here," then added "You Doc?"
"I guess I was.........." the corpsman started to confess a mistake.
"HEY Sarge," Maynard called urgently, "I think we got somethin' here," he said pointing his rifle at a cluster of weeds just below the hotel foundation.
"What is it?"
"Looks like a tunnel entrance."
"Wait there, we'll be right up, don't get too close, ya hear…it might be booby-trapped."
The men formed a semi-circle, keeping their weapons pointed at the well concealed opening in the ground. "What do you think we should do now Sarge?" Maynard inquired. "Blow it?"
"No, we don't know what's in there. Maybe a cache of H.E.," the leader stated meaning high-explosives. "If we blow it we could damned well blow up the whole fuckin' mountain." He handed his M-16 to Maynard, retrieved his .45, then got to his knees to examine the hole closer. "It don't look bobby-trapped," he reported as he got back to his feet. Looking around at the men, his eyes caught Pee Wee's.
"Oh shit, Sarge!" Pee Wee alerted to the fact that he was going to be asked to be the 'tunnel-rat' since he was the smallest man there.
The sergeant handed him the pistol. "Anybody got a flashlight?" he surveyed the group.
"I do Sarge," Arthurs answered, releasing the light from his load-bearing suspenders.

Palmer took the flashlight and with the pistol in hand reluctantly entered the hole head first, belly-crawling downward until his boots disappeared from view. Sitas called to him. "Don't take no chances Pee Wee. If you see or hear anything, get out fast."

The men agonized as Pee Wee made his way deeper into the cavity. Doc couldn't fathom the amount of courage it took for someone to do what Pee Wee was doing. There was no way of knowing what was down there. He could come face-to-face with the enemy, or be killed by a booby-trap, or be bitten by the deadly 'Krait' snake or some other venomous insect or spider. To top off those dangers, the tunnel might collapse and bury him alive. The tension mounted as men anticipated a gun shot or explosion. In the back of Doc's mind was the thought that if something did happen to Pee Wee, someone else would have to go in and drag him out. Knowing that Marines are dedicated not to leave anyone behind he reasoned that since he was the next smallest man, it would most likely be him. *'Oh God, don't let anything happen to Palmer.'* He prayed selfishly.

Even though only a few minutes passed, it seemed an eternity before Pee Wee backed out into the sunlight. His face was pale and sweaty. His breathing was strained and heavy as he gasped for fresh air. It was obvious from the mud-laden uniform that water seeped and pooled within the passage. Doc Lewis witnessed the fear in Pee Wee's eyes as the Marine rapidly huffed out his report between gulps of refreshing air.

"I didn't see anything..........it branched off about.......twenty feet in.......one of them was caved in.......I couldn't breathe....anymore.....I couldn't go any further."

"Take your time," Sitas attempted some comfort while offering his canteen. "Have a drink." Palmer took a swig then asked Lew "Doc, you got a smoke? Mine's all wet."

After he lit up, Sitas questioned him further. "Could you tell the direction the tunnel went? Maybe under the hotel?"

"I think the one that wasn't caved in might be headin' that way, but I'm not sure."

Satisfied with the information Sitas thanked Pee Wee and told him to get some rest.

"What now?" Maynard asked Sitas.

Without hesitation the sergeant gave direction. "Arthurs, you and Johnson go tell the grunts to watch for yellow smoke coming from the ground. We're going to throw it in here and hopefully see where it comes out. Make sure you explain to them that it's us."

"OK, Sarge."

"And tell them to keep their eyes peeled for Charlie trying to escape too."

"Right Sarge," Johnson responded.

Sitas waited a few minutes to give his men time to alert the grunts before pulling the pin and tossing the smoke grenade into the hole.

"You guys scatter too. See if you see any smoke anywhere," he ordered his remaining team.

Sergeant Sitas looked over at the corpsman. "Doc, I don't know what you heard last night but, it could have been VC either going into this tunnel or *dee-dee-ing* from it."

Lew interrupted the comment as a semi-apology for the ass-chewing Sitas gave him earlier. "I don't know either Sarge but, I did hear something," he re-affirmed once again.

"I'm sure you did but, it could have been an animal too. The point is, that if you didn't shoot, we probably never would have found this tunnel."

Doc accepted the sergeant's reasoning with a nod.

"Hey Doc, while you're here, you got any ASA's?" he asked for aspirin. "I got a bad headache."

"Sure thing, Sarge. I have some in my kit. I'll go get it," then advised "You might want to drink more water. Dehydration causes headaches you know."

"Just wait up there for me, I'll be up in a little bit. No sense you coming back down here just to make a house call."

"OK."

When all the men got back to the hotel balcony, none had reported seeing any yellow smoke coming from anywhere around the hotel. Maynard informed the sergeant that the grunts didn't see anything either and suggested repeating the smoke test and running a patrol further down the hillside. Sitas agreed to the suggestion but, not before the men got rested. As the group broke up Pee Wee, Sergeant Sitas and Doc gathered along one of the hotel walls that was still in one piece. There was a flyer with skull and cross-bones printed on it that was nailed to the wall by the grunts as a warning for the VC not to mess with them. It was good place to take some souvenir snapshots before seeking a place in the shade to catch up on much needed sleep.

It was mid-afternoon when Corporal Maynard urgently rousted the corpsman from his nap.
"DOC! DOC! Sitas is having convulsions!"
Lew jumped to his feet, grabbed his kit and rushed to Sitas' aid. The big man was shaking, sweating profusely and mumbling incoherently. Doc placed a hand on the man's wet forehead, finding it extremely hot to the touch and quickly ruled out heat stroke. His experience back at 1st Med. indicated that the sergeant may have come down with a case of Malaria. He calmly issued orders to the men surrounding him. "Quick, take off his boots, pants and shirt. I need some wet rags, the colder the better. We need to cool him down fast. Get some canteens. Hey Unkle, find something to fan him with…here," he tossed Sitas's shirt to him. "Keep fanning him….. Pee Wee, you keep pouring water all over him, especially his chest and groin area." Doc got back on his feet and faced Maynard. "We need to med-evac him STAT."
"Huh?"
"I mean immediately," Lew clarified the medical term.
"I'll have Gilmore radio back to HQ," he advised the Doc.
Lew knelt down beside the patient again, opening his kit and pulled out a rectal thermometer. "Somebody help me hold him still while I take his temp. The last thing he needs is broken glass in his butt."
Private Johnson jumped to the Doc's assistance.
"Bend his leg and hold it steady," the corpsman directed, attempting to get better access to the man's anus.
"Whew man!" Johnson nearly gagged, "He should learn to wipe himself better."
"Don't worry about it Johnson, he's convulsing, he just might release his bowels while we're doing this," the Doc warned as he searched the medical kit. "Damn, no KY."
Lew raised the thermometer and spit on it to lubricate it, then carefully inserted the instrument into the man's orifice. Johnson turned his head away, "Maa-tha fuka."
Maynard returned, "Doc, they're sending a chopper now…ETA about twenty minutes."
"OK, thanks," he withdrew the thermometer and read it aloud "One-oh-four point two." He then elevated the Marine's legs and

placed the wet rags on his forehead and under the armpits. Lew took three subsequent readings while waiting for the chopper. Each one showed a consistent increase in temperature. The last reading was 104. "He needs an IV," Doc spoke to no one as he got up to get a bottle of plasma that was strapped to his web gear. Doc managed to find a good vein on the back of sergeant's hand. Shortly after starting the IV, Sitas withdrew from the convulsions and became alert enough for Lew to inform him that he was being taken back to 1st Med. The chopper was late. By the time the CH-34 landed the sergeant was able to walk with assistance to the LZ. Doc carried the IV high in the air and handed it off to the corpsman inside the chopper. Unkle tossed the man's uniform inside and informed Sitas that he would bring back the weapon and gear later. The men watched until the chopper was out of sight. "Think he'll make it Doc?" Maynard asked.

"To be honest, I don't know. Hell, I don't even know if he has Malaria," the corpsman answered truthfully and went on to explain that there's a condition called F.U.O, meaning fever of unknown origin. "The Docs just don't know what causes it either." No one knew it at the time but, the sergeant wouldn't be coming back to the outfit. With Sitas gone Corporal Maynard was now in charge and it didn't take long for him to get down to business.

"Unkle, you and Pee Wee take Johnson and Arthurs and run a patrol around this place about a hundred meters down. I'll pop a smoke in the tunnel when you're no longer in sight. See if you can locate an exit."

Doc spoke up. "What about me? I think I should probably go too….just in case somebody gets hurt."

"Ok Doc, if you want to," the Corporal continued, "Pee Wee, you lead, Arthurs, hump the radio. Let me know if you find anything. I'll let the grunts know you're going out."

The patrol departed the area passing the 60mm mortar emplacement and followed the footpath that lead down to the winding, Belgian block, access road. Once they reached the road Pee Wee guessed that they were about a hundred meters from the top. He directed Unkle off the road into the jungle and to maintain a steady course and distance from the hotel compound above them. Maynard radioed for them to be on the lookout for red smoke.

Doc didn't mind not having to hump the heavy ruck-sack but, was uneasy about the few men available to fight if they made contact with the enemy. He and the others were all aware that ambush was a favored enemy tactic and were keen on the assumption that *Charlie* had plenty of time to set up booby-traps. As the patrol moved slowly on it occurred to Doc to fix his bayonet. He didn't understand why but, the extra measure somehow made him feel better.

The patrol had circled the entire perimeter of the resort area without seeing any sign of the red smoke. They returned to the compound using the same footpath they had taken outbound but, as luck would have it, their movement flushed out some animal that tripped the pencil flare. The signal alerted the grunts who immediately reached for their weapons.

"WHOA," Unkle called out to them. "RECON PATROL RETURNING."

Maynard hollered down to the grunts from the balcony. "THEY'RE MINE."

As the patrol passed the mortar crew Unkle wise Cracked to one of them that he had befriended earlier, "Wazza matta, we wake ya up?"

The man came back, "No, but we almost put your sorry asses to sleep.....permanently, ha, ha ha."

"Fuck you, pogue," was the best Unkle could come up with.

After hearing from the patrol, Maynard determined that the VC must have been forced to stop digging when the grunts invaded and didn't have the chance to complete it. "We're going to try one more thing then we'll close off the entrance," he decided. "We're going to pop a CS. If anybody's still in there, they won't be in there long."

Corporal Maynard selected Unkle to do the honors. "You throw in the gas and *dee-dee* your ass back up here. If anybody comes out we can pick him off from the balcony." Unkle seemed eager to do the job, outlining his plan. "I'll tape the CS to a long pole with a lanyard tied to the pin and put it in as far as I can before pulling the pin," he grinned at his plan. Maynard agreed to it. "Sounds good. Pee Wee, go let the grunts know what we're up to."

Unkle's plan worked well. Except for a few, barely traceable, whiffs of the tear gas escaping into the air no one experienced any effects of the non-lethal agent. The men watched and waited on the balcony for somebody to exit the tunnel. Their vantage point gave a clear and unobstructed view of the tunnel portal directly below them. After more than two hours of watching, Maynard was satisfied that no one was still hiding in the tunnel. "OK, I guess we'll barricade it tomorrow."

"Hell," Unkle blurted out. "Why don't we just blow it now?"

"We're not going to blow it, Ed. I'll tell HQ about it and let them make the decision. For now, all we're going to do is shove some trees and rocks inside the entrance," Maynard advised.

"Shit Corporal Maynard, you never let me have any fun," Unkle jested, protruding his lower lip in a pouting gesture.

"Now that Sarge is gone, what are we going do about guard duty tonight?" Pee Wee questioned, changing the subject.

"I've been thinking about that too," Maynard answered. "I just don't have enough people for three positions and still man the radio. Gilmore is doing all he can but, he can't do it all. He has to rest sometime." The Corporal paused to take a drag from his cigarette.

"Pee Wee, Unkle and me can operate the radio. That only leaves Arthurs and Johnson to stand guard."

"What about Doc?" Unkle questioned. "He proved last night that he can guard too."

"Yeah," Lew entered into the conversation. "I do good guard." The remark drew snickers.

"No." Maynard insisted. "Corpsmen don't stand guard. If shit goes down we'll need him *boo-koo* fast. Not only that but, the *'legs'* don't have a Doc with them. If they need him, he'll have to take care of them too! We just can't afford to put Doc in a position where he can't move around."

"Maynard's right," Pee Wee agreed. "Doc needs to be able to move around."

Being the center of the guard conflict didn't sit right with Lew. "I really don't mind pulling guard Maynard. Besides, we're all close enough that if something did happen I could get to where I'm needed."

Maynard took another drag and absorbed the corpsman's words before reluctantly rendering a decision. "I know this is my last mission with you guys but, I'm the one in charge so, here's what we're going to do.... We're only going to station two guard positions from here on out. Tonight Pee Wee and Doc will man the same position as last night. Unkle and Johnson take the hole

where me and Johnson were in. I'll keep Arthurs here to get some radio OJT then, tomorrow him and Johnson will switch off."
"That sounds good," Pee Wee agreed.
"Yeah," Unkle concurred. "That's about the best we can do for now."
The two Privates nodded their understanding. With the guard details settled Corporal Maynard told the men to take it easy for the rest of the day.

Most of the men converged on the balcony and gathered around a small fire to shoot the breeze. Gilmore was still manning the radio, relaying whatever traffic came through. He looked haggard. Doc noticed deep bags under the Marines eyes from lack of sleep. He also noticed the redness on his shirtless back from being exposed to the blazing sun all day. It prompted him to comment.
"Hey Bill, don't you know they can court-martial you for sunburn?" he poked fun at the tired Marine.
Gilmore barely comprehended the corpsman's words. "What Doc?"
"I said, you can get court-martialed for damaging government property if you let yourself get sunburned badly."
"That's crap Doc." Gilmore argued. "How many people do you know who ever got court-marshaled for that?"
"Ah…none actually but, that's what they told us," he confessed. "Think about it." He attempted to make a point. "If you get sunburned bad enough to blister and get an infection, you won't be fit for duty. That would be dereliction of duty for not taking care of yourself, since you're considered government property"
Maynard corrected the corpsman. "I think you're half-wrong Doc. It's only a Captain's Mast for an Article 15…not a court-martial offense."
Even though he sensed that Maynard might be right, Doc still defended himself. "Hey, that's what they told us at Corps school."
"That's what they told us in basic too but, I think its bullshit," Pee Wee entered the conversation. "What about you guys?" he questioned the rookies. "You ever hear that?"
Johnson was the first to answer. "Yeah, they told us that shit too. Those mutha-fukin JAG pukes can do anything they want."
"I heard it but, it don't bother me," Arthurs boasted. "I'm too fair-skinned. I have to be careful not to get burned in the first place."

Corporal Maynard decided to put an end to the discussion by addressing the radioman. "Bill, its time you get some rest. Go rack-out for a while. I'll man the radio."
Gilmore didn't hesitate obeying the tacit order. He stood and presented the handset to the leader, advising him that team Heart Breaker was the only patrol that was transmitting then, he weaved his way through the group to retreat in the seclusion of the hotel.

As the men continued their gossip and busied themselves concocting C-ration meals on the balcony someone on the ground shouted out "FIRE-IN-THE-HOLE" followed by a muffled 'fumpf'. All heads turned to watch the 60 mm mortar team launch a few rounds into the jungle below. Doc guessed that the grunts were doing it out of boredom more than actually zeroing-in a defensive bracket. Each round impacted with a 'KA-WHUMPH' that echoed through the valley. The 81 mm crew also got into the act, launching a few of their own projectiles. Doc was amazed that he could actually see the rounds in flight for a few moments before they disappeared in the clouds.
"HEY RECON," Unkle got their attention from the ground. "GET A LOAD OF THIS!"
He waved his hat to signal the recoilless rifle crew. 'BAAM'. The 106mm round slammed into the side of the remains of an outbuilding some 200 meters down the mountain, 'KA-BOOM', easily blasting through the stucco, sending debris flying in all directions. "GET SOME" Arthurs shouted out excitedly. Two more rounds followed. Each impact roused the Marines "HU ROO!"
Suddenly, all hell broke loose. The grunts opened up with everything they had. Two M-60's spewed out a torrent of tracer rounds from opposite directions, M-79 rounds exploded in the tree tops, individual M-16's saturated the jungle haphazardly. It was a brief period of controlled mayhem. When the firing ceased and the jubilation died down, Maynard made a commitment.
"The morning we leave here, we're going to have our own *mad-minute*". The promise excited his men.

That evening the sky darkened as threatening rain clouds moved in; hanging close to the hotel compound. Doc and Pee Wee took their guard position in the fox-hole, anticipating getting soaked. "I

hope you brought some dry socks Doc, it looks like you might need them," Pee Wee prophesized.
"No, it never occurred to me," he admitted. "I'll be back, I'm going run up and get a pair," he said climbing out of the hole.
"OK, I'm not going anywhere," he replied lighting up a smoke.
During the few minutes it took to fetch a pair of socks and return the rain had already begun. The two donned their ponchos and cupped cigarettes in their hands between puffs. The rain pelted the hoods making it difficult to hear normal conversation let alone movement outside of the hole.
"Well," Lew started talking, "Looks like *Charlie* won't be paying us a visit tonight huh?"
"What?" The comment puzzled the Marine.
"The VC don't fight in the rain," the corpsman recalled what he had been told back a 1st Med.
"I don't where you heard that shit Doc, but this is exactly what they like. When it's raining this hard you can't hear 'em sneaking up on you."
What Pee Wee said made sense. It was obvious that what he heard before came from someone who didn't know what they were talking about. He was embarrassed from repeating the stupid comment. He tried to redeem himself by using Marine slang.
"Some 'pogue' corpsman told me that."
"It figures," Pee Wee cracked, tossing the cigarette butt in the mud.
There was a few minute lull between them as the rain continued.
"Why don't you try to sack out for a while?" Doc suggested. "Tonight, I'll wake you when I get tired." Lew didn't want to let on that he was too scared to sleep.
"All right, I'll give it a try, and remember, wake me before you decide to shoot at anything," the Marine instructed as he hunkered down under the poncho for a second before he popped his head out from under the hood again. "Another thing, you might want to keep you piece under the poncho so it don't get too wet."
"Right," the Doc took the Marine's advice.

Several hours passed before the downpour began to let up. During that time Doc didn't have any difficulty keeping alert in the cold dampness. His imagination wasn't as active as it normally was. He guessed that the rain made so much noise that it kept his mind off imagined sounds. He ducked down to light another cigarette. The dim flame reflected the outline of Pee Wee, curled up in a ball under the wet poncho. It suddenly dawned on him that this sleeping Marine is trusting him with his life. It was difficult to comprehend that anyone could have enough faith in him to protect them while they slept. It was at that moment that Lew was overcome with an indescribable sense of pride and wellbeing. It was also when he vowed to never let these men down as a corpsman or friend.

The men switched watch every couple of hours with Doc pulling the last two hours before sunrise. He too had trusted this young Marine to protect him while he slept. The bonds of mutual trust had been forged that night, even though neither of them mentioned it. The rain subsided and the sun was coming up when Doc woke the Marine.

"Hey, Pee Wee, you going to sleep all day or what?"

Most of the morning was spent catching up on sleep. By early afternoon all of the men were awake and sitting around on the balcony, passing time through idle conversation. Despite the heat and scorching sun bearing down, everyone except Doc and Arthurs had removed their shirts, purposely neglecting the corpsman's ambiguous warning.

Their joking and laughter ended abruptly when Gilmore received an urgent transmission.

"Keep quiet you guys, I can't hear." He jumped to his feet and looked down into the jungle valley below their perch. "Roger Heart Breaker, I copy, break break.....this is Bravo November relay, requesting fire mission, over." The men quieted down to listen as Gilmore continued. "Roger that, Willie-peter, coordinates seven-niner-two, six-seven three, I say again, seven-niner-two, six-seven-three, copy?" There was a momentary pause. "Roger, good copy, break-break, Heart Breaker, Heart Breaker this is Bravo November relay, be advised 'on-the-way', I say again 'on-the-way', copy?"

The men watched as Gilmore grabbed a pair of binoculars and scanned the valley, keeping the handset to his ear. They moved over to where the radioman was standing and joined him scoping out the valley. A white puff of smoke appeared rising above the trees far off in the distance. By the time the muffled report

reached their position Gilmore was repeating further instructions from the team in the bush to the artillery fire base. "Add, right, two-five, add right two-five, one salvo, H.E. Fire for effect, Copy?" Gilmore nodded confirmation. "Break, break, Heart Breaker, Heart Breaker, on-the-way….on-the-way, keep your heads down."
Within seconds a volley of barely visible, dark puffs of smoke indicated the rounds found their mark. Another couple of seconds elapsed before the report reached them.
Maynard finally questioned Gilmore. "What's all that shit about?"
"Heart Breaker spotted the gooks movin' supplies," Gilmore answered calmly.
"I'll bet the only thing they're movin' now is their bowels," Unkle blurted out a laugh before Gilmore called back to the fire base to cease fire. He informed the men that two Skyraiders were in the area and were going to give Heart Breaker air to ground support on their target. Since the patrol was communicating directly with the aircraft, Gilmore didn't need to relay for them but, continued to listen in. Two, Navy, Skyraiders appeared over the BaNa mountains and swooped down into the valley below the relay station enroute to their target. The vintage, prop-driven, aircraft seemed out of place in the jet age. Doc and the others watched as the aircraft seemed to disappear in the distant, green foliage as if the jungle devoured them. As the planes released their payloads they came back into view, appearing as small toys climbing upward away from the blasts effect. What looked like a total of eight bombs left the far end of the valley shrouded in thick, dark, plumbs. When the sound waves finally got to them, Doc tried to count the explosions but, they were so rapid he couldn't distinguish individual detonations.
"WUUU-WEEEE, GET SOME," Unkle exuberated.
"OHHH YEAH," Pee Wee accompanied equally excited.
Billie Gilmore continued to monitor the communication between team Heart Breaker and the pilots before signing off. "Roger, Heart Breaker, I copy….Bravo November out." He then turned back to the men, "Looks like they got some good kills outta that," he reported to waiting ears. "They say about 15 dead but, they ain't going to bother with an actual count. Right now they're going to di-di their dirty ass's outta there."

Satisfied that the excitement was over with, the men moved away from the edge of the balcony, back to where they were sitting before the all the ruckus started.
"Who's all in team Heart Breaker?" Unkle asked Maynard.
The Corporal spit out a few names, none of whom Doc knew or heard of.
"Jenkins is the only one I know," Unkle said. "He should be a 'short timer' by now," he added, then laughed over a recollection. "He once told me about the time he was shacking up with this BAM at Lejeune........" Doc interrupted Unkle's story. "What's a BAM?" Everyone turned and stared at the corpsman.
"Doc, Doc, Doc," Maynard uttered, shaking his head. "A BAM is a female Marine. You know, Broad... Assed... Marine...B...A...M... get it?"
Doc naively answered. "OK, I get. I just never heard that before, that's all."
Unkle dropped telling the story.

The remainder of the day was pretty much a carbon copy of the day before. The men read, played cards and just sat around and talked. It was nearly time for the men to take their guard positions when Corporal Maynard announced that they would be relieved by a team from Alpha Company the following morning. The news was well received as the men were becoming bored and restless with the duty they were pulling. The days were long and hot, the nights were longer and cold.

Doc and Pee Wee made their way down to their guard post just before sundown. Neither one of them was tired enough to catch some sleep. They kept themselves busy through idle conversation for several hours before Doc finally succumbed to his partner's insistence to get some sack time. It was after 3 A.M. when Pee Wee woke the corpsman.
The bright moonlight made it easy for Doc to see the time on his watch without squinting at the luminous dots. "Three o'clock!" he exclaimed in a soft voice. "Why didn't you wake me sooner?"
"I wasn't sleepy so I thought I'd let you get some zee's," he whispered back. "You can take over 'til morning."
"OK," Doc simply answered as he ducked down to light up. "Anything going on?"

“Nah. The moon’s too bright…nobody’s goin’ to sneak up on us without being seen,” the Marine surmised but cautioned, “Keep your eyes peeled anyway.”
“You can count on it.”

As the hours stretched, Lew gained confidence the VC weren’t going to strike. His mind drifted away from vigilance into less important thoughts. At first he thought about going over to 1st Med. to check on Sergeant Sitas’ condition when they returned to Reasoner. That thought transitioned into thinking about his friend, Rappaport. He reminded himself to look him up while he was at the medical battalion. He also remembered that he hasn’t written home lately. That thought transitioned into a guilt trip. One obscure thought after another carried him though the watch. He wondered about his brothers and sisters and how they were doing. His older brother was in the Navy aboard the LST, USS Caroline County, that sometimes entered Da Nang harbor. He imagined that it would be nice if they could hook up, providing he could find out when the ship is in port. His thoughts drifted to his younger brother, John, who was living with his sister’s family in Florida. He hoped that John would go on to college after high school, which was still three years away. The daydreaming was interrupted when he heard someone coming up from behind.
It was a shadowy figure of Corporal Maynard. “Everything OK here Doc?” he questioned in normal voice.
Lew hardly noticed that the sun was already peeking over the distant mountain. “Oh it’s you,” he responded casually as if he was focused on his duty. “Yeah, nothing goin’ on here.”
Maynard squatted down, flicking the ash from a cigarette before drawing in a drag. “We’ll give it a few more minutes before you guys call it a night,” his words came out in a stream of smoke. “Pee Wee still sleepin’?”
“Like a baby.”
“You mean shittin’ himself and crying all night?” the Corporal quipped.
Doc chuckled at the humor. Maynard rose and snuffed out the cigarette under his boot as he turned to walk away. “We’ll all muster on the balcony in about half an hour,” he advised.
“Half-hour, aye.”

When the group assembled Corporal Maynard issued the latest skinny. “The choppers are supposed to be comin’ in around ten so, get all your shit together now so we don’t have mess with it at the last minute.” He turned to Gilmore. “We’ll be leavin’ the antenna here, so we don’t have to break it down and hump it back with us.”
Gilmore gratefully responded in radioman jargon. “That’s a good copy.”
“When you got all that taken care of…….” Maynard paused a moment then kept his promise… “Grab your pieces and ammo and muster behind the building. We’re gonna have some fun.”

The men formed a line behind the hotel at the crest of the slope that overlooked the valley below. “Let’s see if we can cut down that tree,” Unkle suggested, pointing to the barren remains of a once hardy, green, tropical giant. All the men raised their weapons, targeting the stump in agreement. Maynard nodded and shouted out loud enough for the grunts to hear, “FIRE-IN-THE-HOLE!” Instantly, the men let go a salvo of fully automatic fire from the M-16’s. The loud, KRACKing reports echoed throughout the valley as the stench of sulphur-like smoke quickly surrounded the group. One magazine after another was expended in a continuous barrage in the effort to fell the tree. At first, each man targeted a different spot on the objective but, soon came together and zeroed-in on one specific location. Splinters flew wildly when the rounds impacted the fibrous skeleton. For most of the men, it was the first time they could actually witness the power of the new weapon on a target, especially when the solidarity of fire was spontaneously accomplished without verbal direction. On previous occasions, their fire was simply sprayed randomly in the jungle without engaging any particular target. It was a powerfully awesome experience for the corpsman who never received formal, in-depth, infantry training. He liked the feeling of the power that he was holding in his hands. As the tree began to sway and list, Doc encountered a brief sense of disappointment, realizing that the exuberance was about to come to an end. All the supporting structure had been chewed away by the volleys and the tree slowly fell, stretching the last strands of its tissue until it collapsed without the expected ‘snapping’ sound.
“CEASE FIRE,” Maynard commanded. “CLEAR YOU WEAPONS.”

Satisfying smiles appeared on the men's faces over the enjoyment of the 'mad minute'.

The team was ready and waiting at the LZ when one CH-46 appeared in the distance. Doc took out a Kodak Instamatic camera to take a group photo before the bird landed. Wanting to be included in the photo he asked one of the mortar-men to do the honors. Gilmore maintained communication with the chopper as it touched down on the pad just moments after the grunt obliged Doc's request. The team quickly scrambled past the replacements with hardly enough time for a courteous salutation. The men were anxious to get aboard and get back to the comfort of their hootch and to take much needed showers. The brief trip back to Camp Reasoner had the team on the ground in time to scarf-down a quick, hot lunch before tending to their own hygiene and cleaning their gear and weapons.

Lance Corporal Whelchel was hammering out marching rhythm on a book with his drumsticks when Doc, Pee Wee and Johnson entered.

Without as much as a polite greeting the corpsman inquired about Sergeant Sitas. "Hey Weasel, you know the *skinny* on Sergeant Sitas?"

"A little Doc. I think they sent him back to the states. You'll probably have to ask Woody or your honcho, LaPorte. They probably have the real *skuttle-butt*."

"Woody? Woody who?" Doc asked.

"Staff Sergeant Woodcock. He came over from the Second Platoon to take over the First. He's our Platoon leader now," Weasel informed the men of the news.

Doc hadn't met the Staff Sergeant before but, he gathered that the others knew him well.

"Oh yeah," Pee Wee began. "When'd that happen?"

"Two days ago. I guess they got a *First Lewy* FNG for their platoon leader so, Woody came over here."

"I think we got the better deal," Pee Wee cracked.

"Yeah," Weasel agreed. "Me too."

Lew casually absorbed the information before changing the subject. "So, Weasel, how'd the thing with the band go?"

"Good actually, "he replied enthusiastically. "It looks like I'll be going up there pretty soon. They said that they have to work things out with replacement problems first but, that shouldn't take longer than a few weeks then, I'll be able to transfer up there."

"Hey man, that sounds good," Doc offered up. "I'm glad for you."

"Yeah Weez," Palmer added. "Looks like you're 'In-like-Flint', huh?"

"Looks that way," Weasel smiled.

Unkle came with news that broke the conversation. "Hey you guys, ya hear the latest skinny?" he asked then followed up the question with the answer. "We're going to do a night-time, combat-jump into Happy Valley!"

"Where'd you hear that?" Pee Wee doubted.

"No bull-shit G.I. Straight skinny," Unkle stressed. "I was just talkin' with the riggers. They're packin' the chutes now, gettin' ready."

"No shit!" Pee Wee attempted confirmation.

"No shit, man." Unkle emphasized. "The Army pukes did a combat jump down south so, we're goin' to do a night-time jump to show 'em up…I guess?"

"When?"

"Real soon is all I know," he answered then added, "They're supposed to pick people from different teams for the 'jump team'. Man, I hope they pick me!"

Pee Wee suddenly became skeptical. "I'll believe it when I see it."

The men spent the remainder of the afternoon cleaning up and getting squared away while continuing to talk about the upcoming jump. It was almost time for chow when the Staff Sergeant came into the hootch.

"Hey Woody," Pee Wee greeted him. "I hear you're our platoon leader now."

"Hey Pee Wee, how you doin'?" he recognized the man. "Yeah, I'm the head- honcho now so, I don't want any shit from you guys for the duration," he joked. "Especially you Unkle," he added playfully. Unkle returned a nod and a smile but said nothing.

It was apparent to Lew that the Staff Sergeant was a familiar figure who earned respect from the men as a senior NCO.

"Looks like we got some new faces here," the sergeant said looking around the hootch.

"Yeah," Pee Wee did the introductions. "We got some F-N-G's here. This is PFC Arthurs and this is PFC Johnson," he announced the Marines first. "And this is our new corpsman, Doc Lewis."

"Men," the sergeant acknowledged the new team members but, didn't bother shaking their hands.

As he nearly always did when he made a new acquaintance, Doc sized-up the NCO and compared him with a movie character. The sergeant was about six feet tall, muscular with coal black hair cut high and tight. His eyes were dark and deeply set into the skull. Even though he was clean-shaven, the coarse dark facial hair looked as if he sported a permanent 'five-o'clock-shadow'. The only character Lew could compare him with was Brutus, in the Popeye cartoon.

"I guess you all heard by now, we're goin' on a night-jump mission. What you don't know is its day after ta-maw-ra," Woody spoke in fractured English. Lew guessed that the man lacked an eighth grade education.

"The 'poop' is that we git ta bracket the LZ for 'em. Us an' three other teams are gonna be inserted in a grid an' light up the LZ with strobe lights. Nobody here is gonna be on the jump team so, don't go askin'. Woody scanned the troop's faces. "Where's Maynard?"

Unkle laughed. "He's prob'ly hiding somewhere Woody. He's short you know."

"Yeah, I know. That's what I wanna tell him. He don't hav-ta go on this one. His replacement is 'sposed ta be here ta-maw-ra."

The door opened and Gilmore walked in. "Am I interrupting something?" he spoke politely when he saw the sergeant standing there.

"That depends," Woody answered. "Who are ya?"

"Lance Corporal Gilmore, Staff Sergeant. I'm the radioman."

"Good. I got some news for ya too, Gilmore," Woody paused. "Your orders got in. As of now you're in Recon."

Surprised by the news, everyone expressed their acceptance by applauding and cheering. Apparently, the radioman had requested a transfer to Recon but hadn't told anyone about it. Sergeant Woodcock let the welcome diminish on its own before continuing.

"Ok, that's it for now men. I'll git with ya all again ta-maw-ra mornin'," he said turning toward the door, then turned back again. "Remember, keep it to yourself. We don't want this shit to git out," he warned before leaving.

From the way the team was talking after chow Doc, gathered that combat jumps were rare and that a night-time jump was unheard of. He sat on the cot composing the letter that he promised himself to write to his mother but, kept being distracted by conversation of the impending jump. Unkle and Arthurs seemed to be the most 'gung-ho' Marines in the team and didn't try to hide the fact that they were disappointed by not being selected as part of the jump team. Pee Wee and Johnson both commented that they would jump if ordered to but neither of them said that they would volunteer to do it. Gilmore and Doc Lewis didn't have a choice since neither of them were parachute qualified. Lew eventually pieced his letter together before Maynard appeared in the doorway holding a treasured case of Budweiser. "Hey you guys, I know you won't be around when I head back to the world so I want to honor you all first." No one objected to having a cold beer but the idea of Maynard buying the brew for his own farewell bash seemed out of place.

"I though we're supposed to buy you the beer," Gilmore grinned.

"Not this time," Maynard answered back. "You can buy me one if we run into each other someday back in the world."

Lew liked the Corporal's answer. Within seconds the familiar sounds of church-keys popping cans filled the hootch. "Here's to you guys," Maynard proposed a toast.

"Back at ya," Unkle countered.

Doc didn't know the Corporal very well but, admired the man's leadership and manner he conducted himself when responsibility was suddenly thrust upon him after Sitas was med-evaced.

It didn't take long before the entire case was consumed and Pee Wee suggested to move the impromptu affair to the Club.

Doc Lewis woke with a pounding headache the next morning. Through blurry eyes he correctly assumed that the others felt the same as each man struggled to wake up. The door slammed when Unkle entered and blurted out, "Too bad you guys missed a good breakfast…Spam n eggs," he grinned, apparently feeling no ill effects from the previous evening. Lew sat up to light a cigarette before heading to the showers. He noticed that Maynard remained asleep while the others stirred about. He also noticed that Maynard owned a folding, lawn chair that would be of no further use to him when he left the unit. Hoping that no one else thought about it he decided that he would try to make a deal with the Corporal for the luxury item.

Maynard was awake, sitting on the edge of his cot, holding his head in both hands when Doc came back from the shower. Unsure whether it would be good timing to bring up the chair he decided to probe a little. "Say Maynard," he stared out subtlety. "Anybody ever tell ya that you're beautiful in the morning?"

"Eat shit Doc," the corporal grunted.

"Never mind," the corpsman half-whispered. "I'll ask you later,"

"Ask me what Doc?" the corporal urged without bothering to raise his head.

Lew hesitated, realizing that he really didn't have anything to bargain with that the Marine could possibly want. He decided on the direct approach. "I was just wondering if you had plans for your chair there."

Maynard raised his head; turning it to look up at the young corpsman. "It's yours Doc. Take it."

The quick, unconditional offer stymied Lew. "Hey, I just can't take. I'll give you a few bucks for it."

"Nah Doc, I don't want anything for it….well, maybe if you have some aspirin?"

"Sure thing. I'll be right back."

Lew made room in his corner for the chair, being careful not to infringe on Weasel's space next to him. He sat down in his newly acquired possession and propped both feet up on the cot. He found it comfortable to just kick back, relax and take in everything going on in the hootch. *'Now, if I could only get a fan,"* he thought, *'I'd be in hog-heaven."* He sat there for a few minutes, quietly enjoying the comfort, thinking about how everybody has to scrounge around for all the little items that make life in Vietnam somewhat bearable. The trance was broken. "Hey Doc, we're goin' to 327. You wanna go?"

He quickly answered Pee Wee's question. "No, not today. I have things to do at the aid station." Before Pee Wee had a chance to get away, Lew stopped him. "Hey man, could you pick me up a couple of cartons of cigarettes while you're there?"

"Sure Doc, Viceroys right?"

"Man, you're sharp," Doc stated, handing the Marine a five dollar MPC. "Thanks."

He was all alone in the hootch after the group departed. A peaceful feeling came over him as he sat there relishing the quiet. He glanced up at a wallet-sized picture of his high school girlfriend, Bonnie, that he pinned to the shelf overhead. She was pretty. He remembered the soft, warm skin of her face and could almost smell the fragrance of the perfume she always wore. It bothered him to think that she was probably dating someone else while he was gone. Even though they broke up, he imagined that when he returned home they would somehow get back together. He couldn't accept the fact that she hadn't replied to any of his letters. Instead, he kept telling himself that they probably got lost in the mail. The notion that he had been rejected prompted him to erase the thought of her. Getting to his feet, he lit a cigarette, grabbed his cover and left the hootch.

He made the few steps to the senior NCO hootch next door and knocked as a military courtesy.

"ENTER," a voice commanded.

Once inside he was modestly acknowledged by Staff Sergeant Livingston. "Doc."

"Sergeant Livingston," he returned the courtesy then made his way to the opposite end where LaPorte resided.

"Lewis, you here to see me?"

"Yes," he answered simply.

"Well, what is it?"

"Ah, I just wanted to know if you might have heard anything about Sergeant Sitas' condition?" he answered softly.

LaPorte dropped the gear he was organizing. "Well, I know that he came down with that FUO shit and that he won't be coming back here." After a brief pause he continued with a few unexpected words. "You done good Lewis. The med evac was the right call." Lew nodded appreciation before the senior added, "If there's nothing else? I have to get ready for the jump tomorrow."

Lew was surprised. "You part of the jump team?"

"That's affirmative. I guess you're going out with LZ teams?"

"Yeah, we're….."

The senior corpsman stopped him. "Well, be careful."

Lew sensed that LaPorte was extremely nervous about the upcoming jump and didn't want to be bothered with small talk. "Yeah, you too. Good luck."

Just as Lew was leaving, Sergeant Woodcock entered, accompanied by a young, healthy looking, Marine buck sergeant.
"Doc, you here to see me?"
"No, actually I needed to speak to LaPorte, Sarge."
Woodcock didn't respond to Lew's answer. Instead, he began an introduction. "I guess while I got ya here you might as well meet Sergeant Holton. He just joined our platoon today."
The young sergeant offered his hand. "Nice to meet you Doc."
"Same here," the corpsman accepted the man's grip.
"Where the hell's everybody at? I was jist at your hootch, ain't nobody there," Woodcock commented sharply.
Lew was afraid to answer truthfully but, decided that he should. "I think they all went to the PX, Sarge."
"Oh yeah. When they git back tell 'em to hang around after chow 'cause I wanna go over ta-maw-ra's game-plan. Got it?"
"I'll let them know Sarge," Doc assured as he anxiously departed.

With time on his hands Lew thought it might be a good idea to go up to the aid station and check on the new men's medical records. As he casually strolled across the grinder he passed some SeaBees building a new handball court. He noticed Captain Dixon and the First Sergeant standing near the foundation, checking on the progress. Out of the blue the First Sergeant belted out, "YOU! You better get your maggot ass over here NOW!"
Stunned, Lew looked around to see if Henderson was actually summoning him. No one else was in the vicinity. He hustled over.
"Yes sir. You called me?" Lew responded with a lump in his throat.
"First," the sergeant squinted his hard, piercing eyes "Don't you see the bars on my captain's collar?"
Instantly, Doc realized he hadn't saluted the officer. "I'm sorry sir," he apologized then rendered a sharp salute. Captain Dixon served up a polite return.
"Now, what the hell are you doing out here without your blouse on?" the sergeant barked again. "Don't you know better than to leave your hootch without putting on your blouse?"
It slipped Lew's mind about putting on his shirt since he didn't intend on leaving the immediate area of his hootch. The only explanation he had was that he forgot.

"You might get away with forgetting the rules in the Navy Lewis but, not in my Corps. I have half a notion to send you before the mast," he threatened.
"Aye, First Sergeant," the corpsman managed a dry-voiced refrain. He looked toward the commander for some kind of benevolent intervention. None came.
The First Sergeant pointed a finger "You go get your blouse on now and don't me let me ever catch you without it again. Do you understand?" he grunted.
"Aye, aye First Sergeant." Doc saluted the captain to return to his hootch.
"ON THE DOUBLE!" the sergeant barked after the first couple of steps.

Relieved that no one witnessed the ass-chewing, Lew lit up a smoke and sat down in his chair, waiting for the trembling to go away. He couldn't believe how stupid he was for forgetting to put on his shirt. He knew that he deserved the admonishment he had gotten yet, for some reason it just didn't seem that important. He imagined that the First Sergeant and Captain Dixon even chuckled over the incident once he was out hearing range. He reasoned that if the sergeant was actually going to write him up he would have done it then and there. Never-the-less, Lew vowed not to let it happen again.

Some of the men began straggling back from the PX one or two at a time. Pee Wee and Johnson were the first. Pee Wee tossed Doc the smokes he requested. "Here ya go Doc."
"Thanks man. I appreciate it."
"Anything new going on around here?" Private Johnson inquired.
"Nothing really. Sergeant Woodcock said for everybody to hang around after chow and a new sergeant, E-5 type, came on board. That's about it."
"You know if the *buck* is Sita's replacement or Maynards?" Pee Wee questioned.
"Beats me?"
"What his name?"
"It's either Horton or Holton…something like that?"
Pee Wee shook his head. "Don't recall that name anywhere."

Lew watched PFC Johnson unwrapping a package that he brought back. “Anybody play chess?” the rookie questioned, raising a game set in the air.
“Not me,” Pee Wee insisted.
“Me either,” Doc confessed, then added, “But I’d really like to learn.”
“OK Doc. I’ll teach you someday,” Johnson promised.
“I never pictured a ‘*splib’* playing chess,” Palmer casually stated.
The corpsman was puzzled. “What ah, what’s a ‘splib’?” he asked seriously.
“Doc, are you trying to say that you never heard of a ‘splib’ before?” Johnson doubted.
“No lie, I don’t know what the hell it means.”
“Well Doc, let me define it for you,” he paused intermittently to puff on his pipe. “A ‘splib’ is a slang word for a black man…..It don’t mean negro…it means black man….a ‘brother’…..not nigger….just a black man.”
“I never heard that before. Is it something new?” Doc spoke sincerely.
“I don’t know how long it’s been around Doc. I do know it’s not as offensive as nigger. You have heard the word nigger before haven’t you?”
“Yeah, sure. Who hasn’t?”
“That’s good Doc. I can tell you’re a man of the world.” He took another puff. “Just so you know, I am not a nigger.” He let the message settle in. “I know some niggers but, I’m not one of them.”
Lew couldn’t know how Pee Wee felt about Johnson’s racial candor but, he was uncomfortable with the direction the conversation was taking and was eager to change the subject. “OK. When we get back from the bush, you can teach me to play.”
Johnson gripped the pipe between his teeth and smiled. “Sure thing Doc.”

The entire team was waiting when Sergeant Woodcock arrived with the new NCO. After making blanket introduction, Woody proceeded to go over the details of the team’s mission in supporting the jump. “Ya’ll know about the combat jump ta-mah-ra. I ain’t happy about us not jumpin’ but, we got our orders so, we'll just do what we're told." Lew detected discontent in the sergeant's voice and assumed all the others did as well.

"First off," Woody continued point by point "We gotta git ready for a three day mission. We'll be inserted just before dark ta-mah-ra night, along with three other teams to mark the DZ with strobe lights. Once we git on the ground we're gonna hump to our corner of the bracket and wait for word to light 'er up. The drop's gonna take place at midnight. Unless some shit happens, we'll harbor there 'til mornin'. If somethin' does happen the gound teams will be the reactionary force." Woody scanned the men's faces, making sure they all understood what he was saying before going any further. "If all goes well, we'll proceed with the patrol 'til we git to our extraction point about a 'click' north." He paused once more before stressing, "It's real important to remember that there's four other patrols in the area, so don't git trigger-happy. We don't want no goddamned, friendly-fire, shit goin' on by killin' our own people!" Despite his lack of eloquence, the sergeant made his meaning clear. Everyone heard stories of G.I.'s mistakenly killing each other in combat.

Woody went on. "We'll draw our 'rats' an' munitions ta-mah-ra mornin' an' muster at the pad ready to go at 1500. Any questions?" No one spoke up.

"OK, then," he added. "Unkle, you git with Sergeant Holton in the mornin' an' show him what he needs to know about gittin' the rations and munitions."

Unkle accepted the order with a nod.

Woodcock issued one more statement before departing. "Nobody better git fucked-up ta-night so stay away from the brewskies."

Pee Wee snickered. "Does that include you, Woody?"

"Maybe." Woodcock simply smiled and walked away.

The following day was filled with extraordinary activity in the compound. Choppers arrived and departed every hour or so, bringing teams in from the bush and taking teams out again.

It was late afternoon when a single, CH-46 arrived to pick up team *Countersign.*

Not long after lifting off than the chopper began its descent into Viet Cong infested, Happy Valley. Weapons lock-and-loaded, the men scrambled from the rear of the helicopter, forming the typical defensive perimeter after it touched down on the top of grass covered knoll. The men shielded their faces from the flying debris as the chopper ascended without receiving enemy ground-fire. Woodcock pointed to each man in succession for the order of march. It came as no surprise to Doc when he was positioned somewhere in the middle of the file. Pee Wee was in front of him while the new man, Sergeant Holton, took up the position directly behind him. Lew turned to Holton. "Don't get so close," he whispered. "We need to watch our intervals." Holton gave the 'thumbs-up' signal and delayed his movement until Doc was about 15 feet in front of him. Realizing that he had just bestowed a bit of important information to an inexperienced, brother-in-arms, Lew took pride in the fact that he was no longer a total rookie and that he had, at that moment in time, become an integral member of Marine recon.

The patrol progressed slowly and quietly through the grass, downward off the knoll until they reached an open, knee-high, grass clearing. Sergeant Woodcock sent one man at a time across the clearing to the tree line that offered concealment. Lew was about half-way across when he spotted a large, brown, animal grazing on the slope about 50 meters to his left. It looked like a majestic elk, with a full rack of antlers. The sight of it made him pause momentarily, thinking that his movement might spook the creature into bugling frantically, which could alert any VC that might be in the area. He didn't know what to do. Looking toward the tree line he saw the team leader signaling for him to keep moving. The animal raised his head and sniffed the air. Catching human scent it bolted and crashed through the brush until it disappeared into the jungle. Relieved that it didn't bugle, Doc moved quickly, relying on the animal's thrashing to cover his own movement.

Darkness came before the patrol reached its destination. Visibility was nil, forcing the men to close their intervals to within arm's reach of each other in order to hold on to the pack of the man in front, enabling them to remain together. Maneuvering was agonizingly slow as the point-man, Unkle, broke a path through the brush and vines. Unable to see what was in front of him, he had to reach out and carefully feel his way through the vegetation with one hand, holding the M-60 with the other, while precariously probing the ground with his foot, one step at a time.

The danger of tripping over or stepping on fallen branches served to increase the tension.

The experience of being totally blind in this hostile environment harvested a surge of fearful apprehension in the corpsman. He assumed the others felt the same. A child-like wish that he had a cat's vision seized his concentration for a moment before a tree branch slapped against his face; bringing him back to reality. All the dangers surrounding them suddenly became acutely embedded in his active mind. He thought that even though the V.C. finding them is a serious threat, the most immediate enemy was the darkness. Any of them could easily have their eye impaled on a low-hanging branch. Anyone could trip and fracture an arm, leg or skull. Slipping on a rock could trigger an accidental discharge from a rifle, injuring or killing someone. Any of these events would require him to respond as a blind man. The last thing he wanted to do was try to aid someone in total darkness.

It was close to jump time when the team found their harbor site. The men searched for a place to settle in, using their hands to locate a reasonably comfortable place to sit and rest on the jungle floor. Woody asked if anyone had experience using tree climbing 'spikes'.

Gilmore let on that he had used them before and volunteered to climb a nearby tree to light up the signal strobe. Woodcock accepted the radioman's offer. The plan was made for Gilmore to perch himself as high up as he could get and to still be able to see the red, flashlight signal from below. When he saw the red light he would initiate the strobe.

Everyone knew that the flashing strobe light would give their exact position away but, counted on the depth of the jungle canopy to obscure visual perception from any enemy force in the area. Gilmore stripped off the radio and web-gear and fastened the 'spikes' securely around his legs. He took the strobe from the sergeant's hand and began to ascend the tree, awkwardly puncturing the bark with the sharp spikes. Upon reaching the highest point he could, he dropped a pebble down to let them know he was in place. Woody then signaled Gilmore with the red lens. Another pebble was dropped indicating that the signal could be seen. The only thing left to do was to sit and wait.

Word came over the radio that the aircraft were approaching the drop zone. Woodcock signaled Gilmore to activate the strobe. Within seconds brilliant, intermittent flashes of light penetrated the darkness from above, illuminating figures of the men on the ground. Doc recognized individuals as quick bursts of the light shone on their camouflage painted faces for tenths of seconds at a time. It was surreal how with each flash, the whites of someone's eyes and exposed, pink lips where the only visible indications that a human was present. Even more eerie was that the person Lew was looking at, moved his head or eyes between flashes and was repositioned when he saw them again. The scene reminded him of an under 21 club that he visited once in Hollywood, where dancers were in a different position every time the strobe-light flashed. Their eyes betrayed the fact that everyone was keenly aware the flashes told the enemy exactly where they were; heightening their vigilance.

Doc listened for the helicopters making their approach to the DZ, hoping that the jumpers would hurry and get on the ground. Woody signaled Gilmore to turn off the strobe. Doc was surprised that the jump had already taken place since he didn't hear the choppers but, was relieved that it had.

Gilmore worked his way down from the tree without incident. Doc was within ear shot when Woody whispered to Gilmore, "You awright?"

"Yeah, but I'm glad that's over with!"

"Okay. Spread the word, nobody sack out yet. Tell 'em to keep alert 'til I say it's OK to get some shut-eye."

Everyone expected the VC to close in and probe their position with rocks. It was a trick they frequently used to get the Americans to think the rocks were grenades and give away their positions. For the next two hours every member of the team remained extra alert but nothing had happened. Sergeant Woodcock passed the word for the men to get some sleep but, stipulated that two men were to be on guard at any one time. Except for Unkle and Weasel, who pulled the first watch, the men laid down for an uneasy rest.

Pee Wee woke Doc and Sergeant Holton after the 4AM sit-rep. "Doc, it's your watch," he whispered while passing along the PRC-25 to the corpsman. "I think one of the jumpers got lost," he quietly informed. "Keep your ears open for anybody trying to rendezvous with us. The password is 'beer can' and the countersign is 'church key'. They say 'beer can'; you say 'church key'. Got it?"

"Got it." Lew confirmed. "Who's lost?"

"Don't know."

For the next hour Lew and Holton sat up, their backs propped against each other, waiting and listening for any signs of the enemy, or more importantly, the missing man trying to find them. Doc's mind usually wandered while he stood watch, this time was no exception. He recalled the universal signal for help was three rounds fired into the air and wondered if he was lost in enemy territory would he dare to fire the three shots. Dwelling on the circumstance he concluded that he wouldn't take the chance and the lost man probably wouldn't either. Instead, he reasoned that if he were to become lost, he would sneak through the jungle, heading east toward the ocean. Logic told him that most American units were somewhere along the coast and that he would most certainly come across one of them eventually. The key would be staying alive but, *'What if...I was badly injured?'* he questioned. *'What if I had a broken leg or fractured skull? Then what?'* That thought transitioned into a more ominous prospect. *'What if whoever is lost was captured when he hit the ground?'* Sergeant Holton, who was listening over the handset, broke the Lew's train of thought. "Doc, One of the jumpers got hurt. HQ said they'll med-evac him in the morning."

"Any idea who?"

"They don't give names over the net Doc." Holton advised.

It made sense. "I wonder if he's the one that got lost?"

"I don't know but, I don't think so."

The two discontinued their conversation, paying attention to the nocturnal sounds of the jungle. Lew had become familiar with whooping, howling, crying and chirping noises as well as the occasional crashing of dead branches falling but, those sounds were all new to Holton. Doc knew that when the noises stopped it was an indication that danger was probably nearby. He could feel Holton's nervous twitch transferring on his back each time a sudden, unexpected noise penetrated the canopy. Certain that the sergeant would soon learn to distinguish normal jungle noises from abnormal sounds; the corpsman maintained his own, seemingly relaxed composure in order to develop the NCO's confidence in him, despite being equally stressed. As the two men sat in silence Doc expected to hear echoing gunfire in the distance. He thought that with so many teams in the area surely one of them would make contact with the enemy, secretly hoping that they weren't the one. A faint squelch came over the radio handset. Sergeant Holton keyed the handset twice, indicating they were safe in their harbor and that it was time for the next two men to assume the watch. Holton passed the radio over to Johnson and Arthurs while advising them of the missing man situation. Knowing it was already five in the morning, Lew wondered if he could even catch up on his sleep.

Awakened by Pee Wee nudging him, Doc raised his head to see it was daylight. Several of the men were already eating their C rations. He shifted his body into a sitting position and scanned the surroundings. Holton was sitting next to Woody, having a whispered discussion over the map that Woodcock held in his hand. Pee Wee spooned fruit cocktail into his mouth. Guessing that he didn't have too much time to eat, Doc pulled out a can of ham and eggs and began to down it in over-sized spoons full. He noticed that PFC Johnson retrieved a packet of toilet paper and left the area to do his business privately. After everyone had eaten and disposed of the trash Woody had them gather around in a tight, semi-circle.

"Ya'll git the word that one of us is lost didn't ya?" he looked around making sure everyone was aware of the situation before whispering further. "All we got to go on is ta be lookin' out for a blonde American. All the teams are gonna sweep the area ta try ta find him an' will prob'ly be out here longer than we planned on so, ya'll have ta go easy on your food an water…. an' godammit, don't go shootin' at anything 'til ya know it's not him or the other teams. Got it?" Everyone nodded. "Okay, lets git movin', we got lots of ground ta cover."

On all the previous patrols Doc Lewis had been on rest breaks came about every hour but not this one. This patrol was of an urgent nature. More than four hours passed before Woodcock called for a break. The men were physically tired from non-stop wrestling their way through the thick, underbrush and jungle vines in the relentless heat and humidity. Doc could feel the muscles in his butt and legs starting to cramp up. Claiming a small piece of real estate he sprawled out flat on the ground and stretched his legs as best he could before passing out salt tablets to the men. Raising two fingers and miming drinking, he made sure all of the men understood what he wanted them to do. The warm, chlorinated water never tasted so good as it washed down the back of his parched throat.

He was tempted to drink every drop that was in the canteen but knew that he would have to conserve whatever water was remaining. He closed the lid and returned the canteen to its cover while glancing over to see Holton scrutinizing a map. Curious, Doc leaned sideways to get a better view of the map. Sergeant Holton obliged him by pointing out their location, whispering, "This is where we are now Doc." He moved his finger. "This is where we started out this morning."

Even though the Corpsman wasn't well versed in map reading, he knew that they covered some rugged territory without looking at the map. "This is where we're going to try to make it to by tonight." Holton pointed once again. Doc nodded and gave the thumbs-up sign.

Reaching into his pocket Lew pulled out the plastic box holding his cigarettes but, before he had a chance to light one, Woody signaled to move out.

Shortly after resuming their march the patrol halted abruptly. From as far back in the file as he was, Doc couldn't see what was going on but, he followed Pee Wee's lead by raising a clinched first in the air to alert the men behind him to stop. The sudden, unexpected, halt sent a jab of fear to his stomach. He stood motionless in his tracks, anticipating some deadly conflict. None came. However, word did come back that there was a trail ahead and Woody decided to take it. The order didn't sit well with the men. Even Doc knew better than to follow trails. Reluctantly, the men pressed forward. This was the first time Lew had seen a Viet Cong trail and despite his inexperience, he could tell that it was used frequently since it was bare dirt with no fresh weeds growing on it; indicating that *Charlie* may have used it very recently. Lew recalled the displays of typical Viet Cong bobby-traps set up back at Camp Pendleton, prompting him to pay close attention for signs of *'pungi-stakes'* and trip wires. He was certain the men up front were just as aware of the dangers that he was but, in the back of

his mind were thoughts that they might miss something. He remembered one of the instructors at Pendleton telling them that if a trip wire was too obvious, look up for overhead devices.
The longer the patrol followed the trail, the more intense Doc's fear became. He had no doubt that there would be an explosion any second, probably from the point man, Unkle, stepping on a mine. The dreadful thought stayed with him until the patrol left the trail. The gratification of getting off the trail reached all the men but, it was short-lived as Sergeant Woodcock directed the patrol to set up an ambush. No one understood the logic of the order until Woody made his thinking clear. He stretched the men five meters apart from each other along a depression that paralleled the trail about 25 feet above it, explaining to each man in turn, "We're goin' ta stay here for a little bit. If the V.C. captured our man, they might bring him along here. If there ain't too many of 'em we'll git him back. You gotta stay quiet an' don't shoot 'til I do. If there's a bunch of 'em jist stay down an' keep still."

Lew observed the others closely as they removed their packs and took prone, firing positions; muzzles pointing down toward the trail. He watched as Pee Wee laid an extra, full, magazine beside his rifle. Doc followed suit and hid behind a lush, green fern that was large enough to conceal several men. Instinctively, he knew enough to keep still and silent. Time dragged on. Every so often he had to reposition his body slightly to remedy cramping, being extremely careful not to make the slightest noise. Once he found a degree of comfort he maintained that position for what seemed like hours. Boredom crept upon him. At one point he amused himself by watching a column of red ants passing in the dirt a few inches from his face, busily carrying on with whatever their instincts programmed them to so. Lew felt the urge to toy with them, just to see their reaction but, knew he couldn't risk a physical movement. Instead, he blew a silent, gentle breath unto their formation. There was just enough force in his breath to push several of the creatures off their path. Lew marveled at how they ignored the man-made breeze and fell right back into formation. He continued to entertain himself by repeating the process every few minutes, occasionally pausing to look over toward the men on either side of him, hoping they wouldn't see him behaving in such an adolescent manner. The intense focus on the ants failed to alert him to the fact that the circulation in one of his legs was being pinched off. He came out of the spell when Pee Wee tossed a pebble at him. He caught sight of the Marine signaling for them to move out. In-turn, he signaled Holton. Attempting to get to his feet, his leg gave out, sending him to the ground. Luckily, the impact from his fall didn't create too much noise. He massaged the leg ferociously until enough feeling returned to enable him to move.

The patrol searched for the missing Marine for two more days before receiving orders to return to Camp Reasoner. The order didn't sit well with the men. Even though the water and rations were nearly spent, they wanted to continue with the search. Marines don't leave Marines behind. Everyone knew that they could survive without rations for a couple more days and that there were plenty of small streams where water could be found. Doc only guessed that the others shared the same feeling of betrayal as he did.

It was late afternoon when the choppers landed to extract the team. The ride back to camp was quiet and the mood was somber. Doc lit up a smoke and scanned the men's expressionless faces staring at the floor.

Stottlemyer was the first to greet Lew when the team disembarked from the chopper.
"HEY LEW," he screamed over the rotor blast. "DID YOU GUYS FIND LA PORTE?"
"Huh? What are you talking about?" Lew answered, bewildered by the question.
"LaPorte is the M.I.A. You didn't know that?"
Lew stopped in his tracks and turned to look Stottlemeyer in the eye. "No shit man. We didn't know who the hell we were looking for!"
"Maybe one of the other teams will find him."
"Yeah," Lew stared, "Maybe one of the other teams will find him."

It didn't take long for the rumors to spread throughout the compound, the most predominant being that LaPorte had planned to desert to be with his Vietnamese girlfriend. Word got around that he packed his belongings and cleaned out his area of the hootch the day before the jump. Other people made comment that he had defected to North Vietnam to eventually make his way to the Soviet Union. Still, others reasoned that he was just a Navy Corpsman who wasn't trained in escape and evasion that either got lost or was captured. Lew preferred to believe the latter. He couldn't comprehend a Corpsman willingly desert his troops or his country.

Sitting comfortably in the chair that Corporal Maynard gave him, he glanced over to the space vacated by the corporal who, by now he presumed, was back home with his family. Lew traced the 'Skulker" image on the patrol flag and recalled a time when he was aboard ship berthed at Yokosuka, Japan when a sailor was physically removed from the ship for visiting the Soviet Embassy in Tokyo. The man was never seen on the ship again. Lew's thought was broken.

"Hey Doc," Weasel got the corpsman's attention. "There's goin' to be a USO show at the stage tonight. Spread the word."

"Oh yeah!" Lew perked up. "I never saw a USO show before. Anybody famous lined up?"

"I don't think so Doc. I heard it's some Aussie group."

"Maybe there'll be some blonde girls dancing around in bikinis," Lew wished.

"Maybe Doc. Maybe?"

The small, battalion amphitheater was filled to capacity shortly before sunset. Anyone who wasn't on duty was either seated on hard, wooden, benches or on the dirt slope, anxiously anticipating the start of the show. A Vietnamese rock-n-roll band appeared on stage setting up their equipment when some of the Marines began to get rowdy, orchestrating cat-calls and loudly calling out "WE WANT THE SHOW...WE WANT THE SHOW." The chant continued as the band tuned their cheap, electric guitars to a uniform, screeching, twang. Seconds later a poorly, performed drum roll silenced the men and a pudgy, bald-headed man sporting red, Bermuda shorts and a bright, yellow, flowered, Hawaiian shirt appeared center stage to start the show.

"GIDDAY BLOKS," he screamed out.

"GIDDAY," the Marines sang back.

The performer then made some kind of well-planned comment about how glad he was to be asked to entertain the fine men of the

U.S.ARMY. The remark incited the audience as the entertainer hoped. The Marines countered with loud boos and hissing, unknowingly setting themselves up for a mini-skirted, busty, blonde, girl to come out from behind the screen and begin singing a version of Brenda Lee's hit, *"He's sorry....so sorry....please accept his apology."* The men stopped their booing and began applauding and whistling, obviously enjoying the view more than the song.

The show continued with jokes, naughty burlesque skits, terribly amateurish song and dance, but the men didn't care. They were enjoying it.

Lew's attention drifted away from the performance when he spotted Weasel a few rows in front of him, holding drumsticks. He guessed that the *Jay Hawk* was hopeful that he would be given an opportunity to go up on stage and join in on a set or two. It didn't happen. Lew re-focused when the pudgy Australian man moved behind the blonde and faked pumping her rear end in a vaudevillian manner while lilting out a melodic refrain.

"Oh, I've got a little Irish lass
She's filled with Irish laughter
Li'l does she realize
It's her Irish ass I'm after"

The audience howled.

Once the show ended and the performers took a final bow, the high-spirited men disbursed to return to their hootches. Lew walked back alone, passing by LaPorte's shelter to peek through the screening, hoping to see the senior corpsman there.

The next morning everyone had the opportunity to sleep in, as was the custom after returning from patrol, providing nothing important was scheduled. Doc woke first, immediately grabbing a cigarette he sat up and looked around to see if anyone else was awake. Nobody was, not even Unkle, who usually never missed chow. The corpsman grabbed a towel, put on shower shoes and made his way to the showers, cigarette dangling from his lip.

Standing under the gentle stream, he closed his eyes and let the cold water refresh his sweaty frame until others began to show up. Reluctantly, Doc surrendered the stream to

Pee Wee. One by one, the men took turns sharing the two, gravity-fed, shower heads; each relishing the few minutes it took to get clean.

"Pee Wee, you want to scrub my back?" Unkle joked.

"Here, scrub this, you faggot-maggot," Pee Wee joked back.

"Scrub what? I don't see anything." Unkle smirked.

"Eat shit Unkle."

Doc and the others took the playful barrage in stride knowing the two men always jag each other as a daily routine.

After everyone returned from the shower and dressed, the conversations turned into a forum of planning their day. Most had nothing on their agenda, except Weasel, who wanted to check on the status of his transfer to the band and Doc, who wanted to find more information about LaPorte. Typically, the day after a patrol meant a trip to the PX, barber shop or disbursing office. Occasionally, someone would attempt to find a friend in another unit. Lew had the feeling that this day could to be one of total boredom but, he wasn't about to spend the day idle. His plan was to hitch a ride over to 1st. Med and call on his friend Rappaport but first, he wanted to stop the aid station and talk to Stottlemyer and see if he heard any news about LaPorte.

"Doc," Johnson spoke. "Do you want me to teach you how to play chess today?"

"Maybe later. I have some things to do first, okay?"

"I don't know Doc. I got a pretty busy schedule today," Johnson jested.

Lew stepped inside the aid station looking for Stottlemeyer. He was nowhere in sight. Hearing a noise coming from the rear of the building he made his way to the back door where he found the petty officer outside attempting to disassemble some wooden pallets.

"Hey man, what ya up to?" Lew questioned.

Stottlemeyer lowered the claw hammer. "Hey Lew," he acknowledged the corpsman. "Sorry man, I didn't hear you there," he semi-apologized before answering the question. "I'm trying to build a shower for the aid station. I made a deal with the Sea-Bees for a hot water heater. The only thing I need to do is scrounge around for a few more parts and build it. You want to help?"

"You're barking up the wrong tree man. Hell, I don't know anything about construction."
"You don't need to. I'll do all the work. All you'd have to do is be a helper."
Lew thought a moment. "Okay but, I can't today. I have some things I need to do first."
"That's fine. I'm not ready to start on the heavy work yet anyway."
Lew nodded then asked the question he came to ask. 'You hear anything more about LaPorte?"
"No. Nobody heard anything," he replied shaking his head. "I suppose you heard the rumors?"
"Yeah, I heard," Lew replied lighting up a smoke. "What's your thoughts?"
"Hey man, I don't think he *chu-hoyed* to the V.C. if that's what you're asking."
"Nah, I don't either," Lew exhaled the answer in a cloud of smoke before asking another question. "Well, who's in-charge until LaPorte comes back?"
"I'm not real sure but, I guess I am. Roshong has been here longer but, he's still an E-3."
"What about Conners?"
"Hey man, where you been? He rotated back to the world two days ago!"
"Huh? Shit, I didn't even know he was that short!"
"He wasn't. His ticket was a third Purple Heart. I heard he burned his hand on a rifle barrel during a firefight. Talk about the 'Luck-of-the Irish' huh?"
Befuddled but, satisfied with the response Lew set up his exit. "Okay. Well listen, I gotta go now but, I'll be back tomorrow to give you a hand."
"Sounds good."
"Catch you later," Lew bid as he left.
"Later."

As Lew walked back to retrieve his M-16 before leaving the compound to make the trip to 1st Med. he was encountered by Private Arthurs. "Doc, you need to get back to the hootch. Sergeant Woodcock wants to see us."
"Why? Whats up?"
"Looks like we're going back to the bush again tomorrow."

"What! Already? We just came in yesterday," the corpsman spouted out.

The entire team was gathered around Sergeant Woodcock when Lew and Arthurs entered the hootch.
"Good, we got everybody here now," Woody commented. Dropping the small-talk that he was engaged in he began to cite the reason for this meeting. "I jist got word that we got us another mission ta-mah-ra." He went on to explain that the team was going to on a 'damage assessment' mission in Happy Valley following a B-52 bomber 'Arc-light' mission. They were to be inserted in an area that was identified as a Viet Cong and North Vietnamese Army stronghold immediately after the bombers dropped their load of 500 and 1000 pound bombs. The mission called for a 3 A.M. wake-up since the payload was to be delivered at dawn. The plan was for the team to be in the air and ready to swoop down and be inserted in the jungle within minutes after the last explosion.
"We got ta git in there an' check out the damage. We're gonna try an' capture us a *gook* too!" Woody paused before looking straight into the young corpsman's eyes. "Doc, you got any heartburn if we blow away some kneecaps?" he sneered.
The question shocked Lew. It jerked and twisted his gut. He noticed everyone staring at him, waiting for a response. Sensing that Woody might just be injecting some sort of masochistic bravado, Lew gave his answer. "Nah, I don't give a shit," he lied. Deep down, he didn't want to be party to maiming anyone, not even the hated enemy but, he didn't want challenge the sergeant's stature either. He guessed that if it came down to it, Woody wouldn't actually carry out the horrific act anyway.
"Good," Woody continued. "We're goin' ta have a officer observer comin' with us---some captain type. My guess is that we're gonna find some bodies…a lot of 'em. Them Arc-lights do some kinda boo-koo damage. No body's ta go lookin for suv'neers neither an' don't go touchin' any dead bodies. They jist might be booby-trapped." Woody looked around, making sure everyone understood. "Now, we need ta git our shit together ta-day an' be ready ta go at the chopper pad at oh-four-hundred. Ya'll git that?"
"How long are we goin' out for Woody?" Unkle asked.

"Plan on five days unless, we git in some shit." Woodcock replied, then smirked, "Personally, I'd like ta mix it up with 'em bastads an' blow 'em all ta hell."

The team spent the remainder of the day preparing for the upcoming mission. Lew was disappointed that he didn't get the chance to go over to 1st Med. or have Johnson teach him to play chess. He assumed that Stottlemeyer would find out about the mission and know why he wasn't there to help with the shower.

It was a few minutes after 3 AM when Sergeant Holton came to the hootch to waken the men. "Up and at 'em girls. Everybody up," he rousted them and turned on the lights. His tone wasn't harsh like drill instructor. It was just loud and firm enough to generate some stirring. "Thanks to one of the cooks, if ya'll hurry you can get a coffee and sandwich at the mess hall before we go."

It was still dark when the team met Sergeant Woodcock and the observer at the ammo point. Each man picked up an issue of grenades and moved to the helo pad to wait for the choppers to arrive. Those who smoked took the opportunity to light up before the birds got there. Doc chain-smoked three in succession. No one was very talkative, preferring to keep individual thoughts to themselves. A solitary CH-46 made its approach to the pad in total darkness. Woodcock ordered Pee Wee and Unkle to use flashlights as a beacon to guide it in while Gilmore maintained radio contact with the pilot. The pilot caught the team off-guard by turning on the helicopter's landing lights; temporarily blinding them as it descended to touch down. The men scurried to get inside the aircraft, each man taking a seat in reverse order of march so that the first one on would be the last man off, as Woody dictated while the men waited. The crew chief closed the ramp door as the bird ascended above the compound and over the hills that marked the Da Nang valley.

A strange feeling came over Lew as he looked out the porthole into the cold, darkness as the chopper gained altitude and headed westward. It was impossible to distinguish how high up they were as no reference was visible on the ground. Somewhere, far below was a vast, unfriendly jungle, waiting to devour them at their first mistake. When the chopper made a subtle heading change, a faint, pink glow of sunrise barely touched the distant horizon. The relative calm was suddenly broken by a chain-like reverberation of shock waves emanating from thousands of bombs detonating. The men could feel the helicopter shake slightly as it collided with the invisible effect. Almost immediately after the first wave hit the chopper the pilot skillfully controlled it's descent to the predetermined LZ. Two enlisted aircrew members manned the .50 cal., waiting to lay down suppression fire if needed. Despite the fact that the LZ was barely visible the chopper landed safely, and more importantly, without taking enemy fire. The team quickly ran off the ramp and formed a perimeter. Luckily, no one got injured in the darkness.

Once the chopper rose and disappeared from view, the jungle became totally silent. There were no animal sounds; no birds calling out; no insects chirping…nothing except beating hearts pounding inside men's chests. The air stank; heavy with lingering smell of spent explosive, chemicals. Woodcock signaled for Unkle to lead the way out of the exposed LZ and into the unwelcoming domain of enemy guerrillas. As the men stepped out their intervals, Lew turned around to see Sergeant Holton instructing the captain, who was in position behind him, to maintain the spacing.

The patrol moved slowly; quietly; deliberately, through mass of vegetation and vines. The stench got stronger the closer the team got to the impact area. Opaque, clouds of nitrate-laden smoke clung close to the surface, partially obscuring the barely visible trees surrounding them. Within minutes they came across the first, fresh bomb crater. It seemed to disappear into the depths of the earth as a pool of smoke settled at the bottom. More and more craters lined their path as the patrol inched through the devastated terrain.

Doc was awed by the destructive power of the bombing. Huge, ancient, trees were uprooted, broken and splintered and scattered about like tooth picks. Large boulders cracked and shattered into thousands of smaller, projectile-like pieces. As the team maneuvered through the organic debris, they moved downward into a narrow, pock-marked valley. The bombs opened up the thick, double layered, canopy, allowing subdued rays first light to mix with the smoke that turned the entire valley into a surrealistic vision of someone's tormented mind. Hundreds of small fires carpeted the valley floor, adding to the smoke and stench. Lew spotted a twisted, mangled carcass of an unfortunate deer dangling from a tree branch overhead, dripping blood in his path. He couldn't help but feel sorry for the innocent creature.

As the team trekked deeper into the mess, signs of habitation became more obvious. Shattered pieces of hand-laced, bamboo structures were strewn everywhere. Parts of utensils were embedded in the trunks of trees. Miraculously, several untouched, cooking fires remained smoldering with food left simmering in pots. One could stop anywhere and find puddles of blood mixed with pieces of human flesh, bones and organs. The greatest mystery was the complete lack of bodies; dead or otherwise. It was unmistakable that the V.C. was occupying the encampment. The question on everyone's mind was "*Where are the bodies?*" One thing was certain....the team was definitely in the enemy's midst.

Doc made a complete turn, surveying everything. He couldn't help but think that the bastards didn't even know what hit them. He noticed that the observer was jotting things down in a small notebook. Lew guessed that the man must an Intelligence Officer and his meticulous note taking only delayed the team from getting out of the area. Each man knew that the enemy would come out of hiding soon and didn't want to take on what was left of a probably overwhelming force. Doc surmised that if the *Charlie* found them, he would be in no mood to take prisoners. The thought suddenly disappeared when a rustling sound near his foot startled him. His eyes and weapon instantly zeroed in on a charred, snake twisting in agony in the burnt underbrush. The lump in his throat vanished but, his heart kept racing. He hated snakes yet, somehow felt compelled to put an end to the creature's misery although, he didn't.

The signal was relayed back for everyone to step it up because they had to get out of the area quickly to avoid enemy contact. The file followed a tiny, trickling stream that cut though the encampment. It was the obvious water source. Private Johnson directed Doc's attention to a severed foot resting in a bloodied pool of water. The foot still had a sandal attached to it. For some reason, the sight of it didn't seem all that gruesome. Six months before it might have made him squeamish.

It took nearly an hour for the patrol to get clear of the crater field. Each step heightened the alertness of every man. *"Surely, the gooks know we're here."* Lew secretly reminded himself. Wide-eyed, he scanned every tree and hiding place. Every so often he turned to check and see if the men behind him were still there. By mid-day the patrol welcomed their first break. Woody passed the word that no one was to eat or smoke.

Resting against his pack, Doc noticed that the creatures were making their normal animal sounds. Taking several refreshing swallows of tepid water it also occurred to him that all the men weren't completely at ease. The veterans seemed to be more vigilant than he recognized on past patrols. No one was engaged in whispered conversation or scrapping out tic-tac-toe games in the dirt. He looked past Private Johnson to see what Pee Wee was doing up in front. It didn't surprise him to see the Marine poised on one knee with his rifle at the ready; looking deep into the undercover. Doc took the queue and copied Pee Wee's posture. Even though he sensed danger, he didn't want to give the Marines the impression that he did. It was obvious that he was not alone. From the way everyone else appeared uneasy in these surroundings, the notion sprouted in Lew's mind that humans must possess an ancient, animal instinct that gives man an uncanny ability to sense danger. *"Damn it!"* he scolded himself. *"There you go again. Pay attention"*

The break ended all too soon. Again on the move, the patrol traversed a rugged ridgeline that separated the bombed encampment from the adjacent valley. Lew guessed that they had ventured about 1000 meters, "as-the-crow-flies", from the enemy stronghold, even though they actually 'humped' farther, given their meandering route through the thick vegetation. The temperature soared to more than 100 degrees by mid-afternoon with about the same humidity. Lew expected some of the men to get muscle cramps or possibly suffer from heat exhaustion. He made a mental note that if Woodcock didn't take more frequent rest breaks, he would say something to him. The last thing he wanted to do was call for a preventable, med-evac this deep in enemy territory. He suddenly noticed that the patrol was deliberately following a trail. *"Shit! What the hell is Woody doing?"* he thought. The tactic gave the corpsman jitters. He didn't relish the call and was certain the other men felt the same, recalling that Sergeant Woodcock pulled the same stunt on the last patrol, which irked the men. Never-the-less, Woody was the leader and Marines obey their leaders.

Everyone looked for booby-traps while, at the same time, scouted out locations where the V.C. might set up an ambush. There were plenty of good sites that gave cover as well as concealment. The situation prompted Doc to nervously scan all around and keep looking behind him. The patrol stopped abruptly. Doc's eyes widened when Johnson relayed a mime message. The Private cupped an ear, then hand-gestured the 'V' sign then formed the letter 'C' with his fingers, followed with the universal, puppet-like, hand signal of 'talking' and finished the message by pointing in the direction in front of the patrol. Lew interpreted the signal as "Unkle could hear V.C talking up ahead." Doc relayed the message back to Sergeant Holton. Everyone 'froze' motionless. Even as far back as Lew was, he too could faintly hear the Vietnamese still squawking. They were obviously unaware of the recon team's presence. *"What now?"* he wondered. The anxiety built; sending his heart pumping full force.

Word was finally whispered back that there were only two V.C. and Woody and Unkle were going to try to get close enough to throw concussion grenades in order to stun the unwary guerillas then, run in and capture both of them. When Doc heard the plan he feared that Woodcock might make good his threat to blow way some kneecaps. Everyone else was to remain in place until the grenades exploded then, move in to repel any other attackers before making their get-away to an extraction LZ.

Along with the others, Doc waited nervously for the explosions. When there weren't any everyone realized that something didn't go according to plan. Woody returned and spread the word that the gooks must have found them out and escaped into the jungle. The team realized that they had been detected and would now have to run for their lives. The was no question in anyone's mind that they were going to be pursued; the question was "By how many?" Woodcock decided to remain on the trail in order to save time on getting to a suitable extraction point before sundown. They traveled a couple hundred feet when they came across a primitive bamboo structure hidden under a stand of heavily canopied trees. Thinking it might contain a cache of weapons, the sergeant stopped the patrol long enough to check it out. He sent Weasel and Unkle in to look around. Weasel came back and reported that there weren't any weapons, only an abundant supply of rice stored in a large, woven basket. Orders were given to booby-trap the container. It was done and the patrol moved on.

The teamed quick-stepped along the trail but, not so fast as to ignore possible booby-traps. The demanding pace tired the men quickly, requiring a couple minutes rest every few hundred meters traveled. Assuming that they were being followed Sergeant Woodcock called for stops only long enough to catch their breath. Desperately in need of water, Doc sat on a boulder beside the trail and pulled out his canteen. KRACK. A single shot rang out; whistling inches past his ear. He felt a sting on his chin just before he dived to the ground. Instinctively, all of the men dove for cover and instantly directed their weapons in the general direction of were the shot came from but, held their return fire. Then a voice shouted out from somewhere, "CACA DAO, G.I…YOU DIE NOW."

Doc trembled. He had never been shot at before and the verbal threat reminded him of World War Two movies where Japanese soldiers psychologically toyed with Americans they surrounded. Lew looked into the faces of the men nearby and recognized that they were just as afraid as he was. They waited and waited for the enemy to attack but no other shots rang out. Woodcock decided that it was time to move out. Lew didn't believe that the leader still wanted to use the trail. He looked back at Holton who only shrugged his shoulders in common disbelief.

The team stayed on the trail another couple hundred meters. The path cut through an open grass covered field on the top of a rise, requiring increasing the spacing of their intervals as they single-filed through the open field. KRACK. Another shot rang out. Once again the men dove to the ground. KRACK- KRACK-KRACK, more shots came their way from what sounded to be a semi-automatic rifle. Unlike the earlier incident, instead of being

somewhat concealed in trees, the men were caught out in the open in barely knee-deep grass.
Even though the sniper knew their exact location, Woody avoided letting him know if he hit his mark. "Anybody git hit?"He asked in an urgent but, calmly subdued voice. Doc listened closely and was greatly relieved when no one spoke out. Woodcock informed the men to stay low in the grass and not to fire back unless they received a heavy volume of incoming fire and knew where it was coming from.
The notion suddenly occurred to Doc that it was only one Viet Cong who was harassing them. He figured that the solitary shooter was attempting to delay the team until more of his kind could come in and surround them. He wondered if Woodcock was thinking the same thing. Once again he felt his body trembling but knew that he wasn't alone in his fear.

The men remained concealed in the deep grass until dusk when Woody low-crawled to each man; informing them of what was happening. When he got to Doc and Holton he told them the same bad news that he told the others. "We ain't goin' ta make it to the LZ ta-nite. Looks like we have ta harbor somewhere 'til mornin'. They're gonna send the choppers to an LZ jist over that ridge. All we gotta do is hold on 'til then. We're gonna git down in that elephant grass over there on the bottom of this rise an' harbor there jist before it gits real dark." Both men nodded that they understood. Woody moved toward the captain and Arthurs.

The last few remaining minutes of daylight had the team crawling through the field toward the tall elephant grass that was growing on the opposite side of the rise. Once concealed deep inside the patch, Woodcock had the men form up in a tight, defensive perimeter. He instructed them to remove the ruck sacks but to keep the web gear and ammo belt on. The logic was that if they had to make a run for it, the stuff carried in the packs was just expendable extra weight but, the ammunition was a vital necessity. He had Pee Wee, Weasel and Unkle position all the Claymores to face the most likely enemy approach at the crest of the rise....a mere hundred feet away. If they had to detonate them, most of the dangerous back-blast would probably go over their heads.

With everyone settled in, the only thing left to do was wait. It was going to be a long, excruciating wait until morning. Doc sat next to Gilmore who was whispering something over the radio. He couldn't hear what the radioman was saying but, imagined it wasn't good. During a pause he asked Gilmore, "What was that bastard hollering back there? What's a crocodile?"
"It's Caca Dao. It more or less means they're going to cut our throats." Gilmore whispered back.
The translation sucked the corpsman's mouth dry. He unconsciously moved his hand up to feel his throat as the gravity of their situation hit home. The Viet Cong knows where they are and were probably surrounding them now! He couldn't accept the fact that all ten of them would most likely be killed sometime during the night. He didn't want to die here, in this dirty, little, corrupt, backward country. Reaching down in the deepest part of his gut he prepared himself for the inevitable outcome. If he was going to die tonight, he wouldn't go without fighting it out with his last ounce of strength. He was going to take a few of them with him. What bothered him most though, was the hurt and anguish that his mother would suffer when she learns of his death. He was grateful that the darkness hid his tears from the others. He guessed that all the others were agonizing over the same emotions and thoughts that were going through his own mind.

The moon gave enough light to make out the figures of the others, who were either reclining or sitting up in sleepless anticipation of the attack. Nocturnal creatures were chattering. That was a good sign but, did little to calm the men's nerves. No one dared to sleep. Gilmore stayed with the radio instead of passing it along. Lew wondered if the V.C. were going to play mind games before attacking. He heard that they sometimes did that. He also heard that they had, on occasions, sneaked in and turned Claymores around on Americans. His mind envisioned that screaming hordes of pajama clad guerrilla fighters would soon be charging over the rise with AK-47's blazing. The image of him having to fight hand-to-hand un-nerved him even more. Though, he was strong for having such a slight, physical frame, he never had much experience as a fighter and realized the he would most likely be killed going one-on-one against a trained, fanatical insurgent. Unconsciously, he felt for the K-Bar knife that was strapped to his suspenders.

The vision repeated itself over and over as the night passed slowly, which made him think that maybe the V.C. were keeping intentionally silent; permitting the Americans to 'psych' themselves into surrendering. At one point he conjured up the notion to sneak away from the team and escape into the jungle to avoid being captured or killed. *"Maybe we all should try to escape; each man for himself?"* he dared to think. *"Surely some of us could survive on our own wits...."* He disregarded the notion as it teetered on being cowardly... *"Although, it might have some degree of merit in other circumstances",* he reasoned. He felt his eyes getting heavy but, it was too dangerous to even close them for a few minutes.

Upon realizing that it was nearly dawn, Doc couldn't understand why *Charlie* hadn't attacked them, after all, they were sitting ducks. Woody gave word for everybody to quietly get something to eat before they moved out. As Doc opened a can of Ham and Eggs, Gilmore made a face at the corpsman's breakfast selection. The men ate quickly, as they were anxious to get moving toward the LZ.

Gilmore leaned toward the corpsman and whispered, "Doc, when we get back, I'll buy the beer."

Lew smiled. "You buy the first case. I'll buy the second."

Gilmore returned the smile and gave a 'thumbs-up'.

By the time the men finished eating the sun was coming over top of the mountains and was beginning to burn off the mist that settled in the valley overnight. After the men retrieved the Claymores, Woodcock gave the signal to move out. The team formed up single file in their order of march and began to come out of the elephant grass with Unkle running point, hugging the M-60; finger poised on the trigger. At Woody's direction he lead the patrol back unto the trail that ran downward into lush, green, boulder filled ravine. There was a strange silence in the air as Unkle stepped across a trickling of water that cut though the bottom of the ravine.

KRACK…KRACK…KRACK…KRACK….KRACK.. A barrage of AK-47 rounds pierced through the morning air. Hundreds of rounds fell upon the team, sending the Marines diving for cover. It was an ambush! Doc jumped behind the nearest tree. Sergeant Holton landed on Doc's back. Both recovered and raised their rifles, joining the others in returning fully automatic salvos toward the general direction of the incoming fire. Doc saw plumbs of dirt kicking up at his feet and heard the impact of enemy rounds penetrating on the front side of the tree while more rounds whizzed by his head. The noise of all the gunfire was the loudest thing that Doc ever heard. He emptied three magazines at the unseen enemy on the high ground on the opposite side of the ravine.

"CA CA DAO YOU MA-THA GI's...CA CA DAO....YOU!! The V.C screamed out as they fired. **"YOU DIE....YOU DIE NOW."**

Doc felt sure the threats were meant only for him. He locked another magazine into the rifle and continued to spray through the concealing vegetation in up in front. That's when he saw Sergeant Woodcock standing up on top of a large boulder; fully exposed to enemy fire, sending M-79 grenade rounds in their direction as fast as he could reload while countering the V.C. threats withy threats of his own. **"COME ON YOU MOTHER FUCKERS...COME GIT US YOU BASTARDS."**

"OH shit!! What the hell's he doing?" Doc thought. *"He's going to get nailed."*

Out of nowhere came the screaming words that Doc didn't want to hear. **"GILMORE'S HIT.....GILMORE'S HIT!"**

The greatest surge of fear he had ever know cut through the corpsman's body. Frantically, he fumbled with the straps on his pack in order to retrieve his Unit One medical kit. He knew he had to get up and get to Gilmore fast but, he didn't want to. He didn't want to run through all the gunfire. Being frightened was mild. He wasn't frightened...he was absolutely terrified yet, he had to go. He took a quick second to scan around but couldn't see Gilmore.

"WHERE THE HELL IS GILMORE AT?" he screamed above the noise.

"DOWN THERE DOC," Pee Wee screamed back, pointing to a cluster of large, moss covered boulders below him.

Lew spotted Gilmore sprawled over one of the large stones on his stomach. *"OH God, help me with this,"* the corpsman begged before jumping out from behind the shelter of the tree and wildly dashed toward the fallen Marine through a rain of increasing enemy gunfire, the Unit One in tow. In full view of the enemy he jumped, hopped and danced his way down over the slippery stones to reach his Marine friend. In one moment of sudden strength he grabbed Gilmore's pack and pulled his body down off the exposed rock to protect him from anymore bullets.

At the same time that he reached his friend, Woodcock hollered out, **"DOC, I'M OUT OF ROUNDS, GIVE ME YOURWEAPON."**

Lew tossed the M-16 up to Woodcock then turn his attention to Gilmore. He struggled to turn the limp body over to assess the injuries when he spotted extreme amounts of blood squirting from the man's jugular vein. Doc's stomach dropped. He knew that his friend was about to die and there was absolutely nothing that he could do to save him.

The captain hollered down, **"HE'S GONE DOC. BETTER FIND COVER"**

The comment angered the corpsman. As oddly as it seemed, he didn't want the last thing that Gilmore would ever hear was his fate. Doc screamed back a lie. **"HE'S NOT GONE! HE'LL MAKE IT."** He then turned to his dying buddy. All the noise seemed to disappear as Doc gazed into Billy's rapidly-dulling, blue, eyes; knowing that any second the young Marine would expire as he held him. Doc listened closely as Billy struggled to speak his last words. In one muted, fading breath, Gilmore uttered, "Help me Momma," then peacefully let go of his very young life. That moment was permanently etched in Doc's mind but he didn't have time to dwell on it. Another call came out, **"DOC, WEASEL'S HIT TOO!"**

Lew was again being forced to show himself to the enemy. And again, he didn't know where this Marine fell either. **"WHERE?"** But, before a reply could come back, he located the Marine laying on the ground about ten feet from him. **"I SEE HIM."** Doc shouted out. Once again he bounded out from behind cover in a hail of bullets to get to a fallen comrade. He reached Weasel and immediately knew that the man was already dead. He must have died instantly. Doc was grateful that Marine didn't suffer. He turned to Woodcock to let him know that Weasel was gone by moving his head from side to side. Woody understood. The youthful corpsman then called out, **"ANYBODY ELSE HURT?"** The survey yielded that no one else was hit. Doc was relieved. The firefight diminished to an occasional shot. Doc didn't like being so isolated from the others so, he jumped up and scurried back behind the tree that he dove behind on the initial

burst of fire. Holton told him that they couldn't call in 'arty' because aircraft were in the area but, a couple of Phantoms were coming in for close air support. He explained to the corpsman that that's what is called 'danger close'. Woodcock remained on the radio handset to coordinate the mission. He instructed the men to retrieve Weasel's and Gilmore's bodies and carry them up to the same elephant grass area they had harbored in the night before. He also told everybody to discard their back packs.
The V.C. let up on their gunfire but not their verbal taunting. They continued shouting the Ca Ca Dao threat as the aircraft swooped down only feet above the canopy.
"KEEP YOUR HEADS DOWN!" Woody shouted.
Suddenly, an instant roar of jet engines filled the air, then, a Cracking of three branches followed in a millisecond by thunderously loud explosions. The rapid change in air pressure made it feel like Doc's head was going to blow up on its own. His eyes nearly bulged out of their sockets and his nose began to bleed. The blasts lifted his body several inches off the ground while hundreds of pieces of shrapnel cut through the surrounding landscape. The concussion shook internal organs and sent uncontrollable muscle twitching throughout his body. Another Phantom followed in behind the first, duplicating the first terrifying experience. Doc feared that another sortie would fall right on top of them. After the planes released their loads Woodcock announced that choppers would be coming in to extract them shortly. The LZ would be the open field above their "harbor site." He wanted everybody to move close to where choppers were going to touch down. Without a weapon Doc made himself useful by carrying Gilmore's body. He couldn't believe how much limp bodies weighed as he struggled to drag the dead Marine up the hill.

It seemed like an eternity before the popping sound of helicopters came from behind the trees on the crest of the ridge. Woody directed the pilot and identified their position with yellow smoke. The large airframe was an inviting target has it descended to retrieve the recon team. Once again all hell broke loose as the V.C. concentrated their fire on the chopper. The crew chief returned fire with the .50 caliber as the pilot managed to nest the bird on the slope. The tail ramp door was inaccessible for the troops. They had to climb up into the chopper through the side door on the exposed side of the aircraft. Doc needed help raising Gilmore's body up to the opening about six feet above the ground. Pee Wee got unto the chopper first then took over for the crew chief as he assisted the men to climb onboard. Pee Wee concentrated the .50 cal. fire into a tree line about fifty meters away. The crew chief reached down and gripped tightly on Gilmore's bloody shirt. He pulled hard to bring the body inside while Doc pushed from below. Everything was happening in slow motion. Doc climbed inside then turned to help the crew chief with Weasel's body. After the bodies were aboard the other men climbed in and found a porthole to return fire from. Unkle filled the deck with empty rounds from the machine gun as he sprayed the tree line while the others did the same with M-16's. As all the portholes were manned by the Marines, Doc grabbed Gilmore's rifle and began firing into the trees on the opposite side of the chopper, even though the enemy fire was coming from there, yet. The pilot started to rev up the engines and the chopper began to shake violently as it struggled to lift off the ground. It shifted in such a manner that it knocked the men on board off balance, causing a momentary delay in their return fire. Smoke, noise, stench, adrenalin and fear filled the cargo compartment as the craft shuttered it's way upward. Enemy bullets riddled the metal beast as it rose just above the tallest tree. Suddenly the crew chief hollered out, **"WE'RE GOIN' DOWN...WE'RE GOIN' DOWN, HANG ON!"** The crew chief's warning sent shock through Doc's mind. *"OH God, we're going to die. Oh God,"* he prayed. *"If you get us out of this, I promise you I'll always go to church."*

The craft impacted the ground hard, knocking the men off their feet but, without the expected explosion. The men regained their positions and continued the counter-fire through the portholes. Empty shell casings and magazines flew all over the deck. Unbelievably, the crew chief climbed out of the aircraft and up unto the engine compartment, exposing himself to the barrage of small arms fire. Doc was bewildered that the man was actually trying to make a hasty repair to the aircraft under such a heavy volume of fire. After making a field expedient repair the brave man wiggled his way back though the gunner's window. Lew held his breath, waiting for the crazy man to fall victim to an AK round. Miraculously, he made it inside unscathed. The pilot once again revved up and attempted to force the helicopter to climb.

The machine strained and rose higher as everyone on board kept pouring bullets into the unseen enemy's position. The craft groaned as it struggled for altitude and distance. An unbelievable feeling of relief came over everyone when the bird made it up and over the ridgeline and out of enemy sight.

There was relative calm when the shooting stopped. The men slumped down unto the troop seats, exhausted from their two day ordeal. Immediately, Doc reached for a cigarette. Drawing a deep puff he held it in his lungs a few treasured seconds before releasing the smoke in a gesture-like signal of relief. As he attempted gain control of his senses his eyes found the lifeless bodies of the two young Marines lying on the deck in the midst of hundreds of spent shells and discarded magazines. His eyes turned to the other men's faces. Everyone else was also staring somberly at their expired, brothers-in-arms. There was no way that the corpsman could know each man's exact emotions but, he knew his own. Woody interrupted Doc's concentration. "Here's your piece back Doc," he said handing over the corpsman's M-16. As Lew gripped the weapon the helicopter moaned and dropped unexpectedly. Woodcock fell to the deck while Doc clinched unto the seat rail as his stomach came up into his throat. The immediate thought was that the chopper was going down! It felt as if someone was learning to drive a stick-shift automobile and kept popping the clutch as the chopper rose and fell in a sustained jerking motion. The crew chief shouted out to alert the recon Marines. **"OUR HYDRAULICS IS ALL SHOT UP. LOOKS LIKE WE HAVE TO FIND A PLACE TO SET DOWN. HANG ON!"**

After a few anxious minutes the pilot coaxed the chopper to land safely on a gently sloping, grass covered field and shut-down the engine. Fully knowing that they were still within the enemy's realm, everyone reloaded their weapons and took up positions at the portholes, waiting to counter another attack. Lew didn't know if the others realized it but, to his way of thinking, they were sitting ducks inside the crippled aircraft. Two Marine Lieutenants climbed out of the cockpit unto the ground. One spoke out. "Sergeant, get your men out of there. We got another bird on the way to take you and your men back."

"Yessir, Lieutenant," Woodcock complied, the barked out the order. "OKAY YOU MEN, GIT OFF THE CHOPPER AN"

FORM A PERIMETER." He turned to the pilot. "Sir, kin we leave our dead onboard 'til the other chopper gits here? They shouldn't be left out in the sun," he asked respectfully.
"Sure."

The team didn't have long to wait until two more CH-46's arrived at the make-shift LZ. Doc helped Johnson carry Gilmore's body unto the first chopper after it landed. Arthurs and Holton carried Weasel. Just as soon as the team members sat down on the troop seats the helicopter lifted off smoothly. Doc glanced out though the porthole as the chopper rose above the downed craft. He thought to himself that if anybody ever deserved a medal, it was that crew chief.

The cold air filled the cargo bay, bringing out the most welcome sense of relief. Doc knew he was out of danger now. They had somehow escaped from should have been certain death for all of them. He lit another smoke and pushed back into the seat, staring at the bodies all the way back to Da Nang.

Before taking the team back to Camp Reasoner the bodies needed to be taken to 1st Med. for a Medical Office to legally pronounce them Killed In Action. The helicopter descended toward the landing pad at 1st Med. Lew looked through the porthole as the aircraft slowly touched down on the metal grating outside of Triage. The sight brought back memories. Four litter bearers entered the helicopter to carry the two dead Marines to Graves Registration. Doc Lewis felt compelled to escort them. As he rounded the corner he recognized Eberson-Witmore as the duty M.O. talking to Captain Dixon and First Sergeant Henderson, who had made the short trip over from Recon to wait for the bodies to arrive. Sergeant Woodcock approached the commander and 1st Sergeant while Eberson-Witmore walked over to examine the remains. Lew could tell that the doctor recognized him from somewhere but just couldn't place him. "Where's the goddamned tags?" the physician belted out in his typical obnoxious manner. "These bodies should be tagged!"
Clinching his teeth Lew tightened his grip on the rifle, thinking he would do a service to humanity if he would just pull the trigger. Controlling his anger Doc ignored the doctor's rant then turned and walked back unto the chopper. He sat back down on the seat

and huffed to himself, *"Tags! Tags! That asshole wants fuckin' tags!"* Exasperated, he let go a large breath of pent up hot air. Woodcock came back onboard and the chopper lifted off toward the Recon compound. In spite of having survived the deadly experiences of the sniper, ambush and being shot down, Lew was sure that all the others shared his grief for the two Marines who lost their lives. The mood was somber as the weary men disembarked from the chopper, turned-in the unused ordinance and sluggishly maneuvered their way up to the hootch.

Lew placed the dirty rifle down on the cot, removed the web gear and plopped his tired body down in the lawn chair. No one was in the mood to talk since nothing could be said that would lessen the pain that each man felt over the loss of their fellow Marines. Taking a moment to reflect and morn, Doc lit a smoke and lowered his head in sorrow; daring not to break the silence. A few solemn minutes elapsed before Palmer softly spoke up.

"That's weird," he remarked.

The comment intrigued the corpsman. "What's weird, Pee Wee?"

"Weasel's and Gilmore's racks are next to each other," he noted. "I think that's pretty weird."

Everyone turned their heads to validate Pee Wee's observation.

"That's just a coincidence man," Unkle assured. "It ain't nothin' but a thing."

The last part of the comment disturbed the corpsman. *"What the hell is that supposed to mean?"* he secretly pondered. *"It ain't nothin'! It IS something."* He dwelled on it for several minutes before he realized that what Unkle said wasn't meant to be frivolous. It dawned on him that, like it or not, this is war; people die in war. It's reality. Friends get killed. One has to accept it and move on. It is certain that others will be killed in battle in the days ahead and one has to mourn the loss, put it aside and keep praying that you survive. You have to develop an attitude to accept that whatever happens, is only a "thing" that occurs on the road of life. Unkle's comment made sense when put in the right perspective. Billy Gilmore and Weasel both died as Marines to be remembered and honored. Lew promised himself that he would never again break the number one rule of corpsmen, that being--Don't ever become too attached to your men.

Sergeant Holton poked his head in the doorway. "Unkle, Palmer…Sergeant Woodcock wants to see you. The rest of you guys can clean up and take it easy."

Mid-way through the afternoon everyone showered and began to field-day their weapons. Everyone took turns sharing the limited supply of cleaning gear while discussing the events of the patrol. It was then that Doc learned that all the others questioned Sergeant Woodcock's wisdom of following the trail. The consensus of the group was that they should have never gotten on the trail to begin with; that they should have cut through the jungle instead. The belief was that if they did that, both Marines would probably still be alive. Lew detected strains of anger in the men's voices as they made unflattering comments about Woodcock's decisions. As he sat there taking in the conversation and listening to their points-of-view, Doc decided that he wouldn't join in, reasoning that it would better for the men to just get things off their chests.

After consuming the first full meal in two days, Doc found Sergeant Holton and an unknown Second Lieutenant in the hootch, taking inventory of Gilmore and Whelchel's personal belongings. The unenviable ritual marked the finality of the friendship that he shared with Gilmore. It was difficult to comprehend that only hours earlier he and Billy agreed to buy each other cold beer. He decided to go up to the 'club' and have a few in Billy's honor.

The following morning the men of team *Countersign* reported to supply to get a re-issue of the gear they abandoned in the field. Stottlemeyer called out as the men passed the aid station. "Lew, got a minute?"
"Not really but, I give it to you anyway. What's up?" Lew answered, breaking away from the group.
"Man, I guess you guys really got in some shit yesterday, huh?
"Yeah," Lew answered, wondering what the petty officer was going to say next. "Why?"
"Well, I just wanted to let you know that if you want to talk about it, I'll be around. That's all." Stottlemeyer thoughtfully offered.
Lew pretended to be hardened even though he secretly appreciated the kindness. "Hey, thanks but, everything's okay.

Shit's shit you know." Thinking that he would build the macho perception he added, "Hey man, it ain't nothin' but a thing."

The NCO saw though the façade but chose to ignore it. "Well, okay. I just thought I'd offer." He turned back toward the aid station when Lew stopped him. "Hey, you still need help with the shower?"

"Sure. Any time you want."

"I'll have to check my appointment book," Lew tried to lighten the air.

The men were all gathered in the hootch getting their newly issued replacement gear together when Sergeant Woodcock entered, bellowing out, "TEN-HUT".

Seeing fresh, young officer accompanying Woody the men quickly got to their feet.

"As you were men," the "butter-bar" insisted.

Everyone relaxed but remained standing.

Woodcock took over. "Men, this here's Second Lieutenant Williams. He's our platoon commander startin' yesterday. I ain't gonna introduce ya all individually 'cause he'll git ta know ya all in no time." He turned it over to the officer. "Lieutenant."

"Men," he acknowledged the group. "As Sergeant Woodcock stated, I'll get to know each of you in due time so, right now just take you seats. I see you all are busy so I'll be brief." He waited until the men were seated before continuing. "I'm aware of everything that happened on your last patrol and even though I didn't have the opportunity to know them personally, I deeply regret the loss of two fine Marines. They died for the Corps. On the other hand, you men fought courageously and survived to fight another day and most likely will." Williams paused momentarily. Doc's mind translated the message as an attempt to establish a bond of understanding with the enlisted troops. It was a typical, newly minted, gung-ho, officer speech that he expected.

"What a bunch of crap."

"For your information," the L.T. continued. "By all reports, you men tangled with a company-sized enemy element. You displayed an enormous amount of courage and bravery under fire. Sergeants Woodcock and Holton have nominated some of you for decorations and promotions. I will review each recommendation thoroughly and based on the merit, will give full consideration on

forwarding them up the chain." There was no reaction by the troops.
"I'm proud to be you platoon commander and look forward to running patrols with you," the lieutenant nearly finished up. "Now, the most important item…there'll be a memorial service for Lance Corporals Gilmore and Whelchel at sunset this evening at the chapel. I expect to see all of you there. That's all."
"TEN-HUT," Woody barked as the lieutenant turned to leave.
The young officer's last remark disturbed the corpsman. *"Why in hell wouldn't we be there?"*

That evening as the sun was beginning to set, warm breezes fluttered white, cotton curtains hanging from the tiny, chapel's windows. Marines representing every company in the battalion quietly filed inside, filling all the unpainted, wooden seats that were available until there was only room enough to stand. Members of team *Countersign* were afforded seats up in front. Lew expected to hear muted, organ music but, there wasn't any. The Spartan surroundings exemplified the Marine Corps idea of bare necessities. A walnut stained, plywood podium, draped in a band of purple colored cloth served as the pulpit. Two inverted M-16 rifles, crowned with camouflaged covered helmets and supported by empty jungle boots, held the prominent position in front of the pulpit.

Doc stared intensely at the rifles, scarcely noticing the Chaplin calling the congregation to prayer. He became so absorbed with the memory of his friend that he didn't even hear the Chaplin's message. He couldn't get the image of Billy's lusterless eyes staring at him; silently begging for help. It flashed repeatedly through his mind during the entire service. He became angry with himself for not being able to save the Marine's life and guilty for having survived. His anger shifted toward God. It was the same anger he felt as a boy when his father died. Yet, in another moment he remembered praying for God several times in the past two days to save his own life. The young corpsman was never so confused. He snapped out of the endless stare in time to pick up on the Chaplin's final words, "Greater love hath no man than this--that a man lay down his life for his friend."
In unison, the gathering ended the service, "Amen."

SO OLD TOO YOUNG

The memorial service for the fallen Marines marked a turning point in Lew's tour-of-duty. Despite all the wounded and dead he had seen while working at the medical battalion, they were all strangers, arriving in wholesale numbers; he had no personal connection with any of them. With Gilmore and Weasel it was different.....it was personal. He lived with them and had gotten to know them well. He shared his life with them and they shared theirs with him. He vowed never to get too close to anyone again.

Team *Countersign* was given several days respite following the ambush. During that time Lew attempted to distance himself from the men in the platoon by spending more time at the battalion aid station rather than hanging around the hootch. It was there that he met several other corpsmen in the battalion who came in mostly to just shoot-the-breeze but, occasionally needed to conduct business there. One of them came around the corner while Lew was helping Stottlemeyer make a final connection on the shower piping.

"Hey sailor," he addressed Stottlemeyer. "When you going to finish this thing?"

Lew turned to see a robust looking young corpsman beaming pleasant a smile toward them. He was holding swim fins in one hand and a diver's weight-belt and swimming mask in the other.

Stottlemeyer responded to the man. "Hell, it could have been finished a long time ago if you kept you word and gave me a hand like you said you would. I had to get myself some good help," he gestured toward Lew. "You know Doc Lewis?"

"No, we haven't met but ......" he paused, "aren't you with the team that got in some boo-coo shit last week?"

"Yeah, it really hit the fan," Lew answered.

The man wrinkled his brow. "Man, from what I heard you guys are lucky that any of you got out."

"It was pretty intense."
"I can imagine. Incidentally, I'm Chapman. You can call me Stan."
"Okay Stan, call me Lew," then added "You going swimmin'?"
"Not really. We're going to do some bridge security down south of Da Nang…making sure *Charlie* didn't plant any mines under the bridge. Do you want to go along?" Chapman explained, nonchalantly extending an invitation.
"No thanks brother…I've seen what floats in that water"
Chapman snickered. "Oh well, I got to get moving. Good to meet you Lew. Catch you guys later. Maybe by the time we get back I'll be able to take a hot shower, huh?"
"Maybe," Stottlemeyer said. "But it'll cost ya a few beers. See ya later."
Lew watched Chapman a few seconds before turning to Stottlemeyer. "Seem like an O.K guy."
"Yeah, he is but, he's also a little too Gung-ho for a corpsman. I think he'd rather be a *jarhead*." The man set the wrench down. "There," he confidently announced. "That should do it. Now, all we have to do is see if we got any leaks. Go over there and open that valve."
Lew took a few steps over to a spigot and turned the handle. The sound of water flowing through the pipe gave encouragement that the system would work. Water gurgling inside the tank subsided, indicating it was filled to capacity. When neither of the men found any leaks they both displayed broad smiles. "All right!" Stottlemeyer happily exclaimed. "Let's fire this muther up." He flipped the switch. "Now, all we have to do is wait a few minutes for the water to heat up and we'll be ready to go."
Lew lit a smoke as they waited. "You hear anything more about LaPorte?" he casually asked.
"No…. nothing confirmed anyway. Somebody heard that a blonde-hair Caucasian was spotted leading a Viet Cong patrol but, I think its bullshit."
"Where did you hear that?"
"It's just floating around. If it's true, it might not be LaPorte. It could be a Russian you know."
"I guess it could be?"
Stottlemeyer reached inside the stall and turned the handle. A shot of escaping air belched out a couple times before a weak flowing stream of fairly hot water spewed out of the shower head. "All

right!" Stottlemeyer yelped. "We're in business. I'm going to get a towel."

Happy with their success, Lew proudly declared, "We did it! You're one hell of a plumber man."

"Go get your towel. You can get in after me."

"Are you crazy? Don't you realize it's about a hundred degrees out here already? Nah, I think I'll pass."

"Yeah. Maybe you're right. I'll try it out tonight when its cooler."

Lew changed the direction of the conversation. "Hey, I think I'm going over to First Med. a little later this afternoon. You want to go?"

"No man, I got a backlog of stuff I need to do. I've been putting it off too long since working on this thing."

Lew donned his utility shirt. "Okay, just thought I'd ask. Anyway, I got to get back to the hootch so I'll catch you later, O.K?"

"Sure. Hey, thanks for your help man. I really appreciate it."

"Buy me a beer."

"You're on."

Lew had the driver stop the six-by in front of the medical battalion. He jumped down from the bed onto the dusty road and crossed over to the guard post. The Marine Private standing guard at the entrance halted him. "Sorry Doc, you're gonna have to remove the magazine and unload your weapon."

"No problem," Lew complied clearing the chamber and putting the magazine back into the ammo pouch. The Marine checked to see the selector switch was on 'safe' before letting Lew pass.

When he got to the orderly room he didn't hesitate entering.

"What do ya need Doc?" the duty corpsman behind the counter asked.

Before answering, Lew scanned the room hoping to surprise Rappaport. He didn't see his friend. "Ah, I'm looking for Rappaport. Is he around?"

The corpsman searched his memory.

"Rappaport…Rappaport..Ah, I don't know any Rappaport."

"Maybe you know him as Heeb," Lew tried to provoke a recall.

"Oh yeah. Heeb. Now I know who you're talking about," then abruptly added. "He's not here anymore."

Surprised, Lew inquired. "Not here? Do you know where he is then?"

"Best guess…New York City." The corpsman casually responded. "He rotated back home a couple weeks ago. Lucky bastard."
The news was disappointing. He didn't realize that his buddy was due to rotate out so soon. His mind was at ease though. He promised Heeb that he'd stop by some time and at least he kept his word. He thanked to orderly room corpsman and headed back to Camp Reasoner.

Waiting alongside the busy, dusty road for somebody to offer him a ride the realization that the two people he truly could call friends were no longer around. Mild despair settled into his crawl. A convoy of trucks rolled past kicking up a dust storm that coated him from head to foot with fine powdery particles. It stuck to his sweaty face and arms while working its way into every crease, fold and pocket. Worse yet, it had completely covered the rifle, accumulating on all surfaces. A Marine jokester riding in back of one of the trucks called out, "HEY BUDDY, TAKE A BATH YOU PIG." He could only imagine what he looked like but threw a good-natured finger wave back at them, figuring that they were on their way to an operation somewhere and most likely some of them wouldn't go home alive. Shortly after the convoy had passed an Army sergeant riding a Honda motorbike stopped and offered him a lift. He accepted and they scooted down the road toward the Recon compound.

"Holy shit Doc!" Pee Wee blurted out when he saw the corpsman enter the hootch. "You look like …….."
"I know," Doc interrupted. "Like a pig."
"Maybe we should call you 'Dusty Doc' from now on," Unkle tossed in his two cents worth.
"Maybe Dirty Doc," Johnson joined in the ribbing.
"Yeah, yeah, yeah. Go ahead, dish it out. I can take it."

The cold shower felt good in the heat of the afternoon. After cleaning up and changing uniform Lew set about to work on cleaning his rifle. Exasperated from knowing that he worked so hard on getting it immaculate the day before, he now had to do it all over again.

While busying himself cleaning the weapon, Doc heard helicopters making their approach toward the landing pad. He looked through the screening to see the CH-34's descend and vanish just beyond the showers.

"*Dogma's* back," Unkle shared his knowledge. "Wait 'til they hear about what happened to us. They'll be glad they didn't go with us."

"You goin' to tell 'em?" Pee Wee asked.

"Nah. Woody's up there. He'll tell let 'em know. Right now, I'm goin' to chow…anybody else goin'?"

Arthurs grabbed his mess gear to accompany Unkle.

"Hey Doc, maybe a little later on you and me can start your chess lessons," Private Johnson offered as he fetched his mess gear to join the other two.

Lew took a drag, "Sure, why not?" he half-heartedly accepted.

"Good. I'll get with you later."

Pee Wee stayed behind and sat down across from Lew. "You not going to eat Doc?"

"I'll go later when the line goes down, besides I'm just not all that hungry."

"Me neither. I guess I'll go when you go." The corporal picked up the rifle barrel. "Here, I'll do the bore," he volunteered.

"If it'll make you happy you can do the whole damned thing," Lew quipped.

Pee Wee let out a little laugh "Just the barrel Doc, just the barrel."

As they neared completing the task, Pee Wee casually mentioned that he heard the rumor of a blonde man reported being seen with the *gooks.*

"Yeah, I heard that earlier today too," Doc advised. "I don't think it's true."

"Who knows?"

Later that evening, under the dim light of a 60 watt bulb, Private Johnson explained to Doc the various ways that chess pieces have to move on a chess board, along with the rules of the game. The corpsman caught on quick and the two began a game for practice. Doc felt confident that he would give Johnson a game; prematurely boasting "Watch out now Mr. Johnson, you're playing against Bobby Fischer's future nemesis." Two moves later Johnson had him checkmate. In total surprise over Johnson's easy win, Lew spouted out, "How the hell did you do that man? You didn't even give me a chance!"

Johnson's dark face beamed a big, split-toothed smile as he leaned back and raised his pipe to light it. "Doc, I think you should play one or two more games before you go an' take on Fischer."
"Hey damn it, wait a minute. I demand a rematch." Lew insisted.
"Okay Doc, only this time *think*," Johnson emphasized pointing a finger to his head.
The second game lasted somewhat longer but, still produced the same result. "Well, at least I'm getting the hang of it," Doc uttered.
"Yeah Doc, you're doing just great," Johnson grinned facetiously.
Everyone spent the remainder of their free time that night reading, writing letters, playing cards or sacking out early.

Sergeant Holton entered the hootch shortly before everyone sacked out. "Listen up men,"
He drew their attention. "We got a mission set for the day after tomorrow so don't go anywhere tomorrow until we get our briefing, got it?"
An assortment of replies indicated everyone understood.
"Ok, I'll even shut the lights off for. G'nite girls."

It was well into mid-morning when Holton came to brief the men on their next mission. He made sure everyone was present before gathering them in a close, semi-circle. "Okay men, let's gather 'round here," he gave them a minute. "The skinny is that we're going to replace a team on a mountain top, observation post called *Dong Din.* It's not supposed to be too bad up there since we've been using it a long time. Should be plenty of built-up bunkers and fox holes already dug. We'll be there about a week so take along plenty of food, water and reading material."
"We've been there before Sarge. It ain't that bad." Unkle offered as-a-matter-of-factly.
Holton nodded. "Okay, that's good. At least some of you *old-salts* are already familiar with the place and will be able to help us new guys out," he half-grinned. "Staff Sergeant Woodcock won't be coming on this one so; I'll be the patrol leader. If you got any questions, concerns or gripes, come see me first....that clear?"
Assuming all had understood he continued. "Be ready to go and muster at the pad at 1300hrs." Looking around at the pickings he

began assigning tasks. "Unkle, you and , ah....ah...Doc get the frag list."
"DOC?" Pee Wee squeaked. "Corpsmen don't do that shit Sarge," he enlightened the still green sergeant.
"Hey, I don't mind," Doc spoke up.
Pee Wee's remark made Holton change his mind. "No, Palmer's right. I forgot. Corpsmen need to do other things. Arthurs, you help Unkle. Pee Wee, you and Johnson get the C-rats delivered and Doc, you just do whatever you need to do."
The sergeant was about to leave when he recalled another bit of information. "Oh yeah, I almost forgot. We'll be taking a radioman from battalion along for the ride. He'll be helping us out since we're short a couple men but, *scuttle-butt* has it that we'll be getting replacements for Whelchel and Gilmore after we get back from this one. Awright, carry on Marines."
After Sergeant Holton disappeared from view Johnson nudged the corpsman. "Looks like you and me will get time to work on your game, huh Doc?" he smirked.
The corpsman returned a slight smile in response.

The remainder of the day was spent getting ready for the mission. By evening everyone had gotten their gear and weapons in order and except for the ordinance were all set to go. The C-rations and 'jerry cans' of water were to be bulk loaded on the choppers rather than individually carried by each man. The only thing left to do was to get a good night's sleep.

Clanking of metal food trays woke Doc. Sitting up in the cot he reached for his morning cigarette.
"Hey Doc, better get up and get some chow," Arthurs advised. "Can't go on a mission on an empty belly."
"Can't play chess on an empty stomach either," Johnson smirked.
"From what I saw he can't play either way," Pee Wee kidded. "Come on Doc, get ready, we'll wait for you," he added.
Lew blew out a stream of white smoke. "Nah, I'll wait for lunch. You guys go without me."
"Suit yourself," Unkle chimed in. "But, breakfast is always better than that shit they have for lunch."
The four of them left together, leaving Lew alone in the hootch.

After finishing his smoke, Doc grabbed his towel and headed for the showers. When he returned he found Corporal Pistorino tossing letters and packages on the men's cots. "Mail call, Doc," he grinned. "I think I have a letter here for you too," he searched through the stack. "Here 'ya go," he handed the corpsman two envelopes.
"Thanks," Lew smiled accepting the pleasant surprise. "This is the first mail I got in a few weeks."
"Here's a package for Johnson, where's his rack?"
Lew pointed to Johnson's cot then silently made his way over to his lawn chair, checking the return addresses, seeing one was from his mother and the other from his sister. He couldn't decide which to open first. He chose his mother's letter first.

Dearest Son,
I hope you're well and in good spirits. We're all doing fine here. Oh how I wish you were here with us now for I have some sad news. Pupy passed away last week.

Unprepared for the news that his grandfather died, Lew felt his heart sink. He recalled the time when he was aboard ship in the Pacific and received the same news about his grandmother. He was so shaken that he couldn't work. He continued reading the letter.

Uncle John went to visit and found him. He was dead a few days before he found him. He must have died peacefully in his sleep. We buried him next to Grandma. Now, he's in heaven with her. Please don't let this bother you. He lived a long, hard, coal miner's life and is sure to be rewarded. You know God has a plan for all of us.

He stopped mid- sentence, unable to read further through watery eyes

The news hit him hard. Reaching for another cigarette he folded the letter and set it aside. For the moment the only thing he had on his mind was going home. He didn't want to be here. He stared at the letter a few minutes then read it again before finally accepting the fact that it was of no use to dwell on something he had no control over. He resigned himself to grieve privately. Wiping a single tear from his eye he put the letter away and opened the one from his sister. It too contained news about his grandfather as well as a few small, family related items. Extinguishing the cigarette under his boot Lew stashed away the letters in the bottom of the foot locker then kicked back into the chair. He felt obligated to mask his emotions from the others. The last thing he wanted was to give any impression of weakness to his comrades.

The huge CH-53 helicopter arrived at the landing pad at Camp Reasoner shortly before 1300hrs. The team waited for the signal to begin loading the cases grenades, C-rations and jerry cans filled with water. The men individually shuttled the supplies onboard rather than forming a line but, within a few minutes they were airborne and on their way to the Dong Din observation post.

After a short flight from the Recon compound the CH-53 Sea Stallion barely had room to land on the small, dirt, landing area, scraped out of the mountain top. Team *Countersign* exited from the rear ramp with scarcely enough room to negotiate around the large craft without being blown off the mountain from the rotor blast. Unkle and Pee Wee both recognized some of the men on the team from Echo Company as the two teams passed each other for the swap-out. Unkle stopped one of them and screamed something into his ear; sparking a return laugh. After the beast lifted off and the dust settled, the new arrivals commenced to survey their surroundings before to setting up 'house'.

Doc strolled along the well-worn pathway that tracked across the very crest of the hill. It led from the landing pad to a sandbagged fortification at the far end of the crest. Several other surface built bunkers lined each side of the pathway. One, larger bunker had a sandbag covered, metal roof that could shelter several men while smaller, entrenchments provided one or two man 'digs'. There was a fortified, communications bunker topped with tall antenna mast. A small American flag fluttered from one of its guy wires. Thousands of discarded C-rations cans surrounding the barren peak created a knee-deep, debris field in all directions that served as alarm if anyone attempted to breach the outpost. Little regard was given to health concerns that the trash heap presented as the Sun cooked food remnants that invited swarms of flies, as well as rodents and monkeys.

The stench took some time to get used to but, eventually one did.

Pee Wee caught up with Doc as the medic paused at the top of the hill to light up a smoke.
"What a view, huh, Doc?"
"Man, this is remarkable. I'll bet you can see a hundred miles," Lew awed, referring to an unobstructed view of sunlight shimmering off the expanse of water of Da Nang Bay with Monkey Mountain barely visible farther in the distance to the east. A river cut through the green, valley below; discharging the muddy flow into the bay. Near the mouth of the river on the sand flats was a small fishing village and farther inland, flooded rice paddies took up most of the real estate. Surrounding their position were several ranges of lush, jungle entangled mountains and valleys. Between two ridges on the northwest side was the portal leading into the infamous Happy Valley. For the corpsman, the entire view was breathtaking. It was a picture right out of National Geographic.
"Hey, you men," Holton broke the trance. "Better get yourselves squared away."
"Right Sarge," Pee Wee replied.
"I'm going to go with Anderson and set up com.," the sergeant informed them. Anderson was the radioman who volunteered to come along for this mission.

Doc claimed accommodations inside the large, covered bunker, along with Johnson and Arthurs. Despite its large appearance from the outside, the inside was cramped with only enough headroom to allow for a slouching posture.
"Look here Doc," Arthurs flipped open the centerfold from a Playboy. "Somebody left us a library."
Lew took an extended glance at the healthy looking image. "Oh yeah, that's what I'm fightin' for!" he ad libbed, dropping his gear in one corner.
Unkle popped his head inside. "Holton said to tell you guys to get a case of C's for each man and can of water for your hootch."

After everyone retrieved their rations and returned to their "Home-Sweet-Hole" they set about with the arduous task of blowing up the rubber air mattresses. There was a price to pay for any form of creature comfort and inflating the mattress' by mouth was the small toll. The procedure had to be repeated daily since most of the mattresses leaked. Doc worked intermittently; taking puffs from a cigarette, exhaling then drawing a deep breath to force his lungs to expel as much air as possible into the rubber bladder. The process eventually left him gasping for oxygen and light-headed. It took him longer than his peers but finally was able to inflate the object to the desired firmness. "Whew!" he commented. "I gotta quit smoking."

"You certainly should Doc." Arthurs agreed. "Why anybody smokes and ruins their God-given body confounds me."

"You know," the corpsman began. "You're right. Someday I'll quit but, I'm not ready yet."

"Tell me something Doc. What the hells' the difference between catching a bullet in the brain in Vietnam and rotting away your lungs? Either way you're going to die."

"About fifty years difference," Doc came back.

Arthurs shook his head then dropped the subject.

Doc lit another smoke.

After the men had time to get settled in Sergeant Holton called them together at the radioman's bunker.

"Here's the deal men," he began. "We're going to need to man the positions at the north and south sides of this here place. I want two men in each hole from sunset to dawn. I don't care who does it just as long as it gets done. I'm going to be with Anderson most of the time but, I'll make my rounds to check on you all. Doc will be the relief man. If anybody needs a break he'll relieve you. Is everyone clear on that?" he scanned the men's faces.

"What about daytime?" Unkle questioned.

"We still got to man the positions with at least one man during the day. I don't care how you guys do it. We're going to be flexible." Holton's eyes once again scanned their faces. "If you see or hear anything, come get me." He paused to look up toward the sky. "It looks like we're going to have a clear night ahead of us so we might as well get started." He dismissed the men.

Without hesitation Unkle assumed the lead. "I'll take the south side now. One of you guys can come over a little later."

"I'll go with you now," Arthurs spoke. "We got nothing else to do."

Pee Wee followed up. "Yeah, I'll take the north side."

Without saying anything Johnson tagged along with Pee Wee. Doc stood there alone.
"If you need me, I'll be in the bunker playing with myself," he attempted a little humor.
"So, what else is new," Unkle blurted back as he led Arthurs down toward their position.
The corpsman had to counter the remark. "Unkle, you can kiss my dupa."

Darkness fell swiftly on the remote outpost. Unable to nap, Doc emerged from the bunker to check on the men in the fighting holes. The cloudless sky and bright moonlight clearly highlighted the entire area, giving near daylight visibility. Moon beams reflected off the waters of Da Nang Bay and the lights of the city glowed farther beyond it. Even, solitary leaves of the surrounding jungle foliage seemed to illuminate as they absorbed the beams. The river below looked like a strand of flowing silver. Working his way along the well-lighted path he could easily see figures of two Marines casually standing watch from inside the hole overlooking the river. They saw him coming. "Hey Doc," Pee Wee greeted. "Wazza matter? Can't sleep?"
"I got a couple hours. What about you? One of you guys want to get some Z's?"
"Nah. We're okay. Maybe Unkle or Arthurs might."
"I'll check them in a couple minutes," Doc spoke as a piece of equipment that emitted a greenish glow caught his attention. "What the hell's that thing?"
"It's a *Star-lite* scope Doc. It lets you see in the dark as long there's some light out. Want to try it?"
"Sure. How's it work?"
"Just hold it up to your eye and aim it at what you want to look at....gotta be careful though. Don't look directly into any light 'cause it'll blind you," Pee Wee instructed.
"You need to remember that the green light reflects back into your eye," Johnson cautioned. "Makes for a good head shot if *Charlie* sees it."
"Yeah," Pee Wee confirmed. "You should try to cuff the eyepiece with your hand. You can adjust the focus with this ring," he showed the corpsman.

Doc brought the instrument to his eye and commenced scanning the river. The image was grainy and shaky but, it did offer much better vision than the naked eye. Spotting an object floating in the river he held on it. "Something's floating in the river. It looks like a canoe."

"We already seen that Doc," Johnson attempted a jest. "We called it in as a miniature VC submarine. The *Galveston* off shore working on a firing solution right now."

Palmer joined in. "Yeah, and the *Oriskiny* sending a torpedo plane just in case that don't work."

Skeptical of the explanation the corpsman inquired further, "Submarine. I never heard of a VC sub. Why didn't we get the skinny on that?"

"Hell Doc, we did, months ago…before you came on board." Pee Wee insisted, then added, "Actually, they aren't true submarines. They're actually one-man, suicide torpedoes covered with a hollowed-out log to disguise them. They float down river into the bay until they get close enough to an unsuspecting ship for the pilot to take over controls and ram it and die heroically for his buddy, Ho Chi Minh."

"You know," Johnson elevated the explanation. "It's the same thing as the Japanese 'Ky-Tans' used in the big war. Same-o, same-o."

Doc fell for it. "Maybe we should tell Sergeant Holton about it."

Pee Wee searched for a quick response. "He already knows. He's the one calling in the naval gunfire. Just sit down and relax. There should be some fireworks soon."

Doc began to take a seat. "Godammit Doc," Johnson blurted out, pushing the corpsman aside. "Be careful. You almost sat on the Claymore trigger."

"Sorry man. I didn't know it was there," Doc apologized and moved over.

The three of them sat quietly for several minutes, keeping watch on the object in the river. Enjoying the success of their prank, Palmer and Johnson found it difficult not to laugh. Several more minutes passed before Holton came up from behind.

"How's things goin?" he seriously inquired.

"Good Sarge," Pee Wee answered quickly; hoping that the NCO would accept the response and leave them to continue their prank.

"Just waiting to watch the shelling, Sarge" Lew let the cat out of the bag.

"What shelling? What's goin on here?"
Realizing that the jig was up Palmer confessed. "Shit Sarge, you ruined it. We had Doc on the hook and was reeling him in. We had him convinced that the log in the river was a VC submarine."
"Younze bastards," Doc remarked in Pittsburghese, embarrassed that he'd been taken in so easily.
Holton wasn't amused. "You're supposed to be paying attention on your watch, not playing games." he scolded. "Don't let this shit happen again. You hear me?"
Both men agreed but, secretly relished taking the hoax as far as they did.
Doc walked along with the sergeant over to the opposite side of the outpost to where Unkle and Arthurs were positioned.
"I got to admit Doc, that was a pretty good joke those guys pulled," Holton confided.
"I can't believe they sucked me in like that. Man, I should have known better."
"They probably would have fallen for it too if the shoe was on the other foot."
"Maybe?"

As the two approached the south side foxhole Unkle relayed an acute observation. "Hey man, you two would be real good targets for snipers with the moon out like this."
"Let 'em try" Holton retorted. "He'll probably miss; we'll see the muzzle flash and call in tons of arty and overwhelm his dumb, sorry, ass with fire power."
"Is that how you Georgia boys hunt 'possum, Sarge? Overwhelming fire power?"
"Cripes son," Holton mocked a drawl. "Hell no. One shot's all we need."
The sergeant's answer sparked a challenge in Unkle's mind. "Say. Why don't we have ourselves a shootin' match tomorrow? It'll give us something to do and keep our shootin' eye sharp," he suggested.
"We can do that, Holton affirmed. "In the meantime, how you men doin'? Everything O.K.?"
"No problem here Sarge." No sooner than Unkle got the words out than a commotion broke out on the slope below them. The clamoring of empty cans on the hillside alerted them that

something was engulfed in the mess. Holton, Arthurs and Doc poised the weapons toward the noise.
"Relax," Unkle calmly let his experience talk. "It's only monkeys trying the scrape out some food. You'll hear it all night. If it was a man there would be a lot more noise. Nobody can make it up that heap without being heard. Not even *Charlie*."
Feeling at ease from Unkle's reasoning the men lowered their weapons. "It's good we have somebody who knows what the hell's going on," Holton stated. "Anyway, remember Docs available to stand watch if you need him."
"Yeah. Just come and get me," the corpsman confirmed.
"I think we'll be okay, Sarge. We'll take turns getting some Z's," Unkle assured.
"All right then, I'll be with Anderson if you need me," Holton advised as he and Doc began walking back up the path.
"You'd better try and get some sleep Doc," Holton recommended. "You might need it."
"Yeah, I suppose I should while I can," Lew agreed as they approached the bunker. He got to his knees and crawled inside.

Sometime during the night heavy, rain laden, clouds moved in and deposited a constant deluge. Thunder and lightning woke Doc from an uneasy sleep. A torrent of water flowed down along the pathway and into the bunker, pooling in the far corner where Arthurs' gear was stowed. Doc shined a flashlight and moved to put the gear on higher ground then, struggled in the confined space to find and don his poncho. The downpour pelted his exposed face as he worked his way around the outside of the bunker in an effort to find a place to penetrate the sandbagged wall in order to create a drain hole. He realized that if he couldn't construct a drain the entire bunker would be knee-deep in water within minutes. He kneeled down in the mud and began to dig out a hole with his bare hands under the bottom layer of bags. The earth under the bag was compacted nearly as hard as concrete. Sensing urgency, he remembered seeing an entrenching tool earlier up at the radio bunker. Jumping to his feet he sloshed his way up through the muddy mess to the
other bunker. The "E-tool" was still there. He retrieved it and returned to begin the excavation. Even though the temperature dropped drastically because of the altitude and cloud cover, he worked up a sweat as he feverishly coaxed small chunks of earth

away from under the bag. He quickly reached the point of near exhaustion as he strained to carve out the breach. Wind-blown sprays of ice-cold water saturated his bare hands as he clutched the shovel handle tightly, sending shivers throughout his body. Large pellets of water hitting his face and eyes obstructed his vision yet, he continued digging. There was a point that he thought about just giving up, reasoning that this was not the most important thing to concern himself with; that when it's all said and done, no one would even appreciate his effort. Resolute, he kept digging, mainly because he started it and wasn't about to quit. It was a personal test of his mettle. Several more impacts of the E-tool finally tore away the plugging, earthen barrier, allowing the surge from inside to escape through the makeshift portal. Tired but satisfied with his accomplishment he got to feet and watched as the muddy stream washed down the slope away from the bunker. He crawled back inside the bunker to see how much of the water drained out. Except for the steady flow that continued to work its way through the sloping bunker from above the pool had all drained out. Doc sat down, flipped back the hood of the poncho and rewarded himself with a cigarette. Spending the remainder of the night in the shelter, unable to sleep, he tried to get warm by changing socks and brewing up a cup of cocoa mix. By dim candlelight he entertained himself by leafing through soggy Playboys and fantasized about the beautiful women until he eventually was able to close his eyes and doze off.

Sergeant Holton stuck his head inside the bunker. "Hey Doc, what do ya say we relieve the watch in a little bit?"
The corpsman opened his eye to see the sergeant garbed in a wet poncho. Through the entrance behind Holton he saw that it was daylight and the rain was still coming down.
"Yeah, sure. When?"
"How 'bout getting some chow now and relieve Unkle's position at six-thirty" Holton replied. "That'll give you about 20 minutes to shit, shower and shave," he kidded.
"Got it," Lew answered without absorbing the jesting remark.
"Anything I should know?" the corpsman asked half-heartedly, lighting up a smoke.
"Not really. Just try to stay dry and keep your eyes peeled. If something happens, fire off one round. Everybody will hear it. I'll be over in the other hole."

"Right," Doc exhaled the smoke.

Boots heavy with mud, Doc sloshed his way down toward his post through the unrelenting downpour. He saw Unkle and Arthurs sitting outside of the foxhole on a stack of sandbags as he approached. Getting closer he observed that the hole was filled with muddy, brown liquid; making it unusable.
"It's about time you got here Doc," Unkle snipped.
"Hey man, Holton said six-thirty," Lew glanced at his watch. "It's only six twenty-five now. I'm early."
"Well, I hope you got a good night's sleep all dry and cozy in your cave."
As much as Unkle's brash comment irked Lew, he chose not to tell him about the hour or so he spent digging out the drain in the mud. "Hey Arthurs, the cave got flooded. I had to move you gear. You might want to sack out on my rack."
Arthurs nodded without rendering a verbal reply, leading Doc to believe that he agreed with Unkle's comment.
Doc watched the haggard looking men as they slogged up the slippery path then, sat down on the sandbags perch to begin the unpleasant vigil. The rain wasn't letting up as he had hoped. Large drops drummed against the hood of his poncho, dripping onto his face and into his eyes then, cascaded off the tip of his nose. Doc strained to see beyond the curtain of water into the surrounding jungle but, could only make out a subdued, green colored, mass of trees. He spotted two Claymore detonator devices resting on top of the sandbags that fortified the foxhole. It occurred to him that if he had to get to them in a hurry, he would have to jump into the water filled pit. *"Hell, I'm cold and miserable already. What difference would it make,"* he thought. He reached under the poncho and pulled out a cigarette. Shivering uncontrollably, he attempted to light it against the gusting winds with his Zippo. When the lighter didn't produce a flame he realized that it was out of fluid.
"SHIT," he barked angrily then, threw the cigarette away, resolving that he would just have to suffer through the watch without a smoke.

The rain began to let up as noon approached but, the sky remained ugly and overcast.

A few rays of sunlight peeked through the clouds far off to the east, conjuring up hope that the weather conditions might change but, from his vantage point Doc saw the clouds extending far out on the horizon. Logic told him that there was no chance of drying out that day. Dismayed, he started to feel sorry for himself again; thinking about home and wishing he was there; cursing himself for ever enlisting.

"Hey Doc," Johnson's voice interrupted his private rant.
Lew turned to see the Marine coming toward him, glad to see somebody. "Hey bro," Lew greeted the Marine.
"Listen Doc, I like you man but, I ain't your bro, so just put that notion out of your mind until your skin changes color; you eat hog-jowls and you become a member of the A.M.E. Baptist Church in B-more, then, I might……might mind you, let you call me bro."
Knowing Johnson as well as he did, Doc sensed that the man didn't take any real offense by the greeting. "I'll get started on a tan just as soon as the sun comes out," he made light of the situation.
The private smiled, showing the gap between his teeth. "Well, it don't look like you'll get started on it today," then changed the subject. "We just found out that team *Dogma* is going to reinforce us here tomorrow. Holton told me to let everybody know. Now, you know."
"That's good. Maybe we won't be stretched so thin."
"That's if they get here. If the weather keeps up like this the choppers won't fly," Johnson commented. "I'll be back to give you a break in a little while. You need anything?"
"Yeah. Got a light?"
Johnson reached into his pocket and pulled out book of C-ration matches. "Keep 'em Doc."
Lew thanked the Marine for the gift and immediately retrieved a cigarette.

It was late afternoon and still drizzling when Pee Wee showed up to relieve the corpsman.
"Sergeant Holton wants to see ya Doc."
Puzzled, Doc asked. "Wants to see me? Somebody hurt? Where's Johnson? He said he'd be back."

"Aw, he's going to come down later when it starts to get dark. Right now he's catching up on his Z's. Nah, nobody's hurt."
"Okay, I'll catch you later."

Doc sloshed up the muddy path toward the radio bunker, occasionally losing his footing in the slippery quagmire. Pushing the make-shift, poncho door flap aside he found the sergeant alone inside the candle-lit bunker monitoring the radio. Reluctantly asking, "You want to see me Sarge?"
Holton lowered the handset from his ear. "Yeah Doc. Want a swig of hot coffee?" he offered a half-full, canteen cup. The corpsman accepted, welcoming the warm but usually nasty tasting brew. "Thanks."
"You get the word that *Dogma's* going to relieve us tomorrow?" Holton quietly asked.
Doc took a sip. "I was told that they were going to reinforce us."
"Things changed. That was the plan. Now, they're taking over the mission."
"Great!" Lew beamed. "Maybe we all can get dried out."
"Don't get too excited Doc," the sergeant searched for a way to break unpleasant news to the medic. "I hate to tell 'ya this but, I guess you'll have to complete the mission with them."
"What!" the news shocked Lew. "Why?"
Holton took a firmer approach with the answer. "Because you are the platoon Doc and they are our men. They need you with them. You're no use to them back at camp."
Lew dreaded being stuck on the mountain top for another week, especially during the monsoons. Forced to accept the duty he reluctantly uttered, "Well, if I have to...I have to."
Holton understood Doc's dismay but, couldn't alter it. "Look on the bright side Doc. It beats humpin' in the bush."
Knowing the sergeant was right, Doc agreed. "Yeah, I suppose it does."
"You'd better try to dry out and get some rest now."
Lew handed back the cup. "Yeah, I suppose I should."

Inside the candle-lit shelter Lew change his socks and cooked up a can of Beans and Franks from his rations using a bit of C-4 explosive. The two Privates had already left to man their posts. Scooping the food into his mouth he noticed that the pool of water had completely drained, leaving behind a layer of mud that was in the process of slowly drying out. He was proud that his effort paid off, even though it went completely unnoticed. Weary from the long day he quickly finished his meal then, added more air to the mattress. Using the poncho as a blanket, wrapped it around his body, hoping the captured warmth would dry the damp clothing he was wearing.

Sometime during the course of the night, several droplets of cold water splashed unto his face from above.
"Damn," he muttered. "The roof's leaking." Moving out from under the dripping he heard the sound of rain drops bombarding the canvas sheet used to cover the bunker.
"When is this miserable shit going to end?"

It was nearly dawn when Lew woke stiff and sore from the contortions he made throughout his restless sleep. He reached for a smoke. The flickering match revealed that the other two men were still at their posts as a blissful moment of expelling the effect of beans and franks interrupted his lighting the cigarette. The taste of smoke mixing with morning breath compelled him to unconsciously swirl his tongue around the inside of his mouth and across the front of his teeth. "Ugh."
The cigarette dangled precariously from his lower lip as he fumbled in the dark to stuff his feet into the still wet, mud covered jungle boots. The heat from his body managed to dry out the "tiger-striped" uniform as he had hoped for but, he could still feel the dampness in the boots coming though the dry socks. After skirmishing with the boots he parted the canvas flap to get a look outside. It was still cloudy and drizzling but, far out in the South China Sea he saw traces of pink light, glowing from below the horizon. It was a sure sign that the weather was going to get better as the day progressed. Lew flicked the butt away with his finger and exited the bunker with the poncho in hand. Relieved to be able to stand fully upright he gave his body a vigorous stretch then headed straight for the radio bunker.
Taking a few steps he realized he forgot his rifle. "Shit." Making an abrupt turnabout, the corpsman lost his footing and fell butt-first into the muck, giving his entire backside a thick, wet coating. Letting loose a barrage of expletives he righted himself and began scraping away as much as he could with his bare hand, unaware that he was being observed.

"Hey Doc Lewis," Anderson got his attention. "You O.K?"
Embarrassed by having been seen, Doc offered a stupid explanation "Yeah, I'm all right. Just practicing…that's all."
"Huh?"
"Just kidding man…..just kidding," Lew let it go at that and returned to the bunker for the rifle.

Sergeant Holton took one look at the corpsman as he entered the radio bunker and produced a big *shit-eatin'-grin.* "Geeze Doc, you look like you've been wallowing around with the sows. What happened?"
"All I'm going to say is that it's slippery out there," Doc answered simply, divulging the circumstances for his appearance in a roundabout manner.
"Okay. I'll respect your private compulsion to play in mud puddles."
"Looks like the weathers going to get better," Doc turned the subject around.
"It's supposed to. We should be hearin' something pretty soon about being relieved. My guess is that the change-over is going to take place sometime this mornin'. Why don't you go and round up the men. Tell 'em to get their shit together and be ready to go at any time."
"Sure."
"Make sure they don't leave their post unmanned until the chopper gets here."
"Okay. Will do."

A light rain continued to fall throughout the morning but, not enough to prevent the chopper from flying. It appeared from the east, flying under the cloud cover and circled the outpost briefly to locate the LZ. The pilot set the aircraft down slowly on the narrow, inclined pad. Once the heavily burdened aircraft made contact with the muddy surface it began to sink into sludge and at the same time began sliding backward toward the edge of the steep mountain slope. Sensing eminent danger the pilot revved the powerful engines full throttle, sending a forceful spray of mud in all directions; splattering everything and everyone within a hundred feet of it. The slurry was no match for the powerful machine as it plucked itself out of the sloppy muck and pulled clear of the slick mountain top perch.

The craft slowly circled the outpost before the pilot informed the recon team's radioman that he was going to attempt to hover, tail first, at the highest point of the LZ in order to on and off-load the troops and supplies. It was a dangerous maneuver since the rear rotor blades would be nearer the surface of the ground because of the incline, making an approach from the rear too dangerous. The team boarding the craft would have to be pre-positioned along the edge of the LZ; the relieving team would disembark from the rear ramp and exchange positions with the first team.

Doc watched the impromptu coordination from his bunker. Cases of rations, munitions and cans of water were tossed out of the cargo bay directly into the mud prior to the swap-out. The crew chief and pilot showed tremendous skill and coordination in maintaining a hover that allowed about a foot distance between the ramp door and the ground. The teams passed each other exchanging comments and playful expletives. Team *Dogma* hunkered down near the edge of the slope as the chopper powered up and rose into the air. Once the bird was clear of the LZ, the team got to their feet and made their way up the slope toward the bunkers. Standing in the drizzle, still wearing his poncho, Doc greeted them sarcastically. "Hey guys, welcome to bee-u-tee-full, Dong Din."
Unexpectedly, his welcoming remark was received with a casual indifference as the men passed by. Lance Corporal "Rocky" Schmidt was the only one who rendered a smile as he passed by. Doc noticed a few unfamiliar faces in the file, but it didn't matter since he was now accustomed to seeing a regular turnover of troops in the company.

The veteran sergeant, "Findley" Johnson was the patrol leader and ensured everyone was settled in and assigned duties before lunch. PFC Jones and Lance Corporal Mervin moved into the bunker with Doc. Both men were FNG's, joining the platoon three days earlier. Another new man, Sergeant Clifford, joined the *Dogma* team before Jones and Mervin arrived but, Lew hadn't had the opportunity to meet him. Doc knew that in the days ahead he would get to know each of them very well.

Team "Dogma"

Mervyn, Pee Wee Palmer, Allen, Bolinski, Johnson, Jones & Pistorino

By mid-afternoon the clouds disappeared and the sun started to evaporate the moisture from the saturated earth, giving off surrealistic wisps of steam that climbed into the air and dissolved without a trace. Living conditions went from cold and miserable to hot and miserable in less than three hours' time. The veteran "salts" were accustomed to the extreme changes in weather but, the new men were weak and nauseated from the sudden shift. Doc told those men to find shade, take salt tablets and drink plenty of water.

"If any of you guys stop sweating, let me know *mos-skochie.* You need to look out for each other too. If you see your buddy not sweating, come get me fast, OK?"

Findley Johnson overheard the corpsman's instructions. "You men can strip down to your skivvy shirts if you want. That goes for everybody. Doc, why don't you go and tell everybody what you told these guys."

“I was planning to Findley,” Lew calmly mentioned then, suddenly realized he called the sergeant “Findley”, the same as the more seasoned men addressed him. When Johnson didn’t bother to correct him, Doc assumed that the NCO didn’t mind the familiarity, at least in the field.
Suddenly, the big, brown sergeant firmly spoke out, “What the fuck is that?” He scolded the new man, Jones, when he removed his blouse to reveal a bright, white T-shirt. “You dumb-assed puke. Don’t you know better than to wear a white shirt in the bush,” he huffed. “Take that damned thing off right now,” he demanded then walked away, shaking his head in disbelief.
Even Doc had to snicker when he witnessed the FNG become frazzled by Findley’s authoritarian demand.

Doc approached the foxhole overlooking the now swollen river where ‘Rocky” Schmidt
dutifully stood his post manning the M-60 machine gun.
“And how are you today Mr. Schmidt?” he inquired half in jest, half seriously.
“I’m doin’ good Doc. How about you?”
“Ah, I’m a little tired but, I’ll live.” He went on. “Findley says it’s okay to take off your blouses but, you have to leave your skivvy shirt on.”
“Great.” Rocky quickly got out of his utility shirt.
“Listen man, all you guys need to take salt tablets and drink lots of water. I don’t want anyone dropping from heat stroke,” the corpsman insisted.
“I already did Doc, but, thanks for the reminder.”
“See, I told them I didn’t need to be here. You guys already know how to take care of yourselves,” Lew threw his arms into the air, animating the remark.
“Take it easy Doc, you’ll work up a sweat,” Rocky joked.
“Besides, this is one of the few times we actually had our own corpsman along for the ride.”
Doc hesitated at the Marine’s words, “our own corpsman”. The phrase gave him an added sense of belonging.
“Well, in that case, I guess I’ll stick around,” the medic made light of the situation.
Rocky grinned then asked, “Hey Doc, could you do me a favor?”
Lew grinned. “I’m NOT going to have sex with you.”

The comment drew a refrained laugh. "Nah, you're not my type. Would you get me one of those LURPS and bring it here. I forgot to grab one."
The term puzzled the corpsman. "LURP, what the hell is that?"
"Get with it Doc. They're the new-fangled, freeze-dried, Long Range Patrol Rations. LURP for short. All you do is add water. They're pretty good."
"Never heard of 'em. Where they at?"
"There should be a couple cartons mixed in with the "C's" down in our bunker. See if you can find a Beef Stew."
"Beef Stew, aye." Doc advised. "I'll be back after I check on the other position."
"Take your time. I'm not goin' anywhere."

Lew traversed the crest of the mountain top to the opposite position and came upon Corporal "Bo" Bolinski puffing on a cigarette, sitting next to the flooded foxhole rather than getting down inside it. "Wazza matter Bo, don't want to go swimmin'?"
"Hey Doc." Bo greeted him. "What brings you to this neck of the woods?"
"Just came to let you know that Findley said it's okay to take off your utility blouse but, you have keep your skivvy shirt on."
The corporal nodded; flicked the cigarette down the littered hillside and commenced removing his blouse.
"Oh yeah," Doc added. "You need to take your salt tabs and drink lots of water too."
"Got it covered Doc."
"I knew you would," he answered politely. "You're probably used to this kind of weather, huh?"
"No Doc, this ain't nothin' like Florida weather. Compared to this, Florida is mild."
The corpsman wanted to stay and chat a little while longer but felt obligated to fulfill Rocky's request. "Well, I gotta take care of something. I'll talk to you later."
"Yeah man, later."

When Lew returned to the bunker he found Jones and Mervin sleeping soundly, resting up for their turn on watch. Quietly, he rummaged through the carton of LURP rations looking for the Beef Stew that Rocky asked for. He found the brown, plastic package labeled *Beef Stew* and another one for himself to try labeled *Spaghetti.*

"Here's you dinner partner," Doc tossed the packet to Rocky. "That what you wanted?"
Rocky glanced at the label. "Yep, sure is. Thanks Doc," he smiled.
"I think I'm going to try one of these myself. How's the spaghetti?"
"That's good too." Rocky stretched out an arm toward the ground, inviting the corpsman to join him. "Pull up a chair."
Lew watched as Rocky cut open the packet with his K-Bar and poured the contents on the ground. He sifted through the items, selecting which one he'll keep, stuffing the unwanted items back into the empty pouch. He poured water into his canteen cup and held it over a piece of lighted C-4 to bring the water to a simmer. Lew copied the Marine's movements. When the water was hot enough it was poured into the entrée' packet and stirred with a plastic spoon then, set aside to absorb the water. After a minute it was ready to eat. Once the corpsman tasted the fare he was surprised at the result. "Holy shit," he exclaimed. "This is good shit."
"Yeah, it's not too bad. Yours is better if you mix cheese in with it," Rocky submitted.
While the pair sat there, consuming the rations and observing the valley and river below, Sergeant Clifford casually approached them from behind. "How's it going men?"
Rocky swallowed a mouthful of food. "All secure here Sarge."
Clifford nodded acceptance then addressed the corpsman. "So, you're our Doc? Lewis, right?"
"Lewis, aye, Sarge," Doc confirmed.
"Good to finally get to meet up with you Doc. Now I can put a face with a name," he formalized the meeting before continuing. "I got some *skinny* for you guys. See that fishing village?" he pointed out the small village near the beach. "Well, some *grunts* are going to sweep through there in about an hour. You need to keep your eyes open for *gooks* running away from it. If you see them *di-di-ing,* try to get a good bearing where they're heading. We'll call in *arty* on their asses."
Lew asked. "What *grunts?*"
"I think a company from 1/5. Why?"

"Just curious. I have a good friend with 1/1"
"Well, that's all I know Doc. By the way, are you on watch here?"
"Not really. That is, I haven't been detailed a watch… yet."
"No? How would you feel about standing a watch later? We're kinda tight on bodies."
Doc hid the fact that he really disliked standing watch. "Doesn't matter to me. I'm not going anywhere," he tried to answer indifferently.
"Good. I'm going back up to see what Johnson has planned. I'll talk with you guys a little later. In the meantime, keep your eyes peeled."

Doc kept Rocky company for a while, passing time in casual conversation until Clifford returned, informing them that the operation in the village had been cancelled.
"Damn," Rocky softly spoke out. "I was hopin' that I could brush-up on calling in fire missions."
"Yeah, me too," Clifford agreed before turning to the corpsman.
"Doc. How about standing the mid-watch here with Mervyn tonight?" Clifford directed with a question.
The corpsman didn't object. "Sure. I'll go get some sack time and come back later."
"Roger that."

There wasn't a cloud in the night sky. The moon and stars shone brightly and visibility was nearly endless. Far off, the lights of Da Nang etched a faint line across the horizon.
Since the rain stopped and the sun dried the path, the short walk over to the position wasn't as difficult as earlier in the day. Lance Corporal Mervyn was already in position when Doc arrived.
"Mister Corpsman, how the hell are you?"
"I guess as good as can be expected," Doc replied. "How 'bout you?"
"Now that the sun went down I'm feelin' better."
"Good. It takes a while to get acclimated to this place. In a day or two it'll seem like you're a native."
"Not me Doc. I'll never get used to this hell hole."
"Why? Where you from?" Doc asked, lighting up a smoke.
"Alaska," the Marine boasted. "Let me tell you somethin'…..it's the ONLY place to live."

Doc sat down next to the new guy. "Well, maybe someday I'll get there and check it out for myself....once we get outta here."

The pair sat and conversed about their homes and military, duty stations for a couple of hours; learning about each other. Doc let Mervyn do most of the talking until the Marine eventually ran out of things to say. There was a long lull in their conversation before Doc pulled the binoculars away from his eyes. "Holy shit," he murmered, loud enough to pique Mervyn's interest.
"What's up? What do ya' see, Doc?"
Sensing that the Marine was taking the bait Doc answered. "Down there...in the river. It looks like another one of those Viet Cong submarines that we called *arty* in on a couple days ago."
"Huh?
Lew led the new man in circles for a while before confessing to the joke to prevent it from getting out of hand. Mervyn made it clear that he didn't care to be made a fool of.
"Don't go screwing with me Doc. This ain't no place to be playin' games."
Gathering that he touched a nerve Doc apologized and promised that he wouldn't play anymore pranks on the Marine.
The remaining days of the mission was a matter of routine, waiting and watching-watching and waiting. Nothing of significance occurred to break the monotony. Although, Sergeant Johnson did permit everyone to get a couple of shots off using the 30-06 sniper rifle that Mervyn carried in a protective case. The target was a half-submerged, tree stump near the river bank about 700 yards distance since Maggie's *drawers misses* could be seen as splashes in the water. Corporal Pistorino was the *spotter,* calling out hits and misses. Everyone got three shots and all the Marines hit the target at least once. Doc was the last man to shoot and surprised himself and the others by hitting the target twice, placing him in the company of Bolinski, Pistorino and Sergeant Johnson. Only Mervyn got all three direct hits. "That's what life in life in the wilds of Alaska does for 'ya," he boasted with subdued satisfaction. "We got to hunt for our food."

After spending more than ten days on back-to-back missions at Dong Din, Doc was happy to be going back to the compound and take a shower, relax and drink some cold beer. The relief team from Echo Company took over the mission early on the seventh day after team *Dogma* arrived. Once airborne, Doc looked out the porthole and saw that the clouds were forming up to dump more monsoon rain on the outpost. *"Poor bastards,"* he thought as the chopper made a heading due east toward Da Nang.

It was time for noon chow when Doc entered his *hootch*. He didn't know what to do first, eat or shower. Figuring the chow line would close down soon he opted for lunch. Dirty, sweaty and hungry he dropped his gear on the rack, picked up the mess tray and made his way up to the chow hall. No sooner than he got in line that Pee Wee entered the building and hurried over to him. "Doc," he addressed the corpsman urgently "You'd better eat on the run man. There's a platoon of grunts gettin' massacred in Antenna Valley. We're mustering a reaction force. Common, we gotta get movin'."

A fleeting moment of despair jabbed at him. He couldn't believe that he had just gotten back from a double mission and now he had to go back out again without so much as a few minutes rest but, he didn't want to show his reluctance. Without saying a word he reached across the serving line, grabbed a messy rack of spare-ribs to munch on then, took off following Pee Wee down to their *hootch.*

Everyone on the team was in the inside preparing to depart at a moment's notice. Doc noticed Arthurs sitting in *his* chair, intensely monitoring the chatter coming over the radio. "Their getting their asses kicked." he reported. "Sounds like a shit-load of NVA got 'em surrounded." Seeing Doc standing there Arthurs made a move to get up out of the corpsman chair. Doc lowered his hand, palm down, expressing that it was OK for the Marine to stay where he was.

"So, what's going on now?" Doc asked Unkle.

"Hey man, we're just sittin' here on our fuckin' asses…while Marines are getting' killed…waitin' for the word to get movin,'" he snapped back, obviously frustrated from not being able help the Marines in trouble. "That's what happenin' Doc."

The corpsman didn't care for Unkle's attitude but, understood the reason behind.

"Hey man," Pee Wee snapped back at Unkle. "We're just doin' what we're told to do. We all feel the same way about it. Just take it easy man……cool down."

"Fuck you Pee Wee. I'll cool down when I'm ready."
The tension between them broke when Sergeant Woodcock entered. "You men gittin' squared away?"
"Yeah, we're ready," Unkle answered abruptly then asked. "When we hattin' out?"
"Jist as soon as we git the word. Right now all you gotta do is be ready. I'll let ya'll know when the L.T. lets me know," Woody answered in his gruff, animal voice. "Jist hang tight," he added as he left the *hootch*.
The remainder of the afternoon was spent "hanging tight". Every so often Arthurs reported on chatter over the radio until he lost communication. He lowered the handset. "I'm not picking up anything," he calmly stated as he fidgeted with the knobs. "I think maybe the radioman got it"
The *hootch* went quiet as everyone realized that no communication was a bad sign.
Sergeant Holton stepped inside and informed the men to "stand down", explaining that a company of grunts were on their way to rescue the endangered platoon. Frustrated, Unkle clinched his teeth and slammed a fist against his open palm. "Damn it."

After receiving the order the men casually began going about doing other things. Doc finally showered, washing away ten days of crud and shaving off patches of facial hair that resembled fuzz more than whiskers. When he returned he found Arthurs still listening to the radio. "Anything new?" he inquired softly.
"No Doc, nothing coming over the net."
Doc simply nodded then stepped over to his foot locker, pulled out a clean uniform and got dressed. He then lit a cigarette and set about cleaning his rifle as the first priority on the list of things to do in order to get back into a normal routine. Once satisfied that he accomplished all the cleaning up and squaring away his belongings, the corpsman spent the remainder of the evening at the Club enjoying conversation and cold beer.

The next several weeks found the corpsman going out into the *bush* with both team *Countersign* and *Dogma* on several uneventful patrols. During that time many personnel changes occurred within the company. Doc Roshong rotated back to the states; replaced by a corpsman named Robertson. Chief Petty

Officer Freeman replaced the missing senior corpsman LaPorte and a much disliked Major Walker replaced Captain Dixon as Force Company commander. Rumor around the compound had it that Major Walker was heir to the Hiram Walker whiskey empire and could only inherit the family fortune by serving in the Corps. Most of the men in the platoon didn't trust the new commander, thinking that the man's motive for being there was purely selfish. Doc didn't put much weight on the rumor since, to his knowledge, no one had ever bothered to verify the truth but, it didn't stop the rest of the men from hating the new, "old man".

CAN'T HIDE BEHIND A TREE.

By mid-November the corpsman had run a succession of back-to-back patrols with both teams. Fortunately, neither team encountered *Charlie* on any of the patrols. The last unit action the team saw was the patrol where Gilmore and Weasel got killed; that was way back in September. Other teams in Force Company weren't so fortunate. Lance Corporal Jerry DeGray and Sergeant Alan Jensen made the ultimate sacrifice. Their memorial service reminded Doc of the solemn ceremony given for Gilmore and Weasel yet, it somehow didn't seem so personal since he had only a casual acquaintance with them. One man, Sergeant Huff, drowned while on a bridge recon while two men from Alpha Company, PFC Larry Collier and LCPL Rauch and one man from Charlie Company, Sergeant Rudd, were killed in action during the month of October. In the back of Doc's mind was the notion that his team's luck couldn't hold out forever and that they were overdue for another run-in with *Charlie.* Doc likened the situation with Pittsburgh Pirates broadcaster, Bob Prince, who preached the old 'hidden vigorish', meaning, the longer a batter went without a hit, the closer he came to getting one.

During a time in between patrols where Doc was fortunate enough to get some much needed rest, Sergeant Clifford passed the word that two seats were available for anyone who wanted to go on R&R in Tokyo. The only stipulation was that whoever was going had to have the money on hand, since there was no time to go to Disbursing, and had to be ready to leave within the hour in khaki uniform. Doc rummaged through his wallet only to find $45. It

wasn't even enough for a day at China Beach. Arthurs saw the disappointment in Doc's face. "I'll loan ya three hundred Doc."
The corpsman couldn't believe what he was hearing. "You will?"
"Sure. I know you're good for it."
"Yeah, I know I have at least thirteen hundred on the books. I'll pay you back when I return. Okay?"
"No problem."
The Lance Corporal reached into his wallet, pulled out $300 in MPC and handed it to the Doc.
"Just make sure you don't catch no V.D. huh?"
Doc smiled and thanked the Marine but, the smile disappeared when he realized that he didn't have a khaki uniform.
Without saying anything Pee Wee dug out a set of kaki's and tossed them over to the corpsman. "Here ya go Doc. You're a Lance Corporal now!" he said referring to the old rank insignia on the sleeves, "And don't forget the piss-cutter," he added, tossing over the traditional Marine cover.
Clifford interjected, "If you don't have shoes just polish up your boots a little. They ain't too particular down at the terminal."
Doc thanked the men then set about gathering all his stuff together, including the only pair of civilian slacks and shirt he had.
"Hey Doc," Clifford offered up. 'I'll be back to pick you up and drive you to Da Nang just as soon as I can cumshaw a jeep, Okay?"
"Yeah. That'll be great. Thanks." Doc accepted happily.

The 707 was filled with jubilant, young men, excited about their prospects of drinking and debauchery in a civilized country far from the stinking, rotting jungles and rice paddies of Vietnam. Doc supposed that many felt a sense of relief that their life was extended at least one more week. When a beautiful, blonde stewardess offered him a drink he felt his heart race with desire. Despite being underage he asked for and received a cold Budweiser then followed her with his eyes as she moved forward up the aisle with her tight-fitting, mini-skirt clinging to the shape of her round, firm, rear end. His imagination visualized her naked; initiating an immediate tightness surging in his trousers. It was obvious that the girl was enjoying all the attention she was getting from the servicemen. Doc thought one of these guys is going to be lucky enough to spend some time with her in Tokyo but, he knew it wouldn't be him. He experienced a near heart attack when she dropped something on the deck and bent down to pick it up. As she stooped, her short skirt open a little to give Doc a fleeting glimpse of the panty covered mound of womanhood nestled between her legs. Even though he was relieved that he didn't embarrass himself with an unwanted stain he wondered if the girl might have intentionally teased him by spreading her legs a little more than necessary. After all, he heard lots of stories about wild stewardesses.

No one on the flight was prepared for the weather when the plane landed at Tachikawa Air Force Base, Japan a few minutes after midnight. It was winter time and no one gave any thought to bring along appropriate clothing. As quickly as they could the men ran from the airplane and unto the warm buses waiting there to take them to the processing center. After a few minutes of processing the men boarded the busses once again for a lengthy bus ride to their chosen hotels in Tokyo.
Doc chose the Dai Ichi Hotel that was within walking distance to the Ginza and train stations. He learned from his last time in Japan that you could almost go anywhere by train. After checking into his room on the tenth floor, he plopped down on the big, comfortable bed and instantly fell asleep.

It was almost noon when he woke.... time to get moving. He didn't want to waste time sleeping. There were too many things to see and do. The first thing he had to do was purchase a heavy sweater, opting not to buy a coat because of expense. He marched out of the hotel and made his way down a little back alley filled with shops where just about anything could be purchased, some things, very discretely. He found what appeared to be a brown, woolen, Irish, turtleneck sweater for roughly ten dollars, that he felt would suit his purpose nicely. As he left the shop Doc ran into a soldier also on R&R who, after exchanging pleasantries, invited Doc to go with him to the USO a few blocks away. He explained that there was a clothing exchange there where people heading back to the Nam dropped off cloths for those just coming on R&R. He would be able to find a coat there as well as a pair of street shoes instead of the boots he was still wearing.

When the pair walked out of the USO, Lew was decked out in a winter coat and a pair of penny-loafers. Doc thanked the soldier and went on his merry way. He took in the sights and sounds of the bustling Ginza district, the Imperial Palace, the Tokyo Tower and by night fall was drained from all the walking he did. Back in his room he turned the TV on to an English language broadcast. That's when he learned about all the racial conflicts and anti-war protests back in the states. It just wasn't the same place he left six months earlier. The country seemed to be going to hell-in-a-hand-basket. He particularly found distain for the war protestors.

The next day he took the train to Yokosuka, his overseas home port when he was aboard ship. After strolling around the base and meandering through the town's seedy, back streets where he spent nights drinking with his shipmates and carousing with hostesses in the night clubs, he decided he had seen enough and went back to Tokyo by mid-afternoon. At the end of his second day of R&R he was ready to go back to his unit…to be with his Marines but, he still had three days to kill…..somehow.

On the third day of aimlessly, roaming around the city's alleyways he caught sight of a sign in a little, obscure alcove that depicted a kimono-clad, woman giving a man a bath.
It intrigued him enough to enter. Before long he was naked and cautiously, inching his way down into a tub of scalding, hot water. He could barely stand the heat and wanted to forget the whole thing when a pretty young woman forced him down and held him a few seconds until his body got accustom to the water. He felt his body go limp with relaxation. The woman applied lather unto a soft-bristled brush and began scrubbing gently across his back, chest, neck and arms. "You like?" she asked. "Yeah, I like."
"You like more for more yen," she began a proposition.
"How much more?"
"Maybe 500 yen?" she answered coolly as she reached deep into the tub and fondled him as an enticement.
Unable to fend off the feeling he agreed, "OK, 500 yen."
"OK, you stand now," she commanded politely.
Doc grabbed the edge of the tub and raised himself to his feet. The women's soft hands expertly swirled soap up and down his legs, buttocks and then from behind, up under his crotch gently squeezed his testicles and surrounded his stiff, virgin member

with her hand, moving it slowly back and forth for only a few seconds before it exploded with steady streams of long, pent-up seed. The experience made Doc's legs quiver and nearly forced him to collapse from weakness. Almost immediately after his ecstasy the woman instructed him to go to the next room and take a shower. The water was ice-cold. He paid her pleasure ransom and departed in a blissful daze. Later in the day he found a movie theater where *Hombre'* with Paul Newman was showing. He expected it to dubbed in Japanese but it wasn't although, it was sub-titled in Japanese characters that disturbed parts of the picture. That evening he found a dimly-lit place in the cellar of a building just off the Ginza called the *Russian Kitchen.* Even though he thought it too sophisticated for him, he sat and ordered a bowl of Borscht. It was a food he never had but wanted to try it. As he sipped the hot liquid he looked up to see the *Playboy* celebrity, Shel Silverstein, sitting in a booth with a beautiful Japanese woman on each side of him. Doc was tempted to ask for an autograph but, thought that would only serve to lower his own self-esteem.
Low on funds, Doc remained in his hotel room for the remainder of his time on R&R, watching television, except to venture out to find inexpensive food and an occasional local beer. He couldn't wait to get back to his unit.

Finally, back at Tachikawa, the reception center personnel encouraged all troops to give up any contraband in the amnesty box, no questions asked. Within minutes guns, whiskey, pornography, switchblade knives and fireworks were tossed into the box. Everyone suspected that the "permanent party" personnel would keep the objects for themselves but, no one wanted to take the chance of getting court-martialed either so, they gave up their questionable possessions. There was also a clothing rack where returnees could pass along civilian clothing they bought while on R&R to the people just arriving. It was the same courtesy as at the USO in Tokyo but went unnoticed by Doc when he arrived.

A few hours later the air conditioned 707 landed at Da Nang. Doc almost welcomed the heat and familiar stench and was anxious to tell the team about his exploits in Japan. Toting a small AWOL bag he soon hitched a ride on the back of a *six-by* heading in the direction of the Hill 327 PX. When he learned that the vehicle was continuing on toward the Recon compound after it dropped off the other riders at the PX, Doc stayed on board. "WHERE YOU HEADIN' MARINE?" the driver shouted back. At first Doc didn't understand the question but, soon realized that he was wearing Pee Wee's uniform with Lance Corporal stripes sewn on the sleeves. "RECON." He answered over the noise. The driver gave him the 'thumbs-up' signal and proceeded down the bumpy, dusty, highway. Doc almost expected to see changes in the familiar surroundings but, after all, he had only been gone for a few days. The driver down-shifted the beastly machine as it approached the Recon compound then came to a surprisingly subtle stop to let the passenger get off. "Thanks guys," Doc issued a courtesy as he walked past the cab toward the compound gate. The sentry recognized the corpsman and waved him through without a challenge.

Lew recollected Doc Roshong's entrance when he returned from R & R and decided to try it out on his own platoon. Swinging open the *hootch* door the corpsman shouted out, "Honey, I'm home!" There was no reply; only disappointing silence. The *hootch* was empty. He looked around and immediately knew that the team was out on patrol. Everything of value was secure except *his* lawn chair, and that was set up on the opposite end of the building, indicating that someone obviously took advantage of his absence. Figuring out that he was alone and was going to have to wait to share his stories with the men he softy spoke out loud, "It's Okay. It ain't nothin' but a thing anyway."

Next morning he took Pee Wee's khaki uniform up to the trinket shop to get laundered before returning it then, trekked over to the Disbursing Office to withdraw the money that he owed Arthurs. When he returned to the *hootch* he found Sergeant Holton inside with three new replacements.
"Hey Doc, welcome back. How was R&R?"
"Great Sarge," the corpsman lied. "You should have gone."
"Maybe next time," Holton stated uncaringly before continuing. "These here men just came on board this morning." The sergeant casually pointed to each man as he recited their names. "That's Evans, Miller and Pledger. See that they find a rack and get squared away will ya?"
"Sure," Lew offered his hand to each of them.

Knowing that Doc would do what was asked Holton left, promising to return later.
The corpsman pointed out three empty cots for them to choose their own, than went about explaining chow times, wearing the uniform outside the *hootch,* sick call and everything else that he remembered asking when he first arrived. Lew plopped his butt down in the chair, propped his feet on the cot, lit up a smoke and sat back and watched as the *newbies* attempted to get organized and couldn't help but think back when he first came onboard—nervous, wide-eyed and eager. He remembered Shifty helping him and now it was his turn to pass along his knowledge to these young Marines.
"What the hell are those little things?" Private Evan's asked, pointing to Doc's flag with the little Midnight Skulker silhouettes painted on. After Doc explained the meaning Evans commented, "You mean you been on sixteen patrols Doc? How long you been here?"
Doc lost track of time. "I guess about….. five months?"
"You see any action?" Pledger carefully probed.
"We get in some shit once in a while," Doc coolly replied lighting up another smoke, waiting for the inevitable question to follow…..it did.
"Anybody get killed?"
A simple "Yes," was all that Doc was going to answer.
There was silence.

The sun was just about set when two CH-46's landed on the helo pad and discharged team *Countersign*. Doc wasn't aware of the teams return or else he would have greeted them down on the pad with offerings of cold beer.
The door flung open and the men staggered in sweaty and filthy, obviously exhausted from the patrol.
"Hey guys, welcome back. Everything okay?" Doc hesitated, fearing that they got into some shit and someone was injured or dead.
"Yeah Doc, we're OK. How about you. How was *your* vaa-caa-tion?" Unkle expelled sarcastically.
The corpsman didn't have a chance to answer before PFC Johnson intervened with his broad, split-tooth smile.
"Hey Doc, you're back my man. How was Tokyo?"

Doc answered Johnson's question while staring at Unkle. "Good. It was good." He then turned back to face Johnson. "How was the hump?"
The private, along with the others simply dropped their ruck-sacs on the cots and sat down. "Whew brother! Doc, that was the most mutha-fukkin' humpin' we ever did. Nothin' but vertical. No mutha-fukkin' horizontal at all man!"
"Mountain after mountain; cliff after cliff," Arthurs added.
"You didn't miss nothin' Doc," Pee Wee chimed in as he scanned the new faces. "You the new guys?" he inquired.
Doc blurted out quickly. "Nah, I brought them back from Tokyo as souvenirs," hoping to raise a chuckle. No one saw any humor in Doc's remark.

After a few days of rest and relaxation the team got another mission. This time they were to set up an observation post on a hill overlooking the coast of the South China Sea somewhere between Da Nang and Chu Lai. During the mission briefing it was announced that the position was softened up by naval gunfire, artillery and aerial bombardment. The question on everyone's mind was why? The S-2 officer explained it away by stating that it was just a precaution but, warned that the VC may have mined or booby-trapped the hillside earlier. Unlike most patrols in the bush the men were ordered to take flak jackets, helmets and e-tools this time. The men found no comfort in knowing that.

The huge CH-53 set down on the top of the mostly barren, grass-covered hill that afforded a sweeping view of the South China Sea and expansive beachhead to the north and south of the O.P. Behind them was a higher ridgeline that could give definitive advantage to the VC if they wanted to mortar the Marine position. Even Doc knew the high ground was better real estate for either offensive or defensive operations. He had seen enough war movies to learn that and surmised that everyone else knew it also. As the team formed a defensive perimeter the chopper flew out over the water and loitered there until it was determined that it wasn't need for a quick return and extraction. Within minutes after landing Sergeant Clifford assigned the men perimeter positions and gave to order to dig in; each man needed to dig his own fox hole. Doc looked to his right and watched Johnson feverishly excavating the rocky soil with the E-tool before attempting to scrape out his own home-sweet-hole.

"What the hell are you waiting for Doc?" Sergeant Clifford verbalized gruffly.

The comment forced the corpsman to grab the E-tool and begin the project. The soil was hard and dry. Every stroke of the small shovel discovered a rock. It took almost a full hour or laborious effort in the hot sun before Doc had scratched out a hole deep enough to lay down in.

"Hey Doc, you'd better fill and stack some sandbags around if that's as deep as you're going to go," Johnson advised sitting deep his finished hole puffing away on the pipe clinched between his teeth.

Doc nodded then continued filling sandbags until he had enough to skirt the hole with two layers. He threw the excess dirt and rocks in front of the bags and placed a few swaths of grass on front of the dirt for concealment. "*There,*" he said proudly to himself, *"That is a good as any Marine could do."* As an added feature he took the time to string a line between two stakes and covered the hole with his poncho, providing a makeshift roof, sheltering himself from either the blazing sun or possible rainstorm. Doc took a moment to crawl down under the poncho canopy to try the hole on for size. Perfect!

He rested his back against to cool earth, lit up a smoke and gazed out across the placid, turquoise, waters that slapped gently on the broad, white, sandy shore that he guessed was about 500 meters below their position. It was beautiful, so clam and peaceful. Once more he couldn't comprehend that such a beautiful country could be so devastated by war. A slight wisp of cool, ocean breeze teased his sweaty face, distracting him from his melancholy. He tossed away the cigarette, climbed out of the hole and stood up to catch any additional breeze against his overheated body. When none came he remembered being out at sea in the doldrums. There was no breeze except for the occasional weak maverick kind that provided little relief from the heat. Figuring that the only way to find any comfort was to crawl back into the shelter, he carefully slithered down into the trench to avoid collapsing the delicately constructed canopy. Once he nestled himself into the most comfortable position that the confines permitted he retrieved a well-traveled, jacketless, paperback copy of *Please Don't Eat*

The Daisies, lit up another smoke and took advantage of the few, rare moments of uninterrupted solitude.

While Doc Lewis was lazily taking it easy Sergeant Clifford sent a three-man team out to reconnoiter the immediate surroundings. They returned within an hour, reporting that they didn't find any recent signs of enemy activity in the area. There were no worn foot paths, fighting holes, punji-pits, fresh cut vegetation, booby-traps, human excrement or cooking fires. They did report evidence of U.S. troops being in the area but, not recently. Rusted out C-ration cans, moss covered plastic spoons, tarnished 5.56 shell casings and one empty aluminum, 35mm film container, combined to prove that some unit was there before them.
"Probably some Army, leg, pukes," Clifford took the opportunity to swipe the Army infantry. The jab triggered a few snickers. Despite the report of enemy absence, the patrol leader ordered that, just before dark, all eight Claymore mines be set up around the perimeter. His logic was that if *Charlie* was observing them, the darkness would conceal the placement of the Claymores. As an added precaution he also ordered grenade booby-traps and pencil-flare, trip-wire devices be placed below their positions and along obvious approaches from the ridgeline above them.
Doc popped his head out from under the poncho shelter and saw Sergeant Clifford standing next to a large bolder that was protruding from the otherwise barren hilltop, explaining his instructions to the veterans of the team. Not wanting to be left out of the loop Doc climbed out from his hole and took a couple of steps through the waist-high grass toward Clifford.
"STOP right there Doc," the sergeant commanded in a muted shout and pointed directly at the corpsman with a cop-like gesture. Lew instantly froze in his tracks fearing he was walking in a mine field that no one told him about. Wide-eyed and scared he watched as Clifford approached him.
"What the hell are you doing Doc?" The leader scolded. "This ain't the bush. While we're up here everybody *will,* I repeat, *will*, at all times, wear their helmet and flak jacket, unless I say otherwise. I thought I made that clear."
Doc quickly scanned his short-term memory but couldn't find that particular edict.
Clifford continued. "Everybody *will* always have their weapon and ammo with them. Now, go get that gear on and don't come

out of your hole without it. We're too exposed here. Anything can happen…anytime!" he espoused before adding, "I ain't no Jimmie Howard."
Relieved that he wasn't in a mine field, Doc took the scolding as a fair trade in his favor and returned to get his gear as ordered, wondering *'Who the hell is Jimmie Howard?'*

Decked out in a full complement of combat gear Doc strolled past each foxhole, secretly comparing them against the one he dug while disguising his motive by reminding the men to drink a lot of water and take salt tablets. He came away with satisfaction that he had done a good job although, he had to admit that Unkle had the deepest and best concealed fighting hole on the hill. The Marine even staked out his field of fire-a text book example of a proper fighting position.

Doc stopped at Johnson's position to sit and shoot-the-breeze for a while. Johnson was enjoying a can of warm, C-ration, fruit cocktail as the corpsman sat down next to him and lit up a cigarette. Curious, he asked his Negro comrade "Hey man, do you know who's Jimmie Howard?"
"Ma-a-a-n, Doc," the Marine stopped eating. "You never heard of Gunny Howard? Shit man, you need to brush up on what's happenin' in this here war, 'specially the Marine Corps stuff." Johnson took another spoonful then, continued. "Gunny Howard was a Recon Marine who got the Congressional Medal of Honor for action last summer. He's one of us, or maybe we should be one of him? Anyway man, he was a Staff Sergeant patrol leader with Charlie Company when their team got into some real bad shit…ended up with *boo-coo*, hand-to-hand with a shit load of *gooks*. I heard that they fought all night long and everybody got dinged or killed before a reaction force could reach them. Skinny has it that Gunny was wounded real bad but even mustered enough guts to throw rocks when they ran out of ammo. I think their Doc bought it too but, I don't know that for sure." Johnson paused for another spoon of fruit that gave the medic a chance to ask, "How many guys were there?"
"I guess about sixteen or eighteen? Every swingin' dick got a Purple Heart that night Doc."
The corpsman took a long drag before releasing the smoke from one side of his mouth so it wouldn't blow into the Marine's face.

Johnson raised the empty can to his lips to get the last drops of the sweet, syrup-water as Doc asked another question. 'Where did all this happen? Anywhere around here?"

"Well Doc, actually I think we're in about the same area. As a matter-of-fact," Johnson went on, "I'd guess that the situation we're in right now is *boo-coo* close to the situation they were in when their shit happened."

That bit of ad lib information left the corpsman with an uneasy feeling in his stomach.

Lance Corporal Miller approached the duo. The Marine passed the word that Clifford wanted everybody to stay in their hole, keep awake and be quiet. "Sarge said we can catch up on our beauty sleep later.....right now we got to be alert," adding, "said he'd be coming around to make sure nobody's in La-La land," then proceeded to the next position.

Lew got to his feet. "Catch you later man. I'd better *di-di* back to my own neighborhood."

"Yeah Doc.....hey...prep you grenades," the Marine offered a reminder.

"You know it bro."

"What did I tell you about calling me that," Johnson half-heartedly stressed.

"Yeah....yeah," the corpsman uncaringly responded back. "See 'ya later...BRO."

Doc prepared a cup of C-rat coffee before darkness fell. While the water was heating up over the C-4 flame he used the time to remove the tape from the four fragmentation grenades he'd been issued, straighten the pins and set them up in a row next to his hap-hazard fortress, so that he could find them quickly in the darkness if needed. He looked around thinking about what else he could do to prepare for an enemy assault. He pulled ten magazines from the tight ammo pouches and stacked them up against the stone barricade along with a pop-flare, a single tear gas grenade and, as a last resort, unsheathed his K-bar and drove it into the dirt next to the gas mask that was ready to don. Hearing the water simmering in the cup he stopped thinking about the defensive preparation and doctored up the strongly caffeinated brew with creamer and sugar. Resting his back against wall of the cool earth trench work, Lew held the cup in both hands and carefully took a sip of the hot liquid when another thought popped into his head. *'Bayonet.....fix the bayonet stupid.'* Setting the cup down he pulled the blade from its scabbard and attached it to the business end of the M-16. After accomplishing that afterthought he returned to indulging himself with the 'joe'. Suddenly, another thought occurred to him. *'Unit One....I need to get it ready too!'* Once again the medic put down the concoction and pulled the medical kit from the ruck sack and placed it on the ground next to him. Satisfied that he thought of everything he returned his attention to the coffee. After taking a few more sips of the nasty tasting liquid Lew's eyes focused on the flashlight attached to his web gear. *'Damn, something else I need to have ready,'* his restless mind perceived. Rather than attending to it immediately, he decide to finish the coffee before retrieving the flashlight and checking to make sure that the red lens was installed instead of the white light.

Once again the night was going by agonizingly slow. Like so many times before, Doc's brain became preoccupied with thoughts of home rather than the possible life-ending dangers at hand. A faint flash of light far out at sea beyond the dark horizon caught his eye, interrupting his otherwise occupied mind. The first inclination was that the light was nothing more than heat lighting but, when it was followed by several other flashes in rapid succession he knew it was coming from a ship's guns. Barely audible, muffled reports reached his ears long after the corresponding flashes, indicating distance.
'Must be a cruiser....too far out to be a destroyer.' He continued to watch the flashes but couldn't hear where the rounds were striking. The show ended abruptly after nearly an hour of bombardment.

Ducking down behind the make-shift parapet he lit his sixth cigarette of the night, carefully hiding the flame then, raised his head above the rim of the shelter and scanned the open, grassy slope below their positions. The nearly barren hillside afforded a wide-open, field-of-fire against any charging attackers. The situation reminded him of an old, Lloyd Nolan, war movie where a million Japs staged an all-out, banzi charge against a handful of our guys. The flick ended by leaving the audience with the impression that the American defenders were all killed, fighting to the last man. *'What the hell was the name of that one? 'Back To*

Battan?' The recollection triggered another worrisome string of thoughts. *'If the gooks decide to come after our asses, how they gonna do it? Will they try to soften us up first with mortars and RPG's from the ridge above us then commit to an all-out, death charge? Will they come at us in drug-crazed, hordes up the slope? Will they try to sneak up through the grass and get us one-by-one? Maybe they'll probe us with grenades? Yeah, mortars and RPG's. Shit, I wish I dug this hole deeper!'*

Sergeant Clifford kept true to his word. Lew watched him leave Johnson's position and come over to his. "Doc, you doing okay?" the sergeant whispered.
"Yeah, I'm OK but you just managed to interrupt me and Ann-Margaret in a compromising situation."
"Sorry 'bout that G.I. but I suggest you forget about her for now and direct your concentration on us staying alive 'til mornin'. It's only a couple more hours."
"Right. Hey, you know anything about that naval gunfire?"
"Yeah, just H & I on some ville up the coast. Don't worry about it."
"I'm not worried about it Sarge. I was just curious, that's all."
"Awright. Who's over at the next position?
"Evans. He's tucked away in those boulders. Be careful. I don't want to have to reset a broken leg out here in the dark."
"I don't want you to either Doc."

Three more Viceroys laid waste before the Sun began its constant ritual far beyond the endless, watery, horizon. The grueling night had passed without enemy contact. Doc fixed his tired, heavy eyes on the unexpected presence of two ships in silhouette, steaming northward, about four miles off the coast. He recognized them to be destroyers and couldn't help but wonder if one of them was *his* ship, the Mason. Even if he had binoculars he wouldn't be able to make out the hull numbers because of the distance and the port side was still hidden by early morning darkness. Never-the-less, he wondered.

It was almost high noon when Doc was awakened by the noise of helicopter rotors popping. He jumped out from his shelter to see the Marines frantically jumping up and down and waving at two Army, UH-1, *Huey*, gunships that seemed to be getting ready to

make a strafing run on the position, apparently mistaking the Marines for VC. All the animation paid off as the lead bird dove down at them at attack speed, then banked sharply to the left, enabling the pilot to identify them as 'friendlies', and was thoughtful enough to give the Marines a smiling 'thumbs-up' sign. Clifford returned the gesture with one more appropriate. The second chopper swooped down in the wake of the first, this time the pilot smartly saluted the men on the ground then, the aircraft paired up and sped toward the fishing village in the valley below, obviously looking for targets- of -opportunity.
"Fukin' Army pukes," Unkle spouted out for everyone.

The following three days were near carbon copies of the first. Hot, humid days filled with boredom mixed with a couple of hours sleep at a time followed by excruciatingly long nights of nerve racking uncertainty. Sergeant Clifford relaxed the helmet requirement on the second day, permitting the men to wear a soft cap during the day but, the flak jackets had to worn at all times except when sleeping. The fourth day brought an interesting situation. One lone fisherman was spotted strolling along the beach carrying a fishing net over his shoulder, wrapped around long, bamboo poles. From a distance it resembled an RPG launcher. The question rose whether or not to call in arty on the man as a possible VC guerrilla. Several of the men laughed at the prospect and were eager to see the man either get blown to hell or take off running. Doc sensed that Clifford was actually considering calling in naval gun fire on the poor bastard, who was probably VC at night anyway. The sergeant chose to let the man go about his business unimpeded.
Lew speculated that Clifford didn't want take any fire support away from troops who may actually need it, for one, unimposing, Vietnamese fisherman.

By the end of their week long mission the team had neither encountered the enemy nor spotted signs of enemy activity. After all was said and done, Doc considered it a good mission. The highlight of the week however, was that everyone on the team had the opportunity to learn how to call in fire missions from naval gunfire, learning that unlike ground artillery, the height of the target needed to be included with the coordinates. Sergeant Clifford allowed a couple Marines to call in practice missions.

Lew wondered if the skipper of the destroyer knew he was sending expensive 5 inch 38 rounds ashore on bogus targets.

The CH-53 came in to extract the team on the morning of the eight day but, brought no replacement. It was speculated that the 'brass' saw the OP as unproductive and was inclined to abandon it for the time being.

Back at Camp Reasoner word was passed that there was going to be an opportunity for a limited number of unqualified personnel to attend an abbreviated, Army parachute school at Camp Kuwi, Okinawa or attend Navy Scuba School in the Philippines. Not being a good swimmer, Doc Lewis opted for *jump school* but, since a limited number of men were allotted space, he had to compete with the Marines in a five-mile run. Only the first twenty people completing the run under the given time were being considered to go. Doc wanted to go badly to earn the right to wear those prestigious, jump-wings. The young corpsman astounded himself when he came in second on the run from Camp Reasoner to the Hill 327 PX and back. It was a little more than five miles and he had never ran that distance before but, he was in good shape and was a sprinter and a Varsity Letterman in track back in high school. He reasoned that must have accounted for the good show, despite being a cigarette smoker. Two days after the qualifying run he and about twenty others were aboard a Marine Corps C-130 Hercules bound for Okinawa. During the long flight to the island he wondered what the weather was like on Okinawa in December, hoping it wasn't too cold. He hated cold weather. Regardless of the weather or any other conditions he was to encounter at the school, he was bound and determined to get those wings. *'It would be a nice Christmas present,'* he told himself

His luck ran out when after two weeks into the course and just a day before making the first of five qualifying parachute jumps, he contracted pneumonia, which sent him for prolonged treatment at the hospital. He pleaded with the Army doctors to let him continue with the school; promising them that he would admit himself after he complete the five jumps. It did no good. Even, literally begging them with tears in his eyes proved useless. The day came for graduation and *his Marines* paid a visit at the hospital before departing back to the Nam. Lew appreciated their visiting but, seeing the newly earned, silver wings that each of them wore, only served to hurt him more. He knew that each of them will have the opportunity to earn the cherished, gold wings by making only five more jumps in country. He congratulated them and wished them luck back in Nam as they departed then, buried his face in the pillow and shed tears of disappointment after they had disappeared from view.

It took another week to recover from the illness before the doctors released him back to duty. Upon reporting to Camp Butler he learned that the Marines he came to jump school with took his personnel jacket back to Vietnam with them. There he was, stranded in Okinawa, without orders and more importantly, without pay records. At least if he got paid he could take advantage of the social life in the town outside the gate. Instead, he had to sell what few personnel possessions he brought with him, including an expensive, 35mm Cannon SLR camera, to get money in order to purchase toiletries and a few snacks. Every day he reported to morning muster, hoping his name would be called to get manifested on a flight back to Nam. Finally, after more than a week passed without a flight he spoke to a corporal working at company HQ. Lew was shocked to learn that there was no record of him even being there. He explained what happened and the corporal set about preparing the administrative paperwork for a certificate in lieu of orders as well as authorization for partial, advance pay. Now, that he had $35 in his pocket he intended to hit the *beach* for a night on the town. Once again his hopes were dashed; in that he was an E-3 and didn't have a *liberty card* that permitted non-NCO's to leave the compound. Giving up on the idea of going out on-the-town, he settled for spending an evening at the Enlisted Club.

Lew woke the next morning with barely enough time to make the morning muster. With a pounding headache, blood-shot eyes and nasty case of beer breath, he stood in formation as best he could. As luck would have it, his name was called to be manifested on the next flight back to good, old, Southeast Asia. Thank God for *barf-bags*.

It was nearly night fall when the plane touched down in Da Nang. He managed to hitch a ride back to Camp Reasoner in an Army *deuce-and-a-half* before dark. Despite being back in the combat zone, Lew was happy and looking forward to being reunited with *his* platoon. When he entered the *hootch* he was shocked to find it totally empty. There was no one living there. It had no cots, foot lockers…nothing but a bare, dust covered, plywood deck. The place seemed abandoned. Dumbfounded, he rushed to the *Dogma* team's *hootch.* Searching in the darkness he found the light string and illuminated a single bulb. It was in the same condition…empty, except for a solitary AWOL bag set down in the corner next to the door he just came through.

Perplexed, he verbalized to no one, "What the hell's going on here?"

Not knowing what to do next he sat down and lit up a smoke to give himself time to think about this dilemma. *'I think I'll go up to the aid station and talk to somebody. Maybe they can tell me what this is all about.'*

It was then that the door opened and *Rocky* came in. The sight of the corpsman surprised him. "Doc! How the hell are you man? We heard that you were sent back stateside!"

Excited, Lew jumped to his feet. "Shit man, am I glad to see you! What the hell's going on here? Where is everybody?"

"Easy Doc," the Marine insisted. "Relax." He gave the corpsman a second to regain his composure before explaining. "The company moved. Went up north to Phu Bai. I just came in from R & R and decided to lay low here until morning then, try to jump on a flight up there in the morning. Now, how 'bout you? You feelin' better?

"Yeah man, I'm okay, I guess," then quickly added, "Hey, where's my shit? What did they do with my stuff?"

"We packed your gear and took it with us. It should be up there waitin' for you" he cautioned, "that is unless they shipped it back to the *world* while I was in Hong Kong…After all, we did think you might not be comin' back."

"I'll tell you what…..if I had a choice, I'd rather be there than here but, I don't have a choice so, I guess I have to settle for second best." Lew tossed the cigarette on the deck and stomped it out.

"Well, wadda-ya-say we *di-di* up to the 'Club' and have us a couple brews, huh?"

Remembering how terrible he felt earlier in the day Lew accepted the idea with reservation. "Sure, but I'll let you have my second ration."

The next morning the pair found themselves at the MAW transient facility waiting to be manifested on a flight to Phu Bai. During the time the two spent together on the previous evening Doc learned that a couple new men came into the platoon while he was in Okinawa. Rocky recalled one man's name as Lance Corporal Jim Prideaux, from Colorado but, the other named slipped his memory. Lew was also relieved that none of *his* men got *dinged* during his absence. Rocky also informed him that nothing more was learned about LaPorte's disappearance and that Staff Sergeant Livingston had been awarded a battlefield commission to second lieutenant.

The morning blended into the sweltering heat of mid-day before the two got word that they would have to go across the runway to the Air Force side of the base to catch a *hop* to Phu Bai. They were told that the Marine C-130's were too busy transporting cargo to someplace called Khe Sanh.

A Staff Sergeant, who was obviously not doing anything important, offered to take the duo over to the Air Force side. As the jeep skirted around the southern end of the runway along a stretch of busy Vietnamese markets, something caught Lew's attention. He recognized a burned-out hulk of a pink and black DeSoto, sedan abandoned alongside the road. He was sure that it was the same automobile that he saw when he first arrived in country, six months earlier…the one that the blonde European woman was driving. Given the uncertainties of war, he wondered what happened to the woman. Passing the wreckage quickly the trio continued to the Air Force Operations section. Once there, both men got manifested on a two engine, Army, *Caribou* transport plane for a direct flight to the airfield at Phu Bai. The plane's engines were running as the men darted onboard. They were amazed to find the cargo bay mostly filled with Vietnamese civilians sitting on the floor in the company of their chickens and swine. A few South Vietnamese, AVRN, soldiers were included in the mix. The crew chief pointed to empty spaces on the floor where the two of them were to sit, as no troop seats were configured. The pair looked at each other in disbelief. Reluctantly,

the men took up the assigned space. Doc sat down next to a small, undernourished, Vietnamese boy who appeared to have some Negro blood flowing through his veins. The boy smiled at the medic, showing his two missing front teeth. Doc smiled back then looked past the boy to a wrinkled, old woman that he perceived to be the boy's grandmother. She made eye contact with American medic, bowed her head slightly and showed her teeth, blackened by years of chewing the betel-nut. Doc returned a slight, acknowledging smile as the airplane's engines revved up and began to taxi.
The flight north was bumpy, smelly and extremely uncomfortable. Never-the-less, the plane landed safely at the Phu Bai airfield. Doc and Rocky clutched their bags to be the first one's off the plane, hoping to never fly on those contraptions again.

Rocky informed the corpsman that the Company compound was a short walk from the airfield but recommended that they hitch a ride, explaining that he didn't like the idea of being out in the open without a weapon. Doc agreed. The first vehicle that stopped was another Army deuce-and-a-half. It seemed to the corpsman that the Army was more conspicuous now than before he went to jump school. Just as the men climbed aboard the vehicle an unfamiliar, ferocious looking, helicopter appeared overhead at tree-top level, streaking past them in a hurry. The sight of it caught Doc off guard. At first he thought that the enemy had their own choppers. Rocky enlightened him. "That's one of the new Cobras Doc. Pretty mean looking, huh?"
"It's ours?"
Rocky nodded. "That one's the Army's. I don't know if we have any. At least I haven't seen any with Marine markings, yet."
"It looks….ah…..intimidating," the corpsman watched it until it was out of sight.

The *six-by* traveled southbound along Highway One less than a mile from the airfield when the driver downshifted to a stop. "FIRST FLOOR….LADIES UNDERWARE," he hollered out. Rocky didn't know whether the comment was meant to be an insult to the Corps or the driver just belted out something intended to be humorous. Regardless, he cut the man a *huss* and thanked

him for the lift. After a short walk down the dusty roadway the two entered the Recon section of the compound.
"Here we are Doc. Home again."
Lew wasn't impressed. It was filled with the same kind of *hootches* as they had back in Da Nang although, the terrain was much more level. One thing that he did notice though, was the obvious presence of numerous, sand-bagged bunkers between each structure. It was a sure sign that the area was more susceptible to rocket attacks than Camp Reasoner.
Rocky pointed out the third *hootch* from the end of a long row on the right was theirs.

Rocky entered the *hootch* first. "Look who I found in a skivvy house in Da Nang," he joked. Pee Wee, Unkle, Johnson and the new man, Prideaux turned their heads.
"Doc!" Pee Wee exclaimed. "You're back. Shit we thought you were history."
"I almost was," the corpsman replied.
"Yeah, we heard you almost died and was sent back stateside," Unkle suggested a rumor being spread around.
"Not our Doc," Johnson added. "He wouldn't just up and die on us. He might want to get far away from us but, not just die on us....would you Doc?"
"Hell no! I thought you guys heard I was coming back then packed your asses up and *di-di'd* up here just to avoid me." The comment drew a collective chuckle.
Lew drew his attention to the new face. "You Prideaux?"
"Yep. That's me."
The corpsman extended his hand, "Doc Lewis."
"Hey Doc," Pee Wee broke up the greeting. "I'm pretty sure all your shit is in the *hootch* behind us. You might want to check."
"I will but, first I guess I should go to HQ and report in. Where is it?"
"I'll show 'ya." Unkle offered. "I gotta go there myself for a few minutes.
Lew nodded acceptance of the offer.
"We'll have a place ready for you when you get back Doc," Pee Wee assured.
"Okay, thanks."

On the way over to the company office Unkle pointed out the chow hall, aid station and officers country, as well as team Thin Man's *hootch* next to theirs. "Dogma ain't here. We changed our call sign to Thin Man. They're in the bush now," he advised."You didn't miss nothin' here Doc. Same old shit. One thing though, we're a bigger target here, being so close to the air strip…just fukin' knowin' *Charlie* wants to blow all our asses away."
"Well, "Doc began a tongue-in-cheek remark. "That's always good to hear."
"No shit man. Up here ain't the same as down south. Up here they got the North Vietnamese Regulars. They got tanks and artillery. Up here if you get in some shit, you can't hide behind a tree like you can down there. They can plop an arty round in on top of your ass. Man, it's an entirely different war."
"What's the humpin' like?" Doc inquired to keep up conversation more than actually wanting to know.
"Tough. They got a place called A Shau Valley. It's loaded with NVA. We did a couple patrols there……signs of *gooks* everywhere…..regulars….not VC," he then brought up the rumor that even Chinese troops have been staging in North Vietnam , possibly getting ready to join in Ho Chi's battle.
Doc didn't believe the Chinese would dare get involved but, was unsure about the tank and artillery part.
After reporting in at the office he parted Unkle's company and re-tracked the steps back to the *hootch* .

Pee Wee kept his word. There was a cot set up in the center of the row and a space was cleared out to make room for his foot locker. Johnson helped Pee Wee and Doc in carrying the stuff over from where it was stored. Doc even found the lawn chair wasn't stolen as he predicted. That bit of knowledge only served to reinforce his belief that the men in *his* outfit are *tight* and aren't about to steal from their brothers-in-arms. This was completely contrary to his experience in the Navy where nothing was safe if left out in the open- not even the Holy Bible.

The four of them ate supper together then returned to spend the remainder of the evening catching up on everything that took place while Doc was gone. Before turning in, Rocky told Doc that he would take him to the armory in the morning to draw a new weapon when he picked up his own.

It was shortly after midnight when a series of thunderous BOOMS startled Doc out of a deep sleep and had him rushing toward the bunkers, thinking a barrage of rockets were targeting the compound.
"DOC, DOC. STOP!" Rocky shouted out. "It's only arty....ours."
Frightened out of his wits Lew huffed. "OURS?"
"Yeah Doc. I'm sorry," the Marine apologized. "I forgot to tell you, there's an arty battery positioned out behind our compound. They're firin' all the time. You'll have to get used to it, man."
"Damn. That scared the starch out of me. It's outgoing then?"
"Yep....outgoing...not incoming. You'll get to know the difference real quick like. Now, try to get back to sleep." The tremendously loud reports of the artillery firing off and on all night kept Doc from getting a good night's sleep.

Half-awake he managed to pull himself up in the cot to light the first cigarette of the day. It took a moment for him to realize where he was.
Johnson was already awake. "Did anybody tell you where the shower is Doc," he asked
"Ah, no."
"Okay. When you're done with your smoke I'll show you."
Lew reached for a towel, flip-flops and *douche kit*. "Let's go now," he uttered, cigarette dangling from his lip. "I have a lot of stuff to do today."
The shower was a cold trickle, gravity fed from a large reservoir tank about fifteen feet overhead. The corpsman became frustrated with the automatic shower head mechanism as it shut the flow of water off when the pull chain was released, making it impossible to maintain a hands-free shower. It was an obvious water conservation method. Still, he considered it a luxury compared to the grunts in the field. BOOM-BOOM-BOOM-BOOM. The *arty* position let go a salvo, startling the unaccustomed medic into dropping the bar of soap. "Go 'head Doc," Johnson sneered. "Pick it up. I'm not one of your *squid* buddies," he jested reassuringly. Lew chuckled then retrieved the soap from the wet, concrete deck.

He and Rocky walked over to the armory and had their M-16's reissued. Lew received a different one from the one he had before. It was just another serial number he had to memorize. Back at the

hootch, as he sat down to wipe off the excess oils and clean it up, Sergeant Holton appeared. "Doc, see 'ya made it back to the fold," he casually recognized the corpsman's return. "You feelin' okay?"
"Yep. Hunky-dory Ed."
"Good. We were wonderin' about 'ya. Didn't think you'd be back. Now that you 'an Rocky are back we got a full team again." The sergeant stood there waiting for a response. Lew shrugged his shoulder, "What can I say. It's good to be back."
"Lieutenant Williamson know you're back?"
"Ah, I don't think so. At least I didn't see him…yet," he added to imply that he intended to let the platoon leader know of his return.
"I think you should see him sometime today and let him know you're back," Holton verbalized as if it were more a suggestion than an order although, it *was* an order.
Doc nodded to assure the sergeant that he would comply.
Holton duplicated the nod then, directed a message to everyone there.
"Everybody, listen up." The *hootch* went quiet. "We managed to get some rubber boat training scheduled for tomorrow. We got to drive through Hue' City to get to the beach so be sure to take your flak jackets and helmets in addition to your 782 gear….and fill your canteens…..we'll be there all day. Don't forget to bring swim trunks if you got 'em. The indigenous population don't take kindly to skinny-dippin'. Arthurs, why don't you take Prideaux over and pick-up a case of C's."
Before Arthurs had a chance to respond Unkle spoke out. "Hey Ed, why can't have a cook out at the beach? Maybe mix business with a little R and R?"
Holton gave the idea a moment to sink in. "Hey, if you can find the shit to have a picnic, I won't object."
Everyone let go an "Ooo Rah".
The sergeant then cautioned them, "Listen, for the record… this is still a training mission," emphasizing *training*. He scanned the men's faces to ensure that all understood what he meant.
Satisfied that they did, he turned to Unkle, "Make it so."
"Aye Aye Sarge."

Early the next day everyone climbed into the back of the *six-by*, eager to hit the road. They had to pinch between the fully inflated, eight-man, rubber boat and the troop seats. In addition to the boat there was an ice chest with sodas, a small hibachi, a bag of charcoal and a cardboard box containing enough steaks for everybody. Unkle wouldn't say, or rather confess to how he procured the steaks. It didn't matter. No one cared.

The truck and passengers rumbled north on Highway One, joining in as the last vehicle in a convoy ahead of them, bound toward the ancient city of Hue'. The vehicle broke away from the convoy and crossed the murky, oddly named, Perfume River. As it entered the city and maneuvered through the busy, unfamiliar streets Doc was in awe of the beauty of the city. The tree-lined avenue was bustling with life. White, pink and beige stucco buildings reflected years of French Colonial influence. Whiffs of wonderful aromas of fresh baked bread and roasted coffee could be sensed under the prevailing stink of fish, pork, duck, chicken and occasional cat cooking at kiosks and sidewalk, café's. Pretty, young Vietnamese girls dressed in long, white sarongs, peeked out at them from under broad, cone-shaped hats. Other girls were decked-out in modern, western attire but, much to the dismay of the young Marines, not one mini-skirt was to be seen. Some women smiled while others looked at them with contempt. Tri-peds, Vespa scooters, mini-busses, bicycles and taxis congested the streets. Traditional music clashed with American rock-n-roll coming from hundreds of transistor radios, even old songs with French lyrics could be heard through the din. People were everywhere. Businessmen dressed in white suits rubbed shoulders with peasants wearing the ubiquitous, black silk, pajamas. Curiously, there seemed to be an abundance of young, Vietnamese men of military age, not in uniform roaming the streets. Doc had a problem with that, wondering, '*What the hell are we doing over here... fighting their war for them? We're putting our asses on the line and they're just wandering around without a care in the world, letting us die for them....that's bullshit.'* Even though ARVN Military Policemen and soldiers strolled among the crowd, it was difficult for Doc to discern that a terrible war was going on. This was a totally different city from Da Nang.

The *six-by* pulled up about 100 meters short of the beach. "Can't you get any fukin' father away?" Unkle belched out to the driver. "We gotta hump this boat 'ya know."

"Can't do it man. We'll get stuck in this sand."
Everyone climbed out and immediately set about off-loading the goods and the boat. It weighed more than the corpsman thought.
"Holy crap," he muttered, as he joined the men in lifting the boat above their heads. "This thing weighs a ton!"
"It ain't that heavy Doc," Arthurs reassured. "It only takes teamwork."
Lew sensed that the muscular Marine was ripe to be played with.
"Hey man, did you know that air weighs about 14 pounds per square inch?" he puffed under the strain. "Given the size of this thing.....(puff).. it probably actually weighs several tons.....(puff)... only, we don't feel it because.....(puff)...the air pressure is equalized all around us."
"Oooooh," the group sung out.
"Okay professor *squid.* Just put your skinny ass into hoisting your 500 pounds worth and we'll be in the water in no time," Arthurs rebounded.
"Oooooh," they sang in unison once more.
They lowered the inflatable boat on the compacted sand short of the surf. After taking a few minutes to catch their breath and go over procedures, the first six men set about paddling out through the breaking water. Pee Wee, Evans and the driver stayed behind with the medic to keep an eye on the weapons and observe the exercise. Pee Wee pointed out to Doc how the men straddled one leg over the side while attempting to paddle all together against the tide. It was comical when the oncoming rush of waves tipped the boat over, sending everyone into the drink and quickly carried the boat back to shore. The first team recovered the boat and repeated the attempt to get beyond the breakers. Their second effort proved successful as they breached the surf and ventured out about a quarter mile.
The raft team then brought the boat about and began their make-believe, clandestine landing on the beach. From Doc's vantage point it appeared that the return trip, going with the tide, was as nearly a difficult struggle as going against it. He anticipated another capsize as he watched the raft continually ride the crest then, disappear down into the trough.
"Say Doc,...you know mouth-to-mouth?" Evans kidded.
Lew turned and calmly replied, "I'm not kissin' any of 'em. They're all fish-bait," he smirked.
"You be a mean muttha, Doc," Evans laughed.

The boat made it ashore without the men taking another dunking. Thinking it might be fun, Doc agreed to go along on the second round of *amphibious landings.* Despite the surf growing increasingly rougher, the second group managed to ply through the waves to open water without being tipped over. It was a much more difficult feat than Doc imagined. His arms and back strained to keep paddling with the others while at the same time, trying to keep his balance in straddling the massive, round, balloon-like structure between his legs. He wasn't afraid of falling into the water rather, it was the fear of being the team's weak link if he went overboard that concerned him most. The crew managed to transit the breakers and position the boat in the choppy water just about the same location as the first crew. Allowing the men to rest a few minutes before continuing with the drill, Sergeant Holton prepped them. "READY PORT-READY STARBOARD- ALL TOGETHER NOW," then barked out the order to "GO". It was followed up with a resounding chorus of "OOOOH-RAAH". They collectively thrust the paddles into the brine together as if it had been rehearsed beforehand and propelled the boat forward on a steady course toward the beach. Each choreographed stroke pushed the craft a little faster. Once they found their rhythm they maintained it by shouting out "RECON" each time the paddles broke the surface of the water. Doc not only struggled with the physical demand, the blinding sunlight mixed with salt water spraying into his eyes and open mouth made him wish he had stayed on shore. Never-the-less, he was committed to the task and intended to see it through to the end. It was a much tougher task than it looked. They paddled without stopping. Every strenuous, contraction of muscle brought them closer to land. As the boat closed in on the shore the water suddenly disappeared beneath in an unseen swell, leaving it airborne for a spilt second, nearly ejecting the unprepared crew. When it fell back in contact with the water at the bottom of the trough, the fluid captured it into slight reverse direction before pushing it forward again, lifting it up on the surging crest then, back down into yet another swell then, another. Finally, it cascaded from last breaker until the water smoothed out, allowing the boat to settle on the sand in the ebb. The men jumped out, jubilantly striking a chord of "RECON..OOOH RAAH"

Left weakened and wet from the ordeal, Doc was still felt exhilarated from the experience. "Shit man," he proclaimed to Rocky. "I hope we never have to do that for real."
"Me neither, Doc," the Marine confessed.
Several more landings were made during the course of the day but, the corpsman declined to take part. Instead, he helped cook the steaks and basically took advantage of the opportunity to relax and enjoy the renewed camaraderie with the men in *his* platoon.

The driver retraced the route to back to the Marine Combat Base at Phu Bai, once again taking them through the streets of Hue'. The congestion and activity wasn't any lighter in the late afternoon than it was in the morning. The truck suddenly jerked to a stop, prompting the men to stand up and look over top of the cab to see what was happening. A string of shaved-head, Buddhist monks, dressed in bright orange frocks, filed past, crossing the street in front of the vehicle. Many people bowed reverently, giving the holy men wide-berth as the precession passed, taking slow, purposeful steps.

For Doc, the journey was more of a sight-seeing trip than just a ride. He absorbed as much of the landscape and culture as he could from the back of a truck, despite remaining on the alert for possible, yet seemingly improbable attacks. Water traffic in the Perfume River seemed to have increased since they crossed earlier in the day. Flotillas of sampans and motorized, canoe-like, craft transited up and down the filthy, brown tributary.
"I bet there's a lotta brown trout floatin' in there," Pee Wee quipped, suggesting the abundance of both human and animal turds.
Doc flicked a spent cigarette over the side into the water and grinned agreement.

Missing evening chow was no concern to the team. The first priority was to clear out the bed of the *six-by* and return the boat and paddles to the dive locker. Then, the men could get back to the *hootch.* The second priority was to wipe the dust from their weapons that had collected from the trip. Everyone busied themselves at the tasking. Somehow, the topic of conversation turned from the day's events to the Corps, the Commandant and

‘Chesty’ Puller, the premier human icon of the United States Marine Corps. The discussion made transition to *officers* in general. Wanting to throw his two-cents-worth in, Doc started spouting off about his experience with naval officers. “Most of them aren’t for shit... always looking out for themselves and getting promotions. Shit, it doesn’t take anything to be an officer.” He failed to pay attention to Rocky repeatedly clearing his throat. Suddenly, a familiar voice spoke up. “You got a problem Doc?” Lew turned. Lieutenant Williamson was standing in the doorway, apparently overhearing the corpsman’s ill-timed remarks. No one had called the hootch to “attention”. Flustered and embarrassed Doc’s voice cracked in response. “No Sir. I don’t have any problem, Sir.”
“Well, if you do, come see me with it first.” It was a command, not an offer.
“Yes Sir. Aye Aye Sir.”
“By the way Doc,” the L.T. questioned further. “When did you get back?”
“Yesterday Sir,” Lew answered, quickly adding, “I went to your hootch to let you know but, you weren’t there sir.” He continued with the explanation hoping to amend the situation. “I was going back again to find you just as soon as I cleaned my weapon here sir.”
Unsure if the medic was on the level, Williamson suspiciously uttered “Uh Huh.”
Doc sensed that the officer doubted his story and deservedly so. The corpsman forgot to go the lieutenant’s *hootch* the previous day and didn’t intend to go after cleaning the M-16 either but, since no one could prove otherwise, he stuck with the alibi.
The Lt. changed the subject. “I want everybody to listen up. We have a mission tomorrow…..first thing. Get your gear in order and be at the LZ at 0700. I’ll brief Holton and Clifford this evening. They’ll give you the skinny afterward. Let anybody who’s not here know what’s going on. We’ll need every man on this one.” Without going into the specifics of the mission the officer’s words sounded ominous.
He continued partly in jest; partly in admonishment. “Except for Doc.”
Lew looked bewildered. “Huh?”

"Since you didn't report in, I have no way of knowing if you're here," L.T. explained in his typically firm but, non-ass-chewing way.
The corpsman didn't quite understand the platoon leader's remark. "Sir?"
"We'll let it go this time Doc but, next time you report to me before you do anything else,
understand?"
"Yes sir. Will do."
Williamson turned, "Carry on."

Rocky faced the medic. "I'm sorry Doc. He was suddenly standing in the hatch. I couldn't warn you," he apologized from the heart.
Lew understood. "Don't worry 'bout it Rock. It ain't nothin' but a thing."

BOOM-BOOM-BOOM-BOOM-BOOM-BOOM a rapid, unexpected salvo from the arty base gave a sudden start to everyone.
"Damned guns," Doc cursed his jitters more than the guns.
Unkle dropped a veteran Marine's observation. "Somebody's in some shit. All six guns without a marking round first." Another salvo of six outgoing rounds immediately followed the first.
"Must be bracketed in pretty good or"…. the Corporal paused.
'Or what' Doc thought, anxiously waiting for Unkle to finish.
"……there is so much shit they're calling it in on their own asses."
"Who is?" Prideaux questioned.
"How the hell should I know?" Unkle replied. "Probably One/One," he guessed. "They're camped out behind us....probably some of them *legs"*
Doc's ears perked up. "One-One!" he exclaimed. "I got a good friend in 1/1."
"They're there Doc," Unkle assured.
Doc grabbed his blouse, cover and rifle. "Hell, I'm going over there to see if I can find my friend."
"Better hurry Doc. It'll be getting' dark pretty soon," Pee Wee cautioned.
"Better report to L.T. first," Rocky took a friendly shot.
"OOOOOH." They all sang out at the ribbing.

"Kiss my dupa, " Doc shot back.

Rifle in hand, Doc stepped lively along the dust covered road that led to the First Marines encampment. Once he was outside of Recon's perimeter he followed a stretch of open road before coming to a large grid-work of typical hootches. Long rows of concertina wire stretched out, surrounding the perimeter. Lew approached two grunts that appeared to be sentry's, nonchalantly smoking and joking from behind a sand-bagged position next to a break in the wire. They eyed the corpsman but, didn't challenge him.

"Hey guys," Lew summoned their attention. "Do either of you know a Doc Johnson?"

"Yeah, I think we have a Johnson corpsman," one of them answered. "You should try the aid station. They'll tell you for sure."

"Okay, where's that?"

The second grunt pointed in the general direction. "Two hootches behind them ones."

"Thanks man."

Lew entered the hootch identified only with a large 'Band-Aid' painted on the door.

Two, grubby-looking corpsman were inside working on a young, black man's blistered and infected foot. Lew's presence momentarily halted the treatment.

"Need somethin' man?" one unshaven medic asked.

"Maybe. I'm looking for a buddy of mine. I heard he might be here. Jack Johnson?"

"Oh yeah man, He's here. Walk through that door, his hootch is right behind this one. Just go on in."

"Okay, thanks."

Lew's gut filled with anxious excitement thinking of reuniting with his friend. He opened the door and stepped inside, eyes searching for Jack among the men sprawled out on cots.

He felt uncomfortable about intruding on the resting men. Surely they deserved a few minutes of relaxation in a relatively comfortable cot instead of sleeping in wet, muddy hole in the ground. He recognized his friend sleeping on a corner cot but, felt he shouldn't wake him.

BOOM, BOOM, BOOM. The arty battery let go a short, loud salvo. It was enough to stir those who were sleeping. Jack was one who tossed a couple of times before raising his body to a sitting position. Thankful for the guns timing and relieved that he didn't have to wake his friend, Lew skirted around packs and web gear strewn on the deck until he reached the foot of Jack's cot.
"Hey man," Lew announced his presence. "You gonna sleep all day or what?"
As the man turned to respond, Lew was taken aback at the appearance of his friend's combat-worn face. It wasn't the clean, healthy, smiling, happy face of the man he had befriended at the Jacksonville Naval Hospital a year earlier. This face was beaten by the hands of fear....tired, worn and hollow. Lew especially noticed that Jack's once gleaming, brown eyes seemed shallow and darker, set deep in weathered, puffy bags, sculpted by tragedy of war. His unshaven face was thin and gaunt and carved with worries and haunting memories. Even though Jack was four years older than Lew and married with a baby girl, the toll of war aged him well beyond thirty. Jack's eyes met Lew's but seemed to stare past the younger medic's as if he wasn't there. The expected happy reunion didn't materialize. Instead, Jack rose and greeted Lew as if he was merely someone he had met in passing. "Lewis," he forced a half-smile, offering his hand rather than the friendly bear hug Lew envisioned. "What are you doing here?"
Lew answered truthfully. "I heard your outfit was in Phu Bai and I wanted to see if I could catch up with you. Hell, I didn't know if you were still alive or got shot up or something."
"Yeah, I'm still kickin'. Only the good die young you know."
"That's what you always told me," Lew reminded.
Jack maintained a polite but distant demeanor. "Let's step outside so we don't bother these guys too much. We just got back from an operation a couple hours ago and they're bushed."
"Okay. Hey listen, I can come back some other time," Lew offered. "I'm with Recon just across the foot bridge. You probably need some sack time yourself."
"Recon? I thought you got assigned First Med."
"I did but didn't care for the bullshit....volunteered for Recon back in August," Lew replied.
"I guess that makes you the dumb-ass, doesn't it?"
Lew snickered at Jack's remark but, didn't answer.

The two leaned against a sandbagged bunker, smoked cigarettes and brought each other up to date until it started to get dark. Lew informed Jack about the patrol the next day then, insisted that he would be back after they returned from the bush. In a surprise move, Jack drew close to the young corpsman, gave him a manly hug and spoke softly, "You take care of yourself …keep your ass down, ya here?"
Lew showed a sad smile. "You too. I'll catch you later."
Jack nodded and turned back toward his hootch.

During the trek back to Recon camp Lew tried to sum up the meeting with Jack. He learned that one of the medics they both knew at Jacksonville was killed on his first day in country. Neither of them knew the whereabouts of anyone else they came over with. It was good to see his friend alive and well even though he was aware that Jack had undergone much more actual combat stress than himself and that was taking its toll on his friend both physically and mentally. *'Those grunts sure have it rough.'*

Skinny had it that the NVA was laying siege on a Marine fire base at Khe Sanh, northwest of Hue'. Word spread that Division S-2 expected a massive attack on the outpost like the one that forced the French to capitulate at Din Bien Phu. It was also expected that in order to surround the Marines there, NVA and NLF reinforcements were to infiltrate the area from the North as well as from all parts of the South. Division wanted to know the whereabouts of those reinforcements. Recon was to find them.

It only took about twenty minutes flight time when the CH-46's landed to insert the team somewhere in the mountainous region of I Corps west of Phu Bai. All the men knew the area was a haven for the NVA and expected the LZ to be *hot.* Fortunately, it wasn't. If they were going to receive enemy fire it would have been while the chopper was most vulnerable…on the ground. Sergeant Holton collected bearings from the map and directed the point man, Rocky, to lead with the M-60 out front. After the bird lifted off and disappeared the patrol set out. The first hour was the most grueling, especially for Doc, who hadn't been in the bush for nearly a month and steep, rugged terrain proved to be physically challenging but, because of the thick, tangling, underbrush the pace was slowed to a few steps at a time; making the movement bearable. Within minutes after their first break the patrol came across a well-worn footpath. It was an unmistakable sign that the enemy was in or had passed through the area recently. How recently was a different matter. Even Doc knew the fresh 'tread' pattern of sandals worn by the VC that were fabricated from old automobile tires, showed up clearly in the damp earth as evidence of very recent use. Looking up ahead Doc saw Holton mark the location of the trail on his map. He saw the sergeant face a moment of uncertainty deciding whether to follow the trail or not. *'Damn. Don't be an ass-hole like Woodcock was in Happy Valley,'*

Holton turned his head and looked the corpsman straight in the eyes then slowly shook his head to let the medic know that they weren't going to take the trail. Relieved, Lew gratefully acknowledged the sergeant's decision with a simple, uncompromising, 'thumbs-up'. Knowing that the trail's location, direction of travel and usage would be of intelligence value, Holton redirected Rocky run a parallel route about ten meters from the trail on the high side of the slope following the path's southern leg of its north-south direction. The patrol continued to flank the path for the remainder of the day, pausing every couple hundred meters or so to set up ambush just in case they were being followed. Despite the fact that Holton ordered no eating or smoking during the ambush breaks, Doc was satisfied just to rest and taste the tepid water from his canteen. Being out of shape the high heat and humidity caused mild cramping in his legs. He needed the time to recuperate from each acute onset.

Rocky came upon a junction in the trail and signaled the patrol to a halt. Holton moved forward to assess the find. From his vantage point Doc couldn't determine what Rocky and the sergeant were discussing but, he was sure it wasn't the weather. It didn't take long to find out. Soon everyone was once again settled in an ambush posture. It looked like a good place to observe the *gooks* should they happen by as well as giving them the higher ground advantage should they be found out. Both branches of the trail seemed to get equal use, indicating significant personnel infiltration into the Phi Bai area.

Doc recalled the 'tire track' sandal impression leading south…the opposite direction of Khe Sanh. One juncture continued south the other branched eastward….toward Phu Bai.

The team held their position until shortly before nightfall when Sergeant Holton took the men out of ambush and led them up the mountain side to find a *harbor site* nearer the top.
Rocky reached the crest sooner than expected. It was obvious that once again, the map was incorrect. He halted at the edge of a tree line at the top of the hill that opened up to a small patch of elephant grass, thorny underbrush and some saplings. Scrutinizing the real estate Holton decided to *harbor* in the tall grass rather than along the tree line. The vantage point gave them a clear view of the mountainous, jungle terrain to their north, west and south and an unobstructed view of the Phu Bai area far off in the east. Keeping in mind that the trail was at the bottom of the hill to their west, and was the most likely direction for an attack, Holton had the men set up the Claymores in a semi-circle facing that direction. Crawling quietly on hands and knees through the thick vegetation, Doc accompanied Rocky to a location on the slope below their position to set up a Claymore.
Lew held his M-16 at the ready as Rocky placed the mine against a bolder, attached the detonator cord and camouflaged its presence before setting back to the *harbor*. After all four Claymores were rigged and ready, pins were straightened on grenades and the machine gun positioned for a sweeping field-of-fire facing the tree line, Holton gave the O.K. for long awaited chow. "No flame, no noise and no smoking," he passed the whispered word.
Doc was hungry but, longed for a cigarette even more than food. In total darkness he opened the tin of something as quietly as possible with the P-38 then spooned a mouthful before he learned by the taste and texture that it was Boned Turkey….not one of his favorites. Fearing extra noise, he ate the fare without doctoring it up and finished the humble meal with a few swallows of warm, chlorinated water.

The men laid down on the cool ground to catch whatever sleep they could before it was their turn to stand watch and respond to the *sitreps*. Doc managed to get a couple hours of restless slumber when his turn came around. Evans passed the handset over to him, whispering, "Doc, your turn." Lew took the receiver and placed it to his ear. Throughout the watch he kept falling off only to be wakened by sudden head jerks. He wasn't aware that the handset had fallen away from his ear unto the ground when he snapped out of dozing off to respond to the faint radio call. Eagerly, he clicked the receiver twice and passed it along to the next man then, quickly fell back to sleep.

It seemed like Doc just laid his head down when Holton woke everyone. Off in the distance near Phu Bai, flashes of light and muted explosions could be seen and heard. Overhead in the night sky, trails of streaking light preceded the swooshing sounds of rockets heading in the direction of the airfield. There was no mistaking that this was a massive enemy rocket attack. Unkle pointed out to Sergeant Holton that flashes of light were coming from one of the mountain valleys behind their position. Immediately the sergeant pulled out a map and under red light conditions plotted out possible coordinates of the enemy launch site. Hurriedly, the radio got passed back to him. "Iron Hand Bravo-Iron Hand Bravo this is Romeo Charlie Six –fire mission-I repeat, fire mission---probable enemy launch site—do you copy? Over," Holton spoke as loud as he dared, just above a whisper. When the confirmation came back, Holton submitted the best guess coordinates where the flashes emanated from and directed "H.E., fire for effect", hoping that his guess was on the money the first time.

Within seconds a barrage of artillery rounds whistled high above them "on the way" to the target. As the outgoing rounds streaked past the team's position the incoming rockets whizzed by from the opposite direction. Arthurs quietly conveyed to the corpsman, "Wouldn't it be wild if they hit each other in mid-air?" he whispered.

"Yeah, that'd be real cool," Doc whispered back ominously. "Shells and rockets exploding right above our heads."

Two salvos of six rounds each impacted in the general area that Holton identified when another Recon team broke in over the net. "Iron Hand Bravo this is Hotel Mike Six…adjust and continue Romeo Charlie Six fire mission…drop five-zero…left seven-five…fire for effect…should be on the mark…do you copy? Over."

The reply came back. "Roger Hotel Mike Six…wait one…break-break…Romeo Charlie Six….Romeo Charlie Six…do you copy and concur with last transmission? Over."

Everyone was aware of another Recon team patrolling the area but Holton was surprised that it was so close. There was a danger of the two teams firing on each other by mistaking the other for the enemy. It was an uncommon, serious SNAFU. Regardless, the other team obviously had a better fix on the launch site. He called back. "Iron Hand Bravo this is Romeo Charlie Six…concur with Hotel Mike Six, Over."

"Roger….break…Hotel Mike Six….I understand…drop five-zero…left seven-five….confirm? Over"

"Roger that…confirmed."

"Good copy Hotel Mike Six…on the way, Over"

Another flurry of screaming projectiles passed overhead; impacting about a *'click'* west, beyond their harbor site. The adjustments made by the other Recon team seemed to have worked as rockets ceased to launch from that area. The consensus between the men was that the site was either blown to smithereens or the enemy packed up and 'di-di'd' to another location. However, Phu Bai was still receiving a scattered concentration of incoming missiles being launched from elsewhere.

No one slept for the remainder of the night as they kept eyes on enemy rockets hitting in a random pattern around the Phu Bai airfield. Occasionally, barely audible 'popping' of small arms fire reached their ears from far off. Arthurs was the RTO and kept Holton and the others informed of radio traffic. It sounded as if the North had invaded the South, disregarding the traditional Vietnamese New Year 'cease fire.'

Most, if not all, of the men felt helpless sitting atop the ridge, unable to do anything but watch the far away flashes and piece together bits of information coming over the radio net.

As dawn broke over Phu Bai the men kept looking east. A few billowing clouds of smoke rose from the populated areas that surround the airstrip. Apparently, none of the rockets found anything vital but, because of the distance, no one knew for sure.

They anxiously waited for word about the Recon camp, wondering if it had been hit; hoping it hadn't; praying for their friends if it had. Sergeant Holton figured that if the enemy were

moving out of the area they might take the trail in the valley behind them. He ordered the men to retrieve the Claymores after they had something to eat and informed the men that they were going back down to observe the trail.
Doc and Pee Wee asked permission to smoke. It was granted. Both men relished the effect of the smoke in their craving lungs. After everyone had eaten they began to retrieve the Claymores. Once again Doc accompanied Rocky to take in the mine. When he reached the location of the device Doc was shocked to find that the camouflage was removed and that it had been turned around to face the harbor site. Both men jerked in fear at the same time. They had been found out! The gooks had sneaked up sometime during the night and turned it around on them. No one heard them… *'Oh sweet Jesus'*, Doc summoned up a dreadful thought. '*What if they came while I was on watch? What if I fell asleep and didn't hear them?* ' Rocky broke the corpsman's trance. "Get the damned thing and get movin'. I'll cover 'ya. Hurry."
Rocky immediately told the sergeant about what happened. Figuring the gooks would probably attack from the tree line, Holton rushed the men to form a defense facing the trees and prepare to put up a life or death fight. Each man spread out and found the best concealment he could. Doc was willing to put money on Holton wishing that he hadn't pulled the other Claymores so soon.

The NCO radioed back that they had been found out but, had no contact with the enemy and requested an immediate extraction. The reply was negative. He was informed that every operational helicopter was being utilized because of a major enemy offensive and none were available. The team would either have to hold their position or 'hump' their way out of the bush. Neither option was appealing.

The Sun rose higher in the sky. It baked the men as they hunkered down motionless in the grass, waiting for the first shots to be fired. The stress of waiting was nearly unbearable. Hours passed without any sign of an imminent attack. Lew's mind began to drift. *'Why aren't they attacking? What's keeping them? Why didn't they turn the other Claymores around too? Maybe there's only one of them? Hey, wait a minute...the mine was clearly marked' FRONT TOWARD ENEMY'! That's what I read! I think?*

Maybe it wasn't turned around on us after all! Maybe both of us were still in a wake up fog and thought we saw something that we really didn't? The wind might have blown the camouflage away? Man, maybe we did screw things up! I wonder if Rocky thinks that too? Maybe I'd better just keep my mouth shut. If anybody finds out we'll both get our asses reamed, not to mention all the embarrassing ridicule we'd have to live with. Yeah, I'll just keep quiet and hope Rocky does too.' The same thoughts kept recycling through the young corpsman mind until a small pebble struck his arm, bringing him back to earth. Evans got his attention and passed the signal to get up and move out. Holton must have decided that the enemy wasn't going to strike…at least now. Word was passed in whispers that the team was going to try to reach a place down in the valley that would accommodate a helicopter and wait there until a chopper could get to them. The march was awkward and tiring. Heavy, thorny underbrush prevented any hope of swift movement. To make matters worse, dark clouds promised monsoon type downpours. Within minutes the rumbling thunder preceded a curtain of water that pelted the entire valley with large, cold, balls of rain. The slope quickly became slippery with mud. Footing was precarious as every downhill step was a balancing act. Finally recognizing that they couldn't maneuver through the torrent, the leader called for an extended break that would allow the men to rest and get something to eat, albeit cold and soggy. When the deluge continued into dusk, Holton wisely decided to harbor there for the night, grouping the men in tight quarters. Ponchos were donned, only to prevent more body heat from escaping from their thoroughly drenched, shivering bodies. The pounding rain hid the noise of ponchos rustling. For the most part the team seemed secure in the harbor.

Evans passed the radio over to Lew. "Doc. Your turn," was all that was necessary to let the corpsman know it was his turn on guard. Barely able to make out the luminous dots on his watch, Doc figured the time was 0200 and the rain was still falling although, not as hard as earlier. He reached in the dark for the handset and carefully pulled it under the poncho, keeping it as dry as possible. Determined not to risk dozing off, the medic sat upright against a tree, pulled the poncho hood over his head and just sat there shivering, unable to hear anything other than raindrops beating against the hood. As usual, random thoughts and recollections kept him company between spurts of concentrated vigilance. Twice his dreaming was interrupted when he had to shake Evans in order to stop his snoring. As the watch continued he became convinced the enemy wouldn't be able to see the amber or smell the smoke through the shroud of water, and ducked under the poncho to light up a cigarette. Three more smokes helped carry him thought the hour-long vigil before the radio came to life.

"Night Hawk, Night Hawk....if you're nestled with Nellie, click it twice."

Lew was on the verge of sending the signal when he realized that he was running with team *Thin Man* not Night Hawk. It dawned on him that both teams in the platoon were out in the bush at the same time. Two clicks indicated *Night Hawk* was secure in their harbor.

"Copy...Break...Thin Man, Thin Man...I need three."

Lew squeezed the handset three times.

"Good copy....out."

It occurred to Lew that he must have dozed off and missed the *sitrep* the previous night or else he would have known that Night Hawk was in the bush then. *'Damn'*

He passed the radio over to Johnson.

The next morning Sergeant Holton learned that helicopters were now available but low cloud cover prevented them from flying. He advised the men that they would have to wait it out until the weather cleared. Once more consulting the map he determined that the extraction LZ that he chose the day before was the best choice and that they would remain concealed in the *harbor site*. It made no sense to move and possibly alert the enemy of their location. On-the-other-hand, he also wanted to scope out the trail on the other side of the mountain. If Charlie was moving, Division would want to know. He pondered the idea of splitting the team up however, deciding that it would be too risky, he dropped the notion, opting instead just to wait for better weather. They had enough rations and water for a week and knowing that the weather changes dramatically, a chopper could be sent just as soon as there was a window of opportunity. Holton drew the team around him and informed them of his decision to remain in the *harbor*.

Everyone spent the day catching naps or reading. The main thing was to keep as quiet and invisible. By late afternoon the drizzle dissipated and rays of sunlight penetrated the leaves overhead. Holton called for the choppers to take them home. The men harnessed themselves into the gear and backpacks then proceeded to make their way to the nearby LZ. Pushing through wet, steaming elephant grass the eight men reached the LZ only moments before two, CH-46's appeared under a few lingering rain clouds that touched the tops of the highest ridges around them.

One chopper descended to the yellow smoke Rocky had tossed into the center of the LZ then, touched the ground momentarily before quickly lifting off again. The move surprised the entire team into thinking that the bird was taking enemy ground fire but there wasn't any. The second Sea Knight dropped down and planted its wheels and rear ramp in the tall grass; allowing the men to hustle on board.

Once inside the men thrust their rifles through the portholes on both side of the craft in preparation to return any incoming fire. The bird ascended straight up instead of the customary gradual, forward climb then came about in a wide bank to port where it found a course back to Recon camp. Relieved, Doc and Pee Wee lit up as soon as the air cooled.

The men learned from the crew chief that the first chopper that landed picked up *Night Hawk* team a few minutes earlier and wanted to fly both teams in one chopper in order to release the second one for another mission. Apparently, the ramp door on the first 46 wouldn't come open and there was no time to spend having the men climb through the side door thereby, forcing the pilot to handoff the extraction to the second chopper.

Doc expelled a long trail of smoke from his satisfied lungs while catching Rocky staring from the troop seat across from him. The young medic sensed that both of them were thinking that they both screwed up with the Claymore thing; bringing the patrol to a premature termination. It didn't matter to the corpsman. They all got out of the bush safely, without making contact with the enemy.

After the platoon returned to their camp the men learned more details of the massive TeT offensive sweeping throughout South

Vietnam. Every major city and town had secretly been infiltrated by NVA and NLF forces. There had been rocket attacks in Saigon, Da Nang, Hue', Phu Bai and nearly every other town, village and outpost in the country.
Word spread that the beer tent at Phu Bai was hit. *Those bastards.* Rumors accompanied every reported attack. Supposedly, ARVN troops shed their uniforms and took up arms with the NVA in Hue and Da Nang; tank battalions swept across the DMZ and were attempting over run the 26th Marines at Khe Sanh; the North Vietnamese Air Force sent waves of MiGs up to meet and shoot down American planes; tens of thousands of Chinese troops were staging at the DMZ to reinforce the NVA. None of the rumors were substantiated by fact nor, taken seriously by Lew. Unkle called the whole mess the "Big Shit". In an unusual move, the men were told to keep their grenades and Claymores instead of turning them in and be ready to move out on short notice.
While most of the men stayed in their *hootches* waiting for the 'word' to come down to 'saddle-up', Doc took advantage of the 'down-time' to stroll over to the 1/1 camp to visit with his friend Jack for a short while. When he got to the outfit's Aid Station he learned from the attending corpsman that Jack's company had gone out on an operation and there was no way to know when they would return. Disappointed by the news Doc returned to the Recon camp only to find both Night Hawk and Thin Man teams gone. He knew he screwed up by not being there when the teams '*hatted-out'*.
"Damn it," he spit out in disbelief. "I was only gone for a half hour." It occurred to him that the teams might still be waiting at the chopper pad. Grabbing the 782 gear and weapon he scurried over to the pad only to find it deserted. It was too late, he missed them. For the next couple of hours he mulled over his missing the muster and wondered if it was court-martial offense in wartime. It bothered him not knowing where his team went or what their mission was. '*Shit, what if somebody gets 'dinged'? What if they need me? How will be able to face them again?'* The burden of guilt sent him into a depressed mood, sulking alone in the empty *hootch*, wondering what the hell was going on. Suddenly the mood was broken as a runner opened the door and urgently gasped "Doc, get your shit together and muster at the pad now….every swingin' dick left in the compound….needs to go on

reaction team……no packs, just web gear…..tell anyone else you see……no stragglers."

Lew stomped out the cigarette, jumped to his feet, grabbed his weapon, 782 and Unit One and dashed toward the helo pad. He merged with the remaining men from other platoons as they rushed toward the pad. The only thing he learned was that the team, *Purple Heart,* was to muster and provide security for a downed CH-46 somewhere near Hue'. No one took time to brief the group on what the expedient assembly was about. The gathering was a hodge-podge of troops who didn't appear to have a leader even though two sergeants were included in the mix. Lew quickly took the last puffs on the Viceroy as the CH-46 was making its descent.
The chopper started to lift off even before the last man stepped onto the ramp. The crew chief grabbed the Marine by the suspenders and yanked him on board.

The chopper shook and vibrated as it moved in the direction of Hue' as fast as the pilot could coax it. Lew never rode on a helicopter traveling so fast and as close to the deck as this bird was traveling. There was no doubt in his mind that the crew wanted to get to where ever they were going in a hurry. No more than ten minutes elapsed before the chopper quickly dropped from the sky and landed on a dried up rice paddy. The crew chief hurried the men out of the cargo bay. A grunt NCO on the ground took charge and directed the reinforcements to cross a mass of dried-up rice paddies toward the edge of a tree line that hid a small village. Sporadic small arms fire greeted them as they scurried across the open remnants. A contingent of grunts already in place near the *ville* let go covering fire for their reinforcements to get into position behind a dike. Doc broke away from the men when he spotted a downed CH-46 lying crumpled on its port side with a dark cloud of smoke rising from it. Assuming that he was the only corpsman around that could render aid if anyone was still inside the twisted mass of metal; he dashed across the dirt field as fast as his legs could carry him toward the smoking superstructure. His heart was racing and lungs aching as he scrambled in a zigzag pattern, doing his best to avoid the enemy bullets that marked the trail behind him. Clearly, he was the target but, didn't hear the reports from enemy rifles. All he saw was puffs of dust kicking up near him and behind him. Instinct told him to dive for cover behind one of the dikes. He dropped a split-second before a spray of bullets would have been his ticket home….. in a body bag. Return fire from the grunts silenced the AK. Taking in a deep breath Doc rose onto his feet and continued the rush toward the chopper. The impact of his feet landing against the hardened earth jarred his head to where his vision bounced like a basketball. His boots felt like sandbags. He couldn't travel fast enough. There were no trees to jump behind like in the jungle. The run was dreamlike where you ran but didn't get anywhere. He forced to himself to keep moving. Disregarding anything else going on around him, getting to the chopper was the prevailing objective. His brain shifted gears.

He was at the twenty…..fifteen….ten….five…..TOUCHDOWN! The last effort to reach the chopper had him dive against it on the downed side. Taking quick, giant gulps of breath he had to sit a few seconds to regain his strength before looking inside. *'One more deep breath'*.

On his knees Lew managed to find an opening in the thin skin airframe big enough to crawl through. He caught sight of two of the aircrew lying unconscious in the burning wreckage. *'Oh sweet Jesus, I gotta get these guys outta here.'* Taking off the web gear he spread the sheet metal as best he could to make an opening large enough to climb through. He barely penetrated the cargo bay when he spotted a .38 revolver lying next to him. *'I'm keepin' this baby,'* he told himself as he tucked it inside his belt before going farther inside. Nauseating smoke burned his eyes and forced a series of gagging coughs that gripped his lungs, nearly overcoming his will to reach the Marines. Making up his mind to rescue them the Doc beat the temptation to give up and continued crawling through the debris until he blindly found the first man. The smoke wasn't thick but, it irritated his eyes so badly that he had to keep them closed. Lew reached under the man's body to flip him over. *"Shit...he's a heavy bastard!'* The slight framed corpsman weighed about 130 pounds; the Marine was about 200 pounds, dead weight. *'God, how am I going to do this?'* It took all the strength Lew had to turn the man over on his back. He then began to perform an assessment. The man was still alive with no signs of massive blood loss. First thing was to get the unconscious victim out of further danger before attempting to render aid. Kneeling at the man's head Doc gripped the man's flight-suit by its collar and once more mustered up strength to drag the man inch by inch over the tangled mess, cutting his own knees against the sharp objects strewn everywhere. A 'POP' alerted the corpsman that either ammo was beginning to cook off or the VC was still taking aim at the bird. The struggle to move the man suddenly became more urgent. He pulled the man about a foot, paused to get another grip; pulled again; paused, pulled again; slowly inching their way to the opening.

When he reached the portal Doc backed through guiding his legs out first then pulled the man again. The hammer of the revolver protruding from his belt caught a piece of the airframe and pulled it to a half-cocked position, bringing the medic to an immediate stop, fearing that he was about to shot off his penis. He carefully withdrew the weapon from his belt, re-set the hammer and set the piece aside near the opening then, followed through with the rest of his body with the Marine in tow.

Two crewmen from the chopper that brought him in were waiting there. Doc gladly turned the man over to his flying comrades. Desperately trying to regain strength and catch his breath Doc couldn't even holler out for the crewmen to stop from carrying the injured man over their shoulders like a sack of potatoes back to the waiting chopper.

Not knowing if he had enough strength, or courage, left to re-enter the chopper to retrieve the second man Doc nearly abandoned the idea but, his conscious told him that he just couldn't leave the man to die.

Once more Doc climbed through the hole and searched for the second man. He reached the man but didn't bother to try to find out if he was alive reasoning, that it didn't matter, the main thing now was to get the body out. As he began thc same routine as on the first man the victim let out a painful moan. That was a welcome sign. Doc made a weak attempt at comforting the Marine before continuing his ordeal. "OK buddy. Just hang on, I'm getting you out of here," he uttered loudly, hoping the man could hear and understand him. "You'll be home in no time….just hang in there."

Knowing there was a chance of saving the Marine, Doc found the energy to move the man's lighter frame quickly through the debris to the opening. POP…another round went off while smoke continued to fill the cargo cabin. With more resolve than before the Navy man mustered all the strength left in him to exert one more, final pull to the improvised portal. This time he repositioned the injured airman so the other two crewmen could pull their counterpart through to safety. Choking and gasping for breath the corpsman followed the victim through the opening. Doc thought he was on the verge of passing out from poisonous fumes when the fresh air hit his lungs. Through burning, watering eyes he saw the two airmen again carrying the injured man on their shoulders. *'Those sons-of-bitches. The poor bastard don't stand a chance of surviving now.'* Lew cursed the two aircrew men for taking the injured men away before he had a chance to treat them. The helicopter revved up and took off with the injured onboard.

Doc took another minute of rest before getting to his feet. The revolver was gone. "Those puke bastards," Lew spit aloud "They stole my pistol."

Physically drained, he struggled to move around to the cockpit. "Shit," he voiced his emotion when he came across the pilot slumped over in the tangled mess. Reaching into the wreckage he felt the man's wrist for a pulse. The pilot's charred skin sloughed-off in his fingers. Then he grabbed the helmet and lifted the man's head to examine the pupils. A marine Captain came up behind the corpsman.

"He alive Doc?"

"I don't think so." Lew made a preliminary guess before confirming. "No sir. He's gone.

Lew moved over to the co-pilot trapped inside the wreckage and burned from the feet to mid-trunk. A quick glance told the medic that this man was barely alive and will expire any second despite moaning coming from his faint, scratchy voice.

"Him too, any second Sir," Lew advised. "The most we can do is try to get them out before chopper goes up in flame."

No Doc, we can't do anything for these men," the captain reckoned.

The corpsman knew that by how the wreckage was all tangled up, neither body could be retrieved. It hurt knowing that one of them was still hanging on by a very tiny thread. He wished he had the courage to relieve the man from his misery. For a split-second he was ready to raise the M-16 to the flyer's head. The officer removed Doc's impulsive compassion.

"You better get over there Doc," he directed the corpsman to join the grunts at the *ville.* "Those men may need you there."

“Yes Sir,” Lew obeyed reluctantly, reasoning that there was nothing he could do at the chopper and he didn’t want to see them burned anymore.

Lew dashed across the rice paddy expecting an enemy round to find him. He made it safely to the dike where the grunt fire-teams were taking cover. Plopping down in between two flak-jacketed, infantrymen he announced, “I’m a Corpsman…anybody hurt?”

“I don’t think so Doc…..didn’t hear any call for corpsman up,” one replied.

“Me neither,” the other concurred.

“What’s going on here?” Lew questioned between gasps of breath.

“All I know is some dinks are shootin’ at us, an’ we’re shootin’ back.”

The other grunt added, “We think they downed that chopper.”

“How many?” Lew inquired.

“Not too many now. I guess most of ‘em di-di’d when you guys showed up.”

Lew raised his head above the brim of the dike to take a look.

“Better keep your head down Doc.”

Lew took the man’s advice when somebody opened up an automatic burst from an M-16.

“THERE….BETWEEN THE HOOTCHES……BLACK PJ’S…..LAST HOOTCH ON THE RIGHT,” one of the grunts down the line screamed direction.

Instantly, everyone began emptying their magazines into the structure. Lew took the cue and joined in the fracas while catching glimpses of his spent rounds bouncing off the helmet of the grunt next to him. It would be humorous if it weren’t for the situation. Their fire was not countered.

Never having been on line with infantry troops, Lew was astounded by the volume of fire laid-down. *‘Nobody’s going to survive that!’* he thought as he looked up and down the line, estimating that maybe only forty Marines unleashed the awesome barrage.

‘What happens now?’ he wondered. *‘Are we just going to hunker down here? I hope they don’t want us to sweep the ville.’* The question remained unanswered for a long, nerve-rattling but, uneventful hour before someone barked out, “RECON….PULL BACK.”

Doc scanned for who directed the command. One of the sergeants from Recon stood away from the grunts and announced, "Recon, follow me."

'Oh shit...what's up now?' Doc feared that they were being ordered to go in and check out the *ville.* To his surprise, the sergeant was leading them back out into the open space of dried up paddies, seemingly oblivious to the possibility that the paddies could be mined. Fortunately, it wasn't. The NCO directed everyone to crouch low when they reached his position. "Okay, listen up," he began. "They're pulling us out of here now. Choppers are on the way so just hang tight and keep low until then. I want you to spread out form a semi-circle between the *ville* and the LZ. When we get a visual, I'll pop green smoke. Clear?"

A few men responded affirmative, the others just quietly accepted the order and dispersed to form the line. Doc positioned himself midway in order to respond to any "corpsman up" call coming from either direction. Once in place, he lit up a smoke and bided time hoping the enemy didn't regroup for another encounter with the Americans. Small arms fire quieted down to an occasional shot from the Marines still in position on the dike near the *ville.* The chopper arrived near dusk. It landed without receiving fire and the Recon men scurried onboard, each one thinking that they were now being relocated to Hue' City as reinforcements. To their surprise, the chopper transported them back to the Recon camp at Phu Bai. Doc was anxious to learn the fate of the Marine aircrew men that he pulled from the downed chopper. On a whim he asked the crew chief on this chopper. The only response he received was an uncaring shoulder shrug. Lew then assumed that he would probably never find out their disposition and accepted the most probable outcome is that they expired en-route, since both were in bad shape and didn't receive the medical attention that he wanted give before the two helicopter jerks toted them off like gunnysacks.

Dead tired, Lew hobbled inside the *hootch,* unexpectedly finding the men from his team had returned from their mission.

"Doc," Pee Wee called. "Where the hell were you when the shit-hit-the-fan, man?"

Hoping to reconcile any hard feelings for not being there in time to go out with them he replied, "Out on a reaction force. A chopper was shot down near some *ville* between here and Hue'. What about you guys? Where were you?"

He sensed that his ploy worked when Unkle spoke up. "Man, we got into some shit up in Hue'….the ba…"
Pee Wee interrupted, "The bad news is that Prideaux bought it."
Doc couldn't believe what he heard. "Damn! Prideaux? Bought it…it meaning killed?"
"Yeah. KIA Doc."
"How?"
Arthurs went into a complete description. "We're securing this bridge, when the *gooks* opened up. The fuckers were everywhere. Prideaux tried to get up and move to better cover…sniper got him right between the eyes. Died instantly"
"You don't know it was sniper," Unkle challenged.
"It had to be. Too good a shot from that distance," Arthurs argued.
Mervyn quieted the argument. "Doc, I never saw anything like it," he quietly confessed. "A round caught him in the head…he just stood there….frozen in time….like in a picture…for…maybe two seconds before dropping. It was weird man…totally weird."
Johnnie Evans questioned the corpsman. "What about your mission Doc, anybody get hurt?"
"Nobody from Recon, Johnnie. Both pilots were killed and I'm pretty the crew chiefs died too but, I'm not real sure about that. Two other fly-boys hustled them away before I had a chance to do anything for them. They were in bad shape but, breathing when I found them." Doc let it go at that.
"Sorry to hear that Doc," Rocky saw the corpsman's hurt.
Everyone in the *hootch* surrendered to a solemnly quiet evening, each man reflecting on the loss of another Recon brother in his own way.

News of the enemy offensive seemed to prevail in all conversations. Word came around of massive attacks in Saigon and Hue'. The American Embassy in Saigon was supposedly over run while the North Vietnamese Army held the entire city of Hue'. No one knew exactly what to believe since the *brass* wasn't passing along any information. It was typical to keep the troops in the dark. Scuttle-butt had the 26th Marines fending off five NVA regiments at Khe Sanh while 1/5, 2/5 and 1/1 were supposedly fighting door to door and hand to hand in Hue'. When Lew heard 1/1 was in the mix he hoped his friend, Jack was safe. Additional *skinny* was that the Army's 1st Cav and 101st Airborne units were also rushed into the city. Rumors abounded about the VC and NVA killing civilians by the hundreds in reprisal for not joining them against the American and ARVN forces. Somebody mentioned that a CAP unit at a *ville* a couple miles south of the camp got wiped out by NVA commandos sneaking in and cutting the throats of the few men who were there to help citizens.

Doc sat there listening to all that everyone said, mentally dispelling most of the accounts, doubting their reliability although, one rumor hit particularly hard. He reasoned that it must have come from the company aid station, which was the prime, local source of gossip. Word was spreading that a field medical unit called *'Charlie Med'* was being so overwhelmed with causalities that corpsmen were actually being pulled from grunt companies to lend a hand. Lew was skeptical about the plausibility and wisdom of taking corpsman away from 'front line companies' as they didn't have enough medics to begin with. Having never heard of Charlie Med, Lew asked around at the aid station. One of the corpsmen, who he didn't know, offered something about it being somewhere up north, possibly near Khe Sanh or Con Tien.

"What kindda shit's that?" Lew emphasized. "Khe Sanh IS the front line! So is Con Tien! So is Hue'! You can't get any more front line than that!"

"Hey man, the whole stinkin' country is the front if you ask me," the corpsman issued his comment.

"Yeah, yeah," Lew wryly agreed and retreated back to the hootch.

That afternoon a memorial service was held for LCPL James Prideaux. Lew always assumed that, because of the last name, the fallen Marine was from Louisiana although, he never bothered to ask. Actually, the troop was such an FNG he hardly got to know him at all. He was intrigued however, to learn that Prideaux hailed from Colorado.

His mind drifted during the canned eulogy. *"When the hell is all this shit going to end? What the hell did he die for? What did anybody die for? What the hell are we doing here?*

I don't want to die here...not for this shit pile piece of real estate. God, damn those bastards who got us into this mess. Let them or their kids come over here and….." TAPS broke the corpsman's silent rant; the formation saluted their fallen comrade, ending the service.

Orders were given for everyone to remain in the compound and be ready to saddle-up at a moment's notice. Just before evening chow S-2 sent out an advisory to expect an enemy rocket attack followed by a possible ground assault.. The entire Phu Bai area was placed on high alert, especially the area around the prime target…the airfield. Any incoming rockets falling short of the runway would most likely hit within the Recon camp. Someone suggested that maybe it would be a good idea to reinforce the platoon's bunker with more sandbags. Doc didn't buy into the idea. "Why bother?" he casually questioned. "I believe that when you number's up…it's up! There's nothing anyone can do to change it."

The 'Reverend', LCPL Pledger, detected an opportunity to voice his religious views. "Doc's right. Everyone's destiny is pre-ordained by God…..yours, mine, Docs…everybody's."

It didn't take long for the other men to jump on the band wagon with their points of view. The mood shifted as a result. Mild disagreements led to loud, petty arguments. Doc just sat back and took in all the bickering; wishing he hadn't even opened his mouth in the first place.

The Reverend simply became 'Rev' when after a short period of squabbling amongst the troops he intervened with an unwelcome prayer. "Oh Lord God Almighty, we ask that you watch over us and our brothers in this grueling conflict……."

"Amen '*Rev,*" Johnson put a stop to the preaching before it led to a lengthy dissertation.

Suddenly, there was an uncommon hush in the quarters. Everyone went quiet and returned to whatever they were doing before the debate started.

A short time after everyone cooled down Sergeant Holton entered, telling the men that
the guard around the compound was to be doubled that night.

Being the lowest ranking FNG's, Pledger, Vess, Phillips and Miller got the first duty.

It was around 2330hrs. when a whisper woke Doc from a sound sleep.

"Doc, you awake Doc?'

Lew stirred in the cot trying to ignore the voice.

"Hey Doc, wake up man, I got a problem."

The corpsman opened his eyes to see the dark outline of a brawny man leaning over his cot. "Who's that?" he demanded.

"It's me Doc….Rocky. Hey Doc, I'm sorry to wake 'ya Doc but, I got a problem."

The Marine whiffed of alcohol. Coming from Rocky the smell didn't make sense. Lew never saw the big guy drink anything stronger than coffee.

Even though he really didn't want to, Doc reluctantly sat up to listen to the Marine's problem. "What's wrong Rock?"

"I got a major problem Doc; maybe you can help me with it."

"I don't know Rock, if it's money I might be able to help but, if it's clap you'll have to get with me in the morning."

"No, No. No Doc, it's not that stuff."

"Awright. What is it?"

"Ya see Doc, I'm getting short. Pretty soon I'll be going back to the *World*. I'll probably find a job, get married and settle down…maybe start a family."

"Sounds like a good plan to me Rock"

"Yeah but, think about it. My last name is Schmitt."

"Uh huh."

"What if I have a daughter? What the hell kind of girl's name sounds good with Schmitt?"

The question caught Lew off guard. He wanted to chuckle but, out of respect, chose not to. For the Marine it was a serious dilemma. Instead, he made a weak attempt to suggest a few female names.

"I don't know Rock, what about Mary? I know it's probably overused but, it *is* pretty."

"Mary Schmitt…. Mary Schmitt…nah….see what I mean Doc, nothing goes with Schmitt."

"Okay. How about..." Lew paused, buying time to think. "Sheryl? The S-H. kinda blends into the S-C-H in Schmitt ?"

"Sheryl? Not too bad….maybe?"

Lew wanted to get back to sleep but, didn't want Rocky to get the notion that he was uncaring. "Ya know Rock. I'd be willing to bet that your wife might be inclined to name a girl after either her mother or grandmother or your mother or grandmother. That will solve everything."

"Oh, you think so? What if their names are Lucille or Gertrude or somethin' like that, huh?"

Lew pondered a moment. "Listen, it won't matter. You can always give your daughter a nickname. Lots of dads call their little girls Princess or something like that. By the way, what is your mother-in-law's name anyway?"
"Mother-in-law? Doc, I ain't married. Hell, I don't even have a girlfriend yet!"
Befuddled and exasperated, Lew expelled a sigh. "Tell you what Rock, let's discuss it more tomorrow. We'll dig up a dictionary somewhere and go through all the girl's names until we find one that just fits, okay?"
"Okay. Hey why aren't you whispering?"
"Look around. We're the only one's here. Everybody else is out pullin' guard."

The following two days found the platoon preparing for another patrol. Doc kept his word to Rocky about looking up girl's names but, Rocky couldn't decide on a name that he liked. Eventually, he let it *'slide,'* opting to deal with it when the time came.
Word came around that a renegade Army soldier was on the loose in the Phu Bai area; everyone was to be on the lookout for him. *Skinny* had it that he was a Green Beret with three tours of duty in country under his belt. When he returned for his fourth tour he simply decided to go off and fight his own war.
"Whadda thinks up with that nut case Doc?," Private Vess addressed the corpsman.
"Hey man, I don't know. Who knows what goes on in people's minds. Maybe he thinks he can do a better job on his own or maybe he just got tired of putting up with all the bullshit."
"To everything there is a purpose," the Rev spoke up.
"Yeah, yeah, yeah, Rev. My purpose is to get back to the *World* in one piece," Mervyn countered the preacher.
"With God's help, you will......but only if HE wants you to."
"My man," Evans questioned the Rev. "How do you even know God's a he?"
"Good question Marine," Rev responded. "Actually, God is non-genderous…neither male nor female. We just say HE to keep things simple."
"Non-genderous! Don't sound like no real word to me," Evans doubted Rev's vocabulary rather than his answer. "What do you think Doc? Is non-genderous a word?

"Beats me. Sounds like it could be," Lew mumbled while lighting up a smoke.
Sergeant Clifford opened the door and entered, breaking up the semi-intellectual conversation. He was sporting a mischievous looking grin.
"Oh shit Sarge," Mervyn anticipated unwelcome news. "What are we in for this time?"
Clifford held off answering right away, hoping to build a good news-bad news presentation. Extending time, he strolled to the center of the hootch before answering.
"First men, I have good news.....and I have bad news." He paused another moment.
"Give us the bad news first Sarge," Unkle spoke up.
The sergeant scanned the men's faces. "Very well, here it is...... The old man wants the whole company to stand inspection tomorrow at 0900. Clean Utes, boots, covers and pieces."
Jaws dropped at the unbelievable announcement. They were in a combat zone, in the middle of a major enemy offensive and the C.O. orders an inspection?
"You want the good news now?" Clifford set the stage to tell them regardless of an answer. "Well, the good news is......," a hush fell...... "we'll be in the bush."
Lew paid no attention to the chatter going on, instead he fell into an unexplainable surge of anxiety. '*Oh God. I don't want to go out again. I'm tired of the humpin', the heat, the cold and I'm tired of being afraid. I'm tired of losing friends. I just want to go home and forget about this God-forsaken war.*' It was this moment in time that he finally realized that he was 'over-the-hump'. He had completed more than half of his thirteen month tour.
"Only six more months to go. I might be lucky enough to make it.'

At dawn the team mustered at the chopper pad, ready but not eager to venture into the notoriously dangerous A Shau Valley, near the Laotian border. Although no one briefed the men of the exact mission, everyone knew that many smaller trails branched off the Ho Chi Minh Trail in Laos and penetrated into the A Shau. Most of the men speculated that Division wanted to know more about the routes and volume of traffic on them. Since only Lt. Williamson and Sergeant Clifford had maps, some of the team even suspected that they might be secretly crossing the border into

Laos. The mood was unusually quiet as they waited for the choppers to arrive. Not knowing when he'll be able to smoke again, Doc lit up three times during the wait. With a tongue-in-cheek quip Rocky broke the mood. "Smoke 'em if 'ya got 'em, huh Doc."

"You betcha," Lew bounced back. "No tellin' when I'll get another chance to dirty up my lungs."

"FIVE OUT," Arthurs alerted the lieutenant when he made radio contact with the chopper pilot.

"Saddle up gents," Williamson readied the team. "They're coming now."

Doc took one last drag before extinguishing the cigarette on the ground then, turned to Rocky, "How do I look, Hon?" he mused.

"Ravishing. Simply ravishing. I'd be proud to take you out to only the finest of jungles."

"Oh, you silly boy, you."

"Cut the shit man," Unkle scorned in a serious vain. "This ain't no time for jokin' around."

Rocky glared at Unkle as if he was about to tear into the corporal for reprimanding him however, the big guy chose to accept the remark as merely a release of tension that he too was feeling and said nothing.

Lew understood the corporal's anxiety. Unkle was a 'short-timer', with less than 100 days left in his tour. The Marine made it this long without a scratch; he certainly didn't want to 'buy-the-farm' now.

"Hey Doc," Rocky tugged on the corpsman's Tiger-striped shirt. "Come here a second," he said, pulling Lew aside. "There's something I want to ask you before we go."

Lew imagined the Marine bringing up the girl's name thing again. He was wrong.

"Was the Claymore really turned around last patrol?"

Lew was relieved that Rocky was the first to bring it up. "I don't think so Rock," he confessed. "I think we screwed up boo-coo."

"I think so too. It ain't going to happen again."

Sensing mutual satisfaction over the admissions, he nodded agreement then both men moved out to the chopper as its wheels touched down.

In an unusual move the gunner opened up with the .50 cal *'Ma Duce'* as the chopper descended to a clearing in the valley floor then, unexpectedly lifted off to move to another location. The maneuver was repeated twice again before the actual insertion took place. It was obvious that the procedure was used to deceive the enemy.

Once on the ground, Lt. Williamson consulted his map then directed Rocky to *'run point'*, leading the way up the heavily forested, mountainside. "Look for caves or bunkers," he whispered extra instruction before allowing Rocky to move out. The point man nodded understanding. Everyone was well aware that this is the enemy's domain. Even the elusive, *Katu* tribesmen, who hunted in the valley, were just as likely to fight the Americans with their bows and spears as the VC and NVA would with AK's. The primitive people were known sympathizers of the VC but, since they were so secretive an encounter with them would be by chance, not design. Despite knowing that, Doc couldn't escape from having the eerie sensation that they were being watched.

The team barely started the 'hump' when the lieutenant signaled a halt to their movement as they came across a break in the canopy that afforded a clear view of a prominent feature on a nearby ridge. Lew guessed that the leader also sensed something strange going on. When the officer radioed in for a 'marker' round be fired on the adjacent ridgeline, Doc knew for sure that the L.T. expected something to happen. A few seconds later a projectile whistled overhead and with a muted explosion, emitted a large, white, puffy cloud of 'Willy Peter' smoke that served as a reference point should 'arty' be needed in a hurry. Lew observed the leader marking the point of impact on the map before signaling Rocky to continue.

Progress up the steep slope was slow and deliberate. Each step was carefully placed to avoid making noise. Unlike some patrol leaders the team had in the past, Lt. Williamson called for frequent breaks as to not over exhaust the men. Doc, for one, appreciated the rests, regardless of the no smoking edict. By mid-afternoon the patrol found no signs of the enemy or trails but, there was plenty of daylight left; enough for the LT to change the patrol route and still cover a lot of ground. The next break he called Sergeant Clifford up from his position at the rear of the column. After conferring with Clifford a few minutes the lieutenant told Rocky to head west along the finger of the ridgeline once they reached the summit. The team moved out again following the finger that descended to the valley floor. The terrain along their path wasn't as steep as the slope they traversed earlier nor, was it as heavily vegetated, making it easier for the patrol to negotiate. The team was near the bottom when Rocky raised a clinched fist, calling for an abrupt halt. Not knowing the reason for the stop, everyone assumed a combat posture. The LT moved up to where Rocky stopped dead in his tracks. Silently, the Marine pointed overhead then continued the message by lowering his arm and sweeping it in a semi-circle. Williamson scanned the area. The team stumbled across what appeared to be an enemy 'harbor site'.

Trees in the canopy were tied together to form a mesh of leaves for concealment from the air and the ground cover was flattened in about a 100 foot diameter circle as if a company sized enemy force had used the location as a resting place or staging area, probably within the past week The lieutenant whispered for Rocky to stand fast while he and Unkle 'snooped' the site. The two fanned out looking for anything that might have intelligence value.

Doc began his own, mental observations. *'No signs of cooking fires- probably a temporary rallying point. Can't see any trash- they probably didn't stay here long.*

What about blood? Maybe this could be an evacuation point? Booby-traps-I wonder if they would even booby-trap their own camp? Trails? There's gotta be a trail!'

Unkle motioned for the lieutenant to come to where he was. Sure enough, there was a footpath leading into and out of the enemy harbor site. *'What now?' What's the LT going to do now?* Williamson approached Rocky and whispered something. The word got relayed back to the column that the lieutenant was going take the men back up the finger and find a place to harbor for the night. During the return to higher ground he assigned the reliable, seasoned veterans, Sergeant Clifford and Pee Wee, the unenviable task of setting up a listening post between the enemy site and their own. He further advised them that Unkle and Rocky would be in position half-way between their LP and the harbor to provide covering fire should they need to *di-di* back up the hill. They had instructions to do nothing but listen. Lew couldn't understand the reason for breaking up the team but, then again, he was just the corpsman. He didn't relish the thought of having to go back down the hill if somebody got hit.

Once the rest of the team settled in the harbor the LT ordered a 50/50 watch at two hour intervals. Half the men rested for two hours while the other half remained on guard. *' It's going to be a long, restless night,"* Doc feared. *'I hope nothing goes down. God, please don't let anything happen.'*

Aside from being wakened every two hours the night passed without incident. First light brought the four isolated Marines back into the fold with nothing to report. The sergeant and lieutenant conferred while the men ate a quick meal before continuing the patrol. The question on everyone's mind was '*What now?'* The answer came shortly. Rocky was directed to return to the enemy campsite for the men to set up a few grenade, bobby-traps, then take an easterly course, paralleling the trail. Remembering the ambush in Happy Valley, Doc and the other survivors looked at each other with worried faces, hoping the lieutenant wasn't thinking about actually taking the trail. Rocky led the way back down the finger to the site where a couple men quickly set the traps. As they worked Williamson slipped over to where the trail picked up and followed it a few steps into the jungle for a closer look. Upon returning he motioned for the team to move out, directing the point man to skirt the trail instead of using it. Doc breathed a sigh of relief along with the others. The lieutenant was careful not to let Rocky cut a path too close to the trail, preferring to barely keep within visual range yet, still remain close enough to hear troops approaching, and being equally careful to maintain strict noise discipline themselves.

Their movement was slower than usual. Every pair of eyes was straining to pierce though the lush, green foliage. Ears were tuned to listen to the slightest variation of jungle sounds and pick up any enemy chatter or movement. Every so often the patrol came to a halt just to stop and listen.

As in all other patrols that Doc had been on, a series of useless, unimportant thoughts popped into his head. *'I wonder if the VC have recon teams? I never heard of it before but, maybe they do? If they do, I wonder if they have corpsmen like me? I'm tired of all this humpin' and livin' in the boonies. I've run enough patrols. I did my share for LBJ. I wonder what my chance is of getting transferred back to First Med? Maybe I'll check it out when we get back. Maybe not. I just can't up and leave these guys. We're all too tight.'*

His lack of concentration caused him to nearly run up the back of Johnson when the patrol made one of its listening stops. This time the stop wasn't just to listen. Rocky signaled the leader to come forward. The trail ended at a dried up stream bed. It appeared that the *gooks* used the bed as a segment of the trail. When the lieutenant pulled out the map Lew guessed that they didn't have to follow the stream it if they knew where it was going. His reasoning proved correct. The LT redirected *point* to ignore the trail and lay a path northward. With only the small, toy-like, wrist compass to refer to Lew guessed that if they traveled north for a while then, west for a while, they would end up making a circle. Figuring that they moved southward after insertion then, east until they reached their present position and now they're taking a northern heading, one move west would put them back close to where they started from. Not that it mattered.

The steady, slow, up-hill, climb in the relentless heat caused the men to weaken to the point where their intervals became extended, leaving too great a distance between each man. Feeling the onset of cramping in his legs, Doc was sure the LT would call for a rest when they reached the top of the hill. Being the point man, Rocky was first to see a half-dozen, cone-hatted Vietnamese on the other side of the hill.

KRACK-KRACK-KRACK-KRACK, he opened up with the M-60. When Doc heard the shots he instantly dived for cover, as did the others. The lieutenant began shouting, "EVERBODY, GET ON LINE. GET YOUR ASSES UP HERE!"

From his position directly behind the point man, Unkle emptied his M-16 on full automatic into the direction of the Vietnamese. Everyone moved forward as fast as their adrenalin revived legs could carry them to the top of the hill only to witness a band of panicked Vietnamese women screaming at the top of their lungs, "NO B.C....NO B.C......NO B.C."

"HOLD YOUR FIRE," Williamson barked. "CEASE FIRE!"

When Lew reached the top he saw the group of women huddled together in an open field of grass, about 90 meters from them, frantically waving their arms into the air. Some were dressed in the black PJ's and others wore bright red pajama-like tops. All on them wore typical, cone shaped, peasant hats.

It appeared that one of them must have been wounded as she was being tending to by another. The first thing that popped into the corpsman's mind was, *'What the hell are they doing here?'* The second thing was, *'I'll bet the LT is going to want me to go down and patch her up.'*

One of the women screamed out again. "NO B.C……..BC NUMBA TEN….NO BC….WE GO NOW…O.K?'"

Doc turned to the lieutenant, anticipating an order to tend to the wounded woman. It didn't come. Instead, the LT thought the situation over then, let the women continue on their way unmolested. Confusion gripped the corpsman. On the one hand, he felt as if it was his obligation to treat the woman under the terms of the Geneva Convention, on the other hand, he realized that the team was now in greater danger of being located and had to move out quickly. Experience told the men that unless the enemy was nearby, their exact location would be difficult to pin-point as the gunfire echoed through the valley. The problem was that they didn't know if the 'gooks' were close or not. There was no doubt in anyone's mind that if VC or NVA heard the shots, they would be out trying to find the team. Williamson gathered the men together.

Without bothering to whisper he spelled out his plan. "Here's the deal men. According to this," he pointed to his map, "there's a few hootches about a '*click'* from here. That's probably were those women are from….no question…they're VC. That's also where that dried stream passes. I suspect they're helping, or even 'comforting' the NVA, if you know what I mean. We're going to find a spot to setup an OP and keep our eyes on what's going on down there. Right now, we have to get out of here. I'm going to assume that they heard us….they know we're here. Our advantage is that they don't know where we're going." The LT stressed speed and stealth. "We have a long way to go before nightfall so step up the pace and be quiet. Clifford, you keep extra alert on rear guard. If they find our tracks they'll definitely follow us. You and Miller try to cover-up our trail." The sergeant nodded.

"Okay, let's move."

Lew brought up the men's physical condition and made a recommendation before they had a chance to move. "Sir, I know we can't stop now but, we're all sweating like pigs in this heat.

We all need to chug down water and take a couple of salt tablets. Sir, we don't need a heat stroke problem out here."
"Right Doc. Let's do it quick and get out of here," Williamson urged.

The patrol moved east again through the steaming tropical forest as quickly as stealth would permit. The terrain became more mountainous and heavily vegetated but, not rugged or impassable. During the march the corpsman's main concern wasn't the enemy as much as it was worry over someone dropping from heat stroke. That became less concerning when their path led to a small, rushing, mountain stream. Crossing the clear, cold, waist-deep, flood cooled them down considerably as each man dipped his bush hat into the cold water and splashed hands full of the liquid on their necks and faces while scooping up a quick, one-handed, slurp from the upstream side. Doc relieved his bladder during the fording, sure that the others did also, making a downstream slurp less desirable. Once everyone crossed, the lieutenant had the men pause only long enough to drain their boots, ring out their socks and check for leeches before moving on. As the single-file column spaced their intervals, the image of Johnson's water-soaked trousers steaming from evaporation in front him gave Lew a sense of just how hot and muggy it was that afternoon. It wasn't too long into the trek when, however reluctantly, the LT even realized that the men had to stop and rest, himself included. Gulping down the last few swigs of water in the third canteen of the six that he carried, Doc savored the tepid liquid flowing against the back of his parched throat. *'Man, the only thing better now would be a smoke.'* All of a sudden it dawned on him, *'Damn, we could have filled our canteens back in the stream. Why the hell didn't I think of that? Why didn't anybody think of that?'* recalling that no one dipped a canteen into the water. The rest ended all too soon. The men were back on their feet, steadily climbing up hill toward the top of a monster elevation. Doc could only assume that everyone else was beginning to feel the strain of the climb as much as he. His heart was pounding from overwork; his lungs sucked in as much air as they could; sweat poured into his eyes; his legs were burning; his head was aching, all signs of the onset of heat exhaustion. Dwelling in the back of his mind was the probability that somebody was going to go down from the heat; just hoping it wasn't him. Even though he desperately wanted to signal for a stop, it was only tenacity that kept him going. In an attempt at the concept of "mind-over-matter" he repeated in his mind, *'It ain't nothin' but a thing. It ain't nothin' but a thing. It ain't nothin' but a thing.'*

Surprisingly, the attempt worked. He made it to the summit along with all the others. Although equally exhausted, the lieutenant stood as each man passed him; whispering to them that this was the location of the OP and pointed to where he wanted them to position. When Lew's turn came the LT broke a slight smile and whispered, "Nice going Doc." He congratulated the medic. "Keep your gear and pack on. When I think it's secure you can take it off. Settle in right there," he pointed out a spot in between two, gigantic, fern plants. Injected with a renewed sense of pride Doc took a step before be overheard the LT whisper to Evans, "Nice going Evans. Keep your gear on….." It was apparent that the lieutenant was rewarding all the men with an "atta-boy" and not just him. It didn't really matter since all the men did deserve a spirit-lifting kudo for *gutting-it-out* on the climb. Doc took his position and continued eyeing the lieutenant, finding a new admiration for the officer's leadership qualities that he hadn't noticed before. When Miller and Sergeant Clifford brought up the rear guard, Williamson had them backtrack and take a position a few meters down the hill to warn the team if they had been followed.

The patrol hunkered down, motionless for what seemed hours before the LT was comfortable enough that they hadn't been followed to give the O.K. for the men to drop their packs and settle in. He silently gave permission to eat by miming spooning food into his mouth and showing a 'thumbs-up' gesture, followed by lipping "No fires".

That particular command didn't present a problem as no one wanted hot food anyway.

Williamson quietly moved to Rocky's position before the Marine had a chance to open a can of 'C's". The officer motioned for the machine-gunner to follow him. Both men stepped out toward where Miller and Clifford were positioned. A few minutes after they disappeared from view the lieutenant returned with the sergeant, passing by the men, down the opposite side of the hill to where they could get a clear view of the hamlet in the valley below. Doc's thinking was that the officer wanted the M-60's fire-power to cover their path while he and the NCO formulate a plan. Everyone had finished eating by the time Williamson and Clifford appeared again. Pee-Wee caught the LT's eye and requested a *smoking lamp* by gesturing puffing on an invisible cigarette. When the lieutenant gave the OK, Doc immediately drew a cigarette from a pack and lit up. The first drag made the corpsman's head feel a little light-headed but, the long awaited pleasure made the effect insignificant.

After the lieutenant and sergeant consumed their meals the officer made the decision that only he, Sergeant Clifford and the RTO, Lance Corporal Arthurs, would take up the observation position a few meters down the slope. The rest of the men would harbor where they were. He sent Evans to tell Rocky and Miller to set up a couple of Claymores and then come back up to harbor with the rest of the men.

Arthurs worked his way over to the corpsman. "I need the battery Doc."

Dutifully, Lew opened his ruck-sack, retrieved the spare PRC-25 battery and handed it over to the RTO.

Clifford gave Unkle and Pee-Wee instructions to have everyone in the harbor-site rotate a two-hour guard, explaining further that since the OP position had the radio, they would take care of the '*sit-reps*'. Lew watched the OP team depart, wishing he could go with them. He wanted to be able to see something other than bushes and trees.

By now, everyone felt fairly confident that they had successfully evaded being found out and weren't being followed. Doc lit up another smoke out of boredom .Aside from taking cat-naps or smoking it was difficult to keep one's mind occupied during idle periods. Some of the men gave their weapons a quick field-cleaning; others brought out paperbacks, if there was enough light to read by but, most were content to just nap.

Lew was repositioning his back pack to lean against as Unkle moved from Johnson's position to his. "Doc, we're goin' to take hour and a half watches…yours is from 2300 'til 0030. Johnson will wake you….you wake Evans. Make sure you can find him and get to him in the dark without makin' a bunch of noise."

It wasn't quite dark yet. Lew glanced at his wristwatch…1921hrs…meaning he could probably catch a few hours' sleep before his turn. "Okay, I got it," he replied before the corporal moved toward Evans. *'I'll have one more smoke before sacking out.'*

Doc felt tugging at his boots. "Wake up Doc…your turn." Johnson whispered.
"Got it," Lew whispered as he sat up and leaned back against his pack. Aside from Johnson shuffling around briefly, trying to get comfortable the jungle was relatively quiet. A few minutes into the watch and feeling fairly secure, Doc pulled out a cigarette. Concealing the flame with cupped hands the brightness blinded him momentarily but, it didn't matter since it was so dark he couldn't see anything anyway. He learned from the many patrols he'd been on that in the darkness one depends on the sense of hearing more than the sense of vision. By now he could distinguish between the scampering of little critters and the crashing noise of larger animals. He recalled months earlier at Ba Na, he thought he heard something and opened fire, and now realized that the origin of that noise was probably an animal scavenging for food. Lew guessed that if the enemy was sneaking up on them now, he could distinguish human noise from animal noise. He believed that animals wouldn't care how much noise they made while human noise would be deliberately slow and intermittent. Logic told him that unless they gave themselves away somehow and VC knew exactly where they were, finding them in the millions of square miles of tropical forest in Vietnam would be extremely difficult. He also guessed that if the enemy would be lucky enough to find them, they would most likely probe their position before attempting an assault. Still, since they did announce their presence with gunfire and the entire A-Shaw, in essence, belonged to the enemy, the element of danger was always present, he had to remain alert. It didn't happen.

His mind drifted to home and family, pondering his future, wondering what he'd do with his life if he survived his tour. It was 'The Big IF', as some 'jarheads' called it. The thought of making it home alive was now gaining more importance than earlier in the tour when such thoughts seldom arose. Then, it was the *"other guy"* who was going to get it but, now he was beginning to sense his own mortality. *'I need to make it home in one piece. I don't want to get maimed. I don't want Mom to agonize. I just want to get back to the World with the same body I left with.'* Even though he wasn't concentrating entirely on the watch, he knew that sub conscientiously; any out of the ordinary noise would snap him back to reality. He continued to ponder his luck so far. He had a couple of close calls but, it would have been worse in a grunt company. They get hammered all the time. Surely, he would have gotten dinged by now if he was with the infantry. *"I've been really lucky so far. How can I keep my luck going? I'm tired of the bush.'* He remembered debating about transferring back to 1st Med., going over the 'pros' and 'cons' *'Why not?'* He would initially tell himself. *'I deserve a break. I'd have to put up with more bullshit, " in-the-rear-with-the gear" but, it'll only be for a couple of months before I rotate back home. I can do that standing on my head.'* Then his thinking would do a flip-flop. '*I'd hate to leave these guys. They're the best I've ever been with. If I transferred it would make me feel like I'm deserting them..... I can't do that.'* Once again his mind changed direction. *'Hey man, think! Most of the "salts" will be rotating back themselves soon... you'd be left here with the newer guys. Unkle, Rocky and Pee Wee are short-timers. Johnson, Arthurs, Mervyn and Holton joined the platoon after I got here. Sure, we shared good times and some shit and I got tight with them too but, damn it, I gotta look out for me. After all, this ain't nothin' but a thing too!'* Conflicting emotions battled back and forth throughout the watch before he firmly convinced himself to ask for a transfer when they got back. *'If I transfer, then I'd at least have a better chance of going home. It's not the same as quitting them...they'll get another corpsman......maybe a better one? Yeah, that's what I'm going to do. I'll talk with the lieutenant when we get back.'* Having burdened himself in thought Lew lost track of time, extending his watch almost fifteen extra minutes. Carefully crawling over the twig-covered, forest floor he reached Evans. *"Hey Johnnie,"* he gently nudged the Marine while whispering as quietly as he could. *"Hey man. It's your watch bro'*. Evans was in such a deep sleep that it took Doc another attempt to wake him. *"Hey Evans...your watch, man,"* he repeated the nudging, secretly hoping the man wouldn't awaken startled enough to yell out something.

"Yeah,, yeah Doc. I hear 'ya man."
Lew didn't bother to tell Evans about the 15 minutes less time he had to spend on watch and waited until the Marine sat up before inching back to his own cubby-hole.
Once quietly settled in a comfortable position the corpsman stared up at the blackness; thinking about the transfer until the notion lulled him asleep.

No one bothered to wake the men in the morning. Instead, each woke at his own leisure. Doc opened his eyes, staring at the canopy he fell asleep under, only now trickles of sun light managed to randomly pierce though the thick layers of leafy foliage, allowing thin, translucent beams to reach the damp, stinking ground. The need to get up and stretch the stiffness out of his aching body brought him to his feet before he was actually ready to surrender the sleep. Forcing himself upright he stretched a minute before dodging around the men to find a nearby, isolated place to empty a painfully distended bladder. Afterwards, he came back to chow-down a LURP ration he had saved from a previous patrol. '*Cold spaghetti...wonderful.'*
Sergeant Clifford came up from the observation position to inform the men that they were going to remain in place for a while; that the LT wanted to continue observing for signs of enemy activity down in the hamlet. Word to the men was to just take it easy.
'Great. We're just going to sit around on our butts all day, doing nothing. Man, I wish I could at least see what's going on down there,' Lew miffed silently, chewing a mouthful of cold pasta breakfast.
Clifford sent Rocky and Miller back down to where they were the day before to act as rear guard with further instructions to leave the Claymores in place. On their way down Miller stopped to visit the corpsman. "Hey Doc, you got any more salt pills? I used all mine yesterday."
Lew nodded, set down the LURP and reached into his Unit One. He issued the Marine 6 tablets with instructions. "Just take one with water every couple of hours. We're not going to be too active today so you probably won't need too many. Tell Rocky the same thing. How you fixed for water?"
"Not bad."
"Okay then, take a couple swallows every hour, OK?"
Miller gave Lew the thumbs-up and departed.

Doc returned to his meal. After finishing the main course he opened the small packet of instant coffee, emptied the contents into his mouth then took a swig a water to wash down the bitter powder. Evans looked at the corpsman and shook his head in disbelief.
During the morning hours most of the men busied themselves field-cleaning rifles, reapplying camouflage face- paint, reading paperbacks or cat-napping. Lew finished an abused copy of John Steinbeck's novel, *Of Mice and Men.* He offered it to Evans.
"Any good Doc?"
"It's a tear-jerker. They shoot the dog and the dumb guy."
"Why would anybody wanna go an' shoot a dog?"
Lew snickered at the Johnnie's unexpected quip.

As the day dragged on Lew dwelled on asking for the transfer. For every good reason he came up with an equally poor reason butted in. *'I wish I had someone to talk to about this. Maybe I could appreciate another opinion better?'* He took a moment to look around to see who wasn't catching up on sleep or otherwise preoccupied. Noticing Johnson sitting there quietly chewing on an unlit pipe, staring a hundred miles away, he decided to crawl over an interrupt the man's meditation.
"George," he grabbed his friend's attention. "You mind if I ask your opinion on something?"
"Depends on what you axe Doc?" his black friend spoke while clinching the pipe firmly between his teeth, showing the little gap.
"Well, I've been giving some thought about finishing up my tour back at 1st Med," he paused a second. "But the only problem I have is leaving you guys. I'd feel guilty if one of you guys got hit and I wasn't around. Man, I got attached to all of you somehow."
"Soooo…." the Marine stretched the word to coax the corpsman to reveal more. "What's the problem again? You'll miss us, is that it?"
"Yeah. That and ….I don't want to get my ass waxed when I'm pretty close to goin' home" he laid out the hard truth.
"Uh huh. I understand what you mean. You want to go back home in one piece. …Me too." He removed the pipe, staring directly into the corpsman's eyes he whispered so low that Lew could barely hear what he was saying. "Listen Doc. If I was in your shoes, I'd do it man. You done did your share. Just in case you don't know it…..this is all about surviving man. Not fightin' for

the good ole U-S of A an' especially not dyin' for no good reason for this mutha-fukin' place."
Johnson's words caught Doc off guard. What he said didn't fit his character. He was beginning to show signs of becoming embittered or disillusioned with the reason for fighting the war. The medic accepted the advice. "Thanks man…appreciate your opinion."
Johnson winked, put the pipe back to his lips and continued staring into the jungle. Lew crawled back into the nest he created between the ferns. Bored from doing nothing he lit up another smoke while surveying the men around him, wondering if they were just as bored as he. Unkle had his back propped against a tree, arms folded and bush hat tipped down over his eyes. Lew couldn't tell if the man was sleeping or just meditating. Pee Wee sat crossed-legged, spreading cheese on crackers, taking one bite at a time. Johnson chewed on the pipe, patiently staring up at the branches above his head. Evans was reclining on his side, propped up on one elbow, reading the paperback Lew gave him. The medic could tell that they were every bit as bored as he was, recalling the cliché' about war's hours of boredom interrupted by moments of terror. He buried the cigarette butt then lowered himself to force a nap.

Only minutes into the slumber he felt the ground shake and heard distant rumbling. It took a moment for him to dispel the thought of earthquake. *'Arc-light'* he told himself, realizing that B-52's were bombing distant, probably un-seen, targets. Undisturbed, he ignored the barely audible muffles and returned to his nap. The medic managed to snatch a couple of hours of 'zees' when he felt someone tapping at his boots. It was Lieutenant Williamson making circle motions with a raised finger, signaling to saddle up and move out. There didn't appear to be any urgency in the leader's silent instruction, it simply meant that it was time for the team to 'hat-out' once again. Thinking that he might not get another opportunity to smoke, Doc lit up and took several quick puffs while donning his gear before extinguishing and burying the butt.

The LT led the men down the slope to rendezvous with Rocky and Miller, re-establishing the same order-of-march, with Rocky running point. After quickly retrieving the Claymores the team stepped out, maintaining sight intervals. A quick glance at his wrist compass told Lew that the patrol was heading south. *'I wish I had a map.'*

The lieutenant indicated the direction but, Rocky set the pace. The farther down the slope they went the thicker the vegetation became, making their travel slow and difficult but, that was nothing unusual. At one point the vines and underbrush became so heavy that Rocky brought out a machete to cut a path. The lieutenant stopped him before he had a chance to start hacking away. After surveying the obstruction and determining that there was no way around it the LT had the men belly-crawl through the thicket, leaving a tunnel-like path in their wake. Progress was measured in inches. Even though he was in the middle of the column and the men ahead of him bored a clearer opening, Doc still got hung up in the entanglement. The concern over a vine grabbing hold and pulling out the pin on a loosely secured grenade was troubling enough but, the extreme heat and humidity only added to his struggle. Salty sweat dripping into his eyes and off his nose into to his open mouth combined with hundreds of thorn pricks drawing tiny spots of blood from his exposed face and forearms sent the otherwise refrained medic into a mental rage. *'Man, I don't need this shit. I'm tired of it. That's it...this is my last patrol. I'm definitely going to request a transfer when we get back.'* Even more disparaging was the noise they were making. Doc's imagination led him to believe that they sounded like a troop of wild boars foraging, despite the fact that he had never even seen a wild boar. *'If Charlie's anywhere near I know they can hear us. All they need to do is toss a couple grenades in here and we'll all be waxed.'* Instinct had him close his eye just as a whipping thorn branch superficially sliced the lid of his right eye. The cut didn't penetrate through the lid but, cut it enough to spill blood. *'Damn it.* The tiny wound quickly became a nuisance as it bled into his eye, forcing him to keep it closed. With one hand clutching the M-16 and the other pushing aside the brush, he couldn't stop to tend to it. Drops of blood mixed with sweat produced small, irritating pools of glue-like substance that clung to his eyelashes. It was enough for him to pause and wipe the lid when a hand was free from pushing back the brush. Knowing that even the tiniest of cuts can become quickly infected in the tropics if not taken care of, he hoped that the patrol would find their way out of the thicket before too long so he could treat it. In the mean time he'd just have to put up with it. *'At least the sweat is diluting the blood so it won't coagulate so quickly.'*

Just when there seemed to be no end to the thicket Rocky floundered his way out of it. The lieutenant called for a short break, giving the men time to rest up before continuing on. Doc immediately pulled out the stainless steel mirror from his pocket and examined the laceration. *'Not too bad,'* he self-evaluated. *'A little cleansing and some Bacitracin should do the job.'*

Williamson came over to check on his corpsman. "How bad is it Doc?

"It's nothing….just a scratch, sir. I'll have it fixed up in no time," the medic assured.

"I want to be moving out again soon so, try to make it quick."

"Yes, Sir."

The bleeding stopped on its own. Doc washed the eyelid and cleared away the little bit of dried blood then, applied a tiny dab of the ointment on the cut. After finishing the treatment he took a swig of water. *' Damn, '* he realized that the canteen was almost empty and that he only had one full canteen left.

The lieutenant looked back to the corpsman. Doc gave the thumbs-up, indicating that he was ready.

No one knew where the officer was leading them as they continued southward yet, they all sensed that he had a definite objective in mind. They also knew that it would be getting dark within a couple of hours and they would have to find another harbor site before too long. The team skulked along the jungle floor at a much faster pace. LT had Rocky step out as quickly as the terrain would permit. The men were tiring and the intervals started to become extended, stringing out the column. When they reached the bottom of the valley they came across another VC trail. As it was being overtaken by weeds it told them this one hadn't been used recently. Never-the-less, the lieutenant marked the location on his map. As each man stepped across the path the man in front pointed out a skull, hanging predominately from a tree. Upon seeing it Doc's first, knee-jerk, reaction was a sudden rush of chills, until he realized that it was a monkey skull. He guessed that the Katu tribesmen probably placed it there for some superstitious reason.

He, in turn, pointed it out to Evans, fully expecting a stereotypical, blackface comic reaction. When Johnnie didn't show any reaction at all it surprised him.

The team climbed another hill, collectively thinking that since it was getting dark they would harbor for the night once they reach the top but, the LT had other plans. Williamson told the men to form a 360 perimeter and wait for the choppers to arrive. The men were completely surprised at the lieutenant's instruction. Tonight, they were going to sleep in their own racks. The LZ was barely visible when the chopper approached, requiring the team to use flashlights to better identify the clearing to the pilot. One man stood at each of the four corners of the LZ with a beacon in hand as the pilot gingerly set the bird down in the grassy clearing. The men rushed aboard and immediately took up firing positions at the portholes to repel any enemy fire. There was none and the chopper quickly lifted off to carry the team back to Phu Bai in the darkness. Doc gazed out the window at the ground below trying to get a perception of altitude but couldn't distinguish anything to use as a reference. It wasn't until they cleared the mountain range west of Phu Bai that lights on the ground gave some indication that they were much lower than he thought. They descended to the well-lighted Recon camp and touched own without a hitch. The men cleared their weapons and made their way back to their quarters to clean up and square away. As Lew plopped his butt down in his chair to remove his boots he glanced up at the mission flag. He lit up a smoke and reminded himself to add another 'Midnight Skulker' for this patrol. *"Damn...that was my 19th mission.....seems like a hundred?'*

The next day word got around that the grunts from 1/5 were involved in some hellacious fighting in Hue' City and taking heavy casualties. The NVA were holed up there and putting up one hell of a fight in a place called the Citadel. None of the men in the platoon knew exactly what the Citadel was except that it was an ancient, walled city that was of significant historical importance to the Vietnamese people. For the Marines, it had no such significance. It was just a place that had to be destroyed in order to root-out the enemy. According to the 'Top Brass,' most of the enemy forces had their asses kicked and had already retreated out of the cities and villages though out the South. Rumor had it that even the ARVN forces were doing some fighting.

Even though Doc wanted to transfer he remained uncertain about it and decided to get opinions from the two men in the platoon he trusted most. Managing to get Rocky and Pee Wee aside he posed the question to them. Both men concurred that the corpsman should do what was best for him and that whatever he decided to do would have no bearing on their trust or friendship. The conversation with them renewed the medic's confidence enough to embark toward Lieutenant Williamson's hootch and request the transfer.

Butterfly's curled his gut when he knocked at the door.

"Enter," someone inside called out.

It was too late to back down. He had to stick to his guns. Opening the door he stepped inside and spotted the lieutenant rolling up the sleeves on a clean, utility shirt that was spread out on the cot. The officer spoke first.

"Can I do something for you Doc?" he asked with firm sincerity.

Not knowing exactly how to relay his desire the corpsman just blurted it out. "Sir, I'd like to transfer back to 1st Med" then, added timidly, "If it's okay with you, Sir."

The officer stopped adjusting the sleeves, straightened up, looked directly at the corpsman and without any hesitation, shot out a firm, "Okay Doc. I'll have the paperwork processed. Anything else?"

Taken aback by the lieutenant's instant, matter-of-fact response the medic just stood there bewildered. Williamson saw that the medic needed something more.

"This is a volunteer outfit Doc. You volunteered to come into the unit…you can volunteer to leave. I don't need an explanation why."

"Yes Sir. I understand that but……"

"Here's the poop Doc. I'll put in the transfer papers, if 1st Med has a billet for you, you'll be re-assigned…if not, you'll stay here until they do….understood?"

"Yes Sir, understood."

"All right then, you're dismissed."

"Aye, aye Sir."

Lew mumbled to himself all the way back to the hootch. *'How the hell did he do that?*
How did he make me feel like a stupid kid? I guess because he's so...so...officer-like?
Maybe I respect him so much that he just makes me feel inferior. Hell, he's only a few years older than me but, somehow he's way ahead of me in maturity. I'll have to admit, he's probably the best officer I ever served with. There's nothing phony about him. We could probably be friends someday.'

HATTIN' BACK TO THE WORLD

February blurred into March. The NVA and Viet Cong were driven from Hue' City but left behind hundreds of uncooperative civilian corpses in their wake. Reports of mass graves being unearthed near Hue' and the surrounding area seemed to be a daily occurrence. Someone in the hootch mentioned a famous quote about "man's inhumanity to man". The words were familiar to Lew but, it was only then that he realized the true meaning of them. It started him to ponder all the famous war sayings he had heard before that, up until now, seemed relatively meaningless. Things like, "hours of boredom interrupted by moments of sheer terror" and "uncommon valor was a common virtue" fit into place as his recollections gave credence to what earlier generations experienced.

Hoping that he wasn't being too obvious Lew casually lit up a smoke and looked around the hootch, watching to see what each man was doing, scrutinizing their young faces, wondering which one will be next to '*buy the farm*'. The thought of himself getting killed didn't enter his mind but, the ever present notion of being severely wounded and maimed for life dwelled heavily on his spirit. From conversations he had with the other men over the past several months, that particular topic seemed to be the prevailing concern of most of them. No one wanted to go back to the '*World' as* an amputee or vegetable. Everyone agreed that a fate worse than death would be having damaged or missing reproductive organs yet, it could happen and when the subject came up it was quickly dismissed as a taboo topic. On one occasion though, it did come up. Miller asked Doc if he had ever seen someone's testicles blown off.

"Actually, no," the corpsman answered truthfully. "I heard about a few cases of it back at First Med. but, I personally didn't see any," he calmly added.

"What would you do if one of us got our balls shot off?" Miller extended his query.

Sensing that the thought was troubling the Marine, Lew blew out a stream of smoke before answering. "Well, first of all," he began, "it's not all that common to have your balls shot off. Usually that particular injury comes from mines or booby-traps…not bullets. I think the chances of being 'dick-shot' are slim. Think about it. How many men in the battalion have you heard had their balls shot off out of probably hundreds of patrols and dozens of fire-fights? I know I didn't hear of any."

"That doesn't mean it can't happen," the Marine came back. "What would you do if it did?" he repeated.

"Other than applying a couple of battle dressings and try to stop the bleeding, there isn't much I could do. Maybe a shot of Morphine if you weren't unconscious from shock and I'd have to throw in an IV and hope the med-evac chopper can get you back to the aid station before you bleed-out. That's about it." Lew then attempted to lighten up the discussion. "Oh yeah. I'd probably confiscate the rubbers out of your wallet too."

Everyone in the hootch orchestrated a concert of good-natured boos and hisses over Doc's humor.

"You're a wrong dude, Doc," Johnson snickered while shaking his head.

The subject never came up again during Doc's tour of duty.

Only two days had passed from the time between the last patrol and receiving word that they were going back out in the bush again the next day. Doc was secretly hoping that his transfer would come through before going out on another patrol but, it didn't. Sergeant Holton was to be the patrol leader. Aware of Doc's request for transfer, he discreetly approached the corpsman outside the hootch as the medic was returning from noon chow.

"Hey Doc," he summoned. "You don't have to go out on this one if you don't want to."

"Why not?" Lew questioned curiously.

"Hell, you pulled your weight and maybe your transfer will come through while we're out. There's no sense in taking any chances at this point," the NCO uttered in a friendly, secretive, tone.
"No, there isn't but….." Lew turned his eyes away momentarily…. "Who said I ever did anything sensible? I'm goin'," he said firmly, even though in his heart-of-hearts he was reluctant.
Pursing his lips, Holton made eye contact with the corpsman and nodded satisfaction with the decision. "Good."

The remainder of the day found the team getting ready for the patrol. Each man stuffed his pack to capacity with food, water, extra ammo, Claymores and M-79 rounds, radio batteries and dry socks until it became the typical 80 pound burden. Doc inventoried his Unit-1 before forcing it in the pack so it wouldn't bulge out from under the top flap. He felt as if he could pack it blindfolded since he had done it so many times before. He kept telling himself that it was just another patrol in order to relieve the uneasy stigma of possibly being his *last patrol.* He heard so many stories of soldiers 'getting it' on their last day in the bush that the notion of him 'buying-the-farm' played heavily on his mind.
He didn't want to convey to the others his fear. Setting the lit cigarette aside he picked up the M-16 and began a token effort of dusting it off and giving it a cursory Ops check. He knew it was clean and ready but, he also knew the importance of showing the others, especially the newer men, that he could be counted on as a rifleman as well as a medic.

The men were already at the helo pad as the Sun rose. It was the typical 'hurry up and wait' scene of men sitting back against their bulky packs; killing time before the helicopters arrived. It was then that Sergeant Holton decided to inform the men of where they were going even though everyone had already guessed it. Holton spouted out the name of some Province in the A Shau Valley that no one was likely to remember anyway. The name just skipped off Doc's mind since it didn't really matter where they were going. To him the only thing that was important was to get back alive and in one piece. His usually calm demeanor gave way to nervous fidgeting, checking and double-checking his 782 gear and rifle; lighting a succession of cigarettes off the butt of the

one before, all the while trying to conceal the anxiety from his comrades.
As he placed the fourth cigarette between his lips to light it from the butt of the third the chopper appeared in the distance.
"Okay men, get ready, the choppers here," Holton announced.
The team came to their feet, adjusting heavy backpacks as they rose. Doc tossed the unlit cigarette to the ground and followed suit, heaving the burden higher on his shoulders while hunching forward slightly to maintain balance. A small dust-storm blasted in their faces as the CH-46 touched down and the men singled-filed their way onto the rear ramp and inside the belly of the quivering bird. Doc found a seat next to the porthole and looked out as the chopper rose and banked to starboard, permitting him to view the un-repaired damage done to the PX where an enemy rocket found it on the first night of TeT. The damage was minor but, the beer that was destroyed angered a lot of troops when they didn't get their ration, at least that was the scuttlebutt making its way around the compound.

The cold air at high altitude sprouted goose-bumps on Lew's thin, hairless arms. The chill lasted through the entire flight. As the chopper began its descent Lew looked out the porthole once again. Off in the distance he spotted two Cobra helicopters strafing a ridgeline with a barrage of rockets. He wasn't sure but, he didn't think the Marines had Cobras so, he figured they were Army birds. As he watched the impact of rockets he wondered if it was their LZ the choppers were softening up. If it was, they were sure to take enemy fire on the descent. The thought spiked a streak of sudden anxiety through his gut. As their own helicopter veered away from the direction of the Cobras he realized that their destination was elsewhere. Somewhat relieved, he slouched back against the web seat, closed his eyes and sat quietly; trying to block any apprehension from his mind.
"LOCK AND LOAD," Sergeant Holton shouted out as the chopper penetrated through a low hanging, stray cloud; revealing a mass of dark green vegetation only a couple of hundred feet below. The bird slowly ascended toward a small clearing that was obviously used as an LZ on a previous occasion. Trees were blown away from their roots by some type of explosives while fresh, new growth of brush indicated that it was a fairly recent, field-expedient LZ, probably created in a hurry. Hovering a few

feet above the debris the chopper's rear ramp was lowered and the men jumped out as they have done many times before; first forming a circular perimeter then, waited for Charlie to send a hail of small-arms fire at the helicopter and them. Luck was with the team again as no enemy fire came upon them or the chopper. As the birds pulled away from the LZ a reoccurring feeling of abandonment came over the medic as it had done on every previous mission. Somehow the choppers were the only tie to civilization and when they departed Lew always experienced the dredge of isolation. Several quiet minutes passed before Sergeant Holton formed the order of march and gave word to move out. The inescapable heat and humidity set the stage for the conditions for the remainder of the patrol.

For two days the team silently inched their way through the steamy, foul-smelling jungle; up and over near vertical mountains; down through thorny thickets and razor sharp elephant grass; fording ice cold mountain streams, all the while keeping vigilant lookout for signs of the elusive, ghost-like, Viet Cong. Everyone was well aware that "Charlie" could pop up anywhere at any time. It was his domain. He knew the terrain. He knew where to hide. He knew where to best ambush unsuspecting Americans.
The Marines, on-the-other-hand, knew their best defense against an ambush was stealth.
Every step and movement was calculated on the assumption that if the enemy could hear you, they could find you; if they find you, they could kill you.
Doc had no idea of where the patrol was going or what their exact mission was. All he knew was that if he survived this patrol he had a pretty good chance of surviving his tour but......in Vietnam, there was no guarantee of surviving from one minute to the next. On every break the men took time to re-apply the camy-paint that sweat washed from their face and arms. During the respites Lew reminded them to hydrate and take salt tablets through miming the ritual to each man although, it wasn't necessary for him to do so since, by now, every Marine knew what might happen if they didn't. He scrutinized each man for tell-tale signs of dehydration. Lack of sweat is a sure sign of impending physical problems that could lead to headaches, muscle cramps, unconsciousness or convulsions. Seeing that everyone was drenched in their own perspiration Doc leaned back and took several healthy swigs from

his own canteen. Resisting the urge to pour a few ounces over his head he returned the container back to its pouch, drew the bush hat down over his eyes, folded his arms and sat quietly while listening to the screeching and lilting songs of tropical birds and skittering's of small creatures rustling through the leafy decaying carpet. Lew found peaceful comfort in the natural sounds of the jungle. He didn't want to hear un-natural sounds or the same complete silence that came over the jungle moments before all hell broke loose in Happy Valley where Gilmore and Welchel got killed. No, this noise was good.

With several hours of daylight left, Holton moved the team in a westerly direction, deeper into the jungle and mountains surrounding the A Shaw. Lew had a vague recollection from a map that he had once seen that the border with Laos ran through a mountain range west of the A Shaw. He wondered if they were patrolling in those mountains.

With Rocky running point the team moved deliberately slow and steady. The more seasoned members of the team who *"snooped and pooped"* with him before trusted him in the point position. He possessed a keen alertness and an uncanny instinct to weave a path through the jungle that avoided much of the ever-present entanglements. Lew remembered a patrol where Rocky detected an old, ineffective booby-trap, over grown with vegetation that no one else would have probably recognized. The corpsman had faith that Rocky would draw first blood if he encountered the enemy in his path, which would give the team an immediate although, possibly not prolonged, advantage in a sudden fire-fight. Every Recon team automatically assumes that they would always be outnumbered and any advantage that they had would initially come from the point man armed with the M-60 being the first to lay down fire. Rocky was that type of individual.

After several long, hot, punishing hours of snaking through the jungle Sergeant Holton decided to make *harbor* well ahead of darkness in a field of large, granite-like boulders near the top of a mountain ridge. It had been a physically grueling day and the men needed rest. Lew found it interesting that instead of forming the customary, circular perimeter Holton instructed the group to form a line parallel to the ridge. Every man found a niche in between the boulders and settled in no more than a few feet apart from each other. Once the Claymores were set out the men immediately began opening C rations. Lew took time to savor a long awaited cigarette before devouring a can of Meatballs and Beans. Afterward, he laid back and fell asleep until Johnny Evans wakened him for watch. Even though there was a chill in the night air Lew abandoned the thought of fumbling for his poncho in the darkness thinking it would make too much noise. It wasn't long before he changed his mind as the temperature dropped rapidly in the mountains, giving him chill-shakes. As quietly as possible he retrieved the poncho from his pack and draped it over his body then continued with his turn on watch. Unknown to him at the time, it would be his last watch in Vietnam. The next morning brought word that the team was to rendezvous with the choppers that would take them back to the compound at Phu Bai.

Back in his *hootch* Doc drew another Midnight Skulker icon on the flag. He counted the little silhouettes that symbolized every time he went out into the bush. *"Damn,"* he thought to himself "*Sixteen times I went out in the boonies!"* The tally didn't seem possible. He recounted and came to the same number. Lighting up a cigarette he sat down on his rack and attempted to recall every time he drew a Skulker. His concentration was broken.

"Lewis, Doc Lewis," a boyish voice called through the screened door.

"Yeah," Lew answered. "I'm Lewis."

"Lewis, you got orders to report for duty at First Med. Come over to the Company Office whenever you get a chance to process out," the voice directed.

Dumbfounded, the corpsman could hardly believe what he was hearing. "What?"

"Your orders came yesterday man. I came over to tell you then but you were out in the field," the high-pitched voice explained as the messenger turned away.

Speechless, Lew turned around and gazed at everyone in the *hootch.* There was an awkward silence that seemed to last an eternity before Rocky stopped cleaning the M-60 and spoke up.

"That's great Doc," he expounded. "You're more than half-way back to the World."

"Yeah Doc," Johnson added. "You'll be home before 'ya know it. Man, I wish I was in your shoes."

Lew reminded them, "Hey, I'm only going back to Da Nang…not di-di-ing out of country yet. I still have a couple months to do at First Med you know."

"At least you'll be out of the bush Doc," Evans countered. "That's better 'an nothin'."

"Is it?" Lew thought to himself, recalling all the petty crap he encountered back when he first was assigned there. *"Maybe it'll be the same bullshit all over again?"*

"Hey Doc," Arthurs broke the medic's thought. "I hate to see you go man but, you need ta just pack up your shit and get outta here…the sooner the better man…..no second thoughts."

"He's right Doc," Rocky agreed.. "You just need to pack your sea-bag and ship out…just the way you planned it….No turning back now."

Lew absorbed Rocky's words and nodded agreement. "Yeah, I gotta stick to my plan but, I want to tell you now…leaving you guys is going to be a real hard thing to do. We've been through some shit together. We're like family….like brothers….."

"Don't go mutha-fukin soft on us Doc," Johnson interrupted. "Everybody ships out when time comes. It's your time…'sides, it ain't nothing but a thing anyway."

"You really have a way with words, don't cha?" Lew grinned.

"Jus talking what's true Doc," Johnson grinned back. "It ain't that we won't miss your sorry ass around here, it's just that everybody gotta di-di outta here sometime. It's your time. That's all I'm sayin'," he explained his drift further, clinching the pipe between his teeth.

Lew smiled, interpreting that his Negro buddy's words actually meant that he was okay with the corpsman's decision to leave Recon and better the chance of going home in one piece.

"All right," Lew continued. "I'd better *hat* on over to the Company Office and find out what the hell the *skinny* is. Catch you later."

The corpsman returned to the hootch after having learned that he was to report for duty at First Medical Battalion in Da Nang at the earliest convenience. There was a lot for him to do before processing out of the unit. In addition to packing his personal gear, he had to turn-in the M-16 and ammunition to the armory, the 782 gear, his helmet, flak jacket and gas mask, the inflatable mattress and sleeping bag, the Unit-1 and account for the

Morphine syrettes. Equally important was deciding on who would be the benefactors of the creature comfort items that he acquired but couldn't take with him or things he didn't need any longer. Rather than giving the impression that he was playing favorites he decided to just leave the foot locker, folding chair, and two sets of faded Tiger Stripes in the corner of the hootch for anyone who wanted them, He kept the prized duck-down pillow and electric fan, stowing both at the bottom of his sea-bag.

Pausing momentarily, Lew sat on the corner if his cot, lit up a smoke and watched the others go about their business. As he did so the realization that he was the *saltiest* man in the hootch. Pee Wee and Unkle had already rotated back to the world, making him the
old-timer in the platoon. Except for Sergeant Holton, Johnson, Arthurs, Evans, Mervyn and Rocky he hardly knew the men who came after Gilmore and Weasel got killed. It was by design that he chose not to get too close to anyone after seeing those two friends lose their lives in Happy Valley. Yet, despite all the advice and warnings he had heard about establishing bonds with the troops, the medic couldn't help but grow attached to his brothers-in-arms who shared so much and worked as a tight-knit team. He exhaled a stream of cigarette smoke and gazed up at the tally flag hanging about his rack. Suddenly an idea popped into his head. *'I'm going to take that flag and get everybody to sign it before I leave here. I'll keep it forever as a treasured souvenir.'* Quickly he jumped to his feet and removed the flag from its perch, then grabbed a pen and approached Johnson.
"Hey man, you mind signing this for me. I want something to remember you by," he asked in a sincere, soft-spoken manner.
"Sure Doc…glad to," the Marine accepted the cloth.
Lew took it around to everyone who was in the hootch then went over the Dogma team's hootch. No one was there. He forgot they were out in the bush. Disappointed, he then strolled to Lt. Williamson's hootch, knocked on the door and entered when granted permission.
"Doc," the lieutenant acknowledged the corpsman's presence. "You still here? I thought you'd be gone by now. What can I do for you?

"I was just wondering if you would sign this flag for me sir," Lew asked making the request sound personal. "I want to have it as a keepsake."
"I think I can manage that Doc," the officer accommodated the young corpsman's request. "It was good to have you with us. Good luck to you," Williamson gave back the flag and pen then extended his hand. Lew accepted it, "Thanks LT. I appreciate it. You be sure to take care of the men, will ya?"
The platoon leader nodded while rendering a slight smile. "Take care." With that, Lew departed. A gut-wrenching sadness came upon him as he made his way back to the hootch . *'I'm gonna to miss these guys,'* he silently thought. *'I never been with a tighter bunch of men...yeah, I'll miss 'em. God, I hope all of 'em make it back.'*

After spending most of the night trying to force himself to sleep Lew managed to get only a couple of hours shut-eye before he finally woke to the noise of a six-by revving up it's powerful, diesel engine in front of the hootch. The morning air was already stifling hot and thick with humidity; releasing beads of perspiration from his forehead, eyelids, underarms and crotch. Instinctively lighting up his first cigarette of the day Lew rose to his feet and moved closer to the door to see what the commotion was all about. It only took a minute to figure out that a work detail was being mustered to fill sandbags as several low-ranking troops tossed bundles of empty bags up into the truck bed, along with shovels, 'C' rats and water. Knowing that the vehicle would have to leave the compound and get on Highway 1 near the Phu Bai airfield Lew hollered to the driver, "Hey, when you guys hattin' out?"
"'Bout ten, fifteen minutes. Why?'
"How about a lift to the airstrip?
"No problem. Get your shit aboard mos-ricky-ticky, I ain't waitin' long," the PFC asserted.
Arranging the ride so suddenly left little time for Lew to do much more than stow what was left to stow and muster with the work party. He didn't have time to say a final goodbye to everyone in the team, only to those men in the hootch. Rather than bidding farewell individually Lew addressed the three men collectively as he got dressed. "Hey guys…sorry I have to say goodbye like this but, I can't afford to miss out on the ride to the airfield." He

hurried lacing his jungle boots." Hey, I'll miss you guys. Tell everyone I'm sorry I couldn't hang around like I wanted to."
Rocky took a few seconds to come over and shake the corpsman's hand. "We understand Doc. We should meet up some time back in the World huh? Take care".
The other two Marines quickly joined in, shaking Doc's hand and bid their own good byes.
Lew let the door slam behind him as he hustled over to the six-by, tossing his over-stuffed, sea-bag up to the Marines already seated then, climbed onboard to join them. The driver clutched the vehicle into gear and coaxed it to move in small jerks as it belched out thick, black plumes of smoke that accompanied the growling, diesel engine. Heavy clouds of fine powdery dust grew immensely in the truck's wake until it eventually obscured the entire compound from view. Doc looked back and watched the dust seemingly engulf everything and everyone that had been part of his life since August. Lew symbolized the image as leaving behind a period of his life that will always be, in essence, a thing.....nothing but a thing.

Doc Lewis reported for duty back at the First Medical Battalion in Da Nang only to find that the entire unit was re-deploying next to the airfield at Phu Bai and he was going with it. He spent the remainder of his tour with the medical unit but, occasionally had opportunity to visit with *his* Recon Marines until he rotated back to the States in July1968.

Greater Love Hath No Man Than This, That He Lay Down His Life For His Friends.

John 15:13

Brothers-in-arms of 1st Force Reconnaissance Company who have made the ultimate sacrifice 1965-1970. They shall never be forgotten.

CPL	**Anthony Allen**	**7-11-67**	
SGT	**Darrell E. Ayers**	**3-19-70**	
CPT	**Eric M. Barnes**	**3-25-67**	
2LT	**Larry M. Beck**	**1-23-67**	
SGT	**Godfred Blankenship**	**3-26-67**	
PFC	**Curtis C. Brown**	**7-15-68**	
LCPL	**William M. Clark**	**8-4-70**	
HN	**Lorning W. Carper Jr. (USN)**	**5-17-66**	
LCPL	**Jerry F. DeGray**	**1-17-67**	
SGT	**Roy G. Dorsett**	**6-29-68**	
LCPL	**Jean-Pierre Dowling**	**1-29-66**	
CPT	**James T. Egan**	**UNK**	**(MIA)**
2LT	**Thomas B. Ferguson**	**3-30-68**	
LCPL	**Victor J. Ford**	**4-29-66**	
LCPL	**William A. Gilmore**	**9-7-67**	
SGT	**Edwin R. Grissett Jr.**	**12-2-68**	**(POW)**
SSG	**Kenneth R. Hall**	**4-24-66**	
LCPL	**Charles E. Harris**	**1-14-68**	
LCPL	**Charles T. Heinemier**	**8-21-69**	
SGT	**James E. Huff**	**10-27-67**	
SGT	**Alan T. Jensen**	**10-17-67**	
CPL	**Raymond S. Joy Jr**	**12-16-65**	
MAJ	**Daniel J. Keating Jr**	**5-22-68**	
HMC	**Michael L. LaPorte (USN)**	**9-5-67**	**(MIA)**
CPL	**Joseph W. Lyons**	**6-5-68**	
2LT	**William E. Martin**	**6-3-67**	
PFC	**James O. McKinny**	**6-16-66**	
PFC	**Francis McLaughlin**	**8-18-69**	

CPL	**Lowell H. Merrell**	**4-23-65**
LCPL	**William R. Moore**	**12-16-65**
CPL	**Patrick J. Murphy**	**5-15-68**
LCPL	**Harold E. Musselman**	**3-3-69**
PFC	**Dennis J. Oliver**	**4-23-69**
HN	**Henry E. Pearce II (USN)**	**1-23-69**
SGT	**Robert C. Phleger**	**5-7-70**
LCPL	**James E. Prideaux**	**2-5-68**
PFC	**Leonard D. Rose**	**1-23-69**
SSGT	**Jose' A. Rosas**	**5-8-67**
CPL	**William J. Schuster**	**6-1-66**
PFC	**James W. Sincere**	**11-22-68**
2LT	**John E. Slater**	**12-15-68**
LCPL	**Luther T. Stowe**	**7-11-67**
GSGT	**Vincent R. Thornburg**	**2-3-70**
SGT	**Craig L. Walton**	**11-7-68**
LCPL	**Russell D. Whelchel**	**9-7-67**
SGT	**David J. Wikander**	**6-25-70**
LCPL	**Ronald A. Williams**	**6-7-67**

Made in the USA
Charleston, SC
13 July 2011